D1080303

The
Modern Domestic Encyclopaedia

THE MODERN
DOMESTIC
ENCYCLOPAEDIA

Dorothy Davis

BOOK CLUB ASSOCIATES
London

This edition published 1976 by
Book Club Associates
by arrangement with Faber & Faber Ltd
© Dorothy V. Davis 1960
New material © Dorothy V. Davis 1970

Printed in Great Britain by
Lowe & Brydone (Printers) Ltd, Thetford, Norfolk

Contents

Introduction

This *Modern Domestic Encyclopaedia* is a completely new edition and it is just ten years older than the first *Domestic Encyclopaedia*. It is five years since the last edition of the book—called *The New Domestic Encyclopaedia*—and a great many changes have taken place in that time.

When I wrote the first *Domestic Encyclopaedia* I was a Home Editor of a woman's magazine and during each year, I not only wrote a great many articles on all aspects of home subjects, I also answered many hundreds of readers' letters.

These were mainly domestic problems and queries repeated *ad infinitum*. I answered the same questions so often and gave the same information about the same synthetic fibres so frequently that I decided it would be a good idea to put all the practical, everyday knowledge needed to run a modern home, into one compact book.

As many housewives like to know the finer points of their tasks, I included quite a lot of technical details and because of these the book was quickly taken up by schools, teachers' training colleges, and by home economists as well as by home editor colleagues.

So when I revised the first edition and brought out the *New Domestic Encyclopaedia* I added more technical data and more information about the latest fibres and fabrics, the newest plastics and a whole chapter on the calorific values of foods.

The new edition was, I am told, gratefully received by teachers, lecturers, students and many industrial firms as well as by housewives and brides. But in our modern life, new things quickly become out of date and up-to-the-minute discoveries of five years ago are frequently out of date and discarded today.

So now I have completely rewritten the book again. Some things have changed little in five years. Others—and especially fibres and fabrics, plastics and laundering techniques—have undergone numerous changes and developments. This new edition covers all the latest fibres, the newest plastics and a great deal of information on the new enzyme detergents. Decimal currency is included in detail and there are comparative charts on the metric system to make it easy for the housewife to compare yards with metres, ounces with grammes and pints with litres.

In most entries I have tried to give as many technical details as possible for those who find them interesting or useful. The same information is repeated in straightforward, everyday language, understandable by younger students or the housewife in a hurry who simply wants to know how to deal with a domestic crisis or how to find out the answer to a problem quickly.

As on previous occasions, I found the technical experts ready and willing to help in checking my information when it dealt with subjects in their own particular field. So many different experts have checked so many different entries for me that it would be difficult to name them all. However, I should particularly like to mention a few and to thank them here for their valued assistance:

Mr. W. R. Beath, the Manager of the Industrial and Technical Marketing Organization of Courtaulds Ltd. and *Mr. P. M. Rowe*, the Press Officer of the British Man-Made Fibres Federation who both helped me so much on the Fibres, Fabrics and Finishes chapter. *Mr. C. Bellingham-Smith* of the Secretariat of the Home Laundering Consultative Council for his assistance with the chapter on Laundering. *Mr. A. Byers*, the Home Appliances Press Officer of the Electricity Council, for his help on the electrical section and both *Mr. T. E. Tebbatt* of ICI and *Mr. G. A. R. Matthews*, Principal Lecturer in Polymer Technology at Borough Polytechnic for their comments on the chapter on Plastics. *Mr. F. W. Arnold*, Chief Inspector of the Leicestershire County Council Weights and Measures Department who checked all my Facts and Figures and in particular the sections on decimal currency and the metric system and *Mr. F. A. Adcock* of Bostik who helped me with the section on adhesives.

Other associations, and industrial organizations helped with checking or research and some of these I should like to thank include:

The Plastics Institute; the Electrical Association for Women; the Gas Council; the Canned and Packaged Foods Bureau; the Silk Centre; Decimal Currency Board; Women's Advisory Committee of the British Standards Institution; British Egg Information Service;

Shoe Care Bureau; McCormick Herb and Spice Bureau; Procter and Gamble Educational Service; Imperial Chemical Industries Ltd.; S. C. Johnson & Son; the Phillips Scott and Turner Company; Du Pont (U.K.) Ltd.; Barber and Nicholls Ltd.; Lever Brothers and Associates Ltd; the Dunlop Rubber Co. Ltd.; Owens-Corning Fiberglas Europe S.A.; and Ciba (A.R.L.) Ltd.

DOROTHY V. DAVIS

Fibres, Fabrics and Finishes

Acetate

This was the second man-made fibre to be produced on a commercial scale in this country (viscose rayon was the first). It is usually regarded as the most silk-like of the man-made fibres in general use. The word acetate is used to denote both staple fibre and continuous filament yarns made from cellulose acetate. At one time these were made chiefly from cotton linters (the short unspinnable hairs of the cotton boll) but today the fibres are usually made from wood pulp.

Acetate is used for waddings, hand knitting yarns and for cigarette filters as well as for a wide range of dress, underwear and furnishing fabrics, both knitted and woven.

Fabrics made from acetate yarns such as Dicel and Lancola are crease-resisting, soft, rich in appearance and drape well. They include satins, taffetas, moires, brocades and also curtain materials and inexpensive linings.

Wash frequently in warm water, never hot. Give a short spin if manufacturer's instructions permit, otherwise drip dry or roll loosely in a towel to remove excess moisture and then hang to dry. Do not wring. This is because some acetate fabrics crack easily and if folded through a wringer this could cause cracking which, on the finished article, would show as fine hair lines. Use only a warm iron, and iron while the fabric is still damp. Handle carefully without wringing. Iron slowly and steadily and not with quick jabs in different directions as this may permanently damage the material.

Acribel

An acrylic fibre made in Belgium.

13

Acrilan

The trade name for an acrylic fibre originally developed in America but now also made on a large scale in Britain. It is made from chemicals obtained chiefly from petroleum. The fabric is soft to touch, mothproof and resistant to mildew. One hundred per cent Acrilan does not shrink, can be easily washed and dries quickly or it may be dry-cleaned.

The fibre can be made into all kinds of fabrics used for anything from baby clothes and blankets to carpets and overcoats. Because it does not shrink, stretch or sag it is ideal for jumpers and jersey dresses.

When Acrilan is *blended with other fibres*, follow manufacturer's instructions.

To wash Acrilan see below under Acrylic fibres.

Acrylic fibres

The various types such as Acrilan, Orlon, Courtelle differ slightly in strength and dyeing properties. Basically, acrylic fibres are produced mainly from acrylonitrile, a liquid derivative of oil refining and coal carbonization processes or from the natural gas present in oil wells together with certain chemicals.

Materials made from acrylic fibres are easy to wash, quick-drying and do not shrink; they are soft and warm and drape well and can be permanently pleated.

Because they have less tendency to stretch and sag, following a pattern is easier. Use nylon or Terylene sewing thread. Press seams lightly and as quickly as possible on the wrong side. Too much heat or pressure may affect the fibres.

Acrylic fibres can be used alone or in blends with other man-made or natural fibres. They can also be woven or knitted into a variety of fabrics including jersey, blankets, underwear, high-bulk fisherman type knitwear and carpets, etc. as well as blended with wool or other fibres in suits, trousers, skirts and dress fabrics. Acrylics are also used to make fleecy materials including warm, soft linings for boots, shoes, slippers and rainwear, etc. The fibres can also be used for filling quilted garments and bedspreads. Long pile fabrics for fun furs and also for actual simulation furs of considerable variety are an important outlet for acrylic fibres today.

Acrylics are unaffected by mildew and are not attacked by moths, although where an acrylic fibre is blended with wool, for example, moths can just as easily attack the wool in the blend and this should be remembered.

The normal process for laundering acrylics would be to wash in warm suds followed by rinsing in cold water and a short spin. The cold rinse is given to cool the fibre down and minimize the risk of creasing during spinning. This is as given in HLCC Label 6.

Pleated garments should be given a hand-hot rinse followed by drip-drying as in HLCC Label 8. Heavy knitwear should be washed as Label 6 and dried lying flat to prevent stretching. For pile fabrics, manufacturers usually recommend a light brushing once the fabric is dry.

If acrylics are washed carefully either by machine or by hand, little or no ironing should be necessary. Where it is preferred, iron with a cool iron at Setting 1. The foregoing are general washing hints only. Wherever possible follow the garment manufacturers' precise laundering instructions for the particular acrylic in question.

Bi-component acrylic fibres such as Sayelle and Courtelle LC are now available. These fibres are used for making bulky yarns suitable for knitwear.

See also under Bi-component acrylic fibres.

See also Modacrylics, page 60, and Man-made fibres, page 55.

Afghalaine

This was originally a wool fibre but a rayon afghalaine is now being made and treatment is similar for both fabrics. Test for colour fastness and then wash quickly in a lukewarm synthetic detergent solution, knead and squeeze but do not twist or wring. Rinse two or three times in clear warm water, ease into shape, roll in a thick towel and squeeze to remove excess moisture. Shake and dry away from direct heat.

Iron afghalaine while still slightly damp, using a warm iron and pressing until quite dry. If the fabric is too dry for ironing, roll it in a damp muslin cloth and leave for half an hour then iron dry on the wrong or right side according to the colour and finish—on the wrong side if the material is dark or matt.

Agilon

This is a type of crimped or bulked stretch nylon yarn produced by drawing the yarn over a sharp edge to give it a coil-spring form and great elasticity. Although used originally on nylon this process is now also being applied to polyester fibres.

Agilon has a matt effect and because of its stretch properties is ideal for socks, stockings and knitted underwear. Stockings made from this fabric look sheer but they are warm to wear and are more absorbent than those made from standard nylon. Wash stockings daily, roll in a towel and dry away from heat.

For washing instructions see under Textured, bulked and stretch yarns, page 96.

Alastra

Rayon manufactured in Belgium.

Albene

This is a matt acetate filament yarn made by French Rhodiaceta but the registered name is also used by associate companies in Italy, Argentina and Brazil.

Alpaca

This is usually a weft-faced plain or twill weave, but may also be plain with a cotton warp and Alpaca goat's hair weft. Wash as for wool.

Amilan

A type of nylon made in Japan.

Angola

A plain or twill fabric similar to flannelette though lighter. Originally it was a blend with cotton and wool but now it is very often made with a blend of rayon and wool and should be washed as for wool or rayon. Angola is mainly used for army shirtings these days but for little else.

Angora

A fluffy type of rabbit wool used for jumpers, hats, etc. Wash carefully by kneading and squeezing in warm soap-flake suds and rinse thoroughly in clear warm water of the same temperature. Squeeze out as much water as possible, preferably by spin-drying, then shake well and spread flat to dry in the fresh air or near an open window away from heat. Shake the garment during drying to raise the fluffy pile.

Nylon and angora mixed are frequently used and although this fabric is as soft and fluffy as pure angora, it is less likely to shed fluff.

Wash nylon angora in lukewarm suds, squeeze gently and do not twist or rub. Rinse two or three times in water of the same temperature and treat as for pure angora, easing the garment gently into the correct shape and size. Shake thoroughly when dry.

Never dry or air angora near heat and if it is necessary to press the garment, use a damp cloth and see that the iron just clears the cloth—never let the iron rest on the actual garment or pressing cloth.

Anti-flame

In a recent year over three hundred and fifty persons died as a result of burns from clothing catching fire. The risk to children is much greater than to adults, but women and girls have three accidents with burning clothes to every one that men and boys have. This is probably due to the fact that frilly party dresses and full-skirted nightdresses which can be drawn into the flame and then act as a chimney are often made at home from material which is highly flammable.

In a properly run household fire risks should be at a minimum and flame-resisting finishes are not a substitute for proper fireguards over fires and open electric heaters.

There are now a number of fibres which are either flame-proof or of low flammability. Teklan, Dynel and Verel are flame-proof and, of course, so is glass. In the low flammability category there is nylon, Lo-Flam Dicel, Fibro F.R. and Evlan F.R.

Fabrics for children's nightwear must, by law, be of low flammability. Teklan, nylon and Lo-flam Dicel are all suitable fabrics and satisfy the regulations. There is also a winceyette made from Lo-Flam Dicel and nylon which passes B.S.I. regulations.

Anti-perspirant

Unpleasant perspiration odour is caused by bacteria which work upon the perspiration and an important advance in hygiene is a finish called Actifresh which keeps textiles odour free by actually checking the growth of the bacteria.

Anti-static treatment

This type of finish reduces soiling as static attracts dirt and also makes it more difficult to remove. Zelec is an anti-static process applied to nylon during manufacture and Permalose is a finish for Terylene. Glencoe is a durable anti-static finish which can be applied to other fibres.

Antron

This is a tri-lobal nylon fibre made by Du Pont. It has lustre, sharper definition and clarity in printed fabrics. These fabrics are rarely made in 100 per cent Antron but usually with a mixture of Dacron. Fabrics are used for dress materials, swimwear and curtains. Wash as for HLCC label No. 4 except for swimwear which should be washed immediately after use in clear water, following manufacturer's instructions.

Antron 24

A special type of tri-lobal nylon fibre produced by Du Pont as a bulked continuous filament yarn for upholstery. Fabrics in Antron 24 are particularly easy to care for and they are hardwearing and resilient. Usually spills and dirt can be wiped away with a damp cloth but follow manufacturer's instructions for cleaning where given.

Antung

A Chinese plain weave wild silk fabric free from slubs. It should be washed in the same way as silk. Iron on the reverse side when the material is quite dry, using a warm iron only.

Arnel

A cellulose triacetate made in U.S.A. and Belgium and similar to the product Tricel made in this country. Wash and treat in the same way.

Astrakhan

A knitted or woven fabric made from curled worsted yarns to resemble the fleece of young Astrakhan lamb. Dry-clean or shampoo as for sheepskin or wash as for wool, depending on the type and thickness of the fabric.

Avisco

An American trade-mark used for various types of rayon. Avisco Vinyon is a trade-mark for chlorofibres made in U.S.A.

Avril

A polynosic fibre manufactured in U.S.A.

Avron

The trade name for viscose fibres made in U.S.A.

Ban-Lon

This name was at one time used for the stuffer-box crimping process but now the actual texturing process carried out under licence from Joseph Bancroft & Sons is known as Textralizing. Fabrics which are approved get the brand name Ban-Lon.

Ban-Lon fabrics may be nylon, polyester or other synthetic fibres and washing should be carried out according to the manufacturer's swing tag or HLCC label. When in doubt, treat according to the fibre concerned.

See also under Textralizing on page 95.

Batiste

Used mainly in the manufacture of corsets, brassieres, girdles, this is a lightweight plain woven fabric made from cotton, silk, rayon or nylon and also from Terylene/cotton and polyester/cotton. Wash in hot, mild suds. For further washing instructions see under Corsets, Brassieres, etc. in chapter on Laundering.

Bedford cord

A fabric having rounded cards running lengthwise with pronounced sunken lines between. Dry-clean or shampoo as for upholstery unless the fabric is guaranteed washable, when launder as for corduroy.

Bel-O-Fast

A non-iron finish used on 100 per cent cotton fabric. Used for shirts, fabric with this finish can be bleached, washed and dried in any way. It needs no ironing at all and is non-shrink.

Bemberg

The trade mark for a cuprammonium yarn made in U.S.A., West Germany and Italy. It is a rayon.

Bi-component acrylic fibres

These consist of two different acrylic polymers with differing shrinkage potential. This means that each fibre is virtually two fibres in one. The two parts of the fibre react against each other when subjected to wet heat treatment, to form a spiral crimp. One part of the fibre shrinks more than the other, thus forcing the fibre structure to change its characteristics. The result is a bulky fibre which is light, easy to launder, non-shrink and ideal for knitwear. Sayelle is a bi-component acrylic fibre.

Blend

This means that a fabric is woven or knitted from blended yarn. This is yarn that is spun from a blend of one or more staple fibres, for example viscose staple fibre and wool. Wash according to manufacturer's label or HLCC swing tag or treat for weakest fibre present.

Bonded fibre interlining

An interlining made from man-made—usually rayon—fibres held together by a special bonding agent. It is crush-resistant, porous, water-repellent and light, and is used to best advantage between two layers of fabric. It can be washed or dry-cleaned and washing is usually fairly easy as the interlining regains its permanent stiffness when dry. Solena and Vilene are examples of this type of interlining.

Wash the garment or fabric in a bath or really large sink to avoid creasing more than is absolutely necessary. Use warm soapy water and press out the moisture without rubbing. Rinse thoroughly, hang to dry or roll loosely in a towel to remove excess moisture. Ironing should be unnecessary but if there are creases, sandwich the material between a damp cloth underneath and a dry cloth on top and press with a warm iron.

Botany

A term used to denote the fine yarns of fabrics made from Merino wool. For washing instructions see under Wool, page 181.

Bouclé

This is the name given to knitted or woven fabrics made from fancy looped yarns. Wash as for wool, page 181.

Bri-Nova

An ICI trade name to describe garments made in tri-lobal ICI nylon, a yarn with a built-in gleam which gives extra depth of colour and a crisp full handle. Wash as for ordinary nylon.

Bri-nylon

This is the brand name for nylon made by ICI and formerly by British Nylon Spinners Ltd.

Brocade

This is a figured fabric which has a pattern of contrasting or self-colour woven in on a special loom. It is used for furnishing or dress materials and can be made from acetate, cotton, silk, rayon or various blended mixtures. Cleaning instructions vary, for very heavy and difficult-to-handle brocades, professional dry-cleaning is probably the best method although isolated spots can be removed with a cleaning fluid such as carbon tetrachloride or Thawpit.

With most brocades, and especially those made from 100 per cent cotton, washing at home is possible providing a little more care is taken. Wash dress brocades according to material; for furnishing fabrics, shake thoroughly to remove loose dust or brush with a vacuum cleaner, then make a lather with warm water and soapflakes and immerse the brocade in this: squeeze the lather through the fabric, scrubbing any very soiled parts such as hems with a soft brush. Wring out soap, rinse and if the material is still dirty, wash again in the same way.

Rinse several times in clear water, wringing between each rinse then hang to dry and iron when the fabric is almost dry. With curtains, continue ironing until the material is completely dry but with loose covers, replace on chairs and finish ironing once the covers are in position.

Buckram

A firm fabric which is stiffened by impregnating a lightweight cloth, usually cotton, with starch, adhesive and other fillers. Dry clean only.

Bulked yarns

See under Textured, bulked and stretch yarns on page 96.

Calico

A widely used plain-woven medium-weight cotton fabric which takes its name from an Indian town where it was first manufactured. Wash as for cotton in hot suds, boiling if necessary. Rinse thoroughly in two lots of clear water, wring and hang to dry. Iron while still slightly damp, with a hot iron.

Add a tablespoonful of turpentine substitute to the water when washing unbleached calico for the first time. This helps to remove the dressing and to whiten it.

Cambric

A lightweight, closely-woven plain fabric, today usually made from cotton with a light dressing or stiffening applied to the finishing process. It was originally a very fine white linen named after the town of Cambray in Flanders where it was first made. Wash as for cotton or linen and dip in a weak starch solution unless the fabric has a special finish, when treat accordingly.

Camel hair

An expensive fabric made from camel and dromedary hair. There are two kinds—the soft undercoat which is short and soft and the outer hair which is coarse, a much deeper tan and longer. Dry clean only.

Candlewick

The candlewick process of manufacturing pile fabrics consists of mechanically pushing tufts of yarn into a fabric backing and then shrinking the ground fabric in the finishing process so that the tufts are locked into the ground fabric. Cotton, nylon, Terylene, Tricel and rayon are used in candlewick which, apart from the popular bedspreads, is used to make scatter rugs, bath mats, housecoats, etc.

To wash, prepare a rich lather with warm water and soap-flakes and squeeze the candlewick in the suds without rubbing the material. Rinse two or three times in clear warm water, squeeze out excess moisture—by hand, or with a spindrier—and hang out to dry in the open air, in a wind if possible, shaking occasionally and pulling into shape during drying. When the candlewick is dry, shake vigorously to raise the pile but do not iron.

Some types of candlewick may safely be machine-washed and wrung. Follow manufacturer's instructions.

Candytuft

Often used for bedspreads, candytuft can be washed at home with hand-hot suds. Rinse thoroughly, dry out of doors and iron while still slightly damp on the reverse side.

Cantrece

A monofilament nylon yarn produced by Du Pont and developed especially for hosiery. It is a high response nylon with a self crimping property which makes stockings more resilient.

Stockings made from this type of nylon cling lightly and look particularly sheer once they are being worn. They are no stronger or weaker than ordinary nylons of a similar denier and should be washed and handled in the same way.

Cashmere

This is the English spelling of Kashmir and the name derives from the fact that the material is woven from the soft hair of the Kashmir goat which lives way up in the Himalayas. The wool is obtained from the combing of the goats and not by shearing. Cashmere is expensive because each goat can produce only about half a pound of Cashmere a year.

Wash very carefully in warm suds, preferably with a liquid synthetic detergent. Squeeze gently and do not twist or rub. Rinse two or three times in warm water only and spin dry or roll in a towel to absorb excess moisture, then place flat on a towel to dry. When washing a cardigan or sweater, stuff shoulders and sleeves with paper towels or with the cardboard rollers on which paper towels are wound—wrapping the rollers in paper first helps to absorb excess moisture. Dry in the fresh air, or near an open window away from heat and shake occasionally during drying.

Cavalry twill

This is a firm, heavy fabric with a double-twill weave and pronounced grooves formed by the weft. Originally used to make cavalry riding breeches but now used also for slacks, raincoats and other heavy clothing. May be of wool, cotton or man-made fibres. Dry-clean unless manufacturers' instructions state otherwise.

Celafibre

Also known as Dicel staple, this is the trade name for an acetate staple fibre derived from cellulose and invariably used in a blend. It is made into a variety of fabrics principally for shirtings and light-weight suitings in blend with viscose rayon and in blend with wool for carpets or knitted underwear, and hand-knitting yarns. It is moth-proof and resistant to mildew. See under Acetate, page 13.

Cellular

A cotton or spun rayon, or rayon/cotton blend such as Perro, shirting or underwear fabric. It is a weave having an open or cell-like structure. Wash as for cotton unless otherwise instructed.

Cellulose fibres

Man-made fibres produced from natural raw materials. Viscose is the most widely known and was the first man-made fibre to be produced in Great Britain on a large scale. Acetate and triacetate are derivates of cellulose and further details will be found under individual headings. See under Acetate, Viscose or Triacetate.

Cellulose triacetate

Known as Tricel in Britain, Arnel in U.S.A. and Trilan in Canada. See under Triacetate on page 97.

Celon

A type 6 nylon made by Courtaulds. It is the newest of the British nylons and has several advantages. The fibre is softer than nylon 66 and it has a super whiteness that stays white even after repeated washing. It is also intrinsically flame-resistant so is ideal for children's nightwear. Celon is used for dress fabrics, knitwear, lingerie, shirtings, overalls, rainwear, upholstery and swimwear. It is also used for men's socks and for fine denier stockings and tights.

Wash in hand-hot water (48° C.) and give warm rinse then drip dry or give a cold rinse and short spin. If ironing is necessary use a warm iron (setting 2).

Charmeuse

Although at one time this was the trade-mark for a material originated by a French textile firm, the fabric has been so widely copied that the term is now a common one and is used to describe a crêpe-back satin woven fabric. It was originally made from pure silk but is now made from acetate or cotton as well as silk. It is used for pyjamas and housegowns and for dresses. Wash according to yarn.

Chenille

This can be a yarn or a fabric made from cut pile yarn. The fabric is soft, tufted and used mainly in furnishings. May be of cotton, viscose or silk. Wash according to fibre.

Cheslon

The trade name for bulked, stabilized acetate and nylon yarns.

Chiffon

This soft light fabric can be of silk, nylon, rayon or other man-made fibres. It is a very sheer fabric made from fine denier yarns and is used principally for handkerchiefs, lingerie, evening gowns and scarves.

If the chiffon is made of *nylon* it can be washed easily and quickly in hot suds. Rinse thoroughly and drip dry and no ironing should be necessary. If garment needs pressing, iron lightly with a cool iron.

Real silk chiffon is not easy to wash at home as it is liable to shrink, and if there is any doubt about laundering or if the garment is an intricately fashioned article needing special ironing, then it should be professionally dry-cleaned.

If you do wash *real silk or rayon* chiffon at home, use warm suds and handle the material gently; knead and squeeze lightly and avoid twisting, rubbing or wringing. Rinse once or twice in warm water and then in cold water, but do not wring.

Roll the garment in a thick towel to absorb surplus moisture and gently ease back to original shape and size. Dry flat on a hanger away from direct heat and iron when the fabric is almost dry, using light pressure and a cool or warm iron. Gently pull the fabric in all directions and finally into shape.

To restore gloss to silk chiffon add a dessertspoonful of white vinegar to the final cold rinsing water, but before next laundering soak the garment for a short time in clear cold water. Treat *new silk chiffon* in the same way. If chiffon becomes limp after washing and requires slight stiffening, use the gum arabic solution mentioned on page 155; or dip in warm water containing liquid glue or in a quart of water containing a tablespoonful of borax. Alternatively, use a weak solution of DIP according to instructions.

Chintz

This is a plain woven printed cotton fabric with a glaze finish which is sometimes permanent. At one time it was usual to send chintz for professional laundering and calendering when the fabric was put through a heavy machine which polished it. Very few laundries now undertake calendering; the process is expensive and there is a long waiting-list for the service.

Chintz which has been treated with a glaze should be dry-cleaned so that the surface is not spoiled but if it has already been laundered at home some of the finish can be restored by rinsing the chintz in a fairly strong solution of ordinary starch or plastic stiffener. Thin or old material will need a proportionately heavier starch.

More gloss can be given to the fabric if a little candle wax is dissolved in the starch and if the material is ironed while it is very damp. Use a hot iron with considerable pressure and slide the iron backwards and forwards across the chintz until it is completely dry. If chintz is left to air while still damp it will lose some of its gloss.

Most new chintz is permanently glazed and can be easily washed in hot suds. Do not rub or twist and never bleach or starch. Give a final rinse in cold water and iron with a warm iron on the right side while the chintz is fairly damp. See also Everglaze chintz on page 39.

Chlorofibres

A term which describes fibres of the polyvinylidene chloride and polyvinyl chloride types. Often known as PVC, this term originally referred to plastics but now includes textiles also. Brand names include the French Clevyl T., a flame-resistant PVC fibre, Rhovyl, Saran and Verel. PVC fibres are not made in the U.K. but the French fibres made by the Rhovyl Company have a following here both as flame resistant fibres for such items as night attire and racing drivers' overalls and also for underwear and socks etc. because it is believed that due to their having a negative static discharge they are helpful in preventing or reducing arthritic and rheumatic conditions. Clevyl T. is the most widely used type of chlorofibres used for these two classes of fabrics. Wash fabrics in warm water, drip dry, don't iron.

Clarino

The trade name for a Japanese poromeric material sold by The British United Shoe Machinery Company. It is used mainly for shoe uppers.

The material will not stain or fade and shoes can be held under a running tap to remove surface mud and dirt. Careful fitting is important when shoes are first bought and worn as the material will give only slightly and the shoes cannot be broken in. Technically, Clarino is a new generation poromeric material made of a three dimensional web of crimped man-made fibres, randomly entwined in a micro-porous synthetic foam, finished with a micro-porous polyurethane top layer. It needs no interlayer to lend it strength. Structurally it is very similar to leather, and it can be processed by conventional shoe making methods.

Clevyl T.

A French PVC fibre which is flame resistant.

Cloqué

A compound or double-woven fabric, often in silk, acetate, Tricel or Courtelle, in which the pattern is raised like blisters. Wash as for acetate, but drip dry and avoid ironing or if unavoidable, finish with a cool iron over a thick towel.

Continuous filament yarns

These consist of a number of separate, unbroken filaments drawn together and given a slight twist. They have a smooth surface and are used for various fabrics such as satins, poults, taffetas and failles.

Corduroy

A twill or plain woven fabric with heavy ribs running vertically down the cloth and a cut pile surface. This hard-wearing material, which has a velvety appearance, may be made from cotton or from cotton blended with rayon, Terylene or Vincel, can be easily washed at home and if the colour is fast it can even be boiled quite safely, although boiling is not necessary for effective cleaning. Use a bath and warm soapy water when laundering corduroy, or give warm, short machine-wash. Try not to wring, squeeze or rub the material but simply swish up and down in the lather. Rinse in the same way without wringing and drip dry out of doors. Occasionally smooth the corduroy with a soft cloth in the direction of the pile while it is drying and shake frequently to avoid creases forming in the folds.

Washed carefully, corduroy should not need ironing but if it is creased, while the garment is evenly damp, press gently on the wrong side under several thicknesses of material or gently press the wrong side of the fabric against an upturned iron. Leave garments hanging in a steamy atmosphere such as a bathroom to restore shape.

Corfam

A poromeric material made by Du Pont from a urethane material reinforced with polyester. It is used for handbags, wallets, sports equipment and shoe uppers. Corfam can be adapted to any design appearance or texture. It offers manufacturers colour, embossability and surface treatments which no other material can give. It is breathable, flexible, water repellent and can be wiped clean. It holds its shape and resists scuffs and abrasions. Generally remove surface dirt and dust with a damp cloth. Occasionally polish with ordinary wax polish.

Cotton

Most cottons will stand fairly hard treatment. Whites are best washed at 185 deg. F., 85 deg. C.; boiling is not essential if you have a good washing machine.

With coloured cottons, always test for colour fastness before laundering. If fast wash at 140 deg. F., 65 deg. C.

Drip dry cottons and those with a stain and water-repellent finish need different treatment, and children's clothes with these finishes are most easily dealt with if washed daily. For laundering instructions see under respective finish in chapter on Finishes. See also page 149 in Laundering chapter.

For special cottons such as voile, organdie, etc., see under respective headings.

Courlene

The trade name for a range of polythene and polypropylene yarns which are resistant to chemicals and completely non-absorbent. They are employed for industrial uses such as ropes and fishing-nets, and easily-cleaned fabrics for awnings, deck-chairs and stools.

Courlene X3

A polythene fibre made by Courtaulds. For further details see under Polythene on page 76.

Cournova

This is the trade mark for Courtaulds' monofil and split film polypropylene yarn.

Courtelle

A British developed acrylic fibre produced by Courtaulds. It has had the most rapid growth of all man-made fibres. It is moth-proof, resistant to mildew, quick-drying, will not stretch or shrink and holds pleats well. It is used in the manufacture of most fabrics including underwear, jersey, curtains, men's suiting and carpets. Courtelle is made up into a number of different fabrics including double and single jersey, tweeds, lightweight coloured-woven fabrics either in 100 per cent form or in blends with cotton as ground fabrics for delicate prints. It is also used to make foam-backed single jersey, deep pile and fleece fabrics, handknitting yarns and knitwear and also for springy pile carpets which are easy to shampoo.

Always follow washing instructions on the label of any particular garment or item. If the label is lost, wash in warm water and give a cold rinse followed by a short spin. Fabrics other than heavy knits can be rinsed in warm water and drip dried if preferred. Iron lightly with a cool iron (setting 1) when fabric is dry.

Courtelle LC

This is a bi-component acrylic fibre made by Courtaulds. A high degree of crimp is developed in the processing giving bulky yarns suitable for knitwear. The LC after the word Courtelle stands for Latent Crimp. Wash as for other acrylic fibres or other types of Courtelle when washing instructions aren't available.

Crash

A heavy fabric, plain woven or with a fancy crêpe weave originally made of linen but now of cotton, spun rayon and unions. It has an irregular surface due to the thick, uneven yarns used. Wash as for yarn used.

Crease-resistant

Cotton, linen and rayons can be treated with a special finishing process involving the application of resins to make them permanently resistant to creasing. This does not mean that creases cannot be made, but it implies that creasing will not occur so readily and that any creases formed will fall out fairly quickly when the garment is hung.

Crease-resist finishes improve the handle and shape of fabrics and also make them less likely to soil and easier to wash as well as reducing laundry shrinkage. On viscose rayons, the finish gives increased strength, especially when the fabric is wet.

Crease-resist finishes remain through regular laundering and dry-cleaning, but, unless specially treated, can be affected by chlorine bleaches and these may also damage the fabric. Treated materials cannot usually be dyed at home and even professional dyeing may mean that the crease-resist finish must first be removed—and it cannot be replaced.

Wash treated fabrics in hand-hot suds, rinse thoroughly but do not wring tightly, bleach or boil. If you spin-dry, cool first and spin for about 15 seconds only for each spin. See page 150 for fuller washing instructions.

The Tootal Broadhurst Lee Co. Ltd. were the inventors of the crease-resisting process and virtually all crease-resist finishes are based on this original process. Finishers using this special crease-resisting process under arrangement with Tootal Broadhurst Lee Co. Ltd. are members of the 'Tebilized' Trade Mark Users' Association. The trade-mark 'Tebilized' denotes tested crease-resistance of a high standard.

Cotton, linen and rayon materials marked 'Tebilized Double Tested' have the tested crease resistance already mentioned and they are also tested scientifically for smooth drying. These fabrics require little or no ironing; they should be washed gently in warm suds, shaken out immediately and hung on a plastic hanger to drip dry.

Crease-retention

Durable finishes are available for 100 per cent wool fabrics. These are different from other crease-retention finishes. The process is embodied in the material during making, although it cannot be seen or felt. When the fabric is made up into a garment and is pressed, the heat and moisture combine with the finish and pleats and creases are set permanently. Garments with this finish can be washed and dry-cleaned but if trousers, for instance, are being pressed, it is important to follow the original creases.

Crêpe

This is the name given to fabric which has a puckered, crinkled or pebbled surface regardless of how this was produced. It may be made by the use of tightly twisted yarns, by a crêpe weave or may be produced by a special process during finishing. Wash in hand-hot water, rinse, remove excess moisture and iron while still damp on the wrong side, using a warm iron.

Crêpe de Chine

This hard-wearing but lightweight crêpe fabric can be made from silk, Terylene or rayon and should be treated accordingly. It is also made now from acetate and triacetate and is particularly successful in KN. Dicel which is a self crimping yarn. Treat according to the fibre but the following hints may help.

Expensive real silk *crêpe de Chine* should be soaked in cool water for half an hour before washing for the first time and this should also be done if the fabric was given an acid (or white vinegar) rinse after the previous laundering.

Wash as for silk and to restore the gloss (for silk) add a dessert-spoonful of white vinegar to the final cold rinsing water. Roll in a thick towel and leave for a short time for the surplus moisture to be absorbed. With fine *crêpe de Chine* this should be sufficient drying as the material needs to be ironed while it is still evenly and slightly damp. Use a warm iron and press on the wrong side until the garment is completely dry.

Rayon *crêpe de Chine* can be washed in the same way as for silk but it should not be soaked first nor should an acid rinse be given afterwards. Handle the fabric gently while wet, rinse thoroughly without wringing and use a cool iron on the wrong side while the material is still slightly damp.

Creslan

This is an acrylic fibre made in U.S.A. and known originally as X.51. Wash as for Acrilan, Orlon or Courtelle.

Cretonne

A printed cotton furnishing fabric of heavier weight than chintz. The name is sometimes applied to the similar printed spun rayon fabrics.

Shake to remove surplus dust, then wash in hand-hot suds and scrub soiled parts lightly with a soft brush. If the material is very dirty, wring and wash a second time then rinse two or three times and if the fabric has not been treated with a special finish, starch lightly. Curtains or covers which are thin and worn should be stiffened with a stronger starch solution.

Iron cretonne with a hot iron while it is still damp. Curtains should be ironed until they are quite dry: loose covers should be partially ironed then replaced on furniture and the ironing finished once the covers are in position.

If the cretonne has a special glazed or crease-resisting finish, see page 47 and treat accordingly.

Crimped yarns
See under Textured, bulked and stretch yarns on page 96.

Crimplene
The trade-mark of ICI for a bulked yarn made from Terylene. It is the lead yarn in double jersey fabrics and is now following this fashion fabric success with men's suitings. Fabrics made from Crimplene are soft, drape well and are used in knitwear as well as for various jersey-type fabrics. Wash as for Terylene jersey or according to swing tag.

Crylor
A French acrylic fibre rather similar to Courtelle or Acrilan but available as a continuous filament and used on a small scale in this country. For washing instructions see page 15.

Cubaleen
The trade name for a washable, printed furnishing sateen with a highly glazed finish. It retains its shiny surface after repeated washings if handled carefully. Use warm suds and a fairly mild detergent; rinse thoroughly but do not twist, rub, bleach or starch. Iron on the right side with a warm iron.

Cupioni
A cuprammonium yarn similar to Bemberg and manufactured in U.S.A. and West Germany.

Cuprammonium
A type of rayon, similar to viscose but made by a different process and manufactured in various parts of the world but principally in West Germany, Italy and U.S.A. It is inexpensive and widely used for linings, lingerie and lightweight dress materials. Wash as for rayon.

Cupro
This is an abbreviation for cuprammonium yarns produced by various manufacturers throughout the world but principally in West Germany, Italy and U.S.A.

Dacron

A polyester fibre produced by Du Pont. Filament yarns of Dacron are widely used in jersey fabrics because of resistance to snagging, shrinkage or stretching. Knitted fabrics of Dacron combine easy wear qualities with lightness and warmth. Dacron is blended with wool, cotton or rayon to give crispness, resilience and durable pleatability combined with comfort and performance.

Dacron absorbs little water so it dries almost at once and spills can usually be wiped away without staining. Wash 100 per cent Dacron as given on HLCC label 4. If necessary use a cool iron on setting No. 1.

Wash gently in hand-hot water and soapflakes or mild synthetic detergent. Rinse thoroughly, drip dry or roll in a towel to absorb excess moisture, then hang to dry away from heat. Many Dacron garments may safely be machine-washed.

Ironing should be unnecessary but if preferred, iron dry with a steam iron set at lowest heat or press with a warm iron over a damp cloth.

Dacron Fiberfill

This is a crimped polyester fibre especially designed as a filling material. It is used in bras, housecoats, anoraks, mattresses and sleeping bags, in cushions and upholstery. As a filling material it is resilient, durable, water resistant, lightweight, odourless, mothproof and non-allergenic. Wash as for HLCC label No. 4.

Damask

This figured fabric was first made in Damascus in the twelfth century. It is made now from cotton, linen and various man-made fibres, and is used for table-cloths, furnishings, etc. Wash according to the fibre concerned. Damask tickings are made from filament and spun rayon together.

Danufil

The name of several different types of rayon produced in West Germany.

Danulon

A Type-6 nylon made in Hungary. Wash as for other nylons.

Daryl

A nylon fibre manufactured in Belgium. Treat as for other nylon.

Delaine

An all-wool lightweight material which is usually printed. Fabrics known as Delaine types are also available in various blends of man-made fibres. Wash as for wool.

Defion

A type of nylon made in Italy.

Delustra

The trade name for a dull-lustre viscose rayon. Wash gently in fairly hot water and iron with a medium hot iron on the wrong side when quite dry.

Denim

This was originally a heavy cotton workwear fabric but it is now also used in a lighter weight for beachwear, jeans, etc., and in a rayon and cotton mixture. Wash cotton denim in hand-hot suds. rinse thoroughly and iron with a hot iron while still slightly damp, With a rayon mixture wash as for rayon.

Depalene

This is the trade name for crimped Terylene yarns used to make half-hose or socks.

Depalon

This is the trade name for crimped nylon yarn used to make half-hose, elastic fabrics, gloves and swimsuits.

Depanyl

The trade name for crimped, high-stretch, bulked nylon yarns used to make gloves, swimsuits and elastic fabrics.

Dicel

The trade name for Courtauld's acetate yarn and staple. Wash and treat as any other acetate. Dicel KN is a self crimping acetate.

Diolen

A polyester fibre similar to Terylene and made in West Germany. Treat as for Terylene.

Dolan

An acrylic fibre made in West Germany and similar to Courtelle which is manufactured in Britain. Treat in the same way.

Dorlon

A polyamide fibre made in West Germany. Wash as for nylon.

Dospun

The trade-mark for yarns made of flax, spun rayon and wool and also for nylon and other synthetic fibres spun by the Doagh Spinning Co. Ltd. of Belfast. Treat according to the yarn in question.

Douppion

This is a fabric made from silk reeled from a double cocoon, that is two cocoons accidentally joined together. The yarn obtained this way has natural irregularities which produce characteristic slubs during weaving. Wash as for silk.

Dralon

An acrylic fibre manufactured in West Germany and rather similar to Acrilan, Orlon or Courtelle. Dralon can be used alone or with other fibres; it does not felt, is hard-wearing, resistant to moths and can be permanently pleated. See page 15 for washing instructions.

Drill

This twill fabric is similar to denim and should be treated in the same way.

Dual toque

This is an obsolete expression now but described a process used on nylon yarns to make stretch fabrics. These were used to make the fully-fashioned welts on stockings and for various circular knit fabrics.

See False Twist on page 40.

Duchess satin

A heavy luxurious fabric used mainly by the home dressmaker for cocktail dresses and evening gowns. Because of the use of unsized yarns, the fabric maintains its crisp appearance and handle after dry-cleaning.

Ducillo

A nylon fibre manufactured in Argentina. Treat as for nylon.

Dulesco

The trade name for an oil-dulled viscose rayon yarn made in Britain, Canada and U.S.A. It is used for giving a dull finish to curtains and furnishing fabrics where there is exposure to light as it has a very good light resistance. Wash in the same way as for Delustra.

Durable pleating

Thermoplastic fibres—nylon, polyester, acrylics and triacetate—can all be durably pleated under heat and pressure whereas cotton and spun rayon must have resin treatments before durable pleating can be applied. Garments which have been permanently pleated are easy to wash and quick to dry. There are various types of pleating including accordion and spring pleating and three-to-one and five-to-one knife-edge pleats. Some designers reverse the pleats at intervals to give a patterned effect.

Launder in warm suds in a large bath and avoid wringing, twisting and rubbing. Do not use bleach or starch and do not boil. Dip the garment up and down in the suds the way of the pleats and rinse thoroughly in the same way.

Many durably pleated garments may be safely machine-washed —follow manufacturers' instructions.

Hang to drip dry with the garment opened out and hanging the way of the pleats. Ironing should not be necessary and instructions should be followed but if really sharp knife-edge pleats are required, the fabric and pleats may usually be pressed lightly with a *cool* iron and many manufacturers recommend this to preserve the crispness of the pleats.

Duracol

This is a trade-mark used by Courtaulds and British Celanese Ltd. to denote any of their spun-dyed fibres and yarns. The trade-mark is generally used in conjunction with another trade-mark. Coloration is produced by dispersion of fast coloured pigments in the spinning dope or melt.

Durafil

A tough, hard-wearing modified rayon staple suitable for blends with cotton or wool for adding strength and abrasion resistance. Used instead of cotton for shoddy and heavy woollens also.

Duraglas

A glass fibre made in Great Britain.

Dynel

Although Dynel was the first modacrylic fibre to be marketed, there is some argument nowadays as to whether it should, in fact, be classed as a chlorofibre. It is an American fibre developed and produced by Union Carbide Chemicals Company while Teklan is a modacrylic made in this country. Dynel is chemically quite different from Teklan, however, which is much tougher and has a higher melting point.

Dynel is a man-made textile fibre produced chemically from such basic raw materials as natural gas, salt, ammonia and water. It is made from 60 per cent vinyl chloride, a gas which is an ingredient of the important vinyl plastics and 40 per cent acrylonitrile, a clear water-white liquid that is the chemical basis of all modacrylic fibres. When the gas, vinyl chloride and the liquid acrylonitrile are combined under heat and pressure, they form a white powder called a resin. This resin is dissolved in acetone, the same liquid used in nail polish removers. The solution is forced through a spinneret (a multi-holed metal disc) into a water bath where it coagulates to form continuous strands.

These Dynel strands, called tow, are dried, stretched, cut and crimped. This crimped-cut fibre, known as staple fibre, is then subjected to tests for quality control and then baled for shipment to spinning mills.

One of Dynel's most important characteristics is its flame resistance but it is also highly resistant to chemicals including almost all acids. It is, of course, affected by acetone so never use nail varnish remover near Dynel. The fibre stands up well to sunlight, it is moth-proof, mildew-proof and is undamaged by salt water, perspiration, dry cleaning solvents, soaps and detergents. It washes easily, dries quickly, gives permanent pleats and creases and it is warm. It can be dyed or whitened.

Dynel is used in this country for children's nightwear and dressing gowns, for hearthrugs and upholstery and for simulation furs. It is also widely used for wigs.

Wash according to the fabric or garment concerned, following manufacturer's instructions where available. Otherwise wash in hand-hot suds, give a cold rinse and short spin or drip dry.

Efylon

A thick filament nylon yarn made in Hungary.

Egyptian cotton

Fine cotton of very high quality grown in the Nile Valley.

Elastomeric fibres

This is a generic term used to describe fibres with a very high extensibility (200 per cent or more) and which recover rapidly from that extension. There are two subdivisions of this class; one is rubber (elastic) and the other covers fibres usually made from polyurethane such as Lycra and Spanzelle. These fibres are sometimes known as Elastofibres. In America, the generic term Spandex is used and in this country they are frequently referred to as synthetic elastomer fibres. Agreement has not yet been reached on a universally accepted name.

Polyurethane yarns are becoming increasingly important for imparting stretch to a wide range of textiles. Polyurethane synthetic elastomer fibres are essentially textile fibres with elastic properties, being extruded as continuous filament in a range of deniers comparable to other man-made fibres.

The chief characteristic is elasticity and they have much greater power than extruded rubber for elastic recovery. Yarns also have a high resistance to chemicals and other factors which degrade rubber.

As synthetic elastomer fibres are always used with other fibres in the manufacture of swimwear, foundation garments, support stockings, etc. washing instructions must depend on the other fibre present. Follow manufacturer's instructions or HLCC label or when in doubt wash in hand-hot water and iron only if necessary at setting 2.

See also under Polyurethane on page 76.

Embossed finishes

Thermoplastic fibre fabrics (such as nylon, polyester, acrylics, etc.) can be permanently embossed without difficulty but, as with durable pleating, cotton and rayon require special resin treatment before the process can be applied. Fabrics with a waffle, embossed or similar textured finish are passed between hot, embossed rollers, and under a process rather similar to that for crease-resisting. The waffle or embossing is usually permanent if washing instructions are followed and the material is generally shrink-resisting also.

Wash in hand-hot suds, rinse thoroughly and drip dry. Do not twist, rub, bleach, boil or starch. Press on the wrong side with a warm iron when dry. Avoid sliding iron over embossed surface.

Enant

Nylon made in U.S.S.R.

Enkalon

This is a Type-6 nylon, originally made in Holland but now also produced in Britain. Wash as for other nylon.

Estron

This is the American generic term for acetate although it is not used in U.K.

Everglaze chintz

The trade name for a permanently glazed fabric which has a special finish to give it dirt-resisting qualities. It can be cleaned easily by wiping with a damp sponge. When the fabric is really dirty it should be dry-cleaned but it will stand up to a number of home launderings providing a strong synthetic detergent is not used. Use warm water and soapflakes or a mild synthetic detergent and rinse thoroughly. Do not twist or rub nor use bleach or starch. Iron on the right side with a warm iron.

Evlan

A modified rayon fibre specifically developed for the carpet trade and widely accepted by the British Carpet Industry. It is used on its own and in blends with nylon, wool and Courtelle and is used in all types of carpets including heavy Axminsters and Wiltons, as well as for lighter weight tufted carpets. The fibre is now also extensively used in upholstery fabric.

Faille

A fine ribbed fabric with the ribs running across the cloth. It was originally made in silk but is more often now made in acetate rayon or other man-made fibres. Wash as for silk or rayon according to the material.

False Twist

The main crimping process for making textured yarns for stretch nylon, bulked nylon, high bulk Tricel, Lancola etc. and stabilized textured polyester yarns.

Felt

This material which is a closely matted collection of wool fibres is difficult to wash or dry-clean as it quickly shrinks or pulls out of shape. Felt garments should be professionally dry-cleaned, but some cleaning firms may refuse to accept responsibility for them. Remove odd stains or spots with a cleaning fluid but follow instructions exactly.

Fiberglas

This is the trade name for fibreglass made by Owens-Corning in U.S.A. It is used in the production of 30,000 different end products for industrial and home furnishing uses. In this country Fiberglas is mainly used for soft furnishings and curtain fabrics. These are made from 100 per cent glass fibre yarn and they do not stretch, shrink, sag or crease. Fabrics are mothproof, fade-resistant and flame-proof. They should be hand washed and drip-dried then put back into use. No ironing is necessary.

More details are given under Glass on page 45.

Fibravyl

A seldom used name for PVC fibre made in France. Clevly T. is the type sold in U.K. This is a chlorofibre with excellent flame resistance.

1111

Fibreglass

Also spelt Fiberglas. A 100 per cent glass fibre yarn made by Owens-Corning originally in U.S.A. but now in this country also. It is mainly used for curtaining material. Fibreglass makes excellent curtains.

For further details see under Glass on page 45.

Fibrenka

Rayon manufactured in Holland.

Fibres

These are the strands from which yarns are made prior to fabric production. They may be natural fibres such as cotton, linen, wool or silk or they may be man-made such as nylon, rayon, acetate, etc. from natural materials or from chemicals. Fibres are usually spun into yarns and the yarns are then made into fabrics.

Fibro

The trade name for a viscose rayon staple fibre manufactured in this country and in Canada and U.S.A. Wash or clean articles made with viscose rayon frequently and follow manufacturer's instructions.

Fibroceta

The trade name for an acetate staple fibre manufactured in this country and used for industrial purposes.

Fibrolane

This was a protein fibre made from casein (from skimmed milk) but it is now no longer produced.

Filaments

These are the long continuous strands of man-made fibres made by chemical processes from natural materials or from synthetic chemicals. Filament can be cut into short lengths to produce staple fibres prior to spinning into yarn. A tremendous amount of filament yarn is produced although it is true to say that nowadays there is more staple fibre than filament yarn. Nylon, Terylene, rayon and the acetate fibres appear as both filament and staple but practically all the acrylics are in staple fibre only, although there is some filament Crylor.

Fixaform

A permanent press finish. For further details see page 71.

Flame-resistant

See under Anti-flame, page 17.

Flannel

A plain or twill woven fabric made wholly or partly from wool. Heavy flannel items such as trousers should be professionally dry-cleaned but items such as lightweight slacks, shorts and skirts can be washed at home.

Use a warm synthetic detergent solution or soapflakes and wash in the same way as for wool. After rinsing, roll in a thick towel to remove excess moisture, shake and dry out of doors away from direct heat. Iron on the wrong side while still slightly damp; use a warm iron and continue pressing until the garment is quite dry. If the fabric dries out too much, do not sprinkle with water but wrap in a damp cloth for half an hour.

Flannelette

A soft, warm, lightweight, flannel-like fabric with a slightly raised face in cotton. Today, flannelette is frequently made in various blends including rayon. Wash as for wool or rayon, unless manufacturer states that the flannelette may be hand- or machine-washed in very hot or even boiling water.

Flare-free

See under Anti-flame, page 17.

Flare-free nylon net

This is treated by a process which makes nylon net quite safe for children for party wear. Wash as for ordinary nylon net then rinse and drip-dry. Treated fabric can be professionally dry-cleaned but it should be clearly labelled with the finish and the cleaners should be reminded not to re-stiffen the net after cleaning.

Flax

The name of the plant from which the flax fibre, used for making yarns is extracted.

Flisca

Rayon manufactured in Switzerland.

Flock-printed fabrics

Materials overprinted with flock, lacquer, gold and other special printings giving the pattern a raised effect should be washed gently in hand-hot mild suds. Rinse well then roll in a towel to remove excess moisture but do not wring. Iron on the reverse side only, using a warm iron. The fabric can be drip-dried and should not then need ironing.

Fluflene

This is modified Terylene yarn which is bulky and yet not heavy. Fluflene is highly absorbent and warm. Garments made from Fluflene include socks, stockings and underwear, as well as various thick-knit outer-wear garments.

Fluflon

The trade name for a particular type of nylon crimp yarn made by a process similar to Helanca. Fluflon is warm, light and has a high degree of elasticity; it is used principally for sweaters, underwear, swimsuits, men's socks and crêpe-stretch nylons.

Wash frequently in hot suds, rinse and drip dry or roll in a thick towel to absorb excess moisture. Dry away from direct heat. The fabric should not require ironing if washed carefully but may be touched up with a very cool iron if necessary. If the material contains rayon, wash in warm suds, but otherwise treat similarly.

Folkweave

A loosely woven material made from coarse yarns—usually cotton or blends of rayon and wool—and used mostly for furnishing fabrics. Test striped or brightly coloured folkweave for colour fastness and wash in warm suds; rinse, wring and hang out to dry immediately. Iron while still slightly damp with a medium hot iron and stretch the material gently where necessary. Plain folkweave may be safely washed in hot suds and immediate hanging is not so essential.

Fortrel

This is an American polyester fibre similar to Dacron or Terylene. Treat in the same way.

Foulard

A fine twill fabric often printed and which is usually called surah nowadays. It was originally made in silk but today is made mostly in acetate or Tricel. Wash according to fibre.

French ninon

Wash as for Ninon.

Frostex

The trade name for knit-de-knit Tricel and nylon bouclé yarns.

Fur fabric

Fur fabrics made for fun furs or to simulate real furs can be made from nylon, rayon or cotton but are most often made now from acrylic fibres such as Orlon, Courtelle or Acrilan or from polyester fibres such as Tereylene or Dacron. In acrylic fur fabrics, mod-acrylic fibres are often included in the fabric to reduce flammability. Cotton and rayon fur fabrics are best sent for dry cleaning. Nylon, acrylic or polyester fabrics should be washed according to the instructions given with the garment. Where these are missing treat as for Nylon fur on page 67.

Gaberdine

A smooth twill fabric used extensively in raincoats and made from cotton, wool and blends of cotton and wool and also blends with the man-made fibres such as Sarille and nylon. It is closely woven with the twill running at a steep angle and thus has a high degree of shower-proofness. Proofing finishes may also be applied to gaberdines to increase resistance to rain. This is the favourite fabric for wax-proofed rainwear. Warm wax-proofed gaberdine by a fire occasionally to maintain the spread of wax-proofing. For rainwear or a coat send for professional dry-cleaning. Light slacks or skirts can be washed in hand-hot suds and ironed when slightly damp with a medium hot iron.

Georgette

A fine sheer fabric something between a crêpe and a voile. It may be made of pure wool, cotton, silk or almost any of the man-made fibres including Tricelon. Fabric made from pure silk or wool is likely to be delicate and difficult to wash at home unless manufacturer's instructions state otherwise so if in doubt send for professional dry-cleaning. Most of the man-made fibres will be fairly easy to wash especially nylon or polyester. Follow swing-tag instructions with regard to washing, water temperature and iron setting. Where no HLCC label is shown, wash as below.

Wash gently, using warm soapflakes or a mild liquid synthetic detergent but measure the garment carefully in case of shrinkage and test for colour fastness. Squeeze and knead the fabric in the suds then rinse two or three times at least in clear water.

Next lay the garment flat on a thick bath towel and carefully ease it back into shape and to the original measurements, then roll it in the towel and squeeze to remove excess moisture. Shake slightly, hang to dry away from heat and gently pull into shape again if necessary.

When the garment is almost dry, iron very slowly and carefully on the wrong side, using a heavy pressure and an iron as hot as the particular fabric will allow. The garment must be ironed until completely dry and to the correct size or it may shrink during the final airing.

Gevetex

The brand name for a glass fibre made in West Germany.

Gingham

This striped or checked fabric is usually woven of cotton or spun rayon but may also be in Terylene/cotton or in a wool blend. It washes easily in hand-hot suds. If there is any doubt about the fastness of the colour, use warm suds only. Rinse, hang to dry and iron with a medium hot iron while fabric is still slightly damp.

Glass

This is a man-made fibre produced by drawing out thin filaments of molten glass. Although it was originally used in the plastics field it is now produced as a textile. To make glass fibres, $\frac{3}{4}$ inch glass marbles are melted over intense heat and eventually 95 miles of filaments are drawn from each marble. The yarn is processed by twisting or plying filaments. Bulk yarns are produced by shooting jet streams of air into the yarn, thus blowing it up. Glass fibre yarn is then woven on standard commercial looms and converters add the design, style and colour to the fabric which is then made up into curtains or curtain fabric for home sewing.

Colours and designs are fast on glass fibre fabrics and they are resistant to light, moths and fire. Curtains of this type increase heat and sound insulation. At one time they were inclined to be brittle or to wear on folds but this problem has now been eliminated and glass fibre fabric is soft and drapes well. A big advantage is that the fabric does not stretch or sag and it is wrinkle free.

When measuring windows for glass curtain fabrics there is no need to allow for shrinkage or stretch. When measuring for floor-length curtains, subtract 1 inch so that curtains do not rub on the floor.

Curtains are usually hung unlined but if lining is preferred, another glass fibre fabric should be used to eliminate the possibility of shrinking. If other lining fabric is used it should be hung as a separate inner curtain or else made to be removed for washing. Weights, if used, should be covered with cloth and then tacked inside the hem to avoid rubbing. Or they can be slipped into detachable pockets at the hem.

To sew fibre glass fabric, use a mercerized cotton thread and a sharp needle. Alter bobbin and top thread tensions of sewing machine to the largest stitch and loosest tension. Experiment on a piece of scrap fabric first trying out lighter and heavier pressure adjustments before actually sewing curtains. See that the stitching does not draw up the fabric and that one piece of the fabric doesn't slip. Sew slowly and guide fabric through the machine allowing the material to feed at its own speed.

As fibre glass fabrics are non-iron, it is best to join widths with a regular French seam but if both seams are selvedges, a plain seam is usually sufficient. Make sure that all headings and trimmings are washable and non-shrink.

Glass fibre curtains should be hung away from radiators and window-sills and clear of the floor to avoid constant rubbing. Ideally, use a pull-cord to draw curtains to prevent undue wear.

Do not machine wash, spin, wring, dry clean or iron glass fibre fabrics.

To launder, swish curtains around in warm water using a mild soap or detergent but no bleach. Dirt will float off the fabric because it cannot penetrate the fibres so do not rub or scrub. Rinse thoroughly in clear, warm water. Do not spin or wring, simply allow excess water to drain off.

Wrap a towel around the clothes line and drape the curtains over it. Do not use clothes pegs. Smooth hems and leave for a short while. Curtains can be re-hung while still damp. If preferred, after rinsing, curtains can be rolled in a towel to absorb excess moisture and they can then be re-hung immediately. Do not iron. Fabric is permanently wrinkle resistant and will fall into natural folds when hung.

Glass fibre fabrics should be washed separately and not with other fabrics. Afterwards, rinse out sink or bath with clear water as the fabric may shed a few loose particles during washing.

Glazes, sheens and lustres

Glazed finishes can be applied with varying degrees of stiffness or softness and are not all stiff like the old-fashioned glazed chintzes.

There are various finishes and processes which give cottons, linens and rayons a sheen which can be anything from a high glaze to a dull or subdued lustre, while some fabrics are treated so that the glaze is applied to one section of the pattern only. Materials treated are usually given extra qualities also such as shrink- and crease-resistance, and many will resist soiling and spotting.

The manufacturer's laundering instructions must be followed when supplied or, if they are not available, wash gently in hand-hot suds without boiling, rubbing or twisting. Rinse thoroughly in clear water but do not wring and never use starch or bleach. Squeeze very gently to remove excess moisture then hang to drip dry, or if possible, hang immediately while still dripping wet. Iron according to instructions. There is no way of reglazing these fabrics at the moment if the special finish is spoiled through excessive creasing or wrong laundering, although stiffening with a strong solution of starch followed by ironing with a hot iron and using firm pressure while the material is damp may help.

Glo-Span

This is a type of elastomeric fibre based on polyurethane. For further details see page 38.

Grilon

Like Mirlon, this is a type of nylon manufactured in Switzerland but a similar nylon is made under the same name in Japan.

Grosgrain

A plain woven fabric which has a definite rib running in the weft direction. The material can be of various fibres and weights and should be laundered or dry-cleaned accordingly.

Guanaco

The hair of a species of llama and rather similar to alpaca.

Habutae

This is a soft, lightweight plain weave fabric, chiefly used for linings and often known as Jap silk.

Helanca

Like Fluflon, this is a process which was originally used to crêpe or crimp nylon, and is now used for Terylene and similar fibres. Helanca is soft, warm and very elastic and is used mainly for men's socks, the heavier type of nylon stockings and for swimsuits and underwear as well as figure-hugging sweaters.

For washing instructions see under Fluflon on page 43.

Helion

A type of nylon made in Italy.

Hemp

A strong but light natural fibre obtained from the hemp plant and rather similar to flax.

Hessian

Coarse, strong cloth, plain-woven from jute or hemp.

High Bulk Tricel

See under Tricel, page 98.

Hipolan

Viscose manufactured in Japan.

Honan

A wild silk fabric used mainly for dresses and blouses. Until recent new finishes were used on it, it was inclined to spot easily but this has mainly been remedied.

Wash as for silk and restore sheen with vinegar in the same way if necessary. Iron Honan while still slightly damp by pressing on the wrong side, using fairly heavy pressure and a moderately hot iron. If the fabric is too dry, do not sprinkle with water but roll in a damp towel for half an hour. Continue pressing until the fabric is quite dry, then hang to air.

Hopsack

This is a loosely-woven fabric of plain weave except that yarns are used in pairs instead of singly. It can be in linen, cotton or rayon and is particularly widely developed as a spun rayon in the Northern Ireland linen industry. Dry-clean.

Inoxor

A metallic yarn made in viscose rayon with a coating of aluminium foil. Unlike most metallic yarns, Inoxor is not washable and fabrics decorated with it should be dry-cleaned only.

Jap silk

A soft lightweight plain weave fabric, chiefly used for linings. It can be made from silk or from other cheaper fibres. Wash according to fibre.

Jersey

A plain weft knitted fabric which can be made from wool, silk, nylon, cotton, Tricel, Courtelle, Orlon, Dacron, Crimplene, rayon and other fibres. Jersey travels well without creasing, can be packed into a small space; it is reasonably warm depending upon the fibre used, yet frequently it is not too hot on a warm day.

Some jersey fabrics and especially those made from rayon and wool, are difficult to wash at home and where the manufacturer states this, garments should be sent for professional dry-cleaning.

Tricel, Courtelle, Orlon, cotton and nylon jersey, etc., are easily washed and garments should be laundered frequently before they are really soiled. Use warm suds and squeeze the fabric gently in the suds without rubbing or twisting. Press out as much soapy water as possible (spin-dry if wished, cooling first and giving short spins) and rinse two or three times. Roll in a towel to absorb excess moisture or spin again and hang to dry.

If cotton jersey is badly soiled—on collars and cuffs for instance—wash in the same way but first rub dampened bar soap (household or toilet soap) into the dirty parts and leave for a few minutes, then scrub lightly with a soft brush and continue as above.

Jute

This coarse natural fibre is obtained from plants and is used principally for sacks and for carpet backing.

Kanekalon

An acrylic fibre slightly similar to Courtelle or Acrilan but made in Japan.

Kapok

A fine hair-like fibre obtained from the seed pods of the kapok tree. As it cannot be spun, it is used mainly as a stuffing material. It is naturally waterproof and for this reason was widely used for Mae West type life jackets. Its extreme lightness makes it particularly suitable for sleeping-bags and for cushions etc. Dry-clean.

Kapron

A nylon manufactured in U.S.S.R.

Knit-de-knit

This is the name given to a process whereby yarn is knitted, set and then de-knitted (unroved or unravelled). The result of which is a yarn which has characteristic loops or waves. Frostex is an example of this type of process used on Tricel.

Kodel

Polyester fibres made in America and similar to Terylene or Dacron.

Koratron

A post cured resin process for imparting permanent shape retention to all types of garments. An important feature of the technique is that all parts of the garment—shell fabric, linings, interlinings, waist band, pocketing, zipper tapes etc. must conform to Koratron standards. The process is licensed by Koratron Technique (U.K.) Ltd. It is used for various garments including men's trousers where it gives slight stiffness and permanent crease retention. Manufacturers claim that the garment will always be perfectly shaped and never need ironing. For washing instructions follow swing label or sewn-in instructions. Where these are missing, wash in hand-hot water by hand or in a machine on medium wash setting, Give a cold rinse and short spin, tumble dry or drip dry. If tumble dried, remove immediately cycle is completed and place on a hanger.

See also Permanent press finishes, page 71.

Lace

Lace varies very much in weight and type, some being very delicate and others—such as those made for curtains—being quite tough.

There are three main types of lace: *Bobbin net* which comprises a wide range of fine net fabrics; *Leaver's lace* which is used for everything from trimmings for underwear to actual dress materials and *Curtain lace* which is made on giant flat machines with Jacquard patterning. To a very large extent, the traditional Leaver's lace machine has been replaced by fine gauge Raschel knitting machines. In fact, most of the Leaver's types have been replaced by Raschel's and only an expert could tell the difference in the finished lace.

Almost all lace made today is machine lace. Hand lace is still made occasionally but it is only a scattered cottage industry, in the U.K. in the west of England around Honiton, for example.

But even though it is made by machine, lace is still fragile and should be laundered with care although much will depend on the fibre used. Lace can be made from cotton, nylon, polyesters and in Vincel/cotton blends.

Launder according to swing tag provided by manufacturer or according to fibre. Take particular care with lace trimmings, blouses, evening wear and also pastel-coloured lace.

Synthetic detergents and soap powders are likely to contain a fluorescer which may affect the colour of pastel shades, so for pastels it is best to use a washing product designed for delicate fabrics. Cotton lace can be starched to restore its crisp, new look. Other lace fabrics should not be starched but may be stiffened with gum arabic or borax or with one or two lumps of sugar in a basin of hot water.

Old or fragile lace should be placed in a plastics stocking washer or a jam jar and covered with warm water whisked to a lather with mild soapflakes. Shake the washer or jar gently so that the suds can penetrate the lace, pour off the soapy water and run clear warm water into the jar for rinsing. Repeat the rinsing process two or three times, then roll the lace in a towel to absorb the excess moisture. Stiffen carefully if necessary.

Fairly strong lace, such as that used for curtains, can be washed in hot suds, and really dirty cotton lace curtains can be boiled if necessary. Rinse thoroughly in two or three changes of water then wring and pull gently into shape before hanging to dry. Iron the lace while it is still fairly damp, using a hot iron and heavy pressure on the wrong side. Continue pressing until the fabric is completely dry.

Some lace fabrics tend to shrink during laundering: counteract this by easing into shape gently before leaving to dry and again during ironing. Hang a lace blouse, dress or other garment on a plastics hanger to dry. An alternative is to hang a frock across a line pegged by the waist seam but protect the lace first with tissue paper both from the line and the pegs. If the dress has a full skirt, peg this to the line along the hemline, again using tissue paper to protect the lace.

Ideally, lace should be pressed on a padded board with the wrong side of the fabric uppermost. Press or iron cotton lace with a moderately hot iron while the fabric is still slightly damp; iron lace made from rayon or a rayon blend when it is almost dry, using a warm iron. Nylon and polyesters should not need ironing but if they do, use a warm iron on setting 2.

Lactron

This is the trade name for uncovered natural rubber thread. DC. 2000 Lactron is a special super-heated resistant version.

Lambswool

Strictly speaking this is material which has been made from the wool of a lamb, or in other words, of a sheep that is not more than eight months old. Wash as given under Wool on page 181.

Lamonyl

A Type-6 nylon manufactured in Switzerland.

Lancola

A spun-dyed textured acetate yarn extensively used in knitted dress and outerwear fabrics. Treat as for acetate, page 13.

Lancolon

A blended filament yarn composed of filaments of Lansil acetate and nylon. It is used for woven and knitted dress fabrics.

Lanital

A protein fibre made in Belgium and France and similar to the Fibrolane fibre produced in this country.

Lansil

A trade name applied to some acetate yarns produced in this country.

Lastex

This is not a polyurethane fibre as is sometimes thought. It is a natural rubber thread with a natural or synthetic textile covering.

Latex

This is the usual generic trade name for extruded rubber threads, which are made from liquid latex rubber. They are still extensively used in corsetry etc. being braided or doubled with nylon, rayon, cotton etc, as they are not suitable for use next to the skin.

Lawn

A fine material which may be made from cotton, 100 per cent polyester or a blend of polyester and cotton as well as from Vincel/cotton blends. It should be washed by hand or for only a very short time in a machine. Use hand-hot water and a rich lather. Rinse thoroughly and wring or spin dry.

Iron while still slightly damp with a hot iron for cotton or a coolish iron for Terylene or Terylene blends.

If the fabric has a minimum iron finish, wash by hand and drip dry. Where ironing is necessary use a warm iron when the material is dry.

Leacril

An acrylic fibre manufactured in Italy.

Lilion

A nylon 6 made in Italy.

Linen

The name linen should actually be applied only to fabrics made from linen yarns spun from flax fibres.

Linen should not be laundered if it is stained; stains and marks should be dealt with first. Most stains can be removed by following the instructions given in the chapter on Stains.

If linen is very dirty, before washing it in hot water and synthetic detergent or soap suds, soak for about 15 minutes in warm soapy water. After washing, rinse thoroughly in two or three changes of water, hang to dry and iron while still slightly damp, with a hot iron. With linen garments such as blouses and dresses, follow the same procedure but iron on the wrong side to avoid shine.

Linron

This is a processed flax fibre recently developed and is so revolutionary in character—as the bleaching and purifying is done at the raw flax stage—that it is claimed to be a linen fibre. It has new possibilities of intimate blends with other natural and man-made fibres, and linen/wool blends quite unknown previously are now being developed.

Llama

The hair of the South American llama—a goat inhabiting Chile and Peru. Vicuña and alpaca are both types of llama but the hair is much finer. Llama hair is brown to black in colour and is long and very smooth. It is also particularly fine and soft and is used in fine woollen and worsted fabrics as well as for heavy coats. Dry clean.

Locknit

This word, synonymous with tricot, is the generic term for plain warp-knit fabrics. It is made from virtually all the filament yarns but mainly nylon and acetate. At one time, locknit was used almost exclusively for underwear fabric but now dress fabrics in acetate and Tricel are popular. These are sometimes referred to as jersey but this is inaccurate as jersey is a weft-knitted fabric. Wash according to fibre or to manufacturer's instructions.

Lurex

The trade name for a metallic and plastic thread made by giving aluminium foil a synthetic coating which will withstand washing or dry-cleaning. The thread, which cannot tarnish and is made in many colours, is used sometimes for decorative purposes in bedspreads, towels, stoles and in numerous fabrics for garments. Wash according to the main fibre present, i.e. cotton, silk, nylon, etc., or sponge to remove spots from unwashable materials. Use a warm iron only, never a hot iron.

Luron

The brand name for a monofilament nylon made in this country and used solely for lines for fishing-rods.

Lycra

An elastomeric fibre produced by Du Pont. It is used extensively in the manufacture of foundation garments. Lycra is a multifilament stretch yarn with high elastic recovery. This means that it stretches and goes back into place like rubber. It is stronger, more durable, weighs one-third less and gives longer wear as well as having two or three times as much restraining power as conventional elastic thread. Lycra can be covered like rubber or used uncovered. It is easily dyed and is used in the tops of pantee-hose to give control and support. Lycra is also widely used for swimwear. Wash both swimwear and foundation as for HLCC Label No. 6. Rinse swimwear in cool water immediately after use. Do not use bleach on Lycra foundations.

Lyflon

A foreign furnishing nylon fabric said to wear five times as long as ordinary wool moquette. Although the fabric is woven from synthetic fibres it looks a little like velvet and is used on the latest Trans-European trains. Stains of all kinds, including ink, wine and oil can all be wiped off with a damp cloth. To clean, wipe with a cloth dipped in clear warm water. Obstinate marks can be removed with a little dissolved detergent.

Man-made fibres

This is a term applied to any textile fibre which is not of natural origin. There are a great many man-made fibres in daily use including cellulosic fibres—rayon, acetate and triacetate; polyamide fibres—the various nylons; polyester fibres such as Terylene, Dacron etc.; and the acrylics such as Courtelle and Orlon etc. These are all either staple fibres for spinning into yarns on textile machinery or continuous filament yarns in long lengths like silk.

Washing and care instructions vary according to the particular fibre. Where possible follow the instructions given on the sewn-in or swing-tag label by the manufacturer. HLCC Care Labels are sewn into or attached to most garments made today and further details of Care labelling are given on page 134. Further information on the care of individual fibres will be found under the respective headings. Where there is no care label and the fibre content is not known, the following general advice may help:

1. Wash frequently and as soon after use as possible. Remove non-

washable components—belts, shoulder-pads etc. before laundering.

2. Do not mix whites and coloured and do not wash with other
soiled garments. Wash fabrics in cream, yellow or other delicate
pastel shades separately and in mild detergent.

3. Do not boil or bleach. If bleach is essential for some reason then
use well diluted in very small quantities and rinse away
thoroughly afterwards.

4. Wash by hand in warm water (40° C.). Use soap flakes, mild
synthetic detergents or washing powder and make sure these
are completely dissolved before garments are immersed in
suds.

5. Wash, rinse and dry garments without interruption. Do not
leave them lying wet. After washing, give a warm rinse and drip
dry or a cold rinse followed by a short spin. For heavy-knits
squeeze gently to remove excessive moisture and roll in a thick
towel before hanging lying flat to dry.

Never let solid particles of detergents or other chemicals come into
contact with fabric. The soap powder or detergent should be completely dissolved before the garments are put in. Almost every washing product contains a certain amount of a fluorescent compound
(i.e. one designed to make white appear whiter and to give an extra
whiteness to white fabrics). If these detergents are used in great concentration the fluorescent compound will swamp the colour that the
dyer has supplied to the fabric, making it appear washed out and
grey after several washings. If a washing machine is so arranged that
this cannot be done, the powder should first be dissolved in a separate jug of hot water and then added to the machine (unless machine
manufacturer states otherwise).

Hang garments made from man-made fibres to dry as soon as
possible after rinsing or removing excess moisture. Line dry if preferred but make sure that the weight is evenly distributed. Knitted
garments or dresses which may lose their shape should not be hung
to dry whilst heavy with water. Always dry all man-made fibre fabrics
away from intense heat and keep white fabrics out of direct sunlight.

If ironing is required, use a cool iron (setting 1) raising to warm
(setting 2) if necessary. Do not sprinkle with water as this may mark
some fabrics; if garment is too dry to iron, re-damp completely.

Do not use starch on man-made fabrics with special finishes
especially those that are resin-treated, i.e. some rayons and fabrics

labelled 'crease-resisting', 'minimum iron', 'stain-resisting', 'low flammability'. Give these resin-treated fabrics a final rinse in cold water.

When garments are sent to be dry-cleaned it is important to tell the cleaner what the article is made of, if no tag or label is attached and if you know the fibre or blend.

A great many man-made fibre fabrics are now available for the home dressmaker and unless you are very familiar with modern fabrics it is generally better to work with a pattern where guidance is given for the particular material you are using.

Rayons and acetates are fairly straightforward for home sewing and the various brands of mercerized sewing thread available can generally be used satisfactorily. Nylon, polyesters such as Terylene and other synthetic fibre fabrics, however, need more care. Ordinary cotton is not suitable for sewing by hand or machine and sewing threads made from synthetic fibres should be chosen.

Both leading suppliers of home sewing threads market a synthetic fibre sewing thread made from Terylene (marketed as Gossamer and Trylko) and these are suitable for most nylon and polyester fibre fabrics. There is also a schappe-spun Terylene sewing thread marketed with the brand name Perivale spun Terylene.

Cut fabrics with sharp scissors and use fine pins and needles. Wherever possible, cut seams on the bias to prevent puckering and allow at least a $\frac{3}{4}$ in. seam as many synthetics fray easily. Overstitch or turn in raw edges and use French or felled seams if possible. Have machine needle and bobbin tensions slack and guide material through gently; if it is forced through too quickly it may pucker. If material slips, sandwich it between sheets of tissue paper and remove these later. Press hems and seams with a steam iron set at low temperature or with a cool or warm iron (setting 1 or 2 according to fibre) over a damp cloth.

Marocain

A medium-weight crêpe fabric, which was originally made in silk then in acetate/viscose blends but is now usually made in acetate, although Marocain is not in much use these days.

Wash in warm suds, rinse immediately. When almost dry, stretch gently under a warm iron until the garment returns to its original shape and size. If the material becomes too dry, do not sprinkle with water but roll in a damp towel for a short time.

Marquisette

An openwork fabric frequently used for curtains. It was originally silk but now is made in cotton, rayon or Terylene and should be washed accordingly.

Melton

A heavy fabric with a felted appearance, widely used for overcoats. It is usually a twill weave of all wool or woven with a woollen weft and cotton warp. The felted finish is produced by heavy milling and cropping processes during which the fibres in the cloth are tightly matted together. Dry-clean only.

Meraklon

This is a polypropylene fibre fabric made in Italy and similar to Ulstron.

Merino

This is fine wool from pure-bred Merino sheep. Strictly speaking the wool fibres should have a diameter of 24 microns or less. The term is used to define the finest and highest qualities of wool and includes botany wool. Hand wash as on page 181.

Merinova

A regenerated fibre made in Italy and similar to Fibrolane which is produced in this country. This fibre also is always blended with others. For washing instructions see Protein fibres, page 79.

Merlon

A type of nylon made in Switzerland.

Metallic yarns

A man-made fibre which is composed of metal, metal-coated plastic, plastic-coated metal or which is a core covered with metal. It is shiny, with a high lustre and is used for decorative purposes in dresses, furnishings and other fabrics. Brand names include Lurex and Metlon. The metal threads are untarnishable and the fabric should be laundered according to the main fibre concerned.

Metlon

A metallic yarn manufactured in U.S.A. Wash as for the main material, disregarding the metallic thread, which is untarnishable.

Milium

This is not a fabric but a metallic finish usually applied to a rayon lining, thus making an insulating lining which retains body heat and keeps the wearer warmer in cold weather and cooler in the sun. The lining is lightweight, porous and is used in caps, bed-covers, foot-wear, sleeping-bags, curtains and all types of apparel but is most widely used in men's suits. British processors are Walkden, Makin & Co. Ltd. It can be commercially dry-cleaned without harm.

Minalon

An acetate yarn manufactured in Japan.

Minimum-iron

See under Drip Dry, page 150.

Miralene

The trade name for a special bulking process for producing crinkle or bouclé type yarn in Terylene.

Miralon

The trade name for a special bulking process for producing crinkle or bouclé type yarn in nylon.

Mirlon

Like Grilon, this is a Type-6 nylon made in Switzerland.

Misr nylon

A nylon fibre manufactured in Egypt.

Mixture

This indicates that a fabric is constructed of two or more different yarns during weaving or knitting. For instance, this might be a woven fabric with a nylon warp and a rayon or cotton weft.

In a mixture fabric, the predominating fibre should be named first. Thus, if there is 60 per cent rayon and 40 per cent nylon, the description would be rayon/nylon and never nylon/rayon. If there are more than two fibres, the same principle applies. For instance a fabric made from 50 per cent wool, 30 per cent nylon and 20 per cent acetate would be labelled wool/nylon/acetate.

As long as there is at least 15 per cent of a man-made fibre in the mixture, the manufacturer does not have to give the exact percentage of each fibre although he can do this if he wishes. It is sufficient to list the fibres in order of their dominance by weight.

The quality and care of a fabric depend on how it is made as well as on its fibre content. If there is less than 7 per cent of another fibre added for decorative (or processing) purposes, this does not need to be named. When washing a garment, care should be taken to treat for the weakest fibre present, even if this is only in the form of decoration. It is for this reason that the manufacturer's care instructions should always be followed as he will have allowed for this.

Modacrylics

This is an American word meaning modified acrylics and which is now accepted in Britain as well. Generally, modacrylics are fibres which consist of between 50 and 85 per cent of acrylonitrile. The fibres are similar to acrylics but they are not quite so strong although they are particularly suitable for flame-resistant fabrics. For this reason they are widely used for children's nightwear as well as for knitted and woven dresses, underwear and household textiles. Modacrylics are also used to make imitation fur.

Fabrics are easy to wash and require little or no ironing. Launder in warm suds, rinse thoroughly and if necessary press with a cool iron. Brand names include Teklan, Dynel and Verel.

For fuller details of chemical basis see under Dynel on page 37.

Modified rayons

These are viscose rayons which are modified during manufacture to produce a range of different yarns with various qualities, properties and characteristics. Modified rayons fall into different groups such as polynosic, high tenacity, crimped and cross linked. Vincel is a polynosic, Tenasco is a high tenacity and Sarille and Evlan are crimped modified rayons. Wash or dry clean as for viscose.

Modified viscose fibres

See under Modified rayons above.

Mohair

This is the hair of the Angora goat and yarns spun from it. Wash as for Angora. See page 16.

Moiré

Often described as watered, this rippled fabric is ribbed or corded and after weaving is finished by being subjected to heat and heavy pressure from rollers. Because of the ribbing, some parts are not flattened and the two surfaces show different reflections which give the watered effect. Dry-clean.

Moisture-repellent

See Water-repellent, page 105.

Monofilament

This is a fibre produced by forcing a more or less liquid chemical substance through a fine hole in a spinneret.

Moquette

An upholstery fabric with a heavy pile and made from wool, cotton, Evlan and the acrylics such as Courtelle and Acrilan. The fabric has a special pile warp lifted over wires which may have knives. Where there are knives, the pile is cut, where there are not, the pile is uncut but fabric can have both a cut or uncut pile. Most moquette requires to be dry-cleaned but the detachable acrylic versions should be washable. See manufacturer's instructions in each case.

Moss crêpe

A full-handling crêpe fabric which was originally made from viscose and acetate doubled yarns; it is now being made in viscose and triacetate which results in greater stability, i.e. it does not shrink so readily when wet. There are, in addition, various processes for moss crêpes which help the fabric to remain stable.

The latest method of making moss crêpe is by using a Tricelon, which relies for the pebble effect on the differential shrinkage between the two composite fibres, just as happened with the elaborate doubling and twisting of acetate and viscose. The dobby crêpe weave is used for crêpes in a variety of yarns here today.

Launder carefully in warm suds. Rinse thoroughly in warm water and when almost dry, press with a warm iron and gently pull into shape and to the original size.

Moth proofing

There are a considerable number of chemicals which will proof fabrics against moth but most of these have a temporary action only and are removed by laundering, dry-cleaning, wear or even by the action of light. All modern man-made fibres are moth-proof but where these are used in blends then the natural fibre—and especially wool—is still liable to attack by moth unless specially treated.

The Mitin moth-proofing process is durable for the life of the fabric treated. It can be used on any wool or woollen fabric including knitting wool, blankets, carpets, furnishing fabrics, soft furniture and garments, etc. It has no effect on the handle or appearance of the fabric, cannot irritate the skin, has no smell and works by making the wool unpalatable to moths and carpet beetles. A number of manufacturers carry out the Mitin process under licence but a specified standard of moth-proofing must be attained first and periodic checks are made to ensure that the standard is kept.

Movil

PVC fibres made in Italy.

Moygashel

This is the name applied to a wide range of fabrics and is the registered trade-mark of a manufacturing firm. They are usually linen, cotton, or spun rayons or blends of these fibres.

Multifilament

These are fibres produced by forcing liquid chemical substance through fine holes in a spinneret. False twist yarns are usually of this type.

Mungo

This is the lowest quality reclaimed wool or a fibrous material made in the woollen trade. In both cases it is produced from old or new knitted fabrics, hand woven or loosely woven fabrics or from milled cloth or felt.

Muslin

A fine, thin cotton fabric originating in the East and comes from the word Muslim. It should be washed in warm water. Rinse several times in clean warm water then squeeze out most of the water and iron while still damp, using a warm iron. If the muslin needs starching use one part starch to ten parts water or stiffen in a gum arabic solution (see page 155.)

Muslin curtains need careful handling and should be rolled and then tied lightly with tapes at both ends of each roll before laundering. If very dirty, soak overnight in cold water then wash by gently squeezing in warm soapless detergent suds. Rinse in two or three changes of clear warm water, starch if necessary then pass gently through the wringer still rolled. Finally unroll the curtains and pin each corner to a sheet or old table-cloth before hanging to dry. Iron while still damp, going round the edges first to set the shape.

Nailon

This is the Italian generic term for nylon.

Needlecord

A fine cord pile fabric at one time made of cotton but now made in various fibres. It is particularly popular in polyester/cotton and polynosic/cotton blends. Washing will depend on the fibres used. For the synthetics see manufacturer's swing tag or wash in hand-hot water, rinse in warm water and drip dry or give a cold rinse and short spin. For cotton fabrics, handle as gently and as little as possible during laundering. Whisk up a rich lather with warm water and mild soapflakes and swish the garment in this. Gently press out excess soapy water and rinse twice in clear warm water, then hang to drip dry. While the needlecord is drying, shake it and smooth the fabric the way of the pile with a soft cloth. Shake thoroughly when dry but do not iron, except as for corduroy.

Net

Many nets—with the exception of nylon, Terylene and similar fabrics—shrink when being washed for the first time and allowance should be made for shrinkage when making up net.

Dress net (if of cotton) should be washed in hand-hot soapflake suds; rinse, drip dry and iron with a moderately hot iron while still slightly damp.

Curtain nets (if of cotton) need a slightly different treatment and frequent laundering. Shake thoroughly to remove loose dirt, rinse in plain cold water then wash in hot water whisked to a lather with a synthetic detergent. Do not rub or twist but squeeze the lather gently through the net and if the water quickly becomes dirty and the lather disappears, squeeze out excess soap and re-wash in fresh suds. Rinse thoroughly two or three times and iron with a medium hot iron while the fabric is still slightly damp.

The foregoing applies only to nets made from cotton. Net is also made from other fibres, usually polyesters such as Terylene, Dacron and Trevira and these should be washed according to the fabric concerned. The polyesters, for instance, can be washed in warm suds, drip-dried and replaced at windows while still damp or they can be given a cold rinse and short spin and ironed with a cool iron when dry.

Ninon

A sheer fabric made from fine twisted yarns and frequently used for close curtains. Although originally made from silk, ninon is now usually acetate, nylon or polyester fibres such as Terylene, Dacron or Trevira. Tricelon is also used for modern ninons. Nylon ninon would normally be used only as dress, lingerie or blouse fabrics. For laundering nylon ninon wash as for delicate nylon and for polyester ninon launder as for fine Terylene.

For other ninon made into curtains, measure them before laundering, then make a rich lather with soapflakes or a mild detergent. Knead the curtains gently then remove from the lather, holding the weight of the material in the hands. Rinse two or three times in clear warm water, fold carefully and pass through the wringer or pat out the excess moisture in a towel.

Hang ninon curtains lengthwise over a line to dry and iron while still damp, using a warm to medium hot iron. Iron carefully along top and bottom and then along selvedges stretching gently and when the curtains are back to their original measurements, iron diagonally to avoid further stretching.

Niplon

This was a nylon fibre made in Japan but the name is now used for a Japanese PVC fibre.

Noils

Noils are the short (i.e. up to about $\frac{3}{4}$ in.) fibres removed from wool during combing for the worsted spinning process. These noils are normally of high quality wool and are sold to the woollen industry as a blend component for adding softness.

Nomex

A high melting-point fibre made by Du Pont. It has excellent fire resistance and is a member of the polyamide family.

Non-iron

See under Drip dry, page 150.

Non-iron cotton

See under heading Cotton on page 28 or Drip dry, page 150.

Non-shrink

See under Shrink-resistant, page 86.

Nun's veiling

This is a delicate fabric, usually worsted, silk or cotton which should be washed gently in warm suds without being twisted or rubbed, although it may be spin dried briefly or put through a wringer to remove excess moisture. Hang to dry away from heat immediately after rinsing, and iron when the fabric is almost dry, using a warm iron.

Nylo-chiffon

The brand name for a delicate nylon chiffon made by Courtaulds. For laundering care see under Chiffon.

Nylon

Known technically as a polyamide fibre, nylon 66 was originally discovered by Du Pont. There is more than one type of nylon. Type 66—the nylon with which we are most familiar—was the first and brand names include Bri-nylon, Du Pont nylon and Blue C nylon. Nylon 6 was developed in Germany independently during World War Two when there was no liaison between American and German scientists. Basic raw materials are similar to those for nylon 66 but the complex chemical processes are different. Brand names for type 6 include Courtaulds' Celon, Enkalon and the German Perlon. There is also type 11, a special type of French nylon; type 680, an American nylon resistant to sunlight and type 610 which is a bristle nylon.

Nylon is a particularly versatile fibre with more end uses than any other of the man-made fibres so far produced. It also has a tremendous number of advantages; among them—exceptional tensile strength, considerable elasticity (much more than natural fibres), it retains a high proportion of its strength when wet, resists abrasion to a remarkable degree, is naturally light in weight, absorbs less moisture than wool or cotton and as it tends to shrink away from a flame it burns with difficulty and is therefore suitable for children's nightwear. Nylon resists most oils and chemicals and is immune to attack by insects, moulds, fungi or bacteria. Because it is mineral-based, it contains no substance which can form food for insects so it is also mothproof.

Filaments of nylon yarn are completely smooth so there are no tiny roughnesses to trap dirt particles and dirt flows off nylon easily and smoothly. It is for this reason that it is easy to launder. Nylon should never be boiled or bleached and it should be washed frequently and separately from fabrics made from other fibres. White nylon should be washed separately from coloured nylon.

Wash nylon by hand or in a machine in plenty of hand-hot water mixed to a rich lather with a soap product or synthetic detergent. Make the most of nylon's quick-drying properties by rinsing in warm water and drip-drying or rinsing in cold water followed by a short spin before hanging to dry. If hanging on a coat hanger make sure it is made from plastic or has a non-staining finish or covering.

Most nylon articles dry quickly at normal room temperature and in any case nylon should not be exposed to direct heat or to strong sunlight. Ironing should not be necessary especially if garments are knitted or are washed correctly and drip-dried. If the fabric is of the type to require light pressing, wait until the material is dry or almost dry and then use a warm iron (setting 2). These instructions apply only to 100 per cent nylon fabrics. If other fibres are included, follow swing-ticket instructions or follow details given on page 55. The following particulars may also help.

Delicate nylon garments such as blouses, stockings, shirts and underwear should be laundered after EVERY use. Nylon dries quickly, does not usually need ironing and will last a long time if washed daily, although once dirt has penetrated the fibres it is almost impossible to get it out without damaging the material. Wash thoroughly, rinse in one or two clear waters then hang to drip dry or roll in a towel, shake and hang out to dry. Squeeze as little as possible to avoid creases.

Lingerie made from *permanently pleated nylon* should be washed after every wearing in hot synthetic detergent suds. Dip the garment up and down in the soapy water the way of the pleats, then rinse in the same way and drip dry. Do not twist or wring fabric but gently pull into shape when almost dry. Unpleated parts may be pressed with a cool iron but pleated nylon should not be ironed.

Most *stains on nylon* can be removed if they are dealt with immediately by washing or dry-cleaning but, as with dirt, once marks have set into the fabric they are difficult to remove. Ordinary cleaning agents used on other materials, such as carbon tetrachloride, trichlorethylene, petrol, benzine, etc. can be safely used on nylon but bleach must not be used. Garments sent for professional dry-cleaning should be clearly labelled 'nylon'.

When nylon is combined with other fibres the garment should be washed as for the weakest fibre in the blend. With *nylon and wool*, for example, or *nylon/acetate* use only warm suds, squeezing gently without twisting or wringing. Rinse two or three times in clear warm water, roll in a towel to absorb excess moisture and iron on the wrong side while still slightly and evenly damp. Use a warm iron for nylon/wool.

Nylon/cotton used for summer frocks can be washed in hot synthetic detergent suds. Rinse and hang to dry away from any direct heat. Iron while slightly damp on the wrong side, using a warm iron and pressing until the cotton in the material is completely dry.

To counteract electrostatic effects—which make nylon cling in cold, dry weather—see under Terylene on page 94.

Cut nylon with sharp scissors and when sewing, use nylon or polyester (Terylene) thread and very fine needles and pins. Where possible, cut seams on the bias to prevent puckering and because the fabric frays easily, allow at least a $\frac{3}{4}$-in. seam; French or felled seams are best used on nylon but in any case always turn in raw edges. Machine needles and bobbin thread tensions should be slackened and if the material slips, sandwich it between sheets of tissue paper and remove these later. Guide the fabric through the machine gently and do not force it through faster than the needle speed or it may pucker. Press hems and seams with a steam iron set at low temperature or with a cool iron over a damp cloth.

Nylon fur

To launder small items of nylon fur fabric at home prepare a rich lather with hand-hot water and pure soapflakes or mild synthetic detergent. Squeeze fur in the suds for several minutes then rinse in warm water, squeeze out surplus moisture and dry out of doors if possible and away from direct heat.

A nylon fur coat which is stiffened or interlined should not be washed in this way unless the manufacturer states that washing is suitable. Although the fur may be washed, the linings may not, and in this case or if there is any doubt about laundering, dry shampoo the garment instead. Prepare a hand-hot solution of a mild detergent or soapflakes and whisk to a rich lather.

Lay the garment flat and moisten a soft brush or piece of sponge in the surface lather and gently scrub the fur only. Clean a small area at a time and do not allow the moisture to penetrate the backing. Rinse by repeating the process with a clean sponge wrung out in clear warm water, and finally pat dry with a clean towel. Dry out of doors but not in sunlight and away from heat of any kind and shake frequently during drying.

Nymcrylon

Manufactured in Holland, this is an acrylic fibre made in much the same way as Courtelle, Orlon and Acrilan. It should be washed and treated in the same way.

Nymplex

A polythene fibre made in Holland.

Olefin fibres

Olefin and polyolefin are both terms used to cover both the poly-ethylene (polythene) and polypropylene fibres. Generally the two olefins—polythene and polypropylene—are only used industrially, though polythene is used in monofilament form for deckchair covers. A big development has been taking place in olefins in tape yarns made from stretch films for use as an alternative to jute. For further details see page 75.

Organdie

A delicate permanently stiffened fabric at one time made only in cotton but which is now frequently made in nylon. Cotton organdie should be washed by hand. Squeeze gently in hand-hot soapflake suds, rinse thoroughly in warm water, fold carefully in a towel and pass through a wringer; dry away from direct heat. To give organdie a crisp finish, iron it on the right side while still damp, using a medium hot iron.

If the organdie becomes limp and needs to be stiffened slightly, rinse finally in gum arabic solution (see page 155); in water containing liquid glue, or in a quart of warm water containing a tablespoonful of borax.

Nylon organdie should be washed as for delicate nylon.

Organza

A thin, transparent, chiffon type of fabric but with a stiffened finish. It has a plain weave and is made in various fibres including nylon. When made from silk it is produced from silk yarns in which the natural gum has been retained. In some fibres, organza crushes and creases quickly but is easily pressed. It is used for scarves, evening dresses, blouses and for trimmings. Wash according to fibre but handle gently.

Orlon

This was the original acrylic fibre, developed in U.S.A. but now also made in Northern Ireland. Made by Du Pont, Orlon is similar to other acrylics such as Courtelle and Acrilan. It does not shrink, re-sists moths, mildew and perspiration and is crease-resisting. Orlon can be used in 100 per cent form or to a lesser extent blended with natural fibres, particularly wool. Primarily used in the production of high bulk yarns for knitwear where garments are shrink-resistant, easily washed—by hand or machine, depending on manufacturer's instructions.

Garments have an excellent colour range from pure white through pastels to deep rich colours. Orlon is extensively used either in 100 per cent form or blended with wool in the production of single jersey laminated fabrics for dresses and suits.

Sew Orlon as given under Man-made fibres on page 57.

Wash according to the manufacturer's instructions or as HLCC label No. 6 or treat as given under Acrylic Fibres on page 15. Lay *sweaters* flat to finish drying, hang other Orlon materials away from heat. Ironing should be unnecessary but if preferred, iron over a damp cloth with a cool, dry iron.

Wash *Orlon jersey* in warm water and mild synthetic detergent or with soapflakes or powder plus a water softener. Rinse thoroughly and drip dry making sure that any pleats fall in the direction in-tended by the designer. Jersey holds more water than most washable fabrics and if the garment is too heavy, support it at the waist band or roll in a towel to remove excess moisture before handing to dry. Or spin dry briefly. Press if necessary, using a cool iron when dry.

Deep pile Orlon coats should be dry-cleaned unless the manufacturer's instructions state otherwise. Do not steam or press and do not brush unless the coat is dry. If the fabric becomes wet, shake, allow it to dry naturally then brush lightly when dry.

Ortalion

A Type-6 nylon made in Italy.

Osmalane

The brand name for a winceyette material which is a mixture of Merino wool and Egyptian cotton. This soft material is used for children's clothes, dresses and blouses, and it is easily washed. Squeeze gently in warm suds. Rinse, remove excess water (spin dry if wished) then dry away from heat. Iron with a warm iron when the material is almost dry.

Oswilena

The trade name for a bonded fibre fabric. For care and washing see under Bonded Fibre Interlining.

Ottoman

A smooth-ribbed fabric with the ribs running from selvedge to selvedge. It was originally made from silk but it is now frequently made in cotton and in acetate and other man-made fibres and should be treated accordingly.

Panne

A silk velvet.

Paper nylon

This is ordinary nylon fabric treated with a special resin finish and in washing it, the most important point is to avoid cracking this finish.

To launder, fill a very large bath with hot suds and lay the petticoat or other garment in this full length. Dip the garment up and down without squeezing or rubbing and remove any particularly dirty marks by scrubbing lightly. Rinse in the same way but avoid squeezing or wringing and hang the garment to drip dry.

Paper nylon washed frequently and carefully should retain its stiff finish but if the garment does become limp, a 50 per cent solution of plastics starch may help to restore it. Drip dry and press with a cool iron.

Fine hair-like creases in paper nylon can rarely be removed, hence the need for careful handling and hanging between wearing. Ironing with a warm iron while the nylon is damp may help a little.

Papillon

This is a fine plain weave fabric. It can be made from silk or other fibres. Wash accordingly.

Patterned finishes

See Embossed finishes, page 39.

Peau d'Ange

Literally translated this means angel skin. It is a dress fabric with a satin weave but with little lustre and more of a fine suede type. It usually has an acetate warp and schappe silk weft. Dry-clean or wash carefully if manufacturer's instructions allow. Treat as for silk or acetate.

Perlofil

A Type-6 nylon manufactured in Spain.

Perlon

This is the original generic name for nylon-6 which was developed in Germany during the war years independently of the nylon-66 invented in U.S.A. It is the name generally given to all nylon produced in West Germany.

Permanent embossing

See Embossed finishes, page 39.

Permanent pleating

See Durable pleating, page 36.

Permanent press finishes

These depend on applying the crease-resist resination to fabrics containing cotton or other cellulosic fibres but leaving the resin uncured. The curing process takes place after the garment has been made and pressed etc. and is then cured in an oven. The best known processes are Koratron, Fixaform and Tootapress. Used extensively on cotton slacks, rayon plus nylon blend trousers and rainwear, blends of polyester fibre with crimped rayon etc. Wash according to

HLCC label or tag. Usually washable by machine and no ironing necessary.

Permanent stiffening

Many of the permanently stiffened fabrics such as Staflex, Vilene, Oswilena, etc. are actually interlinings made from cotton or rayon held together by a special bonding agent although some of the best contain wool as well as viscose and are bonded with rubber. These bonded fibre fabric interlinings are separate fabrics in themselves and are not to be confused with ordinary materials which have been stiffened by a special finishing process. See also Bonded fibre interlining, page 20.

Pest-resistant

See under Moth-proofing.

Phrix

A range of man-made fibres manufactured in Germany—frequently rayon. Phrix Perlon is Type-6 nylon.

Piqué

A fabric with rounded cords running from side to side. Cotton piqué can be washed, boiled and starched and ironed in exactly the same way as most other cotton fabrics. Iron with a hot iron on the wrong side of the material while the garment is still evenly damp. Rayon piqué should be laundered carefully as given under Rayons on page 79. Blends of Vincel and cotton blends are used frequently and both acetate and triacetate have been developed for piqués. There are now also knitted piqués in various fibres. Wash according to swing tag or specific fibre.

Plastics

Plastics materials (probably polythene or PVC sheeting) can quite easily be sewn if long loose stitches are used and the material is machined between two layers of paper. Use a fairly thick thread, not sewing-silk, and avoid deep hems.

If the machine needle becomes hot while sewing plastics, sprinkling the material well with talcum powder before sewing is often of considerable help.

Sometimes a seam sewn in plastics material tends to drag. This can be avoided by sewing a piece of tissue paper into the seam when it is set. When the sewing is finished, the paper should be pulled out, leaving the seam smooth and flat.

Curtains made from plastics will be stronger if adhesive tape is machined on underneath the heading at the same time.

Special adhesives such as Pac or Plastifix are made for sticking plastics materials. The adhesive provides a permanent bond once dry and it can be used for repairing plastics garments.

Plissé

This soft crimped material also known as seersucker is made from Egyptian-type cotton. In the old days, this was one of the few completely non-crush fabrics. Today it is often made by heat embossing thermoplastic fibre fabrics. Although cotton plissé looks delicate and is often used for underwear, it can be treated like other cottons and may be boiled if the colour is fast. Rinse thoroughly, wring carefully, and smooth the fabric during drying. Plissé should not be ironed, although collars and cuffs may be lightly finished with a cool iron if necessary once the garment is completely dry. For synthetic fibres, treat according to fibre.

Plush

A long-pile fabric, woven or knitted and similar to velvet but with a less dense pile. Mainly manufactured from acrylic fibres such as Acrilan, Courtelle, etc. but it can also be made from silk, rayon, nylon and other fibres. Heavy plush and that made from silk or rayon is best dry-cleaned but nylon and acrylic plushes can be washed more easily. For details wash as instructed on swing tag or as given under Nylon fur on page 67, or Simulation fur on page 88.

Polan

A type of nylon made in Poland.

Polyamide fibres

These are what we know as nylon. Made basically from benzene (from coal or oil). Britain is the second largest producer of nylon in the world.

There are various types of nylon, usually known by number, i.e. Type 66—the nylon with which we are most familiar and which was originally discovered by Du Pont. Type 6, the German Perlon, was the pioneer fibre in this class but it is now produced in this country by Courtaulds as 'Celon' and by British Enkalon as 'Enkalon'. Type 610 is a bristle nylon. Type 680 is an American nylon resistant to sunlight, etc. Some nylons are known by name, Perlon for example, which is the name for German nylon whether Type 6 or 66 and Rilsan which is nylon 11. Nomex, a high temperature melting-point fibre and Qiana a new continuous filament fibre both made by Du Pont are both in the polyamide family.

Polyester fibres

Polyester fibres are manufactured mainly from ethylene glycol (commonly known as anti-freeze) and terephthalic acid, both obtained from the petroleum industry. Terylene was the first polyester fibre in the world. It is manufactured in this country while Dacron is the equivalent fibre produced in U.S.A. and based on the British Terylene patents. Terlenka, previously made only in Holland is now also produced in the U.K. as is Trevira, a German developed polyester. Processed yarns such as Crimplene are also polyesters.

Polyester fibre is very strong with a high resistance to abrasion and this makes possible, sheer, lightweight fabrics with good strength and wearing qualities—just as strong wet as dry. It is resilient with good crease resistance and recovery and needs little or no ironing. Polyester fibre is shrink resistant, resists stretch, it is mothproof and resistant to mildew.

It also has heat setting properties and fabrics made from 100 per cent polyester fibre or fabrics containing not less than 55 per cent polyester fibre intimately blended with wool or 67 per cent intimately blended with cellulosic fibres can be durably pleated.

Fabrics made from polyester fibre have a low moisture absorption which means they are easy to wash and quick to dry. Washing can be done by hand or in a machine. Wringing is unnecessary. Water should be shaken off the surface and the garment hung to dry at normal room temperature when it will dry quickly. If it is preferred to give garments a short spin, give a cold rinse first. Tumbler drying is satisfactory on garments made from polyester fibre and this minimizes ironing.

Garments should be washed frequently to avoid heavy soiling. If they are badly soiled, however, this can be dealt with by impregnating the soiled areas with concentrated detergent or soap and leaving for about fifteen minutes. After this time the stains should be loosened and the garment can be washed by hand or machine as directed. Do not boil.

Pleated garments are best washed by hand and hung immediately to drip dry. They can, however, be given a mild machine wash if preferred.

Crimplene garments should be washed as already given but they should be laundered on their own in fresh suds to avoid pick up of lint.

Ironing is seldom necessary if polyester fibre fabrics are washed correctly but some materials benefit from an occasional press. In this case iron at setting 2.

Further details of washing polyester fibres are given under Terylene on page 94.

Polyethylene

Commonly known under the shorter spelling of Polythene. See under this heading for further details.

Polynosic

This term, meaning 'highly crystallized', covers one of the newest modified viscose rayon groups and the one most resembling cotton. It can be used alone or in blends with other man-made fibres or with cotton. Polynosic fibres such as Vincel, Avril and Xantrel are used for wide variety of items including lingerie, blouses and shirts, slacks, rainwear and household textiles. Wash as for viscose rayon unless manufacturer's instructions state otherwise.

Polyolefin fibres

A term used to embrace both polyethylene (polythene) and polypropylene fibres. See below for further details.

Polypropylene

This multi-filament yarn, also known as an olefin fibre, is produced from propylene gas, a by-product of oil and was originally known to us as a plastic rather than a fibre. It was discovered by an Italian scientist, Professor Giulio Natta in 1954, and later an agreement was reached enabling polypropylene yarn to be produced in this country under the name of Cournova. It is very strong even when wet and is highly resistant to abrasion chemicals, damp and sunlight. The main feature about this yarn is its lightness. It is the lightest of all fibres and will float on water.

A big development has been taking place in tape yarns made from stretch films in polypropylene and also in polythene as an alternative to jute. This is used in the primary backing for tufted carpets and also as a very useful twine or string for tying parcels etc. Sacking, in competition with jute in tape yarns from film is also becoming more popular as it is rot-proof.

Deckchair covers and awnings are frequently made from polypropylene. To clean, wipe with a damp cloth.

See also under Polythene below.

Polythene

This is the common name for polyethylene. It is made from chemicals derived from petroleum and is normally recognized as being used for plastics. It is, however, being increasingly used for fabrics as well, as it is light, moderately strong and is non-absorbent. Courlene is an example. Dry-cleaning is not recommended, although for the fabrics at present in use this is unlikely. Deckchair fabrics, awnings and sun-blinds, etc. are being widely made from polythene fabrics since the material is not damaged by strong sunlight. To clean, wipe with a damp cloth.

See also under Polypropylene above.

Polyurethane

This was originally known to us as a foam plastics material used to make cushion fillings, padding and household and personal sponges. Now, however, polyurethane yarns are becoming increasingly important in textiles and are tending to replace, cut or extrude rubber.

In the United States the term spandex is used to describe any fibres made from polyurethane, such as Lycra, but this is not generally accepted and the world's two largest man-made fibre producers describe their polyurethane fibres as synthetic elastomeric fibres.

These elastomeric fibres have elastic properties and a higher resistance to many chemicals, including chlorinated water. The yarns can be made in fine denier, so that they can be used with sheer fabrics and they can also be dyed, are very light in weight and are also comfortable.

Because of these advantages, elastomeric fibres are used in foundation garments, swimwear and support stockings, also in waist-bands, men's socks and also (blended with a variety of woven and knitted fabrics) for stretch outerwear, such as tights and wool-stretch socks, etc.

Since these polyurethane, or elastomeric, fibres are always used with other fibres, washing instructions must vary according to the other fibre used. For girdles, bras, swimwear, etc. the elastomeric fibres are always used with other yarns which can be easily laundered. Wash in hand-hot water, or give a light machine wash; rinse, remove excess moisture (spin briefly if wished) and drip dry. Ironing should not be necessary, but where it is, use a warm iron only. Trade names for polyurethane fibres include Vyrene, Lycra and Spanzelle.

See also Elastomeric fibres on page 38.

Polyvinyl chloride

Also known as PVC. Originally better known in the plastics field but now used for textiles also, mainly for knitted garments and children's wear. Wash in warm water, drip dry. Never boil; never iron: both may cause excessive shrinkage. Brand names include Dynel, Rhovyl and Movil.

Polyvinylidene chloride

A type of PVC now used on a very small scale and which has been largely replaced by polythene. It is used to make protective clothing, deck-chair and garden-chair covers, car upholstery and dolls' hair. Brand names include Bexan and Saran. Also known as a chlorofibre. Wash in warm suds, rinse, drip dry or wipe dry. Avoid ironing.

Poplin

The name given to a type of plain weave with a heavier warp than weft. This gives it the characteristic rib effect from selvedge to selvedge. True poplins are made with two-fold yarns and are hard wearing. Poplin is usually cotton but can also be made from silk, wool and rayon. The Royal Irish poplin made by Atkinson's is a silk and wool mixture fabric. Treat according to the type of materials, washing cotton in the usual way and using warm suds for silk, wool and rayon.

Expensive silk poplins should retain their sheen after laundering but some silks may dull a little and in this case the sheen may be restored with an acid rinse as given under Silk on page 168, but soak in cool water for half an hour before next laundering.

Do not sprinkle rayon or silk poplin with water if the garment becomes over-dry, but wrap in a damp towel for half an hour.

Poromeric material

This is a new-generation plastics material. Clarino and Corfam are trade names for this type of material, which is used mainly for shoe uppers but also for handbags, wallets and sports equipment. Structurally, poromeric materials are similar to leather with the ability to 'breathe' and to absorb and disperse foot moisture. Unlike leather, however, the material is immune to fungus growth or other microbiological attack.

The materials do not stain nor fade and they can be cleaned by wiping with a damp cloth. Shoes of this type can be washed to remove mud, if necessary. The material expands and contracts to follow slight changes of the foot during the day but, unlike leather, it always recovers its original shape rather than adapting permanently to the foot. This means that the shoes cannot be 'broken-in' as they will be the same size and shape after being worn as when new. For this reason they must always fit comfortably when bought.

Scuff marks can be removed with ordinary paste shoe polish in a colour appropriate to the shoes.

Poult

A plain woven stiff fabric with a decorative rib in the weft direction. It is made from continuous filament yarns, especially silk and acetate, and is used for dress fabrics and for furnishings. Dry-clean or if manufacturer's instructions permit, wash as for fibre concerned.

Prelana

An acrylic fibre similar to Courtelle, Orlon, etc., but manufactured in East Germany.

Proban

Not a fabric but an anti-flame finish which can be applied to cotton and rayon for garments, curtains, furnishings, electric blankets and industrial clothing. Once treated, material will not burst into flame if it comes into contact with fire, and the process will even prevent winceyette from catching fire when a blowlamp is applied to it. Fabric treated is also made shrink-resistant and minimum-iron.

Proban-finished fabric will retain its excellent properties if washed according to manufacturer's directions. But never boil or use bleach.

Prolon

These were synthetic fibres spun from proteins such as casein, the waste product of milk, and soya-bean, now known as Azlon. The fibres are now no longer made.

Protein fibres

These were the result of the chemists' search for a man-made fibre similar to natural protein fibres such as wool, cashmere, and silk, etc.

Ardil (derived from peanuts) is no longer being produced and the other British protein fibre, Fibrolane, derived from casein, the waste product of milk has also ceased production. There are very few protein fibres produced today and Merinova is one of the few remaining. Protein fibres are never used alone but always blended with other fibres. Wash as for wool and press with a cool iron on the wrong side when the fabric is evenly damp. Continue pressing until the material is quite dry.

PVC fibres

See under Chlorofibres on page 26.

Qiana

This is a new fibre introduced by Du Pont in continuous filament form. The production of Qiana is entirely new but the connecting links of the molecular structure are the same as those found in nylon 66. Because of this chemical linkage method, the fibre is a polyamide and can generically be called nylon. It is luxurious and silk-like and is being used as an alternative to silk by the Haute Couture. Wash or dry clean according to swing tag or sewn in label.

Raycelon

This is one of the new filament blend yarns made from filaments of rayon and Celon nylon by Courtaulds. It is used for a variety of fabrics including linings, overalls, shirtings, dress and blouse materials, trouser pocketings and rainwear. Wash according to swing tag or HLCC label.

Rayon

Rayon materials are fabrics in their own right and although they often resemble linen, cotton, wool, silk, etc. they possess different qualities. There are two processes for manufacturing rayons—viscose and cuprammonium. The cuprammonium process is no longer used in the U.K. although Bemberg cuprammonium yarns are imported from Germany. Viscose is widely known and used in U.K. as are the modified rayon staples such as Vincel, Sarille and Evlan. Where the type of rayon is not stated it is fairly safe to assume that the fabric is viscose rayon. Note that acetates are no longer called rayons.

Rayon was the first man-made fibre to be produced on a large scale in this country. It is a cellulosic fibre, its raw material being wood pulp. Rayon is also the most widely used of all man-made fibres and almost 50 per cent of the total world production of man-made fibres is viscose rayon. It is undergoing continuous development as new varieties are introduced.

Modified rayon fibres, as the name implies, are viscose rayons modified during manufacture to produce a range of different fibres, each having properties specially suitable for groups of uses requiring differing performances or particular characteristics.

Most rayons are strong when dry but tend to become weaker when wet and they should not be stretched, twisted, wrung or handled roughly during washing. Some rayons crack easily and putting through a wringer could cause cracking which would show as fine lines on the dry, finished garment. For detailed instructions see under Viscose page 104.

Iron while still slightly damp with a warm iron. If the material overdries, immerse the whole article and dry again until the right degree of dampness is obtained or roll in a wet towel for a short time.

Shiny-faced rayons such as taffeta, satin, etc. should be ironed on the right side; dull or matt-finished rayons such as crêpe should be ironed on the wrong side. Never press over a seam when ironing rayons.

See also under Viscose, page 104 and Modified rayons, page 60.

Redon

An acrylic fibre made in West Germany. It is similar to Acrilan, Courtelle or Orlon and should be washed and treated in the same way.

Reevon

A polythene fibre manufactured in U.S.A. and similar to Courlene made in this country.

Repp

This fabric is made with a heavy weft so that the ribs are formed from selvedge to selvedge. While it is most popular for furnishing fabrics, it is also sometimes used in lighter weights as a dress material as well as for women's suitings. Many repps are all cotton but rayon and cotton are sometimes used together. For a cotton and rayon mixture, wash as rayon.

Curtains and loose covers made from cotton repp can be easily washed providing they are not too cumbersome to handle. Shake thoroughly or brush to remove loose dirt and dust, especially along pipings and hems. Wash in hot suds, scrubbing any dirty parts with a soft brush. Re-wash in fresh suds if necessary, then wring or spin dry, rinse thoroughly and wring or spin two or three times more. If the material is limp and has no special finish, starch lightly. Iron with a hot iron when almost dry.

Rexor

A polyester film, such as Terylene, adhered to an aluminium strip. Alternatively, the metallic yarn can be made by dipping the metal in a solution of polyester. It is strong, has a certain elasticity and garments or fabric decorated with it can be washed or dry-cleaned. Similar to Metlon and Lurex.

Rhodia

A type of acetate made in France, Italy, Germany and Brazil.

Rhodiaceta

A type of nylon made in France.

Rhonel

A triacetate made in France.

Rhovyl

A chlorofibre produced in France, West Germany and U.S.A.

Rilsan

A special type of nylon made in France, Italy and Brazil and known as Type-11.

Roylon

A Swiss Type-6 nylon.

Rubber

See Elastomeric fibres, page 38.

Saaba

This is the trade name for twist crimped yarns with reduced stretch and a bulky handle. They are used to make knitted outerwear garments, as well as underwear.

Sailcloth

As its name implies, this is a very heavy and strongly-made canvas used to make sails. It is made from linen, cotton, jute and man-made fibres. The quality used for sportswear, skirts and dress wear is of a lighter weight although the same plain weave. Wash according to fibre. Test for colour fastness.

Samite

This is a rich, lustrous brocade fabric, usually with gold or silver threads in the design, and is used mainly for ecclesiastical robes, vestments and for ornamental fabrics. It has come down to us from the Middle Ages when it was the most fashionable as well as the most expensive fabric in use. Even then it was chiefly worn for sacred uses, but the Norman kings, courtiers and ladies of high rank also wore it for special occasions and ceremonies. It was mostly silk interwoven with red or green as well as with gold or silver and then heavily embroidered.

Saran

A man-made fibre of the polyvinylidene chloride type but also known as a plastics material.

Sarille

A modified viscose fibre which is permanently crimped, made by Courtaulds. Sarille is used to produce fabrics which look like wool, are warm and have increased bulk, but without weight. The fabrics also resist creasing. Sarille is used for dress fabrics, and blended with polyester is used for men's and boys' suits and trousers. It is also used for children's clothes and household textiles, such as blankets and candlewick bedspreads which are lint-free. Sarille is also blended with nylon to make raincoats and gaberdine school wear. Wash or dry clean as given under Viscose, page 104.

Sarsenet

A soft silk material, usually a ribbon, of plain weave and with a very fine warp and weft.

Sateen

This hard-wearing fabric can be made from cotton, silk and cotton or a strong rayon. It resembles satin except that the smooth grain runs across the material and it is mainly used for curtains and covers and for lining garments. Rayon sateen should be washed as for other rayons.

Cotton sateen can be washed in hot suds and should be ironed with a hot iron on the wrong side, being lightly finished on the right side afterwards.

Sateen made from silk and cotton should be washed in warm soapy water and treated more gently. Rinse thoroughly in warm and then in cold water and wring carefully to remove excess moisture. Iron while still slightly damp on the wrong side, using a moderately hot iron.

Satin

This is a type of weave in which the warp predominates over the weft giving the characteristic smooth lustrous surface. Satin fabrics are shiny on one side with the smooth grain running the length of the material. They can be woven of silk, cotton, rayon, Terylene or nylon yarn although the majority of dress satins sold today are made from acetate and from cotton.

Heavy furnishing satins should be sent for professional dry-cleaning as they are inclined to mark and spot easily. Any stains should be dealt with quickly but a thick absorbent pad should be placed underneath and cleaning should start well outside the stain and work inwards. Pat dry quickly using a thick, clean towel.

Silk satin, such as that used for expensive lingerie, should be washed as for silk, giving a final rinse in cold water containing a dessertspoonful of vinegar to restore the gloss. When next the garment is washed, soak it first for half an hour before laundering to remove the acid. Iron silk satin while it is still slightly damp. Use a fairly hot iron and press on the wrong side until the material is completely dry.

Acetate satin used for afternoon and wedding dresses, blouses, scarves and underwear can be washed at home, following laundry instructions given on page 13. It will not lose its sheen and a vinegar rinse must not be given.

Iron acetate satin while it is still slightly but evenly damp; it should not be sprinkled with water or it may 'spot' and if it becomes overdry it should be rolled in a damp towel for a short time. Use a cool iron and press the wrong side of the material until it is quite dry.

Acetate/viscose crêpe satin is another fabric which has a satin on the face and a crêpe surface on the reverse. It is usually meant as a reversible fabric so that the trimmings can be made of crêpe or satin. This fabric is often used for children's frocks. Wash in the same way as acetate satin and iron while still damp, but use a hot iron, pressing lightly and quickly over as large an area as possible. Once the garment has been completely ironed, any odd touching-up can be done with the iron in the usual way.

Sayelle

This is a new generation bi-component acrylic fibre produced by Du Pont. It has all the main desirable properties of conventional acrylic fibres including bright and clear shades, lightness and complete resistance to shrinking. In addition, Sayelle has outstanding resilience due to the very high crimp of the fibres. It also provides exceptional stability to laundering and by specially engineering the fibres, these gains have been achieved with excellent resistance to pilling in wear. It is used in the production of knitwear for men, women and children. Wash as for HLCC label No. 6, i.e. by hand or machine.

Sea island cotton

An exceptionally fine cotton of very high quality. It is obtained from long-staple types of cotton grown in the West Indies and is expensive. It is used for fine shirtings and blouses. Launder as for fine cotton.

Seersucker

The name of this fabric is derived from an American expression for a type of seaweed. The material itself is based on the original cotton crepon plissé and it was the first of the non-iron dress fabrics. It is also made today by embossing plain nylon and Terylene. To launder, wash in hand-hot suds or for 2 or 3 minutes in a washing machine. Rinse in clear warm water and roll in a towel, or spin dry briefly, to absorb excess moisture. Seersucker should not be ironed although collars and cuffs can be lightly finished. If the fabric is

badly creased, press very lightly with a warm iron when completely
dry.

Serge

A medium- or heavy-weight twill fabric—originally made from
wool but now frequently made in blends of wool and rayon and in
other blends also. Send for dry-cleaning or wash quickly in warm
suds, rinse, put through a wringer and hang to dry away from heat.
When dry, iron under a damp cloth, using a warm iron.

Shantung

This is a Chinese plain weave fabric with slubs. Silk shantung is
made from wild silk from the Tussah moth and it should be washed in
the same way as other silk, using warm soapflake suds and a final cold
vinegar rinse. The only difference is in the ironing as shantung should
not be ironed until it is completely dry, using a cool to warm iron
on the wrong side.

If silk shantung becomes limp after washing it can be restiffened
in the same way as silk. See page 168.

Similar constructions to silk shantung with uneven slub yarns are
made mainly from acetate but can be in most of the filament yarns.

Acetate shantung should be washed in warm suds, squeezing gently
but not twisting or rubbing. Rinse thoroughly. Roll in a towel to
remove excess moisture after rinsing, hang to dry and iron while
still slightly damp, using a warm iron.

Nylon shantung, sometimes used for afternoon or cocktail dresses,
is hard-wearing and can be washed easily providing it is not allowed
to become too dirty. Use hot suds, rinse thoroughly, roll in a towel
to remove excess moisture and hang to dry away from direct heat.
Iron may not be necessary but if the garment requires finishing,
press with a moderately hot iron on the wrong side when the fabric is
evenly but only slightly damp.

Sharkskin

A smooth fabric, either woven or knitted, and frequently made
from acetate. Wash in warm suds, squeeze gently, rinse thoroughly
in warm water, roll in a thick towel to absorb excess moisture and
hang to dry. Iron evenly on the wrong side when the fabric is almost
dry, using a warm iron. This fabric may show watermarks if ironed
over damp patches.

Sheens

See under Glazes, sheens and lustres, page 47.

Sheepskin

A very heavy sheepskin rug or one that is lined and backed is easier to shampoo than to wash. To do this treat in the same way as given for nylon fur on page 67.

For small rugs and other sheepskin articles see page 410.

Shoddy

A fibrous material produced from reclaimed new or old knitted fabrics or loosely woven cloths and similar to mungo, but of slightly better quality.

Shower-proofing

See Water-repellent, page 105.

Shrink-resistant

Non-shrink finishes vary considerably although most prevent fabrics from stretching or shrinking within a specified limit. The limit is very often 2 per cent or with some, only 1 per cent and this is very slight indeed although even shrinking or stretching to these small limits is unlikely if the materials are laundered correctly.

The Sanforized Shrunk process was one of the original anti-shrink finishes for cottons, and many manufacturers carry out under licence their own finishes based on the process.

Washing instructions should be followed exactly or, if these are not available, then the fabric should be laundered according to the material concerned (see under various headings in chapter on Laundering), paying particular attention while fabric is still damp, to ironing out any creases, puckers or rucks in the fabric.

Silene

An acetate produced in Italy.

Silicone-proof

See under Water-repellent, page 105.

Silk

Silk is a natural fibre produced by the silkworm. It is one of the oldest textile fibres known to man and was discovered about 5,000

years ago. For 3,000 years China held the monopoly of silk production but in the fourth century A.D. the secrets spread first to Korea
and thence to Japan then later to India and Persia and all over the
near East.

At present about 60 per cent of the world's raw silk comes from
Japan. One of Japan's greatest industries is sericulture—the large-
scale rearing of cultivated silkworms. China is the next largest producer, followed by India and Pakistan. Silk is also produced in the
U.S.S.R., Turkey, Brazil, Italy and France.

The Tussah moth, the most important of the wild silk moths, is
indigenous to China and India and produces the coarser silk from
which fabrics like shantung, pongee and tussore are made.

Silk produced by cultivated silkworms is fine and uniformly smooth
with no irregularities. The silk produced by wild silk moths is frequently irregular, producing when woven, the slubs or variations of
thickness which are the chief characteristics of the shantung type
of fabric. Wild silk is produced mainly by China, India and Pakistan.

The silkworm extrudes two cobweblike silk threads from spinneret
glands in the head coated with gum, which are then merged into one
thread. This thread, with a length of up to 3,500 yards is used to form
the cocoon. It takes up to three or four days for the silkworm to
complete a cocoon. Cocoons vary from white to yellow and green
and it is from these cocoons that silk is produced.

The word 'silk' on a garment does not necessarily mean that the
garment has been made from *real* silk although silk, meaning the
natural product of the silkworm—has certainly been used. *All silk*
implies that apart from a certain amount of weighting added to give
the material fullness, the fabric is made purely of silk. *Pure silk*
contains no weighting of any kind apart from any metallic weighting
used in the dye. *Pure dye silk* contains no weighting of any kind in
the fabric or in the dye.

Nett silk is applied to the product made from the drawing off
of continuous strands of silk from the cocoon, after which they are
twisted into a yarn. *Spun silk* means that the fabric is made from a
yarn composed of silk fibres of a length approximately 1 to 8 in.
long, produced from silk waste by dressing and spinning processes.

Silk fabrics such as taffetas and brocades and many of the multi-
coloured prints should be dry-cleaned and not washed. Silk ties
should be dry-cleaned. Where a manufacturer recommends dry-
cleaning, the garment should never be washed.

Do not allow garments to become too soiled before washing or dry-cleaning. Perspiration stains on silk are often impossible to remove and may weaken the fabric so great care should be taken to prevent these.

Other stains on silk garments are best removed professionally but always advise dry-cleaners what has caused the stain.

Always wash or dry-clean silk garments before packing them away for any length of time. Like wool, silk is a protein fibre and should not therefore be left to soak in an enzyme washing product.

For details of washing silk see page 168.

Silon

A nylon made in Czechoslovakia.

Simulation fur

High pile fabrics simulating fur were at one time made almost exclusively of nylon but this is used on a limited scale only now and most fun furs or simulation furs are made from acrylics. Modacrylic fibres are often included in the fabric to reduce flammability. Wash or dry-clean according to swing tag, care label or manufacturer's specific instructions. Where none of these is available see under Man-made fibres on page 55 or Nylon fur on page 67.

Deep pile acrylic simulation fur coats should be dry-cleaned unless the manufacturer's instructions state otherwise. Do not steam or press and do not brush the coat until it is quite dry. If the coat becomes wet during wear, shake well and allow to dry naturally then brush lightly when dry with a clean brush.

Slit film

Until about 1964, all man-made fibres were produced by forcing a liquid chemical through fine holes in a spinneret. But nowadays, a number of yarns are in commercial production which are made by stretching and splitting a film of polypropylene or by extruding a flat tape or ribbon of this basic raw material. Slit film polypropylene yarns are always extruded, of course, but for these the equivalent of the spinneret is a long narrow slit. The tape of polypropylene is slit processed and twisted in such a way that it is turned into a textile yarn. The yarn is cheaper to produce, very strong, light, coarse and firm to handle. All these advantages make it ideal for industrial uses. Cournova is a brand name of this type of slit film.

Sliver-knit pile fabrics

Many of the present-day plushes, fleeces and simulation and fun-fur fabrics are made by a special knitting process which utilizes a sliver instead of a yarn. It was invented by Mr. Borg—the founder of Borg Fabrics—who developed the process in collaboration with the Wildman Machine Company whose knitting machines are generally, but not exclusively, used for this process. Sliver-knits are often called Wildman-knit fabrics. It is not easy to tell how a long pile plush fabric is made, by casual handling.

Slub

The name given to a yarn containing thick and thin pieces. Slub yarns are made in many fibres including cotton, repp, silk shantung and slub acetate shantung. Slub materials are used for curtains, furnishings, or, in the case of slub rayons, for dress and blouse fabrics.

Wash as for cotton, silk or rayon, ironing with a warm iron while the fabric is still slightly damp. Cotton types may be treated normally.

Soflons

This is the trade name for crimped nylon yarn used for stockings and pantee-hose etc.

Soil-resistant

Some processes combine a resistance to soiling and staining along with other finishes and this applies particularly to the crease-resist and water-repellent finishes. Treated fabrics stay clean longer and are easier to wash and dry. Wash gently without boiling, wringing, twisting or rubbing and do not bleach or starch. Rinse thoroughly in clear water and drip dry.

Solena

The trade name for a bonded-fibre fabric used for clothing interlinings.

Spandex

Although this is a brand name in U.S.A., in fact this is not a trade name, but a name coined in the United States to describe man-made elastic fibres as opposed to natural rubber elasticity. The word has not, however, met with full acceptance and the world's two largest man-made fibres producers describe their polyurethane fibres as synthetic elastomeric fibres. For further details see under Polyurethane on page 76.

Spanzelle

This is the trade name for an elastomeric fibre produced in this country. For details see under Polyurethane on page 76.

Spun rayon

This term is used to describe rayons made from spun staple fibres as opposed to continuous filament yarns. As far as spun rayon fabrics are concerned, these can be made from rayon staple spun on any of the spinning systems—cotton, wool, worsted, Makie, flax jute, schappe and silk, as well as on the condenser system. Wash as for viscose, page 104.

Spun silk

This is yarn spun from short silk filaments or produced by special processes from silk waste after the gum has been removed.

Staflex

A fusible interlining, pioneered by Staflex. It is an ordinary cotton fabric coated with polyvinyl acetate (a plastics material) and used for stiffening garments. There are two kinds, one may be home-laundered and the other may be safely dry-cleaned and maker's instructions should be followed.

Steelon

A type of nylon produced in Poland and also known as Stilon.

Stiffenings

See Permanent stiffening, page 72.

Stretch yarns

See under Textured, bulked and stretch yarns on page 96.

Surah

This is a fine twill weave fabric with a pronounced diagonal weave. It is usually printed and was at one time mainly known as foulard. Can be in silk but is generally in acetate or Tricel so wash accordingly.

Swansdown

This is made in a variety of soft raised fibres. To wash, dissolve mild soapflakes in warm water and whisk until a good lather is formed. Immerse the swansdown in the soapy water and swish gently. Rinse in warm water, hang to dry. Shake frequently while drying.

Synthetic elastomeric fibres

See under Polyurethane on page 76 or Elastomeric fibres on page 38.

Tacryl

An acrylic fibre manufactured in Sweden.

Taffeta

This plain closely woven fabric can be made from any filament yarn but most common are nylon, acetate and triacetate. Acetate taffeta is the most important medium for women's wear linings. For washable linings Tricel has become prominent and both Tricelon and Raycelon taffetas are used for linings. The biggest outlet for nylon taffetas is for rainwear and overalls—the 2 oz. and 4 oz. types being among the largest uses for woven nylon. Taffeta can also be made from silk, cotton, wool, rayon and polyester such as Terylene.

That made from *pure silk* is usually heavily weighted with metallic salts and as it is difficult to wash at home, it should always be sent for professional dry-cleaning.

Taffeta made from 100 *per cent wool*—such as that used in shirting, blouses, pyjamas, etc. must be treated as wool but should be tested for colour fastness before laundering. Iron on the wrong side while still slightly damp, using a moderately hot iron and pressing until the material is quite dry.

Acetate taffeta, used often for cocktail and teenage party dresses, and *rayon taffeta*, used frequently for bedspreads, cushion covers, etc. can both be washed at home quite well providing there is no moiré or 'watered' finish as this may be removed during washing.

Launder in a large tub, supporting the weight as much as possible during laundering, and avoid creasing, wringing or twisting the fabric. Gently knead the taffeta in warm suds, squeezing carefully to remove dirt. Rinse in two or three changes of warm water, give a final cold rinse, then drip dry or roll in a thick towel to remove surplus moisture. Unroll immediately and dry on a hanger or over a line away from heat. When the fabric is still slightly but evenly damp, iron with a warm iron on the wrong side until quite dry. If parts of the material have become too dry, do not sprinkle with water but wrap in a wet towel for 5 to 10 minutes, then iron.

If the taffeta loses its characteristic *stiffness* during laundering, rinse it in a solution of gum arabic (see page 155) or in warm water containing a teaspoonful of liquid glue to every pint of water. Iron almost immediately, or while the material is still really damp. Use a cool iron on the wrong side and continue pressing until the fabric is dry.

Terylene and nylon taffeta should be washed in hand-hot suds; rinse, drip dry and if necessary iron with a warm iron when dry. Stiffened nylon taffeta, which is often used for petticoats, should be washed with as little handling as possible in a large bowl or bath. Where possible, instead of immersing in suds, place the garment on a flat surface and scrub with a soft brush dipped in hand-hot suds. Rinse thoroughly and allow to drip dry. Ironing should not be necessary but if the petticoat has creased during washing, iron with a cool iron while still slightly damp.

Tarlatan

A thin, transparent dress muslin which is stiffened and used for ballet dresses and underskirts. Tarlatan quickly becomes limp if washed and ideally it should be dry-cleaned to preserve the crisp stiffening. If, however, the fabric has already been washed and become limp, it is possible to restiffen it to some extent with plastics stiffener used according to instructions or with a strong solution of gum arabic (see page 155).

A tarlatan petticoat will hold a dress beautifully stiff but may snag nylon stockings. This can be avoided if the base of the slip is bound with ribbon or bias binding.

Taslan

A yarn texturing process offered by Du Pont. It is usually applied to filament yarns of nylon or polyester. Bulking is obtained by the looping of individual filaments caused by them being passed through an air jet. The process gives yarn greater body and the final fabric is softer, warmer and lighter. Taslan does not stretch and fabrics made from it are usually made up into dresses, blouses, lingerie, shirts, etc.

Fabric is easily washed in hot suds; rinse thoroughly, roll in a thick towel to absorb excess moisture and drip dry. Garments will probably need no ironing but if the fabric does require touching-up, use a cool iron only.

The Taslan process is now being used for treating rayon yarns also. This gives extra advantages to fabrics but they should be laundered as given for rayons.

Teklan

This is an entirely British modacrylic fibre which is based on acrylonitrile and vinylidene chloride—derivations of oil refining and of coal carbonization processes.

Teklan is strong, hard-wearing and easy to wash, but its most important asset is its flame resistance which is even better than nylon, as it does not drop molten fibres when hot. As it satisfies British Standard 3120 requirements for 'flame-proof fabrics', Teklan is particularly useful for dressing-gowns, toys, nightwear and children's wear, as well as in industry for overalls, electrical insulation and so on. It is also used for woven and knitted dress goods and for underwear including brushed fabrics. Household textiles including curtain nets and furnishing materials are also made from Teklan.

Fabrics made from Teklan retain their flame resistance even after repeated washing or dry-cleaning and they also have a good resistance to sunlight and to most chemicals. Wash in warm suds, rinse thoroughly and dry in the usual way. Little or no ironing should be necessary but where preferred, use a cool iron only.

Tendrelle

An ICI trade name used to describe stockings made from ICI nylon specially textured to give a stretch stocking which is sheer.

Tergal

Made in France, Tergal is a polyester fibre similar to Terylene.

Terital

A polyester fibre made in Italy and similar to Terylene produced here.

Terlenka

This is a polyester fibre now also produced in the U.K. having previously been developed under the Terylene patent licensing arrangements in Holland.

Terylene

The trade name for what is technically known as a polyester fibre manufactured by ICI Fibres Ltd. Terylene was the world's first polyester fibre and it was discovered in 1941 in the Research Laboratories of The Calico Printers' Association. It was commercially developed by ICI and is a completely synthetic fibre, made from ethylene glycol (anti-freeze) and terephthalic acid which is derived from petroleum.

Large-scale production of Terylene began in 1955. Crimplene is a special bulked form of Terylene. Terlenka, developed in Holland under licence and based on the original Terylene patents is now being produced in Northern Ireland.

Terylene is hard-wearing and resistant to chemicals but may be affected by grease stains if they are allowed to remain in contact and this applies especially to margarine. It will not shrink, fade or rot.

Blends with Sarille crimped rayon are now an extremely important, and perhaps main, outlet for permanent press garments at present.

Terylene should never be allowed to become really soiled. *Underwear, shirts,* etc. should be laundered daily and household items such as *curtains* should be washed once in every 8 or 10 days. It helps to soak curtains in cold water for 15 minutes before laundering.

Use hand-hot water and soapflakes or a mild detergent such as Stergene. Rinse once or twice without squeezing or wringing and drip dry. Use a cool iron to touch-up if necessary. Unlike nylon, completely white Terylene can be bleached.

Many fabrics show *electrostatic effects* to some degree but materials (such as Terylene, nylon, etc.) which do not absorb much moisture and which dry quickly show the effects more noticeably. This happens particularly in cold, dry weather when these fabrics tend to cling and to pick up dust. Blending with rayon or modified rayons such as Vincel eliminates or considerably reduces 'static' because of their moisture absorbency.

Any synthetic detergent used in small quantities in the *rinsing* water will reduce electrostatic effects but Stergene is particularly effective and half a teaspoonful in a wash basin is sufficient. Rinse the garment in the solution, then drip dry and repeat after every laundering. Or you can use a fabric finisher as an anti-static.

Underwear made from 100 per cent knitted Terylene should be

washed in hot detergent suds or in a washing machine for 2 or 3 minutes, but must not be boiled. Rinse once or twice, roll in a towel to remove excess moisture and hang to dry away from heat. If necessary press with a moderate iron before completely dry.

When laundering a fabric which is a *blend* of Terylene and other fibres, treat always for the weakest fibre present in the blend. The percentage is usually stated on a label sewn or hung on the garment or roll of material.

Terylene/wool or *Terylene/mohair* should be washed in warm suds as for wool and dried flat away from any direct heat. Ironing should be unnecessary but if touching-up is required, press with a moderately hot iron on the wrong side when the garment is almost dry. Heavier weight fabrics such as winter frocks, suits, etc. should always be pressed over a damp cloth or a permanent shine may result.

Pleated garments—such as skirts—should not be rolled in a towel after washing but should be hung to drip dry. They should be pulled gently into shape during drying and should not be ironed. Some pleated Terylene garments, such as children's school skirts, are sold as machine-washable.

If the permanent pleats in a Terylene skirt begin to lose their sharpness after some time of wear and laundering, carefully go over the entire skirt with a cool iron and press each pleat in position. This should make the pleats sharp and quite permanent again.

Stains on heavier Terylene fabrics can usually be removed if they are quickly sponged with plain cold water or with soap and water. Failing this, use a dry-cleaning solvent, such as carbon tetrachloride.

Because the dye is added during manufacture, it is not a simple process to dye Terylene (or Crimplene) and domestic dyeing is not recommended. Many professional firms will also not accept Terylene for dyeing. A service is offered by some specialist professional firms, however, including Johnson Brothers (Dyers) Ltd. of Mildmay Road, Bootle 20, Lancs.

For sewing and other dressmaking instructions follow instructions for Nylon on page 67.

Terylene wadding

A crimped polyester fibre designed as a filling material for anoraks, sleeping-bags, cushions, upholstery etc. It is lightweight, odourless, mothproof and non-allergenic. Wash as for HLCC label No. 4. The wadding is water-resistant so will dry quickly.

Tetoron

This is a polyester fibre made in Japan and similar in type to Terylene made in this country. Treat in the same way.

Teviron

Polyvinyl chloride (or PVC) made in Japan.

Textralizing

This is a process used on synthetic filament yarns. It was previously known as Ban-Lon and is a bulking process mainly used on nylon and polyester. The texturing process crimps the fibre in a zigzag shape making it bulky, softer and warmer. The process is carried out under licence from Joseph Bancroft & Sons and approved fabrics get the brand name Ban-Lon.

Textured, bulked and stretch yarns

A number of man-made fibre yarns can now be altered in character and appearance by various special processes which texture, bulk and stretch the yarns giving them various additional properties. Sometimes these processes are known as crimping or high bulking or stretching-twisting. The processes give extreme lightness, bulkiness, or a close stretch-to-fit elasticity. Agilon, Ban-Lon, Crimplene, Helanca, Taslan and Fluflon are typical examples.

Garments made from yarn which has been treated by any of these processes should be washed frequently as over-soiling may be difficult to remove and the harsh washing necessary may damage the article.

Use hand-hot water with just sufficient detergent, soapflakes or washing powder to make a good lather. Wash white and coloured articles separately and wash without hard rubbing. Never use bleach unless the manufacturer states that this is possible and then use it only exactly according to instructions. Rinse garments at once and thoroughly, and either drip or spin dry according to instructions. If no instructions are given, squeeze out excess moisture in a towel, or place in a spin-dryer to remove excess moisture. Hang to dry immediately, easing the weight of the garment evenly along the line, or hanger, so that there is no distortion or loss of shape during drying. Dry white fabrics away from heat and out of strong sunlight.

Iron on the wrong side only if ironing is necessary using a cool iron, setting 1. If garment is very heavy or bulky, send for dry cleaning, labelling the item with the type of fibre from which it is made.

Tootapress

A permanent press finish. For further details see page 71.

Trelon

A type of nylon made in East Germany.

Trevira

Like Diolen, Trevira is a polyester fibre originally made in West Germany and now made in Northern Ireland. It is similar to Terylene.

Triacetate

Familiarly known in this country as Tricel, this cellulose fibre is made by the chemical treatment of wood pulp or cotton linters and oil and is a development of ordinary acetate. It is easier to wash and like synthetic fibres it has heat-setting properties, which means that it can be embossed or permanently pleated and it resists creasing, shrinking and stretching.

Garments can be drip dried and little or no ironing is necessary. It is ideal for children's clothes, because it also resists soiling.

As well as Tricel which is manufactured in this country there is also Arnel which is a triacetate made in U.S.A. and Trilan which is a similar yarn made in Canada.

Triacetate yarns can be both woven and knitted and they are also used in spun staple form in blends with cotton, viscose rayon staple, nylon and wool, especially in fabrics for pleated skirts, dresses and suits, etc. Triacetate is also blended with nylon and rayon for use in men's wear and children's clothing. Tricel is also widely used as a washable filling material for quilts and quilted clothing.

Garments or other articles made from Tricel or any other of the triacetates can be dry cleaned, providing you tell the cleaner what the fabric is. The reason for this is that trichlorethylene is unsuitable and perchlorethylene should be used.

Items can be easily washed at home, however, whether they are small pleated skirts or double-bed size quilts. Wash in warm water containing ordinary soapflakes, powder or synthetic detergent, but allow a large enough container so that you do not need to crush or squeeze the garment unnecessarily. Swirl gently in the suds, rinse in plenty of warm water and hang to drip dry.

It is possible to use a washing machine for many triacetate garments, and clear instructions are usually given in this case—for example—there are quilts and quilted housecoats which machine-wash beautifully. If in doubt give short warm machine-wash, cold rinses, short spin. Where necessary use a cool iron setting 2 while the fabric is still very damp, or use a steam iron on dry material.

Tricel

This is a triacetate manufactured in this country principally from wood pulp or oil or other cellulose. For care and washing instructions see under Triacetate above.

High Bulk Tricel is a textured (false-twist) Tricel which has become very successful for a variety of knitted garments.

When Tricel is combined with another fibre, follow washing instructions exactly or wash according to the weaker fibre. Where uncertain, wash in warm soapy water, rinse, drip dry and press lightly if necessary with a steam iron or with a cool iron while the fabric is still damp.

If garments are sent to be cleaned, the firm must be told that the fabric contains Tricel. See also Triacetate on page 97.

Tricelon

Introduced by Courtaulds in 1966, Tricelon is a man-made yarn of an entirely new type, made by mingling filaments of Tricel and Celon nylon, making it the world's first filament blend yarn.

It has produced a completely new range of lighter fabrics, both woven and knitted, such as ninons, crêpes, georgettes, fine twills, jerseys and cords and in heavier weights, crêpes and warp knits. Fabrics are finished to give a variety of different effects, either by allowing the nylon 6 to relax fully and bulk out the Tricel for full-handling crêpes, or by holding out the fabric and setting the cloth to give stable and smooth-surfaced materials.

Fabrics can be plain or printed and take brilliant and dark colours as well as pastels. It means that materials have the soft appeal of triacetates with the extra strength of nylon. They can be washed by machine (HLCC label No. 6), have good resistance to creasing but may be ironed if necessary—setting 2.

Tricot

The name is taken from the French word for knitting and is used for warp-knits. It was known as locknit in the early days but this term is not generally accepted by marketing men although the trade uses it for plain warp-knit fabrics. They can be made from a variety of fibres including viscose rayon, nylon and Terylene. Wash according to fibre concerned.

Trilan

This is a triacetate rayon made in Canada and similar to Tricel made in this country.

Triple ninon

For particulars and washing instructions see under Ninon. Triple ninon actually refers to silk ninon and the word 'triple' is added to indicate that the fabric was made from Triple A quality of raw silk which is one of the finer grades. Most ninon today is made from acetate, nylon or Terylene. Wash silk triple ninon as stated under Silk on page 168, including the vinegar rinse to restore sheen, but this applies only to *silk* ninon and must not be used on rayon.

Tropal

The trade name for an interlining which is exceptionally warm but very light. It can be used to line eiderdowns, bed-jackets and outdoor coats and also for lagging water-tanks to prevent the loss of heat.

Truon

If a garment has a label marked Truon, this indicates that the collar, the entire garment or part of it was made on 'Sewmatic' equipment. This equipment enables collars and cuffs on shirts, blouses, etc. to be made entirely in one piece and without any banding seam.

Garments marked 'Trubenized-Truon' have been made on the 'Sewmatic' equipment and have also been rendered semi-stiff by the Trubenized process. Garments may be washed or dry-cleaned in the usual way but when laundering at home, avoid creasing and starching. Iron while still very damp and fold by hand.

Tulle

This fine net fabric which was first made in the town of Tulle in the south-west area of France, is made from cotton, rayon, nylon or other fibres and washing instructions vary accordingly. Wherever possible, follow the manufacturer's instructions and where there is any doubt about the permanency of the stiffening, send garment to be dry-cleaned.

Test first for colour fastness before laundering tulle and if satisfactory, swish garment gently in hand-hot suds. Rinse thoroughly and drip dry. Iron with a moderately hot iron while the material is still slightly and evenly damp.

If the fabric has become limp, dip cotton tulle in weak starch and rinse rayon or nylon tulle in gum arabic solution (see page 155). Tulle hat-trimming which has become limp can be stiffened in the same way. When stiffening with gum arabic (or with ordinary glue in warm water) always press the fabric with a cool iron while it is still damp.

Tussah

This is the coarse silk produced by a species of wild silkworm and used to make the fabric tussore. The silk is brown and as it can rarely be reeled it is usually spun.

Tussore

A wild silk fabric with an uneven surface. It is woven from coarse Tussah silk. For care and washing see Shantung on page 85 and treat in the same way.

Tweed

Heavy wool tweeds used for coats and suits need to be professionally dry-cleaned but cotton tweeds for dresses can be easily home-laundered. Wash in hot suds, rinse two or three times in hot and then in cold or cool water, put through a wringer and dry out of doors, pulling into shape if necessary. Iron on the wrong side with a hot iron while the fabric is still damp, using a fairly heavy pressure. Continue pressing until the garment is quite dry.

There are also a great many tweed types of fabrics made in rayon blends and blends of wool with most of the new synthetic fibres such as Terylene, Acrilan and Courtelle. These blended fabrics should be washed as for the weakest fibre present, usually rayon or wool.

Twill

Fabric woven with diagonal lines on the face side is known as twill, and is now made in all fibres, both natural and man-made, when printed it is often known as foulard. Wash as for fabric concerned.

Tycora

The trade name for a complete range of modified filament yarns which have been given varying degrees of bulk and stretch according to the use for which they are intended. Wash as given under Textured, bulked and stretch yarns on page 96.

Ulstron

This is a polypropylene multi-filament yarn made by ICI for industrial uses only.

Valdora

The trade name for a heavyweight poplin ideal for dresswear. It has a special finish which makes it crease-shedding, dirt-resistant and moisture-repellent. Wash in hand-hot suds but do not wring, twist, starch, bleach or boil. Rinse thoroughly and hang immediately to drip dry. Finish with a warm iron if necessary.

Vectra

This was the trade name for a polypropylene hosiery fibre that had three or four times the snag resistance of nylon. It was claimed that it did not fade and was said to be ideal for women sensitive to dyes, because the colour was incorporated in the fibre and not on it. Unfortunately it was not successful and is no longer in production.

Velour

A heavy-pile fabric in cotton, silk, rayon or other man-made fibres. Velours are now made extensively in acrylic fibres, including knitted types. Nylon brushed knitted 'velours' are laminated to a locknit in nylon or acetate for curtains and there are similar upholstery velours in laminated nylon. Treat according to manufacturer's instructions.

This fabric is better dry-cleaned than home-laundered but some curtain material is sold as washable and this can be washed by dipping it up and down in a large bath of rich suds. Do not wring but press out surplus soap and rinse thoroughly in two or three changes of clear water. Drip dry by hanging double across a line or parallel lines and by securing with safety-pins rather than pegs. Shake occasionally during drying and when completely dry rehang. Do not iron.

Velvet

A cut warp-pile fabric in which the cut ends form the surface. Although originally made from silk, velvet is now made from cotton, wool, rayon, nylon and other man-made fibres. Many types are uncrushable, spot-proof and easily washed. Velvet does, however, vary considerably and the manufacturer's instructions should be followed. Where there is any doubt about washability and where the velvet is very heavy, as for instance with curtains, professional dry-cleaning is advisable.

With nylon velvet or where the fabric is guaranteed washable, choose a warm, windy day and test for colour fastness first. This can be done by dipping a small piece of the velvet in warm water and moving it about gently for several minutes. If the water remains clear or is only faintly tinted, washing should be fairly straightforward.

For curtains or covers, shake first or brush thoroughly to remove surplus dust. Whip up a rich lather of mild soapflakes and warm water and immerse the velvet. Do not squeeze, rub or wring and handle as little as possible, simply swishing gently in the suds.

Press out surplus soap against the side of the bowl then rinse in warm water two or three times in the same way. Hang to dry dripping wet without squeezing or wringing. Shake the velvet occasionally during drying and also smooth the fabric the way of the pile with a velvet pad or soft cloth.

Velvets do not need pressing, so that when they are completely dry they are ready for wearing or, in the case of curtains, for re-hanging. Washed correctly, the pile should be soft and fluffy but if it does flatten it can be raised again by brushing gently or by steaming. When steaming velvet, remember that the wrong side of the material is held to the steam.

Odd stains or marks on velvet of any kind can be removed by dabbing lightly with a cloth moistened with carbon tetrachloride. Start outside the stained area and work inwards, then leave to dry and finally steam for a few minutes to freshen the pile.

An alternative method of cleaning velvet which is generally grubby is to rub it with a cloth dipped in powdered magnesia. Rub this gently into the pile with the finger-tips then remove with a clean brush.

To press seams on velvet, place the material face down on a clean clothes-brush and iron very lightly on the wrong side with a moderate iron.

Velveteen

Velveteen can be distinguished from velvet by the fact that the pile is in the weft instead of in the warp of the fabric as it is with true velvet. For the uninitiated this means that in velvet the pile runs the length of the material, in velveteen the pile runs across the fabric.

Generally made from cotton but sometimes from rayon, velveteen can be washed at home in the same way as velvet. That is, whisk up a rich lather with soapflakes or mild detergent and warm water and gently swish the fabric in this without squeezing, rubbing or wringing. Rinse thoroughly and drip dry. Shake occasionally during drying and also smooth the pile with a soft cloth or velvet pad.

Velveteen should not require ironing but if it appears to require finishing, iron very lightly on the wrong side, while the fabric is still slightly damp. An alternative to ironing is to wait until the fabric is almost dry then draw the wrong side of the velveteen over the sole-plate of a cool iron, allow to dry then gently brush the pile.

Veranne

See Verranne.

Verel

This modacrylic or chloro fibre is very hard-wearing yet it is soft and warm. It is manufactured in America and is used to make man-made furs, trimmings for collars and boots and for linings. It can be knitted to make shirts, sweaters and men's wear. Wash garments made with Verel in warm suds; they should dry quickly and without creasing but may be pressed with a cool iron. See also Modacrylics, page 60.

Verranne

The French generic term for textile.

Vicuña

This is the undercoat hair of the vicuña, a small animal of the llama group of the camel family. It lives in the high mountain areas of Chile and Peru and its hairs are the finest and softest available, even finer than the very finest Merino wool. It is a light tawny brown colour and is used to make very expensive overcoats.

Vilene

The trade name for a bonded fibre fabric. For care and washing see under Bonded fibre interlining.

Vincel

A British polynosic fibre made by Courtaulds and one of the newest in this group of modified viscose fibres. It is being widely used for knitted underwear and outerwear including sweaters, dresses, sports shirts and T-shirts. Vincel is also used in woven materials both alone or blended with other fibres for day and evening dresses, rainwear, lingerie and nightwear. It is easily laundered and has a high resistance to shrinkage.

Viscose

The most widely used man-made fibre in the world and apart from jute, the cheapest. Viscose rayon was the first man-made fibre to be produced on a large scale in this country. It is a cellulosic fibre made from a highly refined wood pulp of spruce and pine trees. Nearly 50 per cent of the total world production of all man-made fibre is viscose and it is still undergoing continuous development as new varieties are introduced.

The very large number of uses which have been developed for viscose rayon are due to its adaptability and to the length of time it has been in production. It is used in continuous filament, spun form and speciality yarns in the manufacture of a very wide range of fabrics. These are used for clothes, furnishings, carpets and other textiles. Curtains made from viscose rayon should be washed or dry-cleaned frequently. When garments or fabrics are labelled 'rayon' with no other indications, wash and treat as for viscose rayons.

Viscose should be handled carefully when wet as the strength of the fabric is then lowered, but it is regained as soon as the material dries. Wash frequently to avoid the necessity for hard rubbing and use water as hot as the hands can stand. Mix up a rich lather, squeeze fabric gently so that the suds penetrate, then rinse thoroughly and put through a loose wringer or give a short spin if washing instructions say that wringing or spinning is permissible. Some rayons crack easily if folded or screwed up tightly and this would show as fine lines on the finished article. Do not boil, twist or wring tightly.

Hang to dry as soon as possible and when slightly but evenly damp, iron with a medium hot iron, on the wrong side if the material is dark or has a matt finish.

When making up viscose rayons avoid making pin holes, and wherever possible pin in the seams. Use a mercerized cotton thread for sewing.

The word 'viscose' is now synonymous with 'rayon' as acetate is now regarded as a separate fibre altogether.

Voile

A fine sheer material made from high twist yarn. While cotton voiles are produced in great quantity there are also viscose, nylon and polyester voiles. Launder carefully in hand-hot suds; rinse thoroughly and roll in a thick towel to absorb excess moisture; iron while still slightly damp with a cool iron for nylon and Terylene and a warm to moderately hot iron for cotton or rayon voiles.

Vyrene

This is the trade name for a silicone lubricated polyester monofilament, or in other words, an elastomeric fibre, or a man-made elastic yarn based on polyurethane.

Although it is a fully elastic fibre, it contains no rubber and it is always woven or knitted with other yarns to give elasticity to fabric. It is extremely light in weight, yet sufficiently controlled to be used in girdles, brassieres and swimsuits, and not only for the small figure.

Wash in hand-hot water, or wash lightly in a machine, but do not use bottled bleaching solution. Like other elastomeric fibres, Vyrene is resistant to sunlight, oil and perspiration.

Waffle cottons

See Embossed finishes, page 39.

Water-repellent

There are a number of different finishes, closely allied but with varying claims. On the whole, moisture-repellent finishes tend to be applied to light fabrics and cottons, etc. while shower-proofing processes are used on heavier materials for rainwear, sportswear and similar garments.

Sometimes silicones are used to proof fabrics, sometimes not and the label will usually state if a silicone finish has been used.

Although both finishes can often be home washed, or professionally dry-cleaned, shower-proofed garments are usually better dry-cleaned unless the label states that the garment may be hand- or machine-washed. Where silicones have been used for proofing, the cleaner should be told as a special cleaning process may be necessary.

Often, moisture-shedding properties are combined with a finish which renders fabrics resistant to wet stains and soiling generally and when this is the case, stains should be removed immediately either by wiping or sponging or with a grease solvent if the type of stain necessitates this.

Remove spilt liquids gently by shaking the garment or by flicking the moisture off with a cloth and sponge away any remaining marks. Never rub stains on these finishes or the marks may be rubbed *into* the fabric. Where possible, follow the manufacturer's instructions exactly.

When washing water-repellent fabrics, use good quality soapflakes or powder or synthetic detergent and rinse *thoroughly* in clear water (insufficient rinsing affects the water repellency). Do not starch, boil, rub or wring but leave to drip dry and iron under a damp cloth.

Wear-resistant

Some processes combine a finish giving increased resistance to wear from rubbing or abrasion along with other finishes. Fabrics treated can be home-laundered or sent for dry-cleaning. When laundering, avoid wringing and boiling and do not starch or bleach. Rinse thoroughly and drip dry. Little ironing should be necessary.

Whipcord

A heavy twill woven fabric with a characteristic cord effect, similar to gaberdine. It was at one time made of wool, worsted or wool blends or of cotton but while most fibres can be used in this construction Vincel/cotton blends are popular at the present time. Dry-clean and wash according to fibre and manufacturer's instructions.

Wincey

A lightweight fabric similar to flannel but finer. It was originally made with a wool weft and a cotton warp but may now be made from wool mixture yarns. Wash in hand-hot water, use a steam iron or a moderately hot iron while still damp.

Winceyette

A soft, slightly raised fabric similar to a flannelette but somewhat lighter in weight—originally cotton or a cotton and wool blend but now also made in rayon blends. Wash gently as for wool or rayon.

Because of the restrictions on the sale of flammable night attire for children, efforts are being made to produce flame-resistant winceyette. There is a successful one in Lo-Flam Dicel with nylon and also one in Teklan.

Wollcrylon

This is an acrylic fibre manufactured in East Germany and similar to Courtelle which is made in Britain. See page 15 for washing instructions.

Wool

The wool fibre is a protein material which forms the coat of sheep and lambs. This substance is very similar to that of our own bodies and is a natural material for clothing.

The fibre itself has quite a complicated structure and its outside is covered in minute scales which overlap rather like roof tiles, pointing in the direction of its root end. When a mass of wool fibre is rubbed or worked, these scales act rather like small barbs, allowing the fibre to travel in one direction only—i.e. towards its root and not towards the tip. Thus the fibres move and become more and more entangled until a felt is formed.

This extremely useful ability to form felts is utilized in many ways, but it is a serious hazard when wool garments are washed without due care, as the felting is naturally accompanied by shrinkage which in this case is most undesirable.

Garments bearing the well-known Woolmark are made from 100 per cent wool with only a very small allowance for decoration. This is easy identification for the shopper.

The British Standards Institution has drawn up a wool glossary so that the proportion of wool in woven fabrics can be easily decided. Any cloth labelled *wool*, *woollen* or *worsted*, for instance, should contain nothing but wool except for a small percentage allowed for decoration.

Cloth marked *blended woollen* or *blended worsted* describes fabric which contains not less than 50 per cent wool. Note that the term 'blended wool' is not used as this could equally describe blends of different types of wool. Finally, cloth marked 'fibre blended with wool' (or containing wool) denotes fabric with a wool fibre content of not less than 15 per cent but less than 50 per cent.

It is worth noting that although the word 'wool' is used for fibres of the sheep or lamb it also includes fibres from the fleece or coat of a number of animals—alpaca, llama, vicuña, camel, the cashmere and the angora goat (mohair) and the angora rabbit. This is because the hairs of these other animals as well as possessing special features of their own, all have the same basic characteristics as those of sheep or lambs when compared with man-made fibres or with natural fibres other than wool.

For washing instructions see page 181.

Woollen

Woollen yarns are made from wool which has not been combed and both long and short fibres may be used in its preparation. Generally, woollen yarns are characterized by bulkiness and 'woolly appearance'. All wool materials with either a felted or raised fluffy finish are made from woollen yarns.

Worsted

Originally the name 'Worsted' came from the Parish of Worsted in Norfolk. Worsteds are made from wool which has been combed to remove short fibres (then sold to the woollen industry as noils) and spun on the worsted system, so that all the fibres are parallel and the result is an even smooth lean yarn. Worsted fabrics are generally closely woven, with a clear surface. Gaberdine and serge are of this type.

Nowadays the word worsted often refers to a method of spinning rather than indicating the fibre. Polyester/wool blends, 100 per cent nylon for hand knittings, acrylics for hand knittings and jerseys are all spun on the worsted system and there are numerous blends.

Wynene

A polythene fibre manufactured in U.S.A. and rather similar to Courlene which is made in this country. It should be treated in the same way.

X-51

An acrylic fibre made in America and used for textile fabrics. Material made from it washes easily, dries quickly and does not stretch or shrink; it is resistant to most chemicals and to sunlight. Wash and treat in the same way as for nylon, using a cool iron only for finishing. X-51 was the early name for this fibre which is now known as Creslan.

Yamma

The hair of a species of llama and rather similar to alpaca.

Yarns

These are a great many short strands of a fibre—natural or man-made—spun or twisted together to make a continuous long strand or yarn which is then woven or knitted into a fabric. Yarns can be single, double or of several thicknesses and they can be twisted together to give extra bulk as well as strength. Bulked yarns—usually from man-made fibres—are specially treated to give fullness and warmth. Fancy yarns—such as bouclé or slub—although they look thicker are made for their looks rather than extra thickness or warmth.

Zantrel

A polynosic fibre manufactured in U.S.A. by American Enka Corporation.

Zaryl

Viscose rayon manufactured in France and Belgium.

Zefran

This is an acrylic fibre manufactured in the U.S.A. See under acrylics on page 14 for further details and washing instructions.

Zepel

A Du Pont finish which is applied to fabrics to make them repel water and resist both water-borne and oil stains.

Zephyr

A fine, lightweight fabric with a plain weave and with a striped effect. Used for shirtings, blouses and dresses and usually of cotton. Polyester/cotton or polynosic/cotton blend yarns. Wash accordingly.

2

Chemicals, cleaners and washday aids

Absorbent powders

These include french chalk, fuller's earth, powdered starch, magnesium carbonate, talcum powder, etc. If spread on grease and other stains, they will absorb fresh stains without harming the fabric. Spread the powder over the stain, work gently into the fibres with the finger-tips and brush off as soon as the powder becomes tacky. Repeat until bulk of stain is removed, then work in a fresh layer of absorbent powder. Leave overnight and brush off next morning with a clean brush. Instead of leaving the last application overnight, time can be saved if a sheet of clean blotting paper is placed over the powder and a cool-to-warm iron is gently applied to the paper.

For further details see under respective headings.

Acacia

Gum acacia when available is used to give a light, pliable stiffening to light-coloured fabrics. Usually in the form of rounded 'tears' of varying size, it is nearly colourless or pale yellow, and dissolves easily in water.

Acetic acid

This acid must not be allowed to come in contact with the skin as it has powerful cauterizing properties.

Acetic acid is a useful solvent for organic substances, and it is used by dry-cleaners as a neutralizing agent. It is also used in the restoration of colours which have been damaged by an alkali.

The solution used by dry-cleaning firms is usually of 28 per cent strength, and in this concentration it can be used safely on most fabrics at normal temperatures. Pure acetic acid will dissolve cellulose acetate.

Ordinary white vinegar can be used for stain removal when acetic acid is called for.

Acetone

This is a solvent derived from petroleum. Acetone is one of the most powerful solvents and will often strip or dissolve stoved or baked paints which will withstand most other solvents. It is also likely to attack plastics articles and some man-made fibre fabrics, especially acetates.

Pure acetone, or a nail-varnish remover containing acetone, can be used for removing nail lacquer stains on most fabrics except cellulose acetate, which it will dissolve. It may also affect some coloured materials and if there is any doubt about the material or the colour, test first on an inconspicuous part or use pure amyl acetate. (See below.)

Acetone is an excellent solvent, too, for fats, lacquers, pitch, plastics and varnishes. It is a clear, colourless volatile liquid.

Use acetone on cotton wool and sponge the stain gently. If any colouring remains, sponge with fresh cotton wool moistened with methylated spirit, but again test on rayons first.

Store acetone carefully—it is highly flammable.

Acid potassium tartrate

See under Cream of Tartar.

Ammonia

This is a mild alkali which can be used for removing stains caused by acids such as fruit juice. It also works well on blood-stains as it saponifies the fatty acids present in the blood.

As it sometimes has an effect on coloured fabrics, ammonia solution should first be tested on an inconspicuous part of the garment, and always with rayons of any colour. To make a solution add 1 tablespoonful of ammonia to 1 pint of warm water and soak the stained area in this for 3 or 4 minutes, then remove and rinse thoroughly. If ammonia does affect the colour of a garment, neutralize it immediately by sponging the affected area with a weak solution of white vinegar and water, then rinse thoroughly and launder.

Ammonia will cause yellowing of white silk and wool if used too strong. Should this occur, neutralize with vinegar as above.

Amyl acetate

This chemical has a pear-like odour and is colourless. It is quite safe on most fabrics and is useful for removing nail-varnish stains from acetate rayons and coloured fabrics when acetone may damage the material or the dye. Rub gently with clean cotton wool dipped in the amyl acetate and if any stain remains, sponge with methylated spirit but test this first on rayons and synthetic fibre fabrics.

Amyl acetate is also a good solvent for cellulose, paint and lacquers.

Purchase a CP (100 per cent chemically pure) grade for preference, as an inferior grade may cause damage to cellulose acetate.

Ariel

The trade name for an enzyme washing powder made by Procter & Gamble Ltd.

Beeswax

One of the best known of waxes. It is produced all over the world —wherever there are bees, in fact. Commonest sources are East and Central Africa, South America, India, Burma and Spain. The wax is produced by the bee for building the honeycomb. It is cleansed by boiling or filtering and can be bleached by chemicals or sunlight for use in light coloured polishes.

Benzene

This is a colourless liquid with the odour of coal gas. It is obtained in the distillation of coal-tar.

It is a solvent for oils, tar, paint, sulphur and rubber and is widely used in many of the paint-remover formulae. It is safe on almost all fabrics and dyestuffs, though it will damage rubber, so keep it away from rubber gloves.

Benzene, sometimes known as Benzol, is not the same as cleaning benzine, below.

Benzene is inflammable and should not be used near a naked light. It is also toxic—do not inhale the vapour.

Benzine

Often called cleaning benzine, this is obtained from petroleum and is widely used in dry-cleaning and for sponging or spotting garments. It is also a good grease solvent for most oils except castor oil. Benzine is very flammable and must not be used where there is a naked light of any kind. It is safest used in a covered container out of doors as it is highly toxic. If affected by fumes from the solvent keep moving about in the open air and on no account attempt to allow anyone affected by vapour, to sleep.

Benzol

See Benzene.

Bicarbonate of soda

See under Sodium Bicarbonate.

Big S

This is a trade name for a biological soak powder containing enzymes. It is made by Phillips, Scott & Turner Company.

Biotex

The trade name for an enzyme soak powder made by Aspro Nicholas.

Bleaches

There are a number of commercially prepared bleaches and they should be used exactly according to directions. Sodium hypochlorite (chlorine) bleaches are those normally used domestically. Then there are the perborate bleaches which can be used for removing stains on white and many coloured fabrics. Bleaching powder, not commonly used by housewives, is actually chloride of lime and, like liquid bleach, must be used carefully.

Bleaches should be used on white articles only and then only on suitable fabrics such as cotton or linen which have not been given special finishes. Drip-dry, non-iron, crease, shrink and dirt-resistant finishes and fabrics with a special resin finish should never be bleached.

Do not use chlorine bleaches on silk, wool, nylon or any man-made fibre. Never use chlorine in the water if you are boiling clothes. Dangerous fumes can be given off if the chlorine bleach is heated.

If you are using chlorine bleach to clean a stained lavatory pan, never use a powder lavatory cleanser (such as Harpic) at the same time or the combination may again give off dangerous fumes. Use one or the other for cleaning and bleaching a lavatory pan—but never both together.

There are special bleaches which are safe to use on wool and nylon and sodium hydrosulphite is one. This should be used only on white nylon and wool unless you are wanting to strip out colour. This particular bleach can also be used on cotton and linen but again only on white articles as it decolourizes many dyes and stains of vegetable and animal origin. Dygon, sold by Dylan for stripping out dyes is based on sodium hydrosulphite. This bleach can also be used as an antichlor.

Follow instructions carefully when using any bleach, particularly with regard to dilutions and strength. The actual strength of chlorine bleach varies considerably with different brands. To bleach with chlorine, dilute well before immersing articles then leave to soak for a short time and rinse thoroughly in several changes of water. Never allow bleach to dry on material. Too strong a solution will cause holes to appear in fabric; not immediately but probably after the next laundering when the original cause is forgotten.

Chlorine bleaches will destroy enzymes so never use them in washing water with one of the biological washing powders.

See also under Chloride of Lime, page 116; Javelle water, page 125; Sodium perborate, page 130; and Sodium hydrosulphite, page 129.

Borax

Known chemically as sodium pyroborate, borax is an antiseptic and is a mild alkali which can be used to remove acid stains such as those caused by fruit, wine, tea, etc. Use 1 oz. of borax to 1 pint of water and soak the stained area in this, then rinse thoroughly and launder. With fresh stains it is usually sufficient to stretch the fabric over a basin, sprinkle dry borax over the mark and pour boiling water through, then rinse and launder. Borax is also an ingredient in the flame-proofing of fabrics and can be used to prevent rust in certain conditions.

Brightening agents

See under Fluorescers on page 122.

Carbon disulphide

This is a colourless liquid used as a solvent in the vulcanization of rubber and in the manufacture of viscose rayon. It is used as a solvent for rubber, sulphur, asphalt and fatty matters. Combined with oleic acid it can be used to remove remains of tar stains once the

oil has been dissolved. It should not be used on rayons. Carbon disulphide is very volatile at ordinary temperatures. It is also highly
flammable—treat with extreme caution.

Carbon tetrachloride

This cleaning fluid is derived from chloroform and its use is being
discouraged because inhalation of fumes in a badly ventilated room
can be highly poisonous causing damage to liver and kidneys. Heat
causes carbon tetrachloride to be converted into these poisonous
vapours which are believed to be phosgene or similar.

Although carbon tetrachloride is non-flammable (it was used extensively in fire extinguishers), it should not be used near any heat or
naked flame as a dangerous vapour may be formed. It is for this
reason that fabric cleaned with carbon tetrachloride should never
be ironed or pressed until it is completely dry. Again, for the same
reason, do not smoke while using carbon tetrachloride and avoid
inhaling the fumes. Fumes may have a slightly asphyxiating effect
especially near heat when the poisonous vapour is formed.

Use carbon tetrachloride near an open window or better still in
the open air. Always pour a little into a covered dish and keep the
bottle containing the remainder tightly corked. To use, make a large
ring round the stain to be treated and work inwards, placing a clean
pad of fabric or blotting paper under the stain and changing this as
soon as it becomes soiled. Use cotton wool or a soft cloth for cleaning and work from the back of the stain. Badly soiled materials can
be soaked in the fluid but the above precautions should be taken.
Afterwards allow dirt to settle, strain off fluid and bottle for re-use,
tightly corked.

As a cleaning solvent, carbon tetrachloride is safe on most fabrics
and most colours. It should not, however, be used on plastics and
both silk and rayon should be tested on an inconspicuous spot first.
It may sensitize yellows and bright reds and cause them to soften or
run so test these colours first on any fabric especially where patterned

Caustic soda (Sodium hydroxide)

This very strong alkali is both poisonous and corrosive and it
should be kept clearly labelled in a high, locked cupboard. The soda
can be used to remove severe stains from ovens, sinks and lavatory
pans. To make a solution, dissolve 1 oz. of caustic soda in 1 gal. of
water and apply with an old mop or brush. Protect the hands, clothing and furniture and neutralize afterwards by rinsing with vinegar

solution or by flushing very thoroughly with clear water. Any remaining solution should be thrown away immediately by flushing down the lavatory pan. Caustic soda is known chemically as sodium hydroxide.

Cellulose thinners

This may be amyl acetate or mixtures of similar solvents. They will dissolve cellulose acetate so test first on rayons and synthetic fibre fabrics. Can be used to remove paints, lacquers and nail varnish stains.

Chloride of lime

This contains chlorine and is commonly known as bleaching powder (though nowadays it is used less domestically). Use 1 oz. of chloride of lime to 1 gal. of water, stir well and strain before using. Soak the fabric in the bleach for a short time and then rinse several times thoroughly. This bleach is safe for cotton or linen and some other fabrics but it must not be used on silk, wool or nylon.

Chlorine

See under Bleaches on page 113 and Sodium hypochlorite on page 130.

Cream of tartar

The chemical name for this product of the fermentation of grape juice is potassium hydrogen tartrate or acid tartrate of potassium. It is used during the making of baking powder, self-raising flour and ginger beer and is used also for dry-cleaning.

C.T.C.

The initials stand for carbon tetrachloride.

Detergents

These days there is a vast range of products for washing clothes, floors and paintwork. There are liquids and powders, some based mainly on soap, some which are synthetic or man-made. All are technically detergents, for in fact any cleaning agent which removes dirt is a detergent—the word is simply derived from the Latin word 'to clean'. Pure soap is the original detergent. But today there are very few *pure* soap washing products—most soap powders and soap-flakes have synthetic products added to improve their efficiency.

There are many terms used to describe synthetic washing powders and liquids: soapless cleansers, soapless detergents, synthetic products, synthetic detergents, even 'syndets', a rather awkward shortening of the two words 'synthetic detergents'. For the sake of clarity this book usually uses the term 'synthetic detergent' to cover synthetic liquid and powder cleansers; 'washing product' to cover the whole range of soap-based and synthetic washing agents.

The first synthetic detergent was discovered before the war, but it was only after the war that the industry really got under way. When there is a new development in any field, the new discovery is expected to have almost miraculous powers, and if it fails to live up to the claims imposed upon it, the public may condemn it. In some cases this has happened with the detergents industry, giving rise to misunderstandings which are often very hard to dispel.

One of the fallacies about soap is that it will not lather in hard water. This is not so, because until the appearance of synthetic detergents all washing was done by soap, in all kinds of water. The fallacy arose because it is much easier to create a lather in hard water with a synthetic detergent. In fact one of the great advantages of synthetic detergents is that they work so well in hard water, though even so you need rather more synthetic detergent than in a soft water area.

Nevertheless, soap does lather well in hard water if sufficient is used, and once a rich lather is obtained it lasts well.

Another fallacy is that too much soap or washing powder etc. is harmful to fabrics. It is uneconomical to use more detergent than necessary but not harmful. In fact, the opposite is true and too little washing agent can spoil fabrics, especially, for instance, when laundering new woollen garments. It is important that a good lather be mixed and maintained throughout the wash. This does not apply to the special low-lather products designed for front-loading automatic washing machines, of course. With these, instructions as to the amount of powder used, should be followed. Poor rinsing results can also be due to using too little soap powder or detergent, as can greying of fabrics.

A soapy smell on garments after laundering is not due to the brand of product but is usually caused by soap residue. This means that articles have not been sufficiently rinsed. Sticky fabrics are due to the presence of fatty acid from soap residue, again due to insufficient rinsing.

One of the charges levelled against synthetic detergents is that they are too strong. This is quite fallacious. There are many kinds of synthetic detergent, heavy-duty and light-duty. It is as bad to blame a heavy-duty product for overwashing a light article as it is to blame a light-duty product for failing to remove all the dirt from a heavily-soiled garment.

The correct use of the washing agent, whether soap or soapless, is the key to efficient results.

Any detergent is satisfactory providing the correct one is chosen for the job and it is important to study the instructions on the packet or bottle before using it. A detergent ideal for heavily-soiled white articles is not necessary for delicate silks, woollens or man-made fibres. On the other hand it is far better, when doing the white wash, to choose a heavy-duty washing powder, as it will be chemically formulated to work well in the very hot or boiling water, with maximum benefits.

Any detergent should be completely dissolved before laundry is immersed in the suds (the exception is some fully automatic washing machines where manufacturers advise putting dry powder into tubs before clothes. In this case you should, of course, follow the manufacturer's instructions.) Washing powder or liquid should never be sprinkled or poured directly on to the fabric while it is in the water. Dissolve it separately in a bowl of water. The reason for this is that many detergents, while completely safe once they are dissolved, are very strong in powder form. Undissolved particles of powder (synthetic *or* soap powder) resting on fabric can cause slight or severe patchiness, and an apparent colour change, due to the fluorescer present in the product. Even liquid synthetic detergents recommended specifically for delicate fabrics can have a high content of fluorescer, so should never be used neat or in concentrated form. Fluorescers can have a particularly marked effect on pastel colours, but deeper colours, too, can be noticeably affected.

Follow instructions on packet as to the amount of washing product to use. If you have a washing machine, follow the instruction book which comes with it.

Often housewives with a new washing machine are puzzled because their washing is not clean enough. 'I used to get it much cleaner by hand', they say, and blame the machine. In really severe cases sheets and towels may come out of the machine with lines of greyish lime scum. The simple answer is that they are not using enough washing product. Generally in hard water districts extra soap powder will be required in comparison with synthetic detergents—often double the quantity. But where a water softener is used, less soap powder is necessary. The softener should be added before the detergent.

Some automatic and semi-automatic machines need special low-sudsing washing products, as a high lather would impair washing efficiency. In fact low-sudsing washing powders are much more commonly used in other countries. Scandinavian housewives, for example, are so used to low-lather powders that they often use them for washing by hand too.

Dichloroethylene

This is a solvent similar to trichloroethylene.

Enzymes

These are highly complex chemical compounds which are present in all living cells. There are various types of enzymes and many uses for them. The enzymes used in the special pre-soak washing powders such as Big S and Biotex and in the enzyme detergents such as Radiant and Ariel are the protein-splitting type of enzyme and they are made industrially by growing particular species of bacteria in tanks of liquid which are temperature controlled. It is a fermentation type of process rather similar to that used in making beer. The process takes several days and during this time the bacteria secrete enzymes into the liquid. The enzymes are then extracted, purified and are added to special detergents and washing powders.

Enzymes are not living organisms and they don't eat stains as some people imagine. Technically, the enzymes act as catalysts. Protein stains are made up of complex protein molecules and these are too large to be handled by detergent molecules. The enzymes chemically react with the protein molecule, causing it to break down into smaller units. These can then be dealt with by the detergent in the normal way.

Temperature is very important when using any sort of enzyme detergent. The warmer the water, the quicker the enzyme reacts but above a certain temperature the enzyme loses its ability to react with protein molecules and is ineffective. Both too high a water temperature and also chlorine will destroy enzymes.

The length of time necessary for soaking to remove protein stains will depend mainly on the temperature of the water. For instance, in cold water, overnight soaking is recommended; at the highest temperature at which the enzymes will work—60°–65° C. or 140°–149°

F.—as little as half an hour to an hour might be sufficient. The following chart gives some idea:

Water temperature:

Cold:		16 hours or overnight
30° C. or 86° F.	(lukewarm)	6–8 hours
40° C. or 104° F.	(warm)	3–4 hours
50° C. or 122° F.	(hand-hot)	1–2 hours
60° C. or 140° F.	(hot)	½–1 hour approximately.

Above this temperature—60° C.—the enzyme loses its ability to react with the protein molecule and is thus ineffective and in addition, the stains themselves will be set by the heat and will be even more difficult to remove.

Enzymes will usually remove both old and new stains but if old stains have been set into the fabric by high temperatures during previous launderings then repeated soaking and washing with an enzyme detergent may be necessary to remove them.

It is important to remember that enzymes need time to work and if you intend laundering immediately, you might just as well use an ordinary laundering detergent which will cost less and will remove most ordinary stains and marks.

There are four exceptions to the soaking rule. (1) Fabrics which aren't colourfast. (2) Wool. (3) Silk. (4) Fabrics with flame-resistant finishes. These four exceptions should not be soaked in any circumstances. They can, however, be laundered quickly in hand-hot enzyme detergent suds such as Radiant or Ariel.

These powders can be used in washing machines, whether twin tub or automatic but they are not suitable for front-loading or suds-sensitive machines. If you have this type of washing machine, pre-soak clothes in bowls or sink before laundering in the machine with a low-lather washing product.

The amount of enzyme detergent used is also important. Too much may remove the stain more quickly but will be wasteful; too little may mean that stains may not be completely removed. In twin-tub washing machines about 1½–2 cups is about right in soft water; use 2–3 cups in hard water. In a top-loading automatic use 2–3 cups in soft water; 2½–4 cups in hard water. For hand washing use about one-third of a cup to a gallon of water, a little more in hard water, a little less in soft water.

Always dissolve the powder thoroughly before adding the clothes whether soaking in a sink or washing machine but don't have the water too hot or you will destroy the enzymes. About hand-hot is the right temperature and the powder should dissolve easily. Enzymes are also destroyed by chlorine so never add bleach to the water.

Enzyme detergents, or biological washing powders, as they are sometimes called, can be used to improve the appearance of yellowed nylon, to whiten nappies and to remove any protein stains. These include blood, gravy, eggs, cocoa, milk, soups and sauces. Urine and other nappy stains are easily removed by soaking in a biological washing powder and so are perspiration and other bodily stains. Most food and wine stains can be removed by soaking at the correct temperature and for the required length of time. Ordinary fat and carbohydrate stains present will be removed by the action of the detergent if not by the enzymes also present.

Most enzyme detergents also contain sodium perborate and fluorescent substances or optical brighteners.

Although they are new to us, the use of enzymes is not a recent discovery. Enzymes were first isolated about one hundred years ago. The idea of including a protein splitting enzyme in a washing powder to help remove protein stains originated in a small Swiss soap factory during the 1930's. The Swiss company realized that if the protein molecules could be split by an enzyme they would become soluble in washing powder and they endeavoured to trace an enzyme capable of standing up to the alkalis used in washing products. In turn, they consulted a Danish firm who are specialists in yeast and enzyme manufacture.

It was not until the early 1960's that the Swiss firm launched the first enzyme soaking product and shortly afterwards a Dutch firm started manufacture. The first two biological washing powders in this country (Big S and Biotex) were intended for pre-soaking only. Garments could then be rinsed and hung to dry or could be given a normal wash. These were followed by two washing powders (Radiant and Ariel) and these are intended for pre-soaking and then for laundering.

Worth remembering is that the enzymes won't only break down protein stains in clothes. The soaking powders (such as Big S) can be used to deal with difficult household stains too. They can be used for soaking burnt saucepans; for soaking saucepans used for cooking scrambled eggs; for cleaning blocked drains; for removing stains from teacups, milk bottles, vacuum flasks etc. and for cleaning flower vases. Follow the same rules—prolonged soaking in not too-high a temperature.

Further details of removing stains with enzyme products are given on page 119.

Eucalyptus oil

This can be used for removing bicycle oil, tar, ship's oil (the black oil which is found on beaches and gets on to beach clothes) and all similar stains from many fabrics, including wool or other delicate materials. Place a pad underneath, then work the oil well into the stain on the wrong side with cotton wool, and rub gently. Repeat until stain disappears.

Fluorescers

These are fluorescent substances which absorb ultra-violet light and convert it to visible light. The fluorescers—which are added to washing powders and detergents—attach themselves to the fabric rather like a dye and they actually prevent yellowing of white materials and make them look whiter than when they were new. They have a brightening effect on white and some coloured fabrics.

French chalk

This is an effective grease absorbent, and being white can be used on white and pastel shades. It is harmless on any fabric and can be sprinkled on to a stain and later brushed out or it may be mixed with carbon tetrachloride or other cleaning fluid to make a paste. Spread this on to the stain, leave to dry thoroughly, then brush out with a clean brush.

Fuller's earth

This powdery clay is an excellent grease absorbent and it can be used in powder form or mixed with carbon tetrachloride or other liquid cleaner to make a paste which is spread on to stains and left to dry. Owing to the brown colour of fuller's earth, it should not be used on white fabrics but it is quite suitable for carpets and is safe on any coloured fabric however delicate.

Genklene

This is a proprietary cleaning fluid used for spot removing and based on 1.1.1-trichloroethane. It is safer than trichloroethylene, perchloroethylene and carbon tetrachloride because breathing the vapours has less effect. Even so, always use in a well-ventilated room. Check this and all stain removers on an unobtrusive part of garment before attacking the stain direct. This is because some modern fabrics can be affected by stain removers.

Glycerine

This clear, odourless liquid is a by-product of soap manufacture, and possesses extensive solvent powers, dissolving most substances which are soluble in water and some others, such as metallic oxides, which are insoluble in water.

It is used a great deal by dry-cleaners as an excellent lubricant to facilitate the removal of stains. It is safe to all fibres and dyestuffs, but flush out thoroughly with water after use, as glycerine is insoluble in grease solvents and cannot be removed by dry cleaning.

Grease solvents

These dissolve grease and oil on any substance—the skin included —so that gloves should be worn or a barrier cream used when handling them. However, some solvents, such as benzene, dissolve rubber also, and leather gloves or those made from PVC such as Glovelies, should be worn.

Grease solvents safe for most fabrics and materials include carbon tetrachloride, benzene, cleaning benzine, petrol and white spirit (sold as turpentine substitute). There are also proprietary dry-cleaning fluids, which should be used according to the instructions on the bottle. Synthetic detergents, too, are grease solvents of a different kind.

Place a thick pad of old towelling, cotton wool, rag or blotting paper under a stain when using a grease solvent, work from the wrong side of the material and always make a large ring outside the stain with the solvent, working inwards towards the centre of the mark. A dry-cleaning grease solvent must not be used on plastics.

Gum arabic solution

See page 155.

Gum tragacanth

See page 156.

Hard surface cleaners

These are sometimes referred to as household cleaners. They are usually crystalline products which, when dissolved in water, make a powerful solution which is designed to clean with a once-over wipe.

Manufacturers usually state that no rinsing or drying is necessary. Hard surface cleaners (such as Flash) are ideal for floors, laminated plastic surfaces, ceramic and plastic tiles, paintwork, vitreous-enamelling and for general spring-cleaning.

Hydrochloric acid

This acid, known also as spirits of salts, is both poisonous and corrosive. It should be clearly labelled and kept in a high locked cupboard; unused solutions should be thrown away immediately and never kept for future use. Hydrochloric acid can be used to remove severe stains from lavatory pans, verdigris stains and soot marks from firebricks and stone fireplaces. To prepare a solution use 1 part acid to 10 parts water and apply with an old dish mop or brush. Afterwards neutralize with washing soda solution—1 teaspoonful to 1 pint of warm water—finally rinse thoroughly. Protect hands, clothing, floor, furniture and the cement surround around brick-work.

Hydrochloric acid is frequently used in lavatory cleansers. Do not mix with chlorine bleaches or this will produce chlorine gas vapour which is dangerous.

Hydrogen peroxide

This colourless, odourless liquid is used for bleaching and can be used, when suitably diluted, on any white material except nylon and some types of rayon. It is often effective in the removal of scorch marks. Use 1 part of 20-volume peroxide in 3 to 6 parts of warm water and add $\frac{1}{2}$ teaspoonful of white vinegar and a few drops of ammonia. Sponge the stain or soak the stained fabric in the solution for 5 to 15 minutes, then rinse very thoroughly to remove every trace of bleach. Finally launder in the usual way.

Strength of hydrogen peroxide solution is usually given in terms of 'volume strength': thus 10-volume hydrogen peroxide will evolve ten times its own volume of oxygen gas. Usual strength used in professional dry-cleaners is 3 per cent (10 volume).

Hypo

See under Sodium Thiosulphate.

Hypochlorite

See under Sodium Hypochlorite.

Iodine

Iodine, a brown liquid, is used principally in the removal of silver nitrate stains, apart, of course, from its medical uses.

Javelle water

Another name for this is Labarraque's solution and it is an efficient bleach although it is poisonous, very strong and should be used with care. Do not use javelle water on silk, wool or nylon. A number of ink removers have a similar action to javelle water.

To make javelle water dissolve ¼ lb. of bleaching powder (chloride of lime) in 2 pints of cold water. In another container dissolve ½ lb. of washing soda in 1 pint of boiling water. When quite dissolved, mix the two liquids together in an old jug and stir thoroughly; allow to settle, then strain through muslin and pour into tightly stoppered bottles, clearly labelled 'poison'. Store in a high locked cupboard.

To use javelle water on white cotton or linen, fill a basin with water, stretch the marked fabric over the top and apply the solution to the stain with a medicine dropper, glass rod or stick. Leave the solution on for a few seconds, but no longer than a minute, then rinse thoroughly.

As javelle water contains chlorine, it should really be neutralized directly the stain is out and this can be done with a weak oxalic acid solution or, better still, with photographer's 'hypo' (sodium thiosulphate). Make a weak solution and add a few drops of vinegar, sponge the treated area, then rinse thoroughly and launder.

Labarraque's solution

See under Javelle Water.

Lactic acid

This is a thick yellow or colourless liquid, manufactured by the lactic fermentation of sugar. Used by professional dry-cleaning firms to remove tannin and ink stains. It is because mil' contains lactic acid that it has always been regarded as a cure-all for ink stains. But the snag with milk is that the lactic acid may remove the ink stain, but then you have a protein stain to cope with!

Linseed oil

This oil, from crushed flax seeds, can be used to darken and polish light woods and is used widely in the manufacture of floor and furniture polishes and in paint. Mixed with turpentine, it is often effective in removing heat marks from furniture.

Lissapol

This is a synthetic detergent or wetting agent made by ICI. It can be used for removing oil, grease and water-borne paints and also for softening water. Added to water before stripping wallpaper it will help wet the surface and assist water to penetrate.

Magnesia

Magnesium carbonate—or powdered magnesia—is an excellent grease absorbent and being white can be used just as it is to clean white wool, felt, fur, etc., or mixed with carbon tetrachloride or other cleaning fluid to make a paste suitable for cleaning felt hats, white kid and so on. When used as a paste it should be rubbed on, left to dry, then brushed off with a clean soft brush.

Methylated spirit

An alcohol distilled from molasses (sugar cane) or wood with a dye added. It is useful for removing shellac, french polish and wax stains. It can be used on most oils and grease but is not effective on paints. It can also be used for cleaning mirrors, pictures and windows, and for removing stains such as those caused by grass, seaweed, ball-point pen ink and perfume. Test an inconspicuous part of the garment before using on rayon but otherwise sponge the stain with neat spirit or soak the stain in the spirit if it is severe; if in doubt dilute meths with water. Rinse and then launder.

Methylated spirit can also be used to clean jewellery and piano keys, to remove emulsion paint and water wax emulsion polish.

Naphtha

This is a by-product of tar production. It is a solvent for tar and for shoe polish as well as for heavy greases such as car grease, fuel oil and crude oil.

Oleic acid

An organic acid found in many animal and vegetable fats and oils. Oleic acid is used by dry-cleaners as a lubricant in stain removal, especially in the removal of paint and lacquer stains. Combined with carbon disulphide it may be used to remove residues of tar stains, although not on rayons.

It must in all cases be well rinsed from garments or a rancid odour will be set up.

Oxalic acid

This is a very strong poisonous acid sold in the form of white crystals. It should be clearly labelled and kept in a high locked cupboard. It is used chiefly to remove ink, rust and iron mould stains and to remove the pink and brown mark often left after bleaching with potassium permanganate. It must never be used on silk, wool or rayon.

To prepare a solution of oxalic acid for *cleaning* or *bleaching* use 1 teaspoonful of crystals in ½ pint of warm water; for most *stain removal* dissolve 1 teaspoonful of crystals in ¾ pint of warm water and for cleaning *rust marks* from a bath use 1 teaspoonful in 1 pint of water. To bleach *stain out of wood* dissolve 2 oz. of crystals in ½ pint of warm water.

Mix the oxalic acid with a stick in an old jar and protect the hands, clothing and furniture. It is advisable to stand the jar on an old enamel plate so that if any of the acid is spilt it cannot do any harm.

Unless bleaching the stain out of wood, when it may be left to dry, always rinse oxalic acid away very thoroughly after a few minutes or neutralize with a solution of ammonia. The treatment may be repeated but it is important not to leave the acid in contact with fabric or porcelain for very long. Damage may be caused to fabrics if the oxalic acid is allowed to dry and recrystallize.

If oxalic acid is used on structural surfaces—bricks, wood etc.—and not completely removed, it can produce bright coloured stains—pink or grey-green in colour—from traces remaining.

Paraffin

This can be used for removing a tide-mark from a bath, rust stains from metal and so on. To clean a bath dip a cloth in paraffin, rub the marks hard and rinse; for removing rust, rub paraffin on to the marked parts or soak the metal in paraffin for several hours, then rub hard with an emery cloth until all the rust is removed. Store paraffin carefully, preferably out of the house, and do not use near a naked flame.

Pepsin

Pepsin is a colourless or light buff-coloured powder containing a proteolytic enzyme of the gastric juice of animals. It is often known in the dry-cleaning industry simply as a digester. It has a slightly meaty odour.

It is useful in stain removal, especially in the treatment of egg stains and blood stains, because it digests coagulated albumin and converts it into more soluble substances.

Pepsin is safe on all fabrics and most dyes—the exception is casein-printed fabrics, where the casein in the print will be digested and destroyed by the enzyme. So with printed fabrics, test first on an inconspicuous seam.

Perborate

See under Sodium perborate on page 130.

Perchloroethylene

A solvent which is widely used for dry cleaning and which has largely replaced trichloroethylene. If used at home, work out of doors or in a well-ventilated room. Do not smoke nor use near heat because of unpleasant vapours which may be formed. Test solvent first on an unobtrusive part of garment before attacking stain direct. This is because some modern fabrics may be affected by solvents.

Permanganate of potash (potassium permanganate)

This can be used to bleach stains from any white fabric except rayon, but its use is not recommended generally, as it is fairly drastic. When it is used, normal method is to dissolve $\frac{1}{2}$ teaspoonful of crystals in $\frac{1}{2}$ pint of warm water. Apply to the stain with a medicine dropper, glass rod or smooth stick. Leave for a few seconds, then blot up surplus solution and rinse. If a pink or brown stain remains this can be removed with hydrogen peroxide solution.

Photographer's 'hypo'

See under Sodium Thiosulphate.

Potassium permanganate

See under Permanganate of Potash.

Proteolytic enzymes

See under Enzymes on page 119.

Radiant

This is a trade name for an enzyme detergent made by Lever Bros.

Salts of lemon

Known chemically as potassium quadroxalate, this salt is extremely poisonous and must be handled carefully. It is used mainly for removing ink stains and can be used in a similar manner to oxalic acid. For details see under Oxalic Acid.

Sodium bicarbonate

Commonly known as baking soda or bicarbonate of soda, this is a mild alkali useful for neutralizing acid stains. Either soak stained fabric in warm water containing as much sodium bicarbonate as the water will hold or sprinkle both sides of the stain with the dry powder and moisten with water. When the effervescence ceases, the acid is sufficiently neutralized and excess alkali should be removed by thorough rinsing. In fact in all applications be sure to rinse away sodium bicarbonate well.

Sodium carbonate

Commonly called washing soda, this is an alkali and grease solvent. Provided it is dissolved in hot water (140 deg. F., 60 deg. C.) soda takes only a minute or two to become fully effective. In cold water soda may take up to 30 minutes to become effective.

Soda can be used to soften hard water for laundering purposes, particularly when soap preparations are being used. (Always add soda before soap powder or flakes.) It is important that the correct amount is used as an excess may cause delicate fabrics such as silk and wool to become yellowed. See page 157.

Soda dissolved in milk for 30 minutes will remove sea-water stains from leather.

Sodium hydrosulphite

This is a mild bleach which can be used safely on wool and nylon as well as on cotton and linen (so long as they have not been given special finishes). It should be used on white fabrics only if it is desired to strip out colour. Dygon, sold by Dylan for stripping out dyes is based on this bleach. The bleach, which can also be used as an antichlor, decolourizes many dyes and stains of vegetable and animal origin.

Sodium hydroxide

See under Caustic soda.

Sodium hypochlorite

This is the chemical name for most of the liquid bleaches sold under various names. In the cleaning and dyeing trades it is frequently called *eau de Javelle*—Javelle water. The strength of these bleaches varies considerably according to the manufacturer and a bottle may contain anything from just over 400 grains of bleach to over a thousand grains. The bottle rarely states the strength of the solution and it should be used according to the instructions bearing in mind that these may not be completely accurate.

The bleach must always be very generously diluted when used on fabrics but it can, of course, be used in a stronger concentration on porcelain-enamelled baths, sinks, lavatories, etc. In general for materials, do not use more than $\frac{1}{2}$ to 1 teaspoonful of liquid bleach to 1 gal. of cold or warm (not hot) water. A stronger solution may cause the fabric to develop holes several launderings later. As a point of interest, most reputable laundries use 5 grains of bleach to 1 gal. of warm water.

Liquid bleach should be kept in a dark bottle with a screw-cap lid. In a light bottle the bleach may lose strength and if a cork is used (instead of a screw-cap) there is a risk of leakage and possibly of explosion due to cork particles.

Sodium hypochlorite is suitable for cottons and linens—it should not be used on wool, silk, rayon or nylon nor on most of the resin-treated fabrics (i.e. those with drip dry, crease-resist and other finishes); it may also damage some plastics materials as well as sponges and brushes. Store in a safe place.

Articles which have been overbleached cannot always be righted by plain water—for example a rayon table-cloth which has been overbleached by mistake. Here an 'antichlor' must be used—sodium thiosulphate, obtainable from a chemist.

Sodium perborate

A white crystalline powder which is a mild oxidizing agent. Used for bleaching plastics tableware and suitable for bleaching most fabrics.

Perborate is a colour safe bleach and for this reason it is used in heavy duty detergents and also enzyme detergents. It gives a high degree of stain removal at high temperatures and is effective in maintaining overall whiteness. It is perborate which helps remove a great many stains—mainly non-protein—during ordinary laundering. It is most effective at high temperatures but will also remove stains at low temperatures during overnight soaking.

Sodium sesquicarbonate

This is a mixture of sodium carbonate and sodium bicarbonate. As it is a milder alkali than washing soda alone it is widely used for softening hard water both for laundry and toilet purposes. It is sold as a proprietary product but can be obtained by name from any chemist. It is worth noting that the price of sodium sesquicarbonate varies widely from chemist to chemist and is cheapest bought in 7-lb. bags from chain store chemists.

Sodium silicate

This is what is normally known as waterglass. It can be used for preserving eggs, for sealing a concrete floor and, added to the washing water, enables soda to be used for cleaning aluminium.

Sodium thiosulphate

This is also known as photographer's 'hypo'. It can be used to remove iodine stains and the chlorine which sometimes remains after using javelle water or chlorine bleach (i.e. it is an 'antichlor'). To use 'hypo' for stain removing dissolve a large teaspoonful of sodium thiosulphate in 1 pint of warm water, soak the stained area in this for a few seconds, then remove, rinse thoroughly and launder.

Spirits of salts

See under Hydrochloric Acid.

Synthetic detergents

Used in fairly strong concentrations, these are excellent grease solvents and can be used for removing stains of a greasy or oily nature from most washable fabrics. Immerse in the solution, or for heavy materials sponge lightly, using the lather only from the detergent solution. Rinse thoroughly and dry.
See also under Detergents, page 116.

Tartaric acid

Used for dry-cleaning and in the making of baking powder, self-raising flour, health salts, etc., this is twice the strength of cream of tartar. It is used by dry-cleaners as a solution for the removal of tarnish on lamé fabrics. Complete rinsing of the solution is essential.

Trichloroethylene

A stain-removing solvent which was once widely used for professional dry-cleaning but which has now been largely replaced by perchloroethylene.

Do not use trichloroethylene on triacetate fabrics such as Tricel. It may cause damage. Cleaning fluids can sometimes have an effect on some of the modern treated fabrics, so it is always advisable to check the effect of the fluid on an unobtrusive part of the garment, say the hem, before tackling the stain itself.

Trichloroethylene is difficult to buy under its own name and is more usually sold under a proprietary label so always check particularly before using on a triacetate fabric. Avoid breathing the solvent vapour and do not smoke or use near a flame as heat can cause unpleasant fumes.

Recently, spot-removing fluids based on 1.1.1-trichloroethane (e.g. Genklene) have become available. These are safer than trichloroethylene, perchloroethylene and carbon tetrachloride because breathing the vapours has less effect. Even so, they should still be used in a well-ventilated room with windows and door open. Don't smoke whilst using solvent.

Turpentine

This is genuine turpentine distilled from gum from the pine tree. It can be used for removing paint, enamel and varnish stains and for removing the tide marks on baths. Rub stains gently with a cloth dipped in the turpentine, then rinse and wash. Turpentine substitute is much cheaper and equally effective as a cleaner.

Turpentine substitute

A general term for white spirit and white spirit mixtures. May contain traces of other solvents. See under White spirit for further details.

Vinegar

This is a mild acid and as such can be used to neutralize stains caused by alkalis such as whitewash splashes and those due to too much laundry blue. Vinegar is also used to neutralize paintwork and wooden floors after these have been washed with sugar soap. It can be used neat for stain removal but usually 1 teaspoonful to 1 pint of water is sufficient.

Washing soda

See under Sodium Carbonate.

Waterglass

See under Sodium Silicate.

White spirit

This solvent is also sold as turpentine substitute. It is a petroleum distillate, one stage finer than paraffin. This is one of the safest solvents, not as violent as other dry cleaning fluids and safe on all fabrics and surfaces. It is the least toxic of any solvent but it is as flammable as paraffin and should be used with care and away from a naked flame. It is used to remove oil paint, enamel, varnish and grease stains.

Laundering

About 70 per cent of households in Britain now possess a washing machine, and housewives naturally wish to make the most use of it. The concept of machine washability has spread and a high proportion of textile articles, including those made from man-made fibres, can be machine-washed safely. Where machine washing is not considered safe, the garment will generally carry a label stating 'Hand Wash Only'.

In this chapter, general recommendations for various categories of clothing are given, without specifying that machine washing is permissible or not. However, since the advent of the HLCC Care Labelling Scheme a large number of garments now carry care labels for machine and/or hand washing. and this number is likely to increase rapidly, as the British Standards Institution's 'Textile Care Labelling Code' (B.S. No. 2747: 1967) has been revised to take into account the HLCC Care Labelling Scheme.

Prior attention should always be given to the care label which may give advice, for example, on temperature and method of washing, method of drying, the iron setting and whether ironing should be on the damp or dry article.

The HLCC

An important move made in recent years was the forming of the Home Laundering Consultative Council. This council is a working body formed from major industries in this country which are concerned with the home washing of garments and textile articles. Its aims are:

1. To provide a medium for the exchange of information based on technical considerations between its members in order to provide co-ordinated consumer advice.

2. To establish agreed terminology and definitions related to technical progress and changing consumer habits for use in home laundering advice for the benefit of the consumer.
3. To provide a public voice for the industries concerned both nationally and internationally in matters of home laundering.

Membership of the Council is open to companies and trade associations in five main groups:

1. Textile Industry
2. Domestic Appliance Industry
3. Washing Product Manufacturers
4. Distributors
5. Allied Interests

Agreed washing temperatures and their descriptions

Brief description	Expanded description	Approximate temperature °C	°F
Warm	Pleasantly warm to the hand	40	104
Hand-hot	As hot as the hand can bear	48	118
Hot	Hotter than the hand can bear —temperature of water coming from most domestic 'hot' taps	60	140
Very hot	Near boiling—water heated to near boiling temperature	85	185
Boil	Self-explanatory	100	212

Agreement on domestic iron settings and terminology

This was followed by the HLCC's ironing test method for classifying fabrics into suitable groups for ironing from which the following guide of four iron settings was formulated:

Setting 1. Cool   Courtelle, Acrilan and Orlon
Setting 2. Warm   Acetate, nylon, Terylene, Terylene mixtures, Tricel, wool
Setting 3. Medium hot   Rayon or modified rayon, e.g. Vincel or Sarille
Setting 4. Hot   Cotton and linen

These settings are being used more and more on domestic irons and on textile care labels and in iron and textile manufacturers' literature.

In addition, iron manufacturers may include a very hot (No. 5) setting for use in special circumstances, at the discretion of the user. This term is not intended for use in textile labels and literature.

It must be stressed that the indication of types of fabrics which can be ironed on each setting, set out above, is only a guide. In a blend fabric, for example, it may be possible to use a higher setting than that normally used when ironing a fabric composed wholly of one of the fibres used in the blend. Similarly, a fabric with a special finish may require a lower setting than that normally used on a similar fabric without a special finish.

HLCC care labelling scheme

The Council has been concerned in bringing together the experience of its members in order to provide practical and, as far as possible, comprehensive washing instructions. The two main aims have been:

1. To simplify care labelling and thus assist the housewife to sort her wash;

and

2. To provide instructions for machine as well as hand laundering where this can be effectively carried out.

There are basically three variables in any total washing process:

1. The temperature of the water.
2. The amount of agitation (i.e. comprising both time and type).
3. The method of water extraction.

The HLCC experts came to the conclusion that the vast majority of washing textiles could be covered by eight different processes (seven machine wash with hand wash equivalents and one hand wash only). These were numbered 1 to 8 with a number in a wash tub which provides both a link device and a symbol.

Each number is important in its own right. Four processes cover the normal weekly wash (mainly cottons)—these are Nos. 1, 2, 5 and 7—and four cover incidental washes ranging from frequent items such as shirts and slips to occasional garments such as skirts and dresses. These are Nos. 3, 4, 6 and 8. Each label also carries an empty box in which a manufacturer can add ironing, dry-cleaning or additional cautionary advice if he wishes.

A general guide to the highest temperatures at which fabrics can be washed

This is only a general guide, taken from the HLCC Care Labelling Scheme giving the maximum temperatures for any fabric. If the garment carries a label giving washing instructions, these should be followed, as there may be trimmings or finishes which require a lower temperature than that given below for the basic fabric.

Specific instructions provided by washing machine and detergent manufacturers relating to the use of their particular product should be noted.

If in doubt as to the type of fabric, use the lowest temperature, i.e. 40° C.

Boil—100° C., 212° F. or Very Hot—85° C., 185° F.

White cotton and linen.

Hot—60° C., 140° F.

Rayon; colour-fast linen; colour-fast and easy-care cottons; white nylon; 100 per cent Terylene*; Terylene/cotton or Terylene/linen mixtures.

Hand-hot—48° C., 118° F.

Coloured nylon; cotton fabrics with special finishes; Terylene/rayon mixtures; Acrilan/cotton and Courtelle/cotton mixtures; lightweight rayon fabrics, including knitted fabrics and nets.

Warm—40° C., 104° F.

Acetate; Acrilan; Courtelle; Orlon; silk; Tricel; wool; any fabric containing these fibres (except as indicated above).

The HLCC labelling scheme covers, with minor exceptions, the whole range of washable fabrics. These are the labels you should find on most British garments, domestic articles and fabrics.

The labels are fairly self-explanatory but the following notes may help in case of doubt:

Maximum Wash means the recommended optimum of agitation for any given machine.

Medium Wash means 40–60 per cent of the maximum.

* There may be less need to iron certain types of Terylene fabric if the washing temperature is reduced to 48° C.

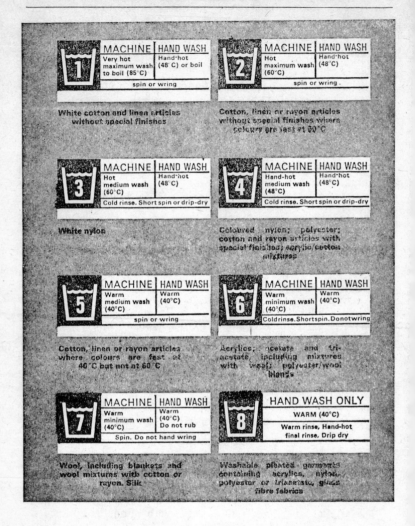

	MACHINE	HAND WASH
1	Very hot maximum wash to boil (85°C)	Hand-hot (48°C) or boil
	spin or wring	

White cotton and linen articles without special finishes

	MACHINE	HAND WASH
2	Hot maximum wash (60°C)	Hand-hot (48°C)
	spin or wring	

Cotton, linen or rayon articles without special finishes where colours are fast at 60°C

	MACHINE	HAND WASH
3	Hot medium wash (60°C)	Hand-hot (48°C)
	Cold rinse. Short spin or drip-dry	

White nylon

	MACHINE	HAND WASH
4	Hand-hot medium wash (48°C)	Hand-hot (48°C)
	Cold rinse. Short spin or drip-dry	

Coloured nylon; polyester; cotton and rayon articles with special finishes; acrylic/cotton mixtures

	MACHINE	HAND WASH
5	Warm medium wash (40°C)	Warm (40°C)
	spin or wring	

Cotton, linen or rayon articles where colours are fast at 40°C but not at 60°C

	MACHINE	HAND WASH
6	Warm minimum wash (40°C)	Warm (40°C)
	Cold rinse. Short spin. Do not wring	

Acrylics; acetate and triacetate, including mixtures with wool; polyester/wool blends

	MACHINE	HAND WASH
7	Warm minimum wash (40°C)	Warm (40°C) Do not rub
	Spin. Do not hand wring	

Wool, including blankets and wool mixtures with cotton or rayon. Silk

	HAND WASH ONLY
8	WARM (40°C)
	Warm rinse, Hand-hot final rinse, Drip dry

Washable pleated garments containing acrylics, nylon, polyester or triacetate; glass fibre fabrics

Minimum Wash means the recommended minimum amount of agitation for any given machine, normally 20–30 per cent of maximum.

Rinsing instructions are only included where these are of special significance.

The fibre examples given under each process are not exhaustive but show that each covers a significant number of textile articles. In the case of a fabric or garment containing two or more fibres, in general the process selected would be the one appropriate to the fibre requiring the milder treatment.

Water temperatures in addition to words can be given in Fahrenheit and/or Centigrade if the manufacturer feels this is desirable.

To the instructions for washing, rinsing and water extraction given against each process number must be added by the manufacturer, where appropriate, ironing, dry-cleaning and general cautionary advice—in that order—in the otherwise empty box at the bottom of each label.

Where an article cannot be washed satisfactorily or without risk by any of the process instructions, manufacturers generally mark 'Dry Clean Only'.

GENERAL

Baby clothes

Baby pants, whether nylon, plastic, rubber or a combination, should be washed after every wearing in warm soapflake suds. Soiled patches can be rubbed gently with a few dry flakes. Rinse very thoroughly, then pat nylon parts dry and wipe plastic or rubber. Leave to dry outside, then reverse for inside to dry—away from heat or sunlight.

Tiny woollies need gentle handling if they are to remain soft and if they are not to shrink. Wash them frequently before they are really dirty, using warm water and mild pure soapflakes or a mild soapless detergent. Squeeze gently in the suds, rinse in warm clear water, roll in a thick towel to absorb excess moisture or spin dry, and lay flat to dry away from heat. Ironing should be unnecessary but if preferred, press on the wrong side with a warm iron when almost dry.

Coloured cotton garments can be washed in hot soapy water, rinsed and spin dried or put through a loose wringer with buttons and trimmings folded inside. Iron cottons when almost dry and rayons while evenly damp. *Cot blankets*, *pram rugs*, *sun-canopy*, etc. can all be laundered according to their fabric. If in doubt use warm water, mild soapflakes or detergent, rinse thoroughly and dry quickly out of doors. Press with a warm iron.

See page 163 for Napkins.

Bed-jacket

Wash a light fabric bed-jacket according to the fabric concerned and a knitted one as given for wool. Outline a woollen bed-jacket first so that it can be coaxed back to its original shape after washing and before being dried flat with a towel between front and back.

If carefully handled, a quilted bed-jacket can be satisfactorily washed at home. Use mild soapflakes or detergent suds of the correct temperature for the fabric concerned. Whisk up a rich lather, immerse the jacket and gently squeeze but do not rub, twist or wring. Put through a loose wringer or spin-dry, rinse carefully, and wring or spin again. Hang to dry out of doors with the weight of the bed-jacket evenly distributed from neck to hem along the line. Iron when dry, avoiding seams and double thicknesses. If the bed-jacket is rayon, iron on the wrong side with a medium hot iron.

Brushed rayon, winter cotton (cotton brushed on the reverse side to make it warm and soft) or brushed wool bed-jackets can all be laundered successfully. Squeeze gently, supporting the weight of the jacket, wring carefully or spin dry and dry flat or over two parallel lines. Shake occasionally while drying to restore fluffiness. Use medium hot iron if rayon, hot iron if cotton and warm iron if wool.

Bed linen

Mend tears or split seams before washing sheets and pillow-cases and remove tea or other stains before laundering in fresh hot soapy water. If any parts are particularly soiled, rub with hard soap or with dissolved detergent suds before washing by hand or in a machine. Rinse twice at least and spin dry, or fold sheets evenly before passing through a wringer. Shake pillow-cases flat before putting them through a wringer and thread them through with the closed end first; pillow-slips ballooned out with air or water may easily burst.

Sheets should not be hung out to dry if there is a fierce wind or they may be whipped into holes, especially if they are wearing thin in places.

If linen is ironed damp with a hot iron—and the heavier the linen, the damper it should be for *ironing*—starching should not be necessary. Fold the sheets and pillow-cases flat as they are taken off the line until they are ready to iron, then if necessary sprinkle lightly and evenly with water.

Creases and folds should never be ironed into bed linen. Fold sheets evenly and then press the folds in by hand and vary the folds with alternate washings to equalize wear. Folded while still warm, linen should of its own weight fall flat with enough crease to hold the shape until use. Iron pillow-slips from the edge inwards.

Air bed linen thoroughly before putting it away, then store in a warm dry cupboard but not in an airing cupboard or it may turn yellow. If sheets or pillow-cases do become yellowed through bad storing or washing, re-launder and dry in sunlight once or twice.

Bleaching should not be necessary, but if it is, use a mild bleach and preferably hydrogen peroxide rather than ordinary household bleaches.

Blankets

New blankets, being washed for the first time, will retain much of their softness if a fabric softener is added to the final clear rinse.

A really dirty blanket is often easier to wash if it is first soaked in water softened with proprietary water softener such as Calgon.

Many modern washing machines cope very successfully and effortlessly with blanket-washing. Follow machine-manufacturer's instructions. To wash blankets when you have no washing machine, choose a warm breezy day; mix up a rich lather, using warm water and soapflakes in a soft water district or mild synthetic detergent where the tap water is hard. Add the blankets to the suds and squeeze gently (or wash blankets in the bath and tread them with bare feet). Avoid over-rubbing the blankets or they will become hard and felted like any other badly-handled woollen article. Rinse in clear warm water until the water is clear, passing through a loose wringer or spin drier each time. Hang over parallel lines to dry in the fresh air but out of sunlight. Iron bindings only—and not the actual blanket—and air thoroughly before using or storing.

If a blanket has become yellowed or discoloured, wash as above but use a special mixture made by adding 1 dessertspoonful of eucalyptus oil to $\frac{1}{4}$ pint of methylated spirit and mix with 3 oz. of pure soap flakes. For a small blanket mix 3 or 4 tablespoonfuls of the mixture (well stirred) into warm water and squeeze the blanket in this.

Bleaching

There are several ways of bleaching discoloured white cotton and other fabrics. A quick method is to dissolve a white dye tablet in the washing water, or a special bleaching powder can be used.

In summer the clothes can be left to dry on a grass lawn; they should then be damped and re-dried in sunlight.

Yellowed and discoloured woollens can be bleached by soaking them in a peroxide and ammonia solution. Mix a $\frac{1}{4}$ pint of ten-volume peroxide in 2 pints of water and add $\frac{1}{2}$ teaspoonful of household ammonia. Soak the woollens for half an hour, then rinse thoroughly. Washing woollens in a mild soapless detergent should prevent further yellowing.

To whiten discoloured nylon use a proprietary nylon whitener. See also in Chemicals and cleaners chapter, page 113.

Blouses

As a general rule for blouses of all fabrics, before washing remove shoulder pads and delicate or covered buttons as well as any detachable trimmings. Zips should be fastened.

Wash a delicate blouse by squeezing it gently through a warm lather made with soapflakes or a mild synthetic detergent. Avoid rubbing the material and if patches are specially dirty—on the collars or cuffs, for instance—dissolve some soapflakes or detergent in warm water and work gently into the material with the finger-tips, or rub on dampened bar soap. Then immerse the blouse in the suds and squeeze the soap through the soiled parts. Rinse in 2 or 3 changes of clear warm water. Roll in a towel to absorb excess moisture and dry on a plastics hanger. For detailed laundering instructions see Nylon, Chiffon, Lace, etc. under Fabrics and Fibres, and recommended temperatures on page 135.

To iron a blouse correctly use a heat suitable for the material (see page 135) and iron on the wrong side. Press the shoulder pads (if these were not removed), then iron any double parts. Continue with cuffs on both sides and then the sleeves, using a sleeve-board or ironing both sides to avoid forming a crease. (For details of ironing a sleeve without leaving a crease see under Dresses on page 150.) Iron inside the top of the sleeves paying particular attention to the shoulder seams. Press the collar on both sides, then iron the right front, the back and finally the left front. Turn blouse on to the right side and finish any frills or gathers with the toe of a cool iron.

Blueing

Blueing is rarely necessary today. The idea of blueing clothes was to counteract the yellowing effect of soaps. Modern synthetic detergents and soap powders do not have this effect so there is no need to use blue. In any case, most washing products contain a fluorescent compound which makes whites appear whiter.

Boiling

Articles laundered regularly in an efficient washing machine and washed in very hot suds (185 deg. F., 85 deg. C.) should not require boiling. If you haven't a washing machine with heater and are unable to wash in very hot water, boiling will remove some stains and maintain a good colour for white articles.

If you wish to boil, remember articles should be washed before they are boiled and they should be boiled in fresh suds and not in the water they were washed in. When using soap powder, it helps to soften the water with soda or proprietary water softener.

Dissolve the washing powder in hot water and add sufficient cold water so that the suds are warm only. Wash the white articles, then immerse them in the soapy water and bring to the boil. Three minutes' actual boiling should be sufficient for most items but badly-soiled articles can be boiled for 10 minutes or if they are very discoloured they can be simmered for half an hour. After boiling, spin dry or put through a wringer, then rinse in the usual way.

Coloured fabrics, cottons with special crease-resisting, moisture-repellent and other finishes, nylon, Terylene and other man-made fibres should not be boiled in any circumstances.

Brassières

Perspiration which rots the elastic is the worst enemy of any brassière so that frequent laundering is essential to prolong the life of the garment and to keep it in shape. Ideally, a brassière should be washed daily and with a nylon bra which will dry completely overnight this is fairly simple. With other brassières, launder at least twice a week.

Use water as hot as the hands can bear and whisk up a rich lather with mild soapflakes. Avoid bleaches of any kind. Do not rub, twist or wring the garment but gently and quickly squeeze through the suds, rinse thoroughly in 2 or 3 changes of clear warm water, then roll in a towel to absorb excess moisture.

Sometimes brassières incorporate synthetic elastomeric fibre in place of rubber, for extra durability and to make them washable.

Gently ease the brassière into its correct shape and hang to dry away from heat. Iron non-elastic parts while the bra is still slightly damp, shaping it over a soft round pad. Gently stretch any net or lace, then reverse the bra and on the inside carefully iron again, pressing the point of the iron upwards into the point of the cup.

Padded brassières of the 'Hidden Treasure' type which have an interlining of rubber need careful handling as it has been found that washing machines, hard water and gas fires all weaken or damage the chemical structure of the rubber. Wash in hand-hot suds as instructed, but use soft water if possible or add a softening agent to hard water.

Dry away from heat and avoid placing the bra near the fumes of a gas fire.

Brunchcoat

See under Housecoat.

Children's clothes

Most children's clothes can be laundered according to the particular fabric concerned and if no hand- or machine-washing instructions are provided see chapter 'Fabrics and Fibres', and washing temperature guide on page 135. Remove chocolate, ice-cream and other stains before laundering; for particulars of stain removal look under the appropriate heading in chapter 'Spots, Stains and Marks'.

A child's outdoor woollen coat can be washed at home, using warm water and mild soapflakes or detergent, but squeeze the garment gently and don't twist, wring or rub. Rinse thoroughly and spin dry or pass through a loose rubber wringer with buttons folded inwards. Hang on a child's coat-hanger to dry in the open air or away from heat. Press lightly when dry and iron the lining according to the fabric.

Nylon pile fabric coats can be immersed in warm suds and the dirt squeezed out. Rinse very thoroughly in warm water, pass through a loose wringer and hang to dry in the open air. During drying, shake the coat frequently and gently stretch it into its correct shape and size. The coat itself will not need pressing but the lining can be ironed with a warm iron.

Some makes of children's coats, including outdoor woollen types and nylon pile fur fabric outfits, can safely be machine washed. Follow washing instructions provided.

Clothes-line

Most plastics covered clothes-lines are extremely strong and hardwearing, but if the rope kind is used it helps to boil a new one for half an hour before using it for the first time. Do not, of course, boil a plastics-covered clothes-line.

A plastics clothes-line can be wiped clean before each use simply by rubbing it with a cloth wrung out in soapy water. If a rope line has been hanging for some time and is really dirty, wind it round a scrubbing-board or something similar and dip the board in hot soapy water softened with ammonia or in hot synthetic detergent suds. Gently scrub the line with a stiff brush, rinse thoroughly in warm and then in cold water and stretch tautly to its full length to dry.

Coats

Heavy outdoor coats require professional dry-cleaning, but *light summer coats* can be safely washed at home and many light nylon and cotton-proofed raincoats can be sponged or hand washed and some even machine washed. Both coats and raincoats should be cleaned frequently and long before they are really soiled so that harsh rubbing is necessary.

Use rich suds (see page 135 for correct washing temperature for fabric) give gentle hand or machine wash. (If machine washable follow manufacturer's directions.)

If any area such as collar or hemline is particularly dirty rub with dampened bar soap and scrub lightly with a soft brush. Rinse thoroughly 3 or 4 times and drip dry on a plastics hanger. Give brief spins if wished, after cooling with cold rinses.

If drip drying is difficult, absorb excess moisture by rolling garment in a thick towel, then hang immediately. When dry, iron according to fabric (see page 135), avoiding seams and double thicknesses; any obstinate creases can be pressed out under a damp cloth, or better still with a steam iron.

With a summer raincoat, if the makers say that the garment can be hand or machine washed, follow manufacturer's instructions or wash in the same way as given for a light coat.

If raincoat is not suitable for immersion in wash-tub, spread the coat on a table, whisk up warm water and mild soapflakes to make a rich lather and gently scrub a small area at a time with a soft nail-brush dipped in the lather. Wring out a cloth in clear, warm water, rinse off the lather with this and go on to the next section. When the whole raincoat has been cleaned, dry it thoroughly with a clean towel and hang to dry on a well-padded coat-hanger in the fresh air.

Whichever way you deal with a raincoat, be sure to rinse out every trace of soapy water or the shower-proofing qualities will be impaired.

Collars and cuffs

If collars and cuffs of garments are particularly *greasy and soiled*, damp them, dissolve synthetic detergent or soap powder in a little water and rub well into the black lines with the finger-tips. Easier still, use a household or toilet-soap. Roll tightly and leave for as long as possible—white cotton or linen can remain rolled overnight, lighter fabrics for an hour. Unroll and launder by squeezing in suds; rubbing or scrubbing should not then be necessary.

Stiff white collars can be made firm and glossy by kneading them in cold-water starch. Kneading allows even absorption of starch into the fabric but the collars should be quite dry when put into the starch and any old starch should be rubbed out first. After starching, leave to dry for half an hour and while still fairly damp, iron with a very hot iron, using plenty of pressure and moving the iron backwards and forwards over the collar quickly. Iron on the wrong side first and then on the right side.

Semi-stiff white collars can be made stiff and glossy in the same way but use boiling-water starch diluted with 2 parts water.

Lace collars need careful handling. Knead gently in warm soap-flake suds, rinse, roll in a towel and dry flat. Another method for washing lace collars of any kind is to wind them round a bottle, swish in warm suds, rinse in the same way and then pin to a flat board to dry. Very old or fragile lace should be tacked on to muslin and then washed in the same way.

To give the lace a crisp appearance, stiffen lightly and iron while still slightly damp with a medium hot iron, stretching the lace gently at the same time.

When stiffening dainty collars and cuffs, sugar and water, gum arabic or a borax solution can be used. Add 1 dessertspoonful of gum arabic or borax to 1 pint of hot water, leave to cool, then use in the same way as starch. See also page 155.

Coloured fabrics

To test a coloured article to see if the dye is fast, damp the inside of the hem and press with a warm iron between two pieces of white cloth. If any colour comes out on to either of the cloths, wash the garment separately.

When washing garments with loose or weak colours remember that speed in washing, rinsing and drying is most important; some dyes which are fast in cold or warm water will run in hot water so use cool water only for washing and rinsing. Pass through a wringer or spin dry, and immediately shake garment briskly, then dry quickly in a breeze if possible but away from any heat—artificial or sunlight. Iron when the garment is almost dry. If you spin dry garment, rinse out spin-can immediately afterwards.

Whenever possible, hang coloured garments to dry inside out;

striped garments should be hung with the stripes running down vertically; garments with varying shades should be hung with the darkest at the bottom. Black and red dyes have a particular tendency to be loose.

If delicate colours are fading or tend to run, it sometimes helps to add a spoonful of Epsom salt to washing and rinsing waters or to give a final rinse in cool water containing vinegar—two tablespoonfuls to 1 gallon.

A little white vinegar or salt in the rinsing water will often make faded blue colours brighter.

For pastel-coloured garments see under Pastel Shades, page 164.

Corselet

See under Corset and launder in exactly the same way. Iron the brassière top over a soft round pad to keep the shape, gently press the point of the iron upwards into the point of the cup and gently stretch any net or lace to the correct size.

Corset

Frequent laundering is essential for any foundation garment to prolong its life, as perspiration will quickly rot the elastic. With modern Latex and nylon girdles daily washing is recommended by the manufacturers and will make them last much longer; with other belts a weekly laundering is sufficient but no corset should go for more than a fortnight without washing.

Before washing, close zip-fasteners, metal clips and hooks and eyes and leave the laces fully open on lace corsets. Use a bowl or bath large enough to take the corset without bending it too much.

Hot water will not damage the elastic, in fact it will benefit it by removing excess body oils and perspiration more easily. Use water as hot as the hands can bear and whisk up a rich lather with mild soapflakes. Avoid bleaches of any kind. Don't rub or twist and remove dirt by squeezing gently or by scrubbing lightly with a soft brush.

Rinse thoroughly 2 or 3 times in clear warm water, then roll in a towel to remove excess moisture but don't pass through a wringer. Pull boned corsets gently along the boning and to dry, hang length-wise along a line or, if possible, with a zip-fastened corset (which should remain closed) thread the line through the corset. Don't peg a garment to the line by suspenders, shoulder-straps or hems and don't dry in strong light or near heat of any kind.

Iron the non-elastic parts with a warm iron on the wrong side when the garment is still slightly damp. Carefully press seams until they are flat and quite dry. Lastex, latex foam and rubberized parts should not be ironed at all and any sections made of nylon should be pressed with a cool iron only, if necessary.

Curtains

Most unlined curtains can be washed at home but lined, interlined and heavy furnishing fabrics such as velour, chenille and brocade, are better dry-cleaned professionally.

Launder light curtains frequently. Take them down from windows, remove hooks or rings, and loosen drawstrings, then shake well or brush thoroughly with a vacuum cleaner to remove loose dust. Mend any holes, sew any gaps in the hems or undo the slip stitches in the hems of new curtains being washed for the first time.

Wash curtains according to the fabric and for details see under appropriate heading in chapter 'Fabrics and Fibres'. Generally, though not for nylon or rayon, smoky curtains should be soaked overnight in warm water whisked to a lather with soapless detergent. Next morning wash in the usual way.

If curtains have been hanging in a sunny window and are tendered by sunlight and humidity, place in a muslin bag or pillow-case and wash them in this, or fold into four lengthwise and tie loosely with 2 or 3 pieces of tape. Soak cotton nets in cold ammonia solution, wash gently in warm detergent suds, rinse thoroughly and roll in a towel. If possible, rehang at windows to dry or dry on a clothes-horse or across a line, press and hang immediately.

Limp net curtains should be stiffened according to the fabric they are made from—using starch for cotton nets and gum arabic solution for rayons.

If white cotton net curtains become grey despite regular laundering, bleach carefully with a safety powder bleach, following the instructions on the packet. A safety bleach will not harm the fabric. It is, alternatively, possible to use a white dye in tablet or powder form after laundering. Chlorine bleach is best avoided. Occasionally boiling cotton net curtains in soapy water will help whiten them and should not damage them if they are handled carefully during laundering. Rinse finally in cold water before drying.

Test coloured fabric curtains for colour fastness before laundering and if the dye is loose wash quickly in warm suds, rinse in warm water and dry quickly in a breeze if possible.

Launder ordinary fabric curtains in rich suds, rinse thoroughly and iron while still slightly and evenly damp. Air completely before replacing hooks or rings. Before hanging the clean curtains rub metal rails with a cloth dipped in silicone furniture polish or paraffin. If curtain hooks or rings are stiff and discoloured, soak them in a little household ammonia.

Plastics curtains can be washed in warm suds and rinsed in clear warm water. Don't rub, wring or twist the curtains, wipe off surplus moisture with a towel and hang to dry, then rub with a clean cloth and rehang at windows.

Walk-through curtains of plastic strips can be cleaned by washing or wiping with a cloth wrung out in warm water and household detergent. Coloured strips usually clean well but white plastic tends to become discoloured after exposure to light and it is impossible to restore the original whiteness.

See also under Glass on page 45.

See also pages 63 and 315.

Dresses

Most dresses can be home laundered—many by machine these days—but check with the manufacturer's instructions, or with the salesgirl when buying a frock, before washing. Remove shoulder pads after marking their position and, unless they are guaranteed washable, remove buttons and belts also.

For washing instructions for each different type of material look under the appropriate heading in the chapter 'Fabrics and Fibres'. Generally, wash in warm rich suds, squeezing gently; rinse then spin dry or pass through a loose wringer or roll in a thick towel, then hang to dry away from heat.

Dry frocks on a plastics hanger where possible, otherwise turn inside out and hang to dry from the waist line, pegging an inside tape or seam. If the skirt of the dress is very full or if it is cut on the cross, peg the skirt also by the hem. This will help the frock to dry more quickly and lessen the risk of the skirt dropping.

Dresses made from modern synthetic fabrics or with special crease-resisting, drip dry or other finishes need special care and handling. Hang these frocks on a hanger the moment they are taken off so that the natural crease-recovering properties of the fabric have a chance to work. Do this even when the dress is soiled and ready for laundering. The fewer creases put into the material before washing, the less ironing will be needed afterwards. See page 135 for washing temperatures.

Pleated dresses should hang by the waistband with the pleats falling straight; use plenty of pegs and peg the frock to the line by a seam or tapes.

If the dress has been handled carefully before laundering and has been washed correctly little or no ironing should be necessary.

Soft crimp seersucker is an exception. Instead of hanging to drip dry, roll in a thick towel to remove as much moisture as possible, then carefully pull the dress into shape, hang to dry and avoid ironing except for collars and cuffs, etc.

For a dress which needs ironing, iron it correctly and quickly by turning the frock inside out, press the shoulder pads if these were not removed before laundering. Iron the sleeves next, using a sleeve-board or point of the ironing-board and beginning at the cuff iron up to the shoulder. If no sleeve or shaped board is available, place a long sleeve flat so that the fold comes exactly at the seam and iron without taking the iron to the outer edge. Turn the sleeve over and repeat the process, then put the underarm seam in the centre and iron the unironed piece of sleeve. Ironed this way, sleeves will not have a heavy crease running down the fabric.

Iron the collar next and then the bodice, going carefully between buttons with the iron point and ironing any double parts first. Pay particular attention to the shoulders as this is where most amateurs show their lack of skill. To iron the skirt, start at the hem and work upwards towards the waist, leaving pleats until last. Never iron round the hem of a bias-cut skirt but always on the straight of the material. Never iron over buttons or over seams.

Finish the frock by turning it right side out and pressing belt, pocket flaps and frills. An added touch can be given by ironing lightly once more over collar and cuffs. Hang immediately.

Dressing-gown

See under Housecoat.

Drip dry

This is basically a method of drying so that creases are minimal and often little or no ironing will be necessary.

Materials labelled 'Drip Dry' are cottons, rayons, cotton and rayon mixtures and linens treated by a special resin process. This usually makes them crease-, shrink-, and dirt-resistant and also implies that they can be drip dried. Cotton fabrics treated in this way are often called 'Minimum-Iron' or 'Non-Iron' fabrics. It is essential that washing instructions are followed exactly where these are supplied. If not, see page 149.

Fabrics made from thermoplastic fibres—nylon, polyester, acrylics and triacetates—are naturally quick-drying and are often recommended to be drip-dried. It was as a direct reply to nylon for shirtings that the drip-dry finish was introduced originally for cottons.

If laundering instructions are not given for drip dries, use warm suds mixed to a rich lather with good quality soapflakes, powder or a mild synthetic detergent. Use as large a wash-tub as possible; squeezing a garment into too small a basin will cause unnecessary creases and does not help the fabric to spring back into its original smooth appearance.

Try not to rub, crease or crush the fabric more than necessary during laundering. Do not boil, starch or bleach and work as quickly as possible so that the garment is in the washing and rinsing waters for a very short time only; do not leave to soak more than is absolutely necessary. After rinsing thoroughly, hang immediately on a plastics hanger, carefully arrange collar and sleeves neatly if the garment has these and leave to drip. Little or no ironing should be necessary but if it is preferred, use a cool iron setting 1 or possibly 2 and iron until the fabric is quite dry.

Where washing facilities do not permit garments to be drip dried, even indoors over a bath or basin, then wash as directed and roll loosely in a large thick towel; pat to remove excess moisture then immediately take out of the towel, shake and hang on a plastics hanger to finish drying. Or give a final cold water rinse and spin dry for a few seconds to remove excess water, then hang neatly.

Drying

Spin dryers can work independently or as part of a washing machine. Clothes can be put into a spin dryer dripping wet and the spinning will extract most of the moisture in a few minutes, depending upon the type of fabric.

It is a good idea, when buying a spin dryer, to look for one in which you can rinse too—it can save hours on wash-day. A pump-emptied spin dryer is more convenient than one which empties by gravity.

With some lightweight materials, articles from the spin dryer are ready for ironing immediately, but with most, further drying for a short time is usually necessary. For the amounts to be spin dried at one time, follow the manufacturer's instructions.

It is now generally agreed that drip-dry garments can be put in the spin dryer—in fact modern fully automatic machines incorporate a programme for washing and spin-drying the minimum-iron, drip-dry fabrics.

The secret is this. When you transfer a washed, soapy garment to the spin can for rinsing and spin drying, first of all hose over plenty of cold water. If you spin a minimum-iron fabric while it is hot you are much more likely to press in creases. Spin off suds, repeat if necessary, still rinsing with cold water. Finally spin dry. Each spin should be restricted to about 15 seconds (count fifteen slowly). Then take out garment, arrange on a hanger, smoothing seams and double thicknesses, and leave to dry.

A great advantage of this method is that drip-dries are still damp enough to dry crease-free, yet they lose that irritating habit of dripping all over the place.

Tumbler dryers are best used in conjunction with a spin drier or good power wringer, so that as much water as possible is extracted before tumbler-drying. The clothes are placed in the special heated cabinet which is controlled by a time switch and the articles are tumbled about in the heat until they are as dry as required. The degree of dryness can be varied from damp dry to completely dry. The filter on the tumbler dryer should be cleaned out regularly. Moist air drawn from clothes can be trunked from the machine through an outside wall, or a flexible vent hose can be fitted and the end led through the window. This is an optional extra for most tumbler dryers.

It is not recommended to turn an airing cupboard into a drying cabinet by taking off the lagging jacket of a hot-water cylinder. An unlagged 25-gallon cylinder set to maintain 140° F. will waste about 100 units of electricity a week, making the cost of a warm airing cupboard about two shillings a day. A 250 watt airing cupboard would do the same job for about 2d. a day.

It costs very little to convert an ordinary cupboard into a dryer/ airer. Small heaters that use less than ½d. worth of electricity an hour are sold for the purpose. The heater goes into the bottom of the cupboard and, as a precaution, fix a sheet of open mesh metal at an angle above the heater. Then, if anything should fall, it will not fall on the heater. Leave a small gap at the top and bottom of the door for ventilation.

The gentle heat, obtained from this type of heater, will also dry wet outdoor clothes and shoes. Specially made metal cabinets with variable heat controls can usually be set for fast or slow drying.

Heated drying cabinets can be operated by gas or electricity and they are made in various sizes from small folding models and wall cupboards to large cabinets. In most the heat can be adjusted and used for drying or airing, but usually drying ready for ironing takes up to an hour or an hour and a half. There is also the folding type of portable dryer, which has a drip tray at the bottom and a safety electric element (usually incorporating 'black heat') which sends up a constant heat to dry clothes.

For indoors, these dryers are a good investment. Alternatively, plastics-covered wire lines or curtain springs which can be fitted to hooks on the wall at either end over the bath are very cheap, quick to put up and take down, and are a big help with indoor drying.

Dungarees

When dungarees and painters' overalls are badly stained, do not wash immediately but dampen thoroughly, then rub all over with hard washing soap, paying particular attention to stained areas. Roll up tightly and leave overnight, then next day scrub with hot synthetic suds. If soap powder is preferred, add soda to the washing water to help dissolve grease and dirt. Pass through a wringer, then rinse twice, wring again and dry out of doors. Iron while still damp with a hot iron.

To make heavy overalls and dungarees easier to launder next time, dip in a thin starch after washing and hang out of doors to drip dry.

Dusters

Launder dusters frequently in hot synthetic detergent suds (use extra powder if greasy) but do not wash other items at the same time as the dye in dusters is often loose.

Eiderdowns

It is possible to wash an eiderdown at home and these days some types (particularly Tricel ones) can be laundered in a washing machine.

If washing by hand, however, a large bath, plenty of room to move the quilt about and a warm breezy day are necessary. Whisk up a rich lather with warm water and mild soapflakes, immerse the eiderdown and gently squeeze up and down for 3 or 4 minutes. Lift out of the suds, run clear warm water into the bath and gently press the eiderdown in the water so that the soap is forced out of the feathers.

Repeat the rinsing process 3 or 4 times but do not rub, twist or wring the eiderdown. When rinsing is completed, pass carefully through loose wringer, taking care not to split the cover, or spin dry if quilt will fit in the spinner, or carefully roll the eiderdown in a large sheet and, with help, twist the sheet at both ends so that the moisture is wrung out gently and slowly. Two people are needed for wringing because an eiderdown is very heavy when wet. In fact home laundering of eiderdowns should only be undertaken if you are feeling strong!

Shake the eiderdown and hang to dry out of doors over parallel lines or sew a piece of tape to each corner and peg these to two lines. Shake occasionally during drying to distribute the down or feathers evenly and finish drying in the airing cupboard or front of a fire to make the eiderdown fat and fluffy.

Electrostatic effects

All textiles show electrostatic effects to some degree and these cause garments to cling and to pick up dust and dirt especially in cold dry weather. This is particularly the case with quick-drying synthetic materials such as Terylene, nylon, etc.

A liquid synthetic detergent used in small quantities in the final *rinsing* water will reduce electrostatic effects. Half a teaspoonful of the liquid in an average size bowl should be sufficient but the treatment should be repeated after every laundering and always in the final rinsing water.

Better still, use one of the new fabric softeners (not to be confused with water softeners) to reduce static.

Embroidery

Embroidery should always be tested for colour fastness before being laundered. To do this, place a damp cloth over the embroidery and press lightly with a warm iron. If no stain comes off on to the cloth, the colour is fast and the article can be safely washed. If the dye is loose, wash, rinse and dry quickly, using cool water. Further details of washing coloured fabrics are given on page 146.

To iron embroidery, place right side down on a thick bath towel or blanket folded 4 or 5 times and covered with a clean cloth. Lay a thin, damp cloth on the back of the embroidery and press with a hot iron until the cloth is dry. Ironed this way, the embroidery should stand out as though new. Alternatively, an ironing-board with foam padding is excellent for ironing embroidery.

Fabric softeners

A fabric softener helps the wool or other fibres to slip over one another freely. It reduces wear, dirt pick-up and static electricity. Fabric softener, added to the rinsing water after washing, also improves the drape of fabric, and increases fabric bulk.

Fabric softeners, such as Comfort for instance, usually incorporate optical brighteners so that white nappies appear whiter. While their most important property is softening, they also offer additional advantages for home laundering.

They make ironing easier and garments remain cleaner longer. The softeners help eliminate static electricity on nylon shirts and underwear, preventing them from clinging and crackling. They also contain a perfume to give laundry a pleasing smell of freshness.

Fabric softeners are particularly useful on woollens and on bulky sweaters made from man-made fibres; on babies' napkins, towelling jackets and on napped fabrics. Follow manufacturers' instructions to achieve best results.

Foundation garments

See under Corset, Brassière, etc.

Frocks

See under Dresses.

Gloves

See under heading Gloves in chapter on Valeting.

Gum arabic solution

Some fabrics are difficult to stiffen satisfactorily after laundering and are likely to become patchy and discoloured if stiffened in the usual way with starch. Materials such as Taiho, silk shantung and taffeta, etc. come into this category. For these fabrics gum arabic is an excellent stiffener and gives a finish often similar to the original.

To make a gum arabic solution, wash 4 oz. of best white gum arabic crystals (plum or acacia tree gum if possible) in cold water and add to 1 pint of hot water in an old saucepan or in a jar standing in a pan of water. Dissolve slowly over a very low heat, stirring frequently and when finally melted, strain through fine muslin and bottle. If possible store in a bottle with a glass stopper.

This gum arabic solution is strong and needs to be diluted with water to the strength required for the fabric. For Taiho, shantung, taffeta and similar materials 2 teaspoonfuls of gum arabic to 1 pint of water is sufficient but other fabrics may need 4 or 5 teaspoonfuls to a pint while delicate lace usually needs only ½ teaspoonful to a pint.

Wash and rinse garment in the usual way, then add the required amount of gum arabic solution to the final rinsing water and squeeze the material in this. Hang to dry and iron while the material is still really damp—within 15 minutes of rinsing for delicate fabrics.

Gum tragacanth

This is much more expensive than gum arabic and it is not soluble in water so that it must first be dissolved in methylated spirit before being diluted with an equal amount of water. Used for stiffening lace and other delicate fabrics, but gum arabic is equally satisfactory.

Gymslips

Many modern gymslips are extra-easy to wash at home. Some are even machine-washable. If you are in doubt however, and there is no care label, tack pleats in position and test a gymslip or tunic for colour fastness before laundering by squeezing the belt or shoulder strap in warm suds for a minute or two. If the colour is very loose, wash garment quickly in warm suds, as given on page 146.

If little or no colour runs, wash the slip in warm soapy water, keeping it moving in the suds the whole time. Wash fairly quickly and do not leave to soak. Rinse thoroughly in warm water, then spin dry or put through a wringer and hang to dry immediately. Arrange on a hanger on line so that pleats are held taut and fall vertically. Press lightly, using a damp cloth—preferably with a steam iron—when almost dry.

Handkerchiefs

Place an old sponge bag in the bathroom or in the bedrooms and ask your family to put every dirty handkerchief in one of these containers. It is more hygienic, saves work and searching and sorting on wash day and if a dirty handkerchief is put in the bag before a clean one is taken, fewer are lost. Better still, of course, urge them to use paper tissues.

Soak soiled handkerchiefs overnight or for at least an hour in cold salt water before washing them, then rinse thoroughly under running water before adding them to hot soapy water. If you have a fully-automatic washing machine, use the Pre-wash or Rinse programme for this pre-soaking, adding salt.

Unless you have a washing machine, boil handkerchiefs every washday or at least once or twice a month. To whiten them if they are discoloured, use safety bleach according to the manufacturer's instructions. (Be careful not to overbleach.) Dry handkerchiefs out of doors and in the sun if possible. Iron with a hot iron and press round the hem first to keep the handkerchiefs square.

Delicate handkerchiefs or those with fine lace edgings should be washed in a nylon bag. Rinse and pass through the wringer still in the bag and, if possible, dry in the same way. Fine handkerchiefs pegged on to a line should be hung evenly across the line and not pegged by the edges or into the lace trimming.

Some housewives find they can save ironing time if handkerchiefs are not dealt with separately but after rinsing are laid flat, one on top of the other regardless of size. When all the handkerchiefs are in a pile, they pass them through the wringer, flat or folded, and then roll and place in the ironing basket. To iron, they place the complete pile flat on the board, iron the top handkerchief, and fold it; the next hankies are by now partly ironed and need less time. The week's handkerchiefs can be dealt with quickly and methodically with no sorting, straightening or arranging on the ironing-board.

Hard water

Water is popularly termed hard when it does not form an immediate lather with soap. There is, in fact, a scientific grading for hardness of water, called Clark's scale.

Water hardness is due to the presence of calcium, magnesium and iron compounds dissolved in the water. When soap is added to hard water, an insoluble scum consisting of salts of these metals with the fatty acids of the soap, is formed.

Using a synthetic detergent for laundering will avoid the scum caused by soap and hard water. If ordinary soap powder or flakes are used the water can be softened first by adding a little soda, sodium sesquicarbonate or proprietary water softener, but it is most important that these are added in the correct quantities, especially in the case of soda.

Soda is an efficient softener but the amount must be calculated very carefully or the surplus may damage the materials. It is best made up in stock solution and then diluted as required. To make a stock solution dissolve 1 oz. of washing soda in 1 pint of boiling water, leave to cool, then bottle.

How much the soda is then diluted will depend upon the degree of hardness, and the local water board or authority will give this information. London water contains up to about 20 degrees of hardness and for this 2 tablespoonfuls of soda solution to each gallon of water is sufficient. If the water has 10 degrees of hardness, add 1 tablespoonful of soda solution to each gallon of water and *pro rata*. Add the soda to the hot water before adding the soap powder or flakes.

Sodium sesquicarbonate is dearer to buy (although fairly cheap at chain store chemists) but it is a milder alkali than soda and is efficient at softening water. It is not so important to gauge accurately the amount used but usually 1 dessertspoonful to 1 gallon is sufficient.

Probably the best water softener is a proprietary type such as Calgon. It is more economical if bought in bulk. This product, unlike soda, does not need to be dissolved in very hot or boiling water. It will dissolve in cold water successfully.

Housecoat

Housecoats, dressing-gowns and brunchcoats (three-quarter length garments which are something between a formal housecoat and an early morning dressing-gown) are made in a variety of fabrics, and manufacturer's instructions should be followed as to the advisability of dry-cleaning or home-laundering.

Most fabrics—including velveteen, needlecord, corduroy, nylon and Terylene quilted housecoats—can be home-laundered, and some can be machine washed if minimum washing and spinning times are allowed. For water temperature for different types of fabric, see page 135. For drying see page 151. For ironing see page 159.

It is most important that quilted housecoats should be hung so that the weight is evenly distributed. If possible, arrange neatly on a plastics hanger (after short spin) and dry out of doors or over a bath. No ironing should be necessary if the garment has been carefully washed to avoid creasing. If finishing is necessary, press lightly with a cool iron.

Velveteen, needlecord, corduroy and similar fabrics should be handled as little as possible during laundering to avoid marking the pile. After rinsing, hang on a line or hanger to drip dry and occasion_ ally smooth the fabric the way of the pile with a soft cloth. Ironing should not be necessary, but if the garment is badly creased, press against a warm upturned iron so that the wrong side of the material is against the soleplate.

Ironing

Always use an iron from a wall socket and never from a ceiling lighting point or from a lampholder.

Before ironing lingerie and handkerchiefs, sprinkle 1 or 2 drops of toilet cologne on the ironing sheet. The heat of the iron will draw the fragrance into the clothes.

When ironing *easily marked materials*, place a piece of tissue paper over the fabric first and iron on the paper.

A special arm to hold the *flex* running to an electric iron is well worth the money. An alternative is to screw a large curtain hook into the end of the ironing-board and run the flex through this so that it is always clear of the ground.

To ease *aching feet* when ironing, either sit on a stool or remove slippers or shoes and stand on a soft cushion till the job is finished.

Whatever the garment or fabric it is important to continue ironing until the material is completely dry. Garments left to air while slightly damp will wrinkle and lack a good finish.

The *temperature of the iron* is important especially with fabrics such as nylon, rayon and Terylene, etc. which would be permanently damaged by too hot an iron. There are set temperatures at which each fabric should be ironed (see page 135 for full details) and most modern irons are thermostatically controlled to give the correct temperature for the fabric indicated.

For an *iron without settings* there are three main temperatures to bear in mind: Cool—for acrylics (Acrilan, Courtelle and Orlon)— and with an iron of this temperature the heat is just bearable against the palm of the hand; Warm—for acetate, nylon, Terylene, Tricel and wool. Here the heat of the iron would be just bearable against the tips of the fingers; Medium Hot for rayon—dampened finger causes a slight hiss; Hot—for cotton and linen—the iron should give a sharp hiss when the soleplate is touched with a damp finger.

A *thermostatically controlled iron* takes a minute or so to drop from a high temperature to a low one or to heat up, so ironing should always be sorted so that items which need a low temperature are dealt with first and you should work up to cottons and linens which need a really hot iron.

Most fabrics can be damped down by sprinkling them with warm water if they become too dry, but silks or rayons should never be re-damped or they may become patchy and spotty. If they become too dry, roll in a damp towel.

Time can be saved on ironing if the basket of washing is placed on one side of the ironing-board with a clothes-horse to take small items and a hanging rack for dresses, shirts, blouses, etc. on the other. A number of plastics coat hangers should be handy.

A rack to hang the coat hangers on can be easily made by screwing a dozen cup hooks one underneath the other on a piece of wood. Leave 2 or 3 inches between each hook and make some provision for hanging the fitment. With a hook screwed behind the kitchen door or on the clothes-horse, a hole or piece of tape in the top of the batten is sufficient.

Ironing can also be speeded up if sheets, table-cloths and other large items are neatly folded and placed on the ironing-board and the rest of the washing ironed in the usual way on top. Half-way through the work, the large items underneath will be sufficiently ironed to be placed aside for airing. Some housewives find that quite a lot of time can be saved on handkerchiefs if they are ironed all together. For details see page 157.

Complete the ironing of one portion of an article at a time and do not dart from place to place. With straightforward fabrics ironing should be a smooth backwards and forwards motion at a fairly slow pace. Each time the iron is diverted to a different stroke it requires extra physical and mental effort on the part of the operator and in the case of delicate fabrics such as rayons, it can damage the material.

Iron children's clothes the same way using the point of the iron to press in to dainty pleats, smocking, etc. The tiny puffed sleeves of a small child's dress can be tricky but not if the sleeves are firmly stuffed with a soft towel first.

The soleplate of an iron will not develop stains and marks from ironing starched items if it is rubbed with a damp cloth while it is still warm after each use.

There is a proprietary liquid for iron soleplates, not cheap but it goes a long way. It is said to speed up ironing by making the sole-plate glide smoothly over the fabric. Rinse additives will also help make ironing easier. Details are given under Fabric softeners on page 155.

For details of ironing a dress, blouse or shirt, see under respective items.

Lace

Details and washing instructions for lace are given on page 51 in the chapter 'Fabrics and fibres' and in this chapter under Collars and cuffs. In addition to the instructions already given under the fabric and garment heading, bear in mind that white cotton or nylon lace should be washed in hot suds but coloured lace of any type should be laundered in warm soapy water.

Laundry aprons

Water will not run down a plastics apron and drip if a thick strip of old towelling is stuck or sewn round the hem of the apron.

Leather shorts and jackets

See page 194 in chapter on Valeting.

Lingerie

Most lingerie should be laundered according to the fabric concerned and these can be found in the chapter on 'Fabrics and fibres'; there are also additional details under garment headings such as Brassières, Corsets, etc. on pages 143, 147, etc.

As most underwear comes into contact with the skin, and therefore with perspiration, it should be washed frequently so that grease, dirt, and make-up cannot penetrate the fibres of the material. Quick-drying fabrics containing, for example, Terylene, nylon, Lastex, etc. should be washed after *every* wearing.

Underwear that is particularly soiled on shoulder straps or hemline should be soaked for 20 to 30 minutes in warm water whisked to a lather with a detergent. White nylon underwear can become discoloured fairly quickly; avoid this by laundering it daily in a liquid synthetic detergent lather. The discoloration can be corrected by similar laundering or with a special white dye in tablet or powder form intended to whiten yellowed nylon. Bleach should not be used as this may damage the fibres permanently. Avoid drying white nylon garments near heat or in sunlight.

For stiff petticoats see under Bonded Fibre Interlining on page 20 or Paper Nylon on page 70. Nylon or Perlon net crinoline petticoats should be washed by hand in hot suds, rinsed and left to drip dry. They should not require stiffening or ironing.

Loose covers

Very heavy fabrics such as velvet, velour, etc. are better dry-cleaned but most other materials used for loose covers can be easily washed at home. Remove the covers and brush with a vacuum cleaner attachment or brush well out of doors to remove loose dust; pay particular attention to pipings, pleats, seams, etc. and mend tears or torn places before washing.

Test coloured fabrics for colour fastness and if the dye is loose have the covers dry-cleaned or wash quickly in warm suds, rinse in warm water, wring and dry in a breeze if possible.

If the dye is fast, mix up a rich lather with soapflakes or soapless detergent and squeeze the covers in this; remove and wash in a second lather if the water becomes dirty quickly and the foam subsides. Rinse 2 or 3 times, pass through a wringer and hang to dry out of doors, pegged between two lines if possible to allow the wind to get into folds.

Iron when almost dry but still slightly and evenly damp, on the wrong side if the material is matt or on the right side for a glossy finish. To iron loose covers, go lightly over the seat, back and arms and then press seams, pleats and frills properly. Replace covers on chairs and finish ironing the flat pieces once they are correctly positioned; if this is done the covers will fit better and have a tailored appearance.

Most cotton and linen covers keep clean longer and have a more attractive finish if they are lightly starched after laundering. In this case dry the covers completely and then sprinkle with warm water to dampen before ironing. However, if the fabric has a special glazed finish or if it is crease-resisting, drip dry, non-iron or has some other added finish do not starch it and handle gently when washing, avoiding twisting, rubbing and wringing. Simply wash by squeezing, rinse and drip dry. Finish with a warm iron.

If loose covers are correctly washed they should not shrink; if they do and are difficult to fit, rinse them in warm water, pass through a wringer and hang to dry for a short time only. While the covers are still fairly damp, gently stretch them on to the chairs and once they are correctly positioned, press with a moderately hot iron.

Loose mattress cover

The loose cotton cover which often protects a mattress tick can be washed easily. Soak it for 10 to 15 minutes in a warm solution of detergent whisked to a good lather, then wash by machine or hand with very hot detergent suds. Rinse 2 or 3 times, then spin dry or wring and hang to dry. Iron while still slightly damp and leave to air thoroughly before replacing on mattress.

Napkins

Babies' napkins should be rinsed out in cold water, then left to soak for at least an hour or overnight. After soaking, spin or wring tightly and wash in very hot or boiling soapflakes or liquid-detergent suds. Rinse very thoroughly in hot water, wring or spin dry and hang out of doors to dry. If you wash by hand, boil napkins once a week for 5 to 10 minutes after bringing the water slowly to boiling point from cold. If you wash regularly by machine with very hot water, boiling is not essential.

Many mothers are finding that a great advantage of modern fully-automatic washing machines is that they incorporate a pre-wash or rinse programme, which gives a cold rinse and then spins. This is ideal for treating nappies before washing, and saves hours of pre-rinsing by hand.

Biggest boon for mothers has been the break-through in enzyme detergents. These biological washing powders are quick and efficient and ideal for the protein stains plus which are synonymous with nappies. Rinse then leave to soak overnight in cold water containing enzyme soak or washing powder or leave for a few hours in warm or hand-hot water and then wash in the normal way. See page 119 for further details and temperatures. Don't have the water too hot or the enzymes will be rendered ineffective and don't use a chlorine bleach. The powders can be used for soaking and hand washing or in a washing machine.

Overalls

For heavy duty overalls see under Dungarees on page 153. Light overalls and children's overalls in corduroy, twill, denim and spun rayon, etc. can be washed in warm suds, rinsed and wrung or, in the case of corduroy, hung to drip dry. Avoid soaking unless the overalls are very dirty and the colour is guaranteed fast. Corduroy overalls should not require pressing; rayon should be ironed on the wrong side while slightly damp, using a medium hot iron. Cotton, twill and denim overalls should be ironed with a hot iron while they are still fairly damp.

Pastel shades

Garments in delicate pastel shades should be laundered separately in mild suds, well dissolved. Many synthetic detergents and washing powders contain fluorescent dye or a special whitening agent and while this will make white fabrics appear whiter it may cause apparent fading or patchiness on subtle pastel colours if the washing product is used dry or in too strong a solution. This change of colour may affect any material, even quite heavy items such as sheets and towels. So never use washing products in concentrated form, especially on pastels.

Pastel-coloured garments should not be soaked before laundering nor should they be left lying around wet after washing or rinsing. Proceed straight from washing to rinsing and from rinsing to drying.

Pillows

If necessary, pillows can be washed at home just as they are, but it is a fairly strenuous task, so if in doubt don't!

If washing by machine, wash only one pillow at a time. If washing by hand, prepare a large bath of warm soapy water and squeeze the pillows in the suds so that the lather penetrates the feathers.

Rinse the pillows in several changes of clear warm water, preferably spin drying between each rinse, then finally spin dry or squeeze in a thick towel and hang to dry in the sun. If the wet pillow is too heavy for the line, tie string to the corners and hang from two hooks like a hammock. Shake frequently during drying, which may take several days. Press lightly with a cool iron if the fabric is creased and air well before using.

Pillows washed at home may develop a not-too-pleasant smell during drying, however well they have been washed. This is mainly due to resins and oils in the feathers having been disturbed.

To avoid this possibility, the feathers can be emptied into another case while the ticks alone are washed. Once they are dry, rub the inside of the ticks with beeswax and press with a hot iron so that small feathers cannot work through.

Latex and polyether foam pillows are naturally germ-proof, moth-proof and completely non-allergenic. This means they need little care beyond washing the outer pillow-slip.

However, accidents do happen and if, for instance, a child is sick on the pillow or if food or drink are spilt and soak through the pillow-slip on to the pillow itself then further attention is necessary.

If the spilt substance has stained the pillow cover but has not penetrated the foam interior then it should be sufficient to unstitch the cover and remove it for normal washing. The foam interior is soft and easily damaged so protect it from damage and from light by placing it in another pillow-slip whilst the cover is being washed. Avoid using the pillow until it is stitched back into its own cover again.

If the stain has gone right through the pillow cover and on to the foam itself, it may be possible to remove the mark by gentle sponging of the surface with soap suds, taking care to wet the foam as little as possible. Sponge suds away with a cloth wrung out in clean water and pat dry with a towel. Re-stitch foam into its own cover or place temporarily in a pillow-slip and leave to dry either at the top of a warm airing cupboard or near a fan heater. Never place the pillow on a radiator or any other form of direct heat.

Where the foam of the pillow has become completely saturated by a spillage and complete washing seems the only answer, great care should be taken. Wash the pillow, preferably without removing the foam interior from its cover, in warm soap-suds, squeezing it gently and never twisting or wringing it. As the foam absorbs so much water, it will become very heavy when wet, and keeping it in its cover will make it easier to handle without damaging the foam.

Rinse until the water is clear, and gently squeeze out as much of the water as possible. Follow this by wrapping the pillow in a towel and pressing out any further moisture possible. Still in its cover, leave the pillow in the top of a warm airing cupboard or near a fan heater until perfectly dry. This can be a lengthy process but it should be done very thoroughly and drying should not be speeded up by placing the pillow near a radiator or any form of direct heat.

Where hair-oil stains are concerned, prevention is better. Use an extra pillow-slip cover. The Dunlopillo Esquire pillow is specially designed to ward off marks from hair-oil or night-creams and it has an extra protective slip cover which can be removed for washing.

Pleats

Permanently pleated garments are, for the most part, easy to wash and care for whether made from nylon, Terylene, rayon, sharkskin, Orlon, Acrilan or any of the newest man-made fibres. For almost any permanently pleated fabric, use a large tub and a mild soapflakes solution (see page 135 for the right temperature). Swish vigorously to make a rich lather, then immerse the garment so that the pleats remain vertical. Dip up and down in the suds without rubbing, twisting or wringing, then rinse 2 or 3 times in the same way.

Many pleated garments can now be machine-washed, and retain their pleats well. Follow care label. Always cool before spinning (see page 152). Give 15-second spins only.

Wash pleated items frequently so that they do not become soiled, but if a garment is particularly dirty round a hemline or collar, rub bar soap into the patches and scrub lightly with a soft brush. Avoid rubbing two parts of the fabric together.

Hang pleated blouses and dresses on a hanger and peg skirts by the waistband tapes to a line so that they can drip dry. If possible, dry garments in the open air and arrange the pleats neatly and always in the direction that they are designed to hang.

Pleated garments should not be ironed but the bodice of a dress or the collars and cuffs may be touched up with an iron of the correct temperature for the fabric concerned (see page 135). For further details see under specialized fabric: Nylon, Terylene, Tri-Shan, etc. and under Dresses, page 150. See also page 36 in chapter on Fibres, Finishes and Fabrics.

Powder puffs

Most powder puffs may be washed in warm water and mild detergent suds, and this applies especially to foam and nylon velvet puffs. Fluffy lambswool puffs or those with a real skin or chamois backing should be washed in warm suds—never hot or the skin will become hard. Add 1 teaspoonful of glycerine to the washing water to help retain fluffiness.

For Swansdown see page 91.

Rinse additives

See under Fabric softeners on page 155.

Sheets

See under Bed linen, page 140.

Shirts

The *spare collars* of shirts should be washed each time the shirt itself is laundered, otherwise when the worn-out collar is replaced the new one may be several shades deeper than the shirt.

Most shirts can be washed in very hot suds but if a shirt is a *rayon blend* hot water only should be used. If it contains *wool*, use warm water.

A really soiled *white shirt* (other than rayon or wool) can be soaked in detergent suds for half an hour before laundering, and bar soap (white toilet soap will do if you have no household soap) can be rubbed on the collar, neckband or cuffs. Wash in very hot or boiling suds (if necessary scrub soiled areas lightly with a brush). Rinse twice, spin or wring and hang to dry until just damp, then roll ready for ironing.

Nylon and Terylene and minimum-iron cotton shirts should be washed every day or after every wearing and they will take only a few minutes to launder; once dirt penetrates the fibres, it then becomes almost impossible to get it out. Remove collar stiffeners and wash in hot suds, then rinse in hot water and again in water containing an anti-static (see Electrostatic effects on page 154). Spin dry or pat in a towel. See page 152 for note on cooling before spinning. Alternatively, hang immediately on a hanger. Finally, smooth any crumpled parts and arrange the collar neatly. The shirt should not require ironing but if it needs touching-up it may be pressed with a warm iron.

If a nylon or Terylene shirt has become discoloured, you can buy a special whitener in a sachet tablet or bottle. Follow instructions then rinse thoroughly, drip dry and when dry press lightly with a cool iron.

Non-iron fabric shirts should be kept on a hanger whenever they are not in use.

To iron a shirt, turn it inside out and iron any double parts first, then turn it back to the right side and iron the collar or the collarband and the cuffs, stretching the material taut and ironing until the fabric is quite dry. Iron the sleeves next, using a sleeve-board if available or iron flat so that no crease shows (to do this correctly follow the instructions given under Dresses on page 150).

Iron the back and then the fronts of the shirt, paying particular attention to the shoulders and edging the toe of the iron carefully under and around buttons and over buttonholes. Fasten the buttons, then lay the shirt front downwards ready for folding. Turn in the sides so that the sleeves lay flat down the back of the shirt level with the collarband, then turn up the tail and fold the same amount up twice more. Give the front a final quick press and put aside for airing.

Silk

Before washing silk, test for colour fastness. (Details of testing for colour fastness are on page 146.) Wash silk by hand in tepid water using a mild lather of liquid soapless detergent, mild powder detergent meant for delicate fabrics or soapflakes. Do not rub, twist or wring and never soak or boil silk.

Squeeze the garment gently in the suds then rinse three or four times in tepid water until the water remains clear. Remove excess moisture by rolling in a thick towel and patting lightly then hang to dry away from direct heat of any kind and out of the sun.

Iron silk fabrics on the wrong side with a warm iron and—with most silk materials—while the garment is still slightly damp. To avoid shine when it is necessary to iron on the right side of the fabric, press over a piece of muslin. Shantung, antung, tussore, douppion and crepon and better ironed when dry.

To restore the sheen to silk, add a dessertspoonful of white vinegar to the final cold rinsing water but before next laundering, soak for half an hour in cool water to remove acid.

It helps when rinsing dark pure silk to add a tablespoonful of vinegar to each gallon of water. Remove acid by soaking before next laundering. Methylated spirit is often added to the final rinsing water when laundering light silk garments.

To restiffen pure silk after laundering, rinse in a gum arabic solution (see page 155). This must be made in advance and if none is prepared, a quick way of stiffening the silk is to dissolve a small tube of liquid glue in the final rinsing water. Iron while still damp and within about a quarter an hour of rinsing.

Skirts

Wash according to the fabric concerned (see chapter 'Fabrics and fibres'), and washing temperature guide, page 135.

With modern resin finishes, the amount of care a skirt normally receives will affect the laundering. If care is taken to smooth a skirt flat before sitting, if it is hung on a skirt hanger the moment it is taken off and if it is not allowed to become creased, stained or soiled, then washing is a quick matter of dipping in suds in a large bath, rinsing and hanging to drip dry.

Hang skirts to dry inside out firmly supported at the waistband. Press or iron according to the fabric but avoid ironing permanently

pleated skirts. For washing instructions for pleated skirts, see under
Pleats on page 165.

Soaking

We have turned full circle as far as soaking before laundering. At
one time soaking overnight was usual then as washing methods and
detergents improved, so soaking became unnecessary apart from
short soaking of about half an hour for heavily soiled items and for
special things such as napkins.

Now, with the introduction of biological washing powders containing enzymes, soaking is once again a helpful adjunct to washday.
Protein stains, such as those caused by egg, gravy, perspiration,
blood etc. have always been difficult to remove. With washing
powders containing enzymes, these stains are broken down and then
removed by the detergent.

When soaking with these biological washing powders, it is important to remember that the enzymes can be destroyed by heat and
also by chlorine. On the other hand, the speed at which the enzymes
work is directly proportional to the water temperature.

In cold water, stained articles should be left to soak in an enzyme
powder solution overnight; in hot water (not above 140° F. or 60°
C.) they should be ready for washing in approximately half an hour
to one hour. A chart of times and temperatures is given on page 120.

There are two types of enzyme washing powder. One type (such as
Big S. or Biotex) is a pre-soak powder and articles only slightly
soiled can be soaked and then rinsed or given ordinary laundering
treatment with ordinary detergents. The other type of biological
washing powder is an enzyme detergent intended for pre-soaking and
for the actual laundering as well.

Do not soak wool, silk, flame-proof finishes or fabrics where there
is doubt about the colourfastness.

It is a good plan to soak new coloured items such as brightly
coloured tablecloths, towels etc. in cold salt water overnight or for a
few hours before the first wash. This helps to set the colour. Spin out
as much of the salt water as possible and then rinse in clear water
before actually laundering. Handkerchiefs can also be soaked in salt
water but again should be rinsed thoroughly before being added to
suds.

Materials which are being laundered for the first time almost
always contain dressing which forms a scum with soap. Quite a lot
of the dressing can be removed if the articles are soaked for half an

hour in cold water before being washed. This advice applies mainly to items such as sheets, towels, pillow-slips, table linen, cotton shirts, etc. and not to woollens, rayons, coloured articles where the dye may run, and to fabrics with special finishes.

The soaking process is quicker and easier if you have a fully-automatic washing machine which has a pre-wash or pre-soak programme. But soaking can also be done in a twin-tub and then the water spun out before refilling with fresh hot suds.

Socks

Stretch socks which are made from nylon or Terylene are sometimes sold in one size and this stretches to any foot. With some makes there may be, say, three sizes—small, medium and large. The socks—which seldom wear into holes—should be washed daily in warm suds, rinsed, spin-dried or wrung and rolled in a towel, then hung to dry away from heat. They dry very quickly and do not need airing.

Cotton and cotton-and-rayon mixture socks should also be washed after every wearing but with wool socks every other day or about three times a week should be sufficient. Woollen socks should never be allowed to become really dirty or soiled with perspiration or they will become flat and hard and lose much of their warmth. They may even shrink for this reason. Wash as for wool in warm suds and without rubbing or twisting. Air thoroughly before wearing.

Sorting laundry

When fabrics could be quickly divided into linen, cotton and woollens and the articles into whites and coloured, sorting laundry was simple. Now, with so many different fabrics it is easiest to divide washing first into two main groups—sturdy fabrics and fine or delicate materials—and wash these separately. These two groups need different methods of washing, different types of soap powder, flakes or soapless detergent and quite different temperatures of water.

Of course, if you have an automatic washing machine you will sort the laundry according to the washing programmes the machine offers. If, however, you wash by other types of machine, or by hand, the following points may guide you:

Strong white nylon and Terylene can come into the sturdy fabrics class as they will withstand hot water and soapless detergents but they should be washed alone or they may pick up any dirt in the water. Continue with other white articles, washing the cleanest things first

—usually table and bed linen (boost the temperature to very hot or boiling for these if practicable). Progress to more soiled white cotton items such as underwear (which should be turned inside out).

Coloured cottons and linens come next and again should be sorted into those with fast dyes and those that might run. Begin washing the cleanest and work downwards to the most soiled. Colours which are suspect should be left until last.

Silks, rayons and woollens all need careful, individual washing and so do many of the other man-made fibres. Details for washing various materials are given in the chapter on 'Fabrics and fibres'.

If there is a considerable amount of washing or the lather subsides and the water becomes dirty, it is more economical to use fresh suds for the next batch of laundry than to keep adding detergent and to continue washing in dirty water.

If you have a fully-automatic machine, sorting will be easier. Just follow the programme guide—e.g. whites, coloureds, minimum iron, woollens and so on. Consult instruction book frequently.

When sorting clothes for washing, empty pockets, remove collar stiffeners, pins and loose buttons, and if possible mend tears or holes before laundering. Close zips but leave hooks and eyes unfastened. Tie loose apron strings together. Remove buttons if affected by high temperatures.

Starching

Although it is principally used for stiffening, starch also adds a crisp newness to other fabrics and it helps materials to stay clean longer. Most cotton and linen fabrics benefit from starching but shantung, tussore, woollens, man-made fibres and cottons with special drip dry, glazed or other finishes should never be starched.

As different articles require different amounts of stiffness it is easiest to sort them first so that anything requiring full-strength starch is dealt with first, working downwards to items needing only a light stiffening with well-diluted starch.

To make *full-strength boiling water starch*, mix a heaped table-spoonful of starch to a smooth paste with 3 or 4 tablespoonfuls of cold water, carefully dissolving any lumps. Pour on 1 or 2 pints of fast boiling water, stirring all the time with a wooden spoon, until the starch 'cooks'. When this happens it becomes a blue-grey colour and looks clear and jelly-like. This is full-strength starch, used as it is for shirt collars and possibly lace doilies.

Dilute full-strength starch with 2 or 3 pints of water for a stiff finish for aprons, table napkins, tray cloths, cotton bedspreads, chintz curtains or loose covers, tablecloths, etc. Add another 1 or 2 pints of water for a medium stiffening ideal for dinner mats, print aprons, frocks, sheets, pillow-slips, cotton shirts, etc. Make a weak starch suitable for handkerchiefs, print blouses, very fine table-cloths or delicate cottons by adding another 2 pints of water.

Water added to made starch can be hot or cold. Generally it is best to have the starch hot for white linens and cottons and warm for coloured clothes. Turn garments inside out and immerse articles in the starch solution one at a time; move them around and dip them in and out 2 or 3 times to ensure that the starch penetrates the fabric, then wring out or spin out all surplus starch.

Starched articles can be rolled in a dry towel and set aside for ironing an hour or two later or they can be dried out of doors and then damped down with a sprinkling of warm water before being rolled ready for ironing later. Have the iron as hot as the fabric permits and use a firm pressure to give a smooth, glossy finish.

Boiling-water starch will not form a skin if the bowl is covered with a damp cloth directly the starch is made. Another way of preventing a skin forming is to stir in a little cold water immediately after the starch is made.

Cold-water starch is used to give extra stiffness and a high gloss and it is particularly suitable for stiff glazed collars and cuffs and shirt fronts. To make it, mix 2 tablespoonfuls of powdered starch with 2 tablespoonfuls of cold water to a smooth paste; add 1 pint of cold water, stir thoroughly and leave to stand, then stir again and strain to remove any lumps. Immerse articles as for boiling-water starch and iron while still wet with a hot iron, using plenty of pressure.

Cold-water starch can be dried and used again; let it stand for several hours, then pour off the water and leave the starch to dry.

To give a garment a *particularly stiff finish*, make up a stronger solution or add less water when diluting. Alternatively, wash and dry the article in question and then, when it is quite dry, immerse it in the starch, roll it up in a dry towel and iron without hanging to dry.

Instant starch is available now and this is very easy to prepare. It is sometimes referred to as cold water starch as it can be mixed with cold or warm water but it should not be confused with the time-consuming cold water starch already mentioned and which gives a much greater degree of stiffness. Instant cold water starch is already 'cooked' and simply needs mixing. It is sprinkled on to the water, is stirred and is then ready. Any left over can be bottled—a wide-necked jar with a screw cap is easiest to use—and is ready again for immediate use.

Plastic starch is useful when a light stiffening without gloss is required. It is not really starch but a prepared plastics solution based on polyvinyl acetate and it is difficult to remove, so instructions should be carefully followed. Plastic stiffener can be used on frocks, baby clothes and blouses which require 'body' and which could otherwise be stiffened with a weak boiling-water starch, and it can also be used for rayon and paper nylon.

The plastic stiffener should remain effective through a number of washes but well-wrung articles should be kneaded in the solution for about a minute before being squeezed to remove surplus starch. Iron while still slightly damp or press under a damp cloth. If the iron sticks, it helps to iron over a piece of muslin.

Spray-on starches are also plastic stiffeners but they are intended for spot starching whilst ironing. They are ideal for collars, cuffs or for touching up shirt or blouse fronts. They are also useful for adding a finishing touch to special items needed in a hurry such as an evening dress or scarf.

If a slight stiffening only is wanted, the water in which rice has been boiled can be used as a substitute. Other substitutes are gum arabic solution, sugar, stationer's gum (half a teaspoonful of glue to 2 pints of water) and powdered gelatine (1 teaspoonful to $\frac{1}{2}$ pint hot water).

See also under Gum arabic on page 155.

To give linen articles an *extra high gloss* dissolve 1 oz. of gum arabic in $\frac{1}{2}$ pint of boiling water and leave to stand overnight. Next morning strain and bottle. Add 1 teaspoonful of the liquid to each pint of starch and use in the ordinary way.

A *sharp wind* will remove stiffness from newly starched washing, so collect articles from the line as soon as they are dry on a windy day.

Use starch, too, to keep white gloves clean for longer, to stiffen the brims of babies' bonnets or sun hats, and on cushions and pillow-cases to stop feathers working through.

Good quality, closely-woven fabrics need only a weak starch solution; poor quality, well worn articles will need a strong solution. Household linen which is almost worn through can be dipped in starch and ironed in order to make the weak patches stronger.

Cotton needs a stronger solution than linen as it absorbs it less readily.

When the ironing is finished rub the soleplate of the iron with a damp cloth while it is still warm. This will prevent damp starch leaving a stain.

Suspender belt

See under Corset and launder in the same way.

Swimsuit

A swimsuit should be washed after every use. After sea- or pool-bathing, a quick rinse through in cold water is usually sufficient but the swimsuit should be dried away from heat and out of the sun to protect both the dye and any rubber.

When storing a swimsuit after the summer, it should be treated more carefully. Close zips and hook fastenings. If the swimsuit has been used mainly for sea-bathing, soak in cold water to remove the salt; if it has been used in a swimming pool soak in $\frac{1}{2}$ gallon of water containing 1 dessertspoonful of borax. These are the only times a swimsuit should be soaked. Rinse and then wash thoroughly in warm mild suds, rinse 2 or 3 times, roll in a towel and dry out of doors in the shade.

A really soiled swimsuit can be lightly scrubbed with a soft brush but the suit should not be rubbed, twisted or wrung as it is very easy to damage boning and fasteners and to strain the fabric. Never roll up a wet swimsuit and avoid staining it with suntan oil. Most non-greasy suntan preparations are quite safe but sun oil may leave a permanent stain and may affect the fabric.

Table linen

Although usually referred to as table 'linen', this tag does identify tablecloths, napkins, tray-cloths and place-mats, etc. made from cotton, rayon and other fabrics as well as linen and it is important to know which fabric is being dealt with before attempting to launder it.

White linen or cotton can be safely soaked for 10 to 15 minutes in warm suds before laundering and articles benefit from this if they are badly marked. Rayons should not, however, be soaked, even if badly soiled. Linen and cotton are at their best when they have been starched, but a gum rinse is the more usual stiffener for rayon if one is needed. Real linen is best ironed with a hot iron while it is still almost wet; cotton should be ironed with a hot iron while it is still damp; rayon needs only a medium hot iron, and the fabric should be slightly but evenly damp.

Remove tea, coffee or other stains before washing table linen, or laundering may set the marks permanently. Especially-soiled areas should be scrubbed lightly with a soft brush and bar soap or dissolved detergent, but do not rub one piece of material against another. After laundering, rinse in 2 or 3 clear waters, spin dry or wring to remove as much moisture as possible and then starch.

Cotton needs a stronger solution of starch than linen and well-worn materials need a stronger solution than new or finely woven fabrics. When finishing the damp articles, iron on the right side and continue ironing until the fabric is quite dry or there will be a slightly rough surface instead of a smooth, polished finish.

Fold tablecloths into three like a screen and iron the creases along the length of the cloth only, simply folding the rest. Vary the position of creases occasionally to avoid wear in certain parts only and avoid ironing any creases into afternoon cloths. Embroidered cloths should be ironed on the wrong side over a soft cloth.

Iron place mats, tray cloths, etc. flat and if it is difficult to store them flat, roll them round a cardboard tube or rolled magazine and keep in position with an elastic band. Store table linen in a cool, dry, airy cupboard but not in an airing cupboard.

Tea towels

Ideally, tea towels should be washed out in hot suds every day and then given a thorough laundering on wash day, using a synthetic detergent and very hot or boiling water.

Dipping tea towels into a thin starch after laundering gives them a smooth finish and prevents them leaving fluff on glasses and china.

Ties

Test for colour fastness by pressing under a damp cloth before attempting to launder a tie. If little or no colour comes out then before washing place the tie on a wire frame or tack through the double thicknesses, unless the tie is made of Terylene when these precautions are unnecessary.

A Terylene, cotton or rayon tie may be washed in hot suds but silk or wool should be washed in warm suds only. If the tie is on a frame, dip a nail brush in the lather and scrub the tie gently; without a frame, squeeze the tie gently in the suds, taking care not to twist it out of shape.

Rinse thoroughly, then fold in a thick towel and pat out excess moisture and hang to dry, unless the tie is knitted when it should be dried flat. Terylene ties should dry smooth and crease-free but those made from other fabrics should be pressed under a damp cloth when completely dry.

Silk ties should always be dry-cleaned, never washed.

Towels

Linen or huckaback towels can be washed and treated like other linen. Use a fairly hot iron for finishing to restore gloss.

New Turkish towels should always be soaked in clear warm water for several hours before being used for the first time or at least before being laundered. Wring, wash quickly in warm suds, rinse and dry. The towel is then soft and fluffy and ready for normal use.

Beach or gaily coloured terry towelling needs a rich mild lather and hand-hot water. Wash the towelling quickly, then spin-dry or wring, rinse twice, spin-dry or wring again and hang to dry in the fresh air immediately. Shake well during drying and do not iron.

White towels can be boiled occasionally to maintain a good colour. Put thin, worn towels into a rinsing water containing the remains of the starch when the rest of the laundering is finished. This will help to crisp them without making them stiff.

Turkish towels should not be ironed nor passed through a wringer once they are half-dry or they will become limp. After airing, shake well to raise the pile, then fold and store, using them in rotation.

Trousers

Whether trousers are dry-cleaned or home-laundered will depend mainly upon the fabric and on whether the manufacturer has attached a label to the garment stating that the gaberdine, flannel, rayon, etc. has been pre-shrunk and can therefore be washed.

Worsted trousers and those made from worsted blended with Terylene, Orlon, etc. are easily washed in warm suds. Scrub any soiled patches with a soft brush and bar soap or dissolved soap powder. Put through a spin dryer or wringer, rinse, spin or wring again and hang to dry away from heat. Press over a damp cloth with a cool iron when the trousers are quite dry.

Corduroy trousers should be washed quickly, and with as little handling as possible, in warm suds. Rinse quickly and hang to drip dry. Smooth the pile with a soft cloth and shake occasionally during drying. Do not press, but iron linings when the trousers are dry or, if the corduroy is badly creased, press lightly on the wrong side against a warm upturned iron, or use a velvet board made for dressmakers.

Washable *gaberdine, rayon or flannel* can be washed in the same way as worsted trousers. With white flannel trousers, wash in warm suds, rinse in warm water, dry away from heat and press with a cool iron only.

Trousers made from 100 per cent *Terylene, Orlon, nylon*, etc. can be washed in the same way as other garments made from these fabrics. Ironing may not be necessary but if there are any creases, press lightly with a cool iron.

For slacks, shorts and trousers made from other materials, look under the fabric concerned in the chapter 'Fabrics and fibres'.

Veils

Wash gently in mild warm suds, rinse in warm water and pin to a sheet of paper or piece of material to dry. If the veiling is very delicate or only lightly soiled it can be dry-cleaned at home. See page 193 for details.

After washing, restiffen a veil by rinsing in gum arabic solution (see page 155). Another method of stiffening is to dissolve some sugar or a small tube of glue in the final rinsing water. Iron damp within about 15 minutes of rinsing.

Washing machine

Washing machines take over most of the tiring work of washing but it is important to get to know your machine well; to know what it is capable of doing, just how it washes your clothes and how to get the best value out of it.

If you have been used to a twin-tub, for instance, and you change to a fully automatic machine then you will need to change your washday habits if you are to get the most out of your new expensive aid.

With a single tub machine with a wringer or spin dryer or with a twin-tub then you will probably find it easiest to wash once or twice a week when you can probably wash whites at one wash and coloureds at the next or possibly whites first and then coloureds each time.

With a fully automatic machine, however, programming means that only one type of laundry can be done at any one time and it will pay you to wash several times a week—possibly every day if your household is large enough. This way you can launder white nylon and other man-made fibre garments one day; bedlinen and table linen another; ordinary coloureds another and delicate coloured man-made fibres on yet another day of the week.

This way you spread the load of washday and as all you have to do is load the machine and finally take out the clean washing and hang to dry—or even take out the dried washing in some machines—the whole process is quick and simple.

If you do mix loads in an automatic, remember that white nylon and Terylene etc. should not be mixed with coloured items. If you cannot launder them separately, put them in with white sheets and pillow-slips etc. and wash them at the temperature appropriate for the nylon/Terylene. Take out after a short spin only and hang to dry, then re-set the machine for a fast spin for the bedlinen. White shirts, for instance, should wash quite satisfactorily this way and should not require ironing.

There are three main types of washing action in washing machines. Pulsating action or turbulating; reciprocating paddle action and tumbling action.

Machines which use pulsators or turbulators to agitate the water are fitted with fast-revolving ribbed discs. These are either in the side or the base of the tub. This is the most powerful type of agitation and washing times are usually much less than for other methods of washing. Pulsators are used in single tubs, twin-tubs and in automatic machines.

Reciprocating paddles are used in all three types of machine too. They are vertical paddles, or blades, fitted in the base of the tub and they move backwards and forwards, swishing the clothes first one way and then the other. The agitation is fairly gentle.

The tumbling action is used in some kinds of automatic washing machines, usually those which are front-loaded. The tub is fitted with projections and these lift the clothes and drop them back into the suds. The tubs usually rotate in one direction and then in the other. The washing action is gentle but produces a great deal of lather and if there is too much this prevents clothes from being properly washed. In these machines a low-lathering washing product is usually recommended.

It is because some machines give more powerful agitation than others that the Home Laundering Consultative Council Care Labelling Scheme now describe the amount of agitation required as Maximum, Medium or Minimum rather than as a length of time.

Further details of the HLCC are given on page 134 but it is useful to know that Maximum Wash means the recommended optimum of agitation for any given machine. Medium Wash means 40 to 60 per cent of the maximum. Minimum Wash means the recommended minimum amount of agitation for any given machine, normally 20 to 30 per cent of maximum. The manufacturer's instructions supplied with your machine should give details of Maximum, Medium and Minimum wash times but if in doubt consult your appliance dealer.

In an automatic machine it is usually possible to wash one load only in each suds solution. In single and twin-tubs then it is possible to wash a second and subsequent loads in the same suds used for the first wash.

Bear in mind that you will get best results by using fresh suds for each load but for speed and economy it is possible to use suds again if the first wash was not very dirty. If you add more water, however, whether hot or cold, you will need to add more washing product. This should not be added if there are clothes in the water. Never wash fabrics such as nylon and Terylene in water which has already been used for other washing.

Manufacturer's instructions should be followed exactly when using a washing machine and this applies especially to the size of the load of washing put into the machine each time. Clothes must have sufficient room to move and overloading a machine will prevent thorough cleaning. On the other hand, with some types of machine severe underloading *can* cause overwashing. Most manufacturers state the weight of dry washing a machine should take each time. For the approximate weights of various articles see page 180.

It is important to choose soap powder, soapflakes or soapless detergent suitable both for the washing in question and for the machine. Some manufacturers state that soapless detergent can be used providing the quantity is judged fairly accurately and there is not too much foam. Some low foaming detergents are designed especially for use in a washing machine.

After use, empty a washing machine completely, then rinse well with clear water if manufacturer advises this. Disconnect machine from electricity supply, then dry inside and out with a dry cloth. It is important to clean the machine and to remove every trace of deter-gent. If the machine has a filter this should be removed, cleaned under running water and replaced.

Wringer rollers should be well rinsed to remove all traces of detergent and this is particularly important if a synthetic detergent is used. If the wringer is fitted with a hand-pressure release, this should be released and the rollers thoroughly dried. To prevent rollers sticking together when the machine is not in use, separate them by placing a clean piece of folded cloth between the rollers or two wads of cloth or cotton wool at each end of the rollers.

The enamel parts of the machine should also be wiped down with a damp cloth wrung out in clean water in order to remove any soap or scum. Finish by polishing with a clean dry cloth.

Many automatic washing machines have interiors which are self-rinsing.

Always connect a washing machine to a three-pin plug and see that it is properly earthed.

Weight of articles

These are the approximate weights of dry articles of laundry. Allowances must be made, of course, for very light fabrics such as nylon or for very heavy materials such as wool or velvet.

	lb.	oz.		lb.	oz.
Apron		4	Matinée coat		4
Bath towel—large	1	0	Nightdress		10
medium		12	Overall—long sleeved		9
Bedspread—folkweave	4	0	Petticoat		3
Blanket—double	6	8	Pillowcase		5
single	5	0	Pyjamas	1	0
Blouse—short sleeve		4	Rompers		4
long sleeve		6	Sheet—double	2	6
Bolster case		8	single	1	6
Bootees		1	Shirt		8
Briefs		3	Tablecloth—54 in.		12
Chairback cover		4	Table napkin		2
Child's dress		6	Table runner		4
Collar		½	Tea towel		4
Cotton frock		8	Tray cloth		2
Face towel		8	Vest—baby's		2
Handkerchiefs, 12		6	child's		3
Hand towel		5	woman's		4
Knickers		6	man's		6

Wool

There are two basic types of wool garments and materials so far as washing is concerned. One is normal wool which has not been treated to make it washable and the other is wool which has been specially treated.

This second type is generally labelled 'Shrink Resistant' or 'Washable Shrink Resistant' or 'Machine Washable'. The phrase 'Washable Shrink Resistant' appearing alongside the Woolmark means that the production of the garment has been controlled and tested to ensure washability to at least safe hand-washing and it should not shrink. 'Machine Washable' is self explanatory, although the washing machine manufacturer's instructions for wool should be faithfully followed. If these are not given, wash for the minimum time possible in the machine and keep water temperature to lukewarm.

Untreated wool may be safely washed provided adequate care is taken. This means that a mild detergent should be used, water should be at hand-warm temperature and an absolute minimum of rubbing or agitation should be used as it is this factor which is the main cause of shrinkage.

Treated wool can be washed much more safely and agitation or rubbing may be employed where necessary without fear of shrinkage. Generally speaking, the shrink-resist treatments last for the life of the garment and do not deteriorate during washing and wear.

The following points should be borne in mind when washing wool of any kind. The water should not be too hot for the hands. The detergent should be completely dissolved before the garment is put into the wash water. Agitation should be kept to a minimum, especially when the material does not bear a label stating that it is treated wool.

Soaking is normally unnecessary, as the protein nature of the fibre means that it readily releases normal soiling during mild washing. Detergents should be rinsed away in lukewarm or cold water until the water runs clear. Excess water may be removed by spin drying, careful wringing using light pressure or by rolling in a thick towel.

Drying should not be carried out in a tumble dryer, but rather, in the case of knitwear, by placing the garment flat, away from direct sunlight. Woven materials such as blankets may be dried normally on a line.

Careless drying can affect colour in wool. The natural colour of wool varies from white to a pale cream. Any other colour has been added by dyeing. Most dyes are fast but some are unstable and the colour may migrate or fade. Wool dried in direct sunlight—whether indoors near a window or out of doors—can cause wet wool to fade and other forms of direct heat can cause blotchiness in the colours.

Test machine-knitted garments for colour before washing and if the colour runs, wash quickly and separately. Tack delicate garments into shape before washing and run a wool thread through the neckline of high-necked jumpers so that they do not stretch during laundering. Remove unwashable trimmings and close zip-fasteners.

If a jumper or other woollen garment is likely to stretch or shrink, take a note of the measurements before laundering or, better still, draw the outline of the garment on plain paper. Ease back to correct size and shape before leaving to dry.

The most common kind of wool shrinkage is felting shrinkage. When this happens the wool garment becomes thick, stiff and matted and also smaller in size. Wool has an outer layer of overlapping scales rather like the tiles on a roof. It is because of these scales that wool fibres move easily in one direction only, causing them to become entangled—thus careless washing can cause felting.

The other type of shrinking—fortunately not so common—is called relaxation shrinkage and this usually happens when new articles are washed for the first time. During manufacture, the wool yarns are sometimes stretched and then held under tension until after the finishing processes.

When this happens, the yarns relax to their natural length the first time the garment is washed or dry-cleaned and the garment appears to have shrunk. This happens often in the case of double jersey, which has not been produced to washable standards.

If you suspect that a garment has been made in this way, the effect of the shrinking can be prevented by keeping the garment slightly stretched during drying and again during pressing. Or most relaxation shrinkage can be recovered by pressing with a steam iron or over a damp cloth working in the direction of the shrinkage, especially with knitted structures.

What is far more common is stretching. Knitted wool garments stretch very easily, especially when they are wet. Usually wool will relax again during drying if it is allowed to but if it is stretched while drying then it will stay that way. It is for this reason that woollen garments should not be allowed to hang during drying, otherwise the weight of the moisture in the fabric will cause stretching.

Drying hand-knitted garments flat also helps to prevent them pulling out of shape. Fasten buttons, zips and hooks and pull seams straight before drying. A hammock can be used to dry garments flat or a towel can be pegged between two lines, in the shade and away from heat. When a garment is very heavy, striped or multi-coloured, place a towel or crumpled tissue between front and back.

If most of the excess moisture is first removed, large baby shawls and stoles may be hung on a line to dry but they should be hung double or over two parallel lines and they should not be pegged. Hang away from sunlight.

White woollens especially should be dried away from sunlight and from other forms of heat or they may discolour and become yellow. If this happens, they can be bleached with a special powder bleach or peroxide (see under Bleaches on page 113) or a little borax can be added to the washing water. Alternatively one of the new enzyme washing products may be used but for a short soak only—half to one hour— at a low temperature no hotter than hand-warm. Future launderings in a mild soapless liquid detergent should prevent yellowing.

Most woollens look best when they are soft and fluffy so that ironing is usually unnecessary. If a particular garment calls for a flat, smooth finish, press lightly on the wrong side of the fabric using a warm iron at setting No. 2. Avoid stretching the garment.

New laundry aids for wool are frequently to be found in shops and some of these can help considerably especially with particularly valuable or hand-knitted garments. A cold water wash, such as Adamite for instance, can be used for special woollens or a fabric softener could be used in the rinsing water.

Fabric softeners help the wool fibres to slip over one another more freely; they give added bulk and extra softness of handle. They usually incorporate optical brighteners and they are therefore additionally useful for white woollens.

Enzyme detergents have already been mentioned but while they may be useful occasionally for removing stains or yellowing, they are not generally recommended for woollens and this applies particularly to shrink-resist wool garments.

Wringer

Protect a wringer by rinsing it in clear warm water each time it is used and especially if a synthetic detergent is used for laundry. Dry the rollers on an old towel and place a small piece of material between them. Release tension or adjust so that there is no pressure on the rollers.

Valeting

Artificial flowers

Revive limp artificial flowers by holding them in the steam of a kettle, then dry in a warm place or in front of the fire. Or spray with plastics starch and iron.

Buttonholes

Loosely woven fabric will not fray when making buttonholes if the material is first painted with a thin line of colourless nail lacquer. Leave to dry before cutting.

Cigarette burn

On a *heavy garment*, professional mending is probably the most satisfactory method of making a burn invisible but with an ordinary dress or other *lightweight fabric* it is possible do do this at home so long as a piece of material of similar weight and design is available.

To do this place the damaged material face down on brown paper and neatly trim away any charred or ragged edges so that a clean-cut hole remains. Cut a piece of matching fabric larger than the hole and a piece of transparent polythene sheeting the same size as the patch (a piece cut from a plastics bag would be suitable). Place the polythene between the hole and the patch and press lightly with a hot iron. The polythene will melt and bond the patch to the damaged fabric so that the mend is invisible.

For a small burn on *upholstery* try pulling a few short pieces of thread from the underside of the chair or settee and weave these neatly over the hole, matching the pattern as far as possible.

A burn on a *carpet* can be professionally mended or it can be done at home. If the burn is very tiny, darn with matching rug wool and teazle with a wire brush or leave the ends free to make tufts; for a small burn this is often successful, but for a larger burn patching is the only remedy. Trim the burned threads so that a neat hole remains and cut a small patch of carpet (to match if possible) so that it will just fit the hole. Drop the patch into the hole and stick a large piece of sacking or hessian over the back with carpet adhesive. If possible, lightly smear the edges of the patch with adhesive before dropping it into the hole.

Clothes brush

A bristle clothes brush should not be washed very often or in time the bristles will become soft. Clean this type of brush by rubbing plenty of warm bran (heated in the oven) into the bristles. Leave for an hour, then shake out the surplus powder and remove the remainder of the bran with a comb followed by rubbing with a clean cloth. Repeat if necessary. A nylon, rubber, foam plastics or similar clothes brush may be washed frequently and is often of most value if washed 2 or 3 times a week.

Coat hangers

Clothes will stay put on hangers if strips of plastic foam are stuck at each end or rubber bands are wound around hanger ends.

Collars

If the collar only of a coat is soiled, this can be cleaned by rubbing with powdered magnesia or by sponging lightly with a cloth dipped in carbon tetrachloride. Make-up frequently marks the neckline of a winter dress and this can be cleaned in the same way or, if the material is in a pastel shade, rubbing with a piece of stale bread is often sufficient.

Crêpe soles

Crêpe or rubber soles which have worn smooth and become slippery can be roughened again to give a firm grip if they are rubbed on a coarse kitchen grater.

Darning

Darning is less strain on the eyes if the darning mushroom is given 2 coats of hard white enamel.

To mend a hole or tear in a *blanket*, darn with thick wool, then teazle the darn with a wire suède brush so that it blends in with the blanket.

When darning *sheets*, a useful trick is to place a piece of fine paper or handkerchief tissue over the hole then stitch backwards and forwards over the hole and paper with a sewing machine. Turn the sheet and stitch across the hole and then launder the sheet in the usual way. The paper will dissolve in water leaving a neat darn.

Sock darns last longer if, instead of using a double strand of wool, one strand of darning wool and one strand of thread are used in the needle. After a few weeks the wool will wear but the thread will remain holding the darn. It takes only a moment to replace the worn wool strands in the darn.

When darning *gloves*, a glass marble dropped into the finger makes an excellent miniature darning egg.

Dry-cleaning

If articles are being sent to a firm of dry-cleaners, mend any tears or holes first; remove buttons unless it is certain that they are made of a substance which will resist cleaning solvents; make a note of any special stains and their cause; add a special note giving details of any stain-removing treatments already tried. If a garment is made from one of the man-made fibres, always attach a label saying which fibre it is made from and if the material has a special finish, add this to the label also. Some fabrics—such as Tricel—and some finishes—such as the silicone ones—need special dry-cleaning treatments or they may be spoilt.

Elastic

The quickest way of renewing elastic in a garment is to tack or safety-pin one end of the new elastic to one end of the old. Pull the other end of the old elastic and the new piece is automatically threaded in.

Embroidery

To copy a design from a piece of embroidery (already embroidered) lay the embroidery flat and cover it with a sheet of clean note-paper. Carefully rub over the outline of the design with the back of a spoon or a soft blunt lead pencil and the pattern will appear on the paper ready to be inked and transferred.

To copy a design on to fabric for embroidering, go over the complete pattern with a broad-nibbed pen dipped in yellow transfer ink (obtainable from artists' supply shops). Let the ink dry, then reverse the design on to the fabric and press with a warm iron. This method means that the design appears on the fabric in reverse and if the right side is wanted then the back of the paper design must be outlined in transfer ink. To make transfer ink see page 468.

Fur

Although fur does not show dirt readily, in fact it collects more dirt and grime than fabric. Grit and dirt work into the roots of the fur, drying the natural oils and making the hair dull and brittle.

It is important therefore, that furs are cleaned regularly. It is better to have the cleaning carried out by an expert and to have the fur professionally moth-proofed. The moth-proofing is permanent and is not affected by cleaning. Furs should *never* be washed and should never be placed near heat of any kind.

Spirit cleaner will remove stains and odd marks from the *lining of a fur coat* but as the lining is apt to become much dirtier or to show the dirt more easily than the fur itself, it is often easier to unpick the lining, remove it completely and wash according to the type of material.

Isolated stains on dark furs can be removed by gentle cleaning with a liquid cleaner such as carbon tetrachloride or with one of the proprietary cleaners.

If an entire fur needs cleaning, this should be done professionally although it is possible to do it at home. *Dark furs* can be cleaned with warm bran, fig dust or hot silver sand. Heat whichever is being used in a pan or in the oven but be careful not to burn it, then rub well into the fur. Leave for 2 or 3 days or repeat several times, then take out of doors and brush and shake the fur until all bran and dust are removed.

Another method especially good for *light furs* is to sprinkle them with powdered magnesia, rubbing it well into the fur with the finger-tips. Ordinary cornflour can also be used but it is not so effective. When the fur is completely covered, roll it in a sheet of paper and leave for 2 or 3 days if possible, then take out of doors and brush and shake the fur until all the powder and dirt are released.

Gloves

Gloves often receive more wear and less care than other items. The newest gloves—both in skin and fabric—are being made with the latest finishes. This means that some gloves are treated to make them moisture- and stain-repellent while others, regardless of their type, can be easily and quickly washed. Wherever possible follow the manufacturer's instructions or ask for care particulars when buying gloves.

It is important to buy the correct size in gloves if they are to wear well. To ascertain this, measure round the palm of the outstretched hand on the actual knuckles. Pull the tape measure fairly tight and do not include the thumb. The number of inches shown is the size in gloves.

To get lasting value out of gloves, do not pull the glove on to the whole hand at once. Smooth on four fingers first and fit the thumb in last. Never pull the glove on by holding a single thickness with the fingers of the other hand; this stretches the glove so that the edges tear or develop wavy lines. Always draw on the glove gently or fold the edges over to give a double thickness and pull on this.

Skin gloves can be gently stretched back into their original shape if the wearer makes a habit of blowing into the gloves the moment they are taken off and while they are still warm.

If *skin* gloves are guaranteed washable they should be washed frequently and before they are really soiled. To do this wear them and immerse the hands in a rich lather made with soapflakes and warm water. Ease out the dirt by squeezing the hands together, then rinse thoroughly in the same way using clean slightly soapy water. Dry slowly away from heat and gently 'work' the skin during drying to soften it. If the gloves should become stiff once they are dry, roll them in a warm dry towel before attempting to wear them.

Ordinary *chamois* and *doeskin gloves* can be washed in warm water and soapflakes. Rinse the doeskin or other washable gloves thoroughly but do not rinse chamois leather. If the gloves are hard, add a tablespoonful of olive oil to the soap suds, boil for a minute, add cold water until the suds are the right temperature, then wash the gloves. Dry away from heat.

Washable kid gloves need fairly careful handling. Make up a rich lather with warm water and soapflakes but do not immerse the gloves. Instead, place one glove on the hand and gently rub the surface with a piece of soft cloth wrung out tightly in the warm suds. Clean one finger at a time, rubbing until the area is free of marks, then treat the palm and back.

Clean the other glove in the same way, then rinse by wiping with a fresh cloth wrung out in clear warm water, treating a small area at a time. Finish by patting with a warm soft towel, then hang to dry— on glove hangers if possible—in a warm place but away from any heat. Before wearing, rub the gloves well between clean, warm hands to soften the kid.

Unwashable white kid gloves can be cleaned by dipping cotton wool in carbon tetrachloride and sponging the surface quickly with this. Use clean cotton wool as it becomes soiled. Dark kid gloves can often be cleaned easily by rubbing them with a cloth dipped in Vaseline.

Use a grease-absorbent powder such as french chalk or fuller's earth for *leather* or *suède* gloves which cannot be washed. Sprinkle the powder over the stains or marks, then wrap the gloves in a towel and leave for an hour or so. Finally brush off with a clean brush. If some of the marks still remain repeat the powdering but avoid more drastic treatment. An alternative method for slightly soiled suède gloves is to put them on, then 'wash' them in a bowl of dry oatmeal and brush them thoroughly.

Home-cleaning will frequently remove marks and stains caused by handling greasy or dirty items but where the finger-creases of the gloves are marked with perspiration and grease stains caused by carrying the gloves in hot, damp hands, cleaning is difficult and frequently impossible.

Some leather gloves benefit from an occasional polish. Hogskin gloves, for instance, can be washed on the hands, rinsed and dried on glove stretchers or with the fingers padded with paper. As soon as the gloves are completely dry, rub in a little white handbag, shoe or furniture cream and polish with a clean duster.

With *string* or *fabric* gloves wash in the same way as for kid but wash off the hands, using hot water for cotton, nylon or Terylene. These gloves should be washed after every wearing.

Some fabric gloves tend to become very limp after washing; this can be avoided if the soiled gloves are laundered in the normal way, then dipped into a thin starch and ironed dry.

Woollen gloves should be washed off the hands and treated like any other woollen goods, using warm water and squeezing gently to avoid shrinkage and felting.

Handbags

Handbags should be completely emptied after each use, or weekly if the bag is in daily use. Brush dust and fluff from the lining with a clean brush and remove grease or lipstick stains with a spot remover.

If the lining is generally grubby and soiled, wring out a cloth in warm soapless detergent suds and wipe the lining with this. Wring a second cloth in clear warm water and rinse the lining and then dry with a soft warm cloth. Make sure the handbag is completely dry before storing or before replacing items in daily use.

Send a handbag for repair if the leather splits or if the handle starts to pull away. Repairs are usually very cheap when they are still small. If a handbag becomes wet or rain-spotted, wipe it dry as quickly as possible. Treat the outside of the bag according to the leather or material.

Calf is a fine soft leather and many handbags are now given a special finish to protect the skin from rain and finger-marks. A bag with this finish can be wiped clean, otherwise a calf bag should be polished periodically with a colourless liquid wax made especially for cleaning fine handbags. If the bag is made from aniline dyed calf then only a special aniline calf dressing should be used as ordinary creams may penetrate the clear finish and have a darkening effect.

Crocodile is the hardest wearing leather and probably the most expensive. It needs little care beyond regular dusting and an occasional clean with a colourless shoe cream or liquid wax. Rub hard to remove surplus polish.

Hide handbags need to be cleaned and protected with a transparent liquid or paste wax, rubbed well into the leather and buffed when dry.

Lizard and snakeskin handbags can be cleaned with a colourless shoe cream or a transparent wax unless the skin has been bleached and has a dull finish. In this case ordinary cream may make the skin yellow and a special cleaner designed for unpolished reptile skins should be used.

Luxan hide. This was originally developed for covering furniture. It has a cellulose finish so that it is as easy to keep clean as it is hardwearing. When it is soiled, simply sponge it with a damp cloth and dry it.

Nappa leather. Handbag care will vary according to the quality of the leather. Nappa is very soft and is used for smart handbags. A good bag will last well but a cheap leather almost invariably cracks after a little wear. The handbag should be used gently, stuffed with a little tissue when not in use and dirty marks should be sponged away as soon as possible with a damp soapy cloth.

Pigskin. This leather should be rubbed occasionally with a white silicone cream or transparent liquid wax. Remove grease marks or stains by sponging lightly with a spot remover or with carbon tetrachloride. If the leather is really soiled, it may be washed with warm water and leather soap. Rinse thoroughly, dry with a soft cloth and then polish.

Plastic handbags can be sponged clean with a damp soapy cloth. Rinse with a cloth wrung out in clear water and rub dry. Do not polish. Wipe away any grease stains immediately.

Suède handbags should be held in the steam of a kettle filled with boiling water, occasionally, to raise the pile. Remove spots and marks with a grease solvent and rub shiny patches with a fine sandpaper. A badly soiled suède bag can be treated with suède cleaner, following the instructions given with the cleaner.

Hats

Berets. At one time a beret implied a round shapeless woollen hat worn by schoolgirls but this is not so today. A beret can be a woolly 'butcher-boy' hat to wear with tweeds or it can be made from Taiho, Orlon, piqué, mohair or any other material.

Apart from the muffin-shaped ones with a leather rim, almost any beret can be washed, but it is as well to inquire when buying. For the washable ones, whether made from wool or other fabric, make a rich lather with warm water and soapflakes and gently squeeze the beret in this. Rinse 3 or 4 times in clear warm water and roll in a towel to absorb excess moisture.

Flat, pancake-shaped styles dry best stretched over a dinner plate but the round or butcher-boy style should be placed over a pudding basin and the bulges padded out with crumpled tissue paper. Dry away from heat.

Unwashable berets can be sponged with soapflakes suds and then with a cloth wrung out in clear water.

Feathers. A hat made from feathers mounted on canvas is difficult to 'spot' or clean as the dry-cleaning fluid may make the canvas limp or it may dissolve the adhesive holding the feathers in place. With this type of hat, sprinkle the feathers and canvas with a cleaning powder such as french chalk, powdered magnesia, fuller's earth or plain talcum powder and work it in with the finger-tips. Leave overnight, then brush out the powder with a soft clean brush and repeat the process if necessary.

Felt. Odd marks can often be removed from a light felt hat by gently rubbing the surface of the felt with fine clean sandpaper. For white felt, rub powdered magnesia into the hat with a clean cloth, leave overnight and then shake to remove surplus powder and brush well with a clean stiff brush.

Fur felt. A white fur felt hat can be cleaned with fine sandpaper or with a cleaning paste. Make this by mixing french chalk with dry-cleaning fluid to make a paste; spread this on to the hat, leave to dry, then brush off with a clean dry brush. Alternatively sprinkle with talc and brush out later.

Straw. Freshen a straw hat by removing trimmings and washing or cleaning separately and by wiping the actual straw with a clean cloth moistened very lightly with a sweet oil.

If the straw is really dirty and freshening is not sufficient, most straw hats can be cleaned by light scrubbing with a nail brush dipped in warm suds. Remove trimmings and stuff the crown first and shake the brush each time so that the straw is not made too wet. Rinse by wiping with a cloth wrung out in clear cold water and leave to dry flat out of doors.

A white straw hat can be scrubbed with an old toothbrush dipped in hydrogen peroxide or in lemon juice and hot water (1 tablespoonful to 1 pint). Rinse well and allow to dry. An alternative is to clean the hat, using the methods given for white felt.

Soiled *Panama* hats should be scrubbed with a nail brush dipped in a mild detergent lather. Rinse in clear water containing glycerine, blot up surplus moisture and dry in the sun.

Another way of cleaning a light straw hat is to squeeze the juice of a lemon into a saucer with a teaspoonful of flowers of sulphur. Brush on to the hat with an old brush, then rinse off with cold water.

For a straw hat that has not lost all its stiffness but is merely a little limp, pack out the crown with paper, place a damp cloth over the straw and iron gently with a warm (not hot) iron. Any parts round the brim which need extra stiffening can be painted with straw hat varnish first.

If a straw hat has completely lost its stiffness through being soaked in rain or after cleaning and the above method is not sufficient, the hat can be restiffened by brushing thin glue, gum arabic or varnish into the straw. Keep the brim flat under pressure until completely dry. If the straw has lost its shape, damp slightly and reshape before brushing with the stiffening solution.

Clean a piqué or summer hat by 'spotting' with dry-cleaning fluid; by rubbing with powdered magnesia (see white felt), or by washing (see Beret).

Hems

When letting down the hemline of a summer frock, do so before laundering. On a thick skirt or coat, let down the hem and before pressing, remove the mark left by rubbing it with a piece of very fine glass paper.

Unpick the hems of children's summer frocks and iron them flat before storing them away for the winter. When they are needed in the following spring they will be easier to lengthen and there will be no 'give-away' mark.

To turn up a hem without sewing, use a latex adhesive or press over polythene, using the method for mending a cigarette burn on page 184, or use double sided adhesive tape.

Jersey dress

Hang up a jersey frock or suit by tapes sewn inside the waistband to avoid sagging. See also under Jersey and Orlon in 'Fabrics and Fibres'.

Lace braid

Silver lace braid or cord on a uniform can usually be cleaned providing the tarnish is not too severe. Cover the braid with bicarbonate of soda or magnesia and work this into the cord with a stiff brush. Leave for an hour, then brush the powder out of the braid with a fine wire brush. If this method is used there is no need to remove the braid from the uniform.

A paste made from french chalk and carbon tetrachloride is also often effective in removing slight tarnish. Apply to the braid and leave to dry, then brush off with a stiff brush. With this method also, the braid can be left in position.

Gold lace *can* be cleaned with liquid cyanide but this is better done professionally as the surface of the gold can easily be damaged. The braid must be removed from the uniform and dipped quickly in and out of the cyanide and then rinsed thoroughly under a running tap. This treatment is unlikely to be carried out at home but if it is, suitable precautions must be taken and the hands should be protected.

Lace veil

For a lace veil that is rather grubby but not very dirty, dry-shampooing is probably the best method as this will not remove the necessary stiffening. The easiest way is to drop the veil into a bag, pour in a good handful of powdered starch and shake the bag well. Another way is to place the veil on a towel, shake on powdered starch and rub it into the fabric with the finger-tips. Either way, leave the veil in the starch for an hour or two if possible, then remove and shake off the excess powder. Powdered magnesia, talcum powder or french chalk can all be used in the same way.

To restiffen a lace veil, rinse in warm water containing a little dissolved sugar or in a weak gum arabic solution (see page 155).

To launder a veil see page 51.

Lamé

Brush with a soft brush to remove surface dust and store rolled in blue or acid-free tissue paper. If the metal does tarnish apply a paste of carbon tetrachloride and powdered magnesia. When the paste is dry, brush off with a firm clothes brush. Test the material before treating.

Leather jacket

Leather shorts and jackets which are labelled washable can be laundered in warm water using good quality soap or soapflakes. The water should be comfortable to the hands and a rich lather should be made before the leather garment is immersed in the suds.

Where the leather is hard, add enough soapflakes to a pint of hot water to make a rich lather; stir in a tablespoonful of olive oil or glycerine, pour into a saucepan, heat and boil for one minute. Add sufficient cold water to make a cool, rich lather and wash the leather garment in this. Rinse in clear, warm water and then in clean warm water containing a few soapflakes so that the water is slightly soapy. Dry in the open air and away from any heat and 'work' the leather between the hands to soften it before it is quite dry. Many reputable dry-cleaners have special leather and suède departments for dealing with such garments.

Leatherette jacket

These jackets are made to resemble leather but need a quite different type of treatment. As they contain rubber, stains cannot be removed with a grease solvent although spots can be treated with a thick paste made from french chalk and water. Leave on until dry and then brush off.

A very light sponging with lather on a damp cloth would do no harm but the jacket must be well rinsed and dried in a cool place and must on no account be pressed or ironed. For a new jacket, professional dry-cleaning is worth the expense involved.

Lingerie

If shoulder straps continually slip and slide, leave the fronts of the straps in position but unpick the straps at the back, cross them and resew. An alternative is to use tiny gilt lingerie strap holders or to use holders made from inch-long pieces of ribbon fitted with press fasteners at either end. These are sold very cheaply at haberdashery counters.

Mackintoshes

See under Raincoat.

Metallic embroidery

To clean metallic embroidery on a satin or other evening gown, dip a soft baby brush in ordinary bicarbonate of soda, brush into the embroidery, leave for a few minutes, then remove with a second soft, clean brush. Cream of tartar or powdered magnesia may be used in the same way.

Needles

To thread a darning needle quickly when the wool is thick, fold a short piece of cotton in two and push the wool through the loop formed. Thread the two ends of cotton through the needle eye and pull gently and the wool strand will follow.

Needlework box

Thread odd hooks and eyes on to a safety-pin and they can be easily found in a full workbox. Small pearl buttons can be kept together in the same way.

Reels of cotton will not disappear if they are threaded on a piece of covered wire formed into a circle or rectangle to fit the shape of the workbox. Cotton can be snipped off without removing the reels from the box.

A small magnet fastened to the needlework box with a long piece of ribbon or tape is invaluable for picking up dropped pins quickly or for finding a lost needle.

Nylon stockings and tights

The sheerness and strength of nylons depend on the denier and the gauge. A fine denier yarn loosely knitted (such as 15 denier 45 gauge) is filmier and not as strong as a fine denier closely knitted (e.g. 15

denier 66 gauge). Stronger still is a thicker thread closely knitted (i.e. 30 denier 66 gauge).

Denier means the thickness of the nylon thread and this may be: the recently introduced sheer 9 or 12 denier which are gossamer fine, 15 denier (very fine—in fact an ordinary hair is three times as thick as one 15 denier strand); 20, 30 denier (medium); 45 or 60 denier (stretchy crêpe). Gauge means the closeness of the knit and the number of stitches across $1\frac{1}{2}$ in. There are seven gauges to choose from— 45, 48, 51, 54, 60, 66 or 75. The loosest knit is 45 gauge (i.e. 45 stitches across $1\frac{1}{2}$ in. of stocking) and the closest knit is 75 gauge (75 stitches across $1\frac{1}{2}$ in.).

Tights are usually made in 20 denier nylon usually in micro-mesh or run-resist. Micro-mesh fabric consists of rotating rows of tuck stitches separated by plain stitches. Thus, when a thread is broken, the micro-mesh fabric will ladder from bottom to top and a ladder will always run upwards and never in a downward direction. This is due to the tuck stitches having a locking effect. Micro-mesh fabric is more open than run-resist and has a sheerer appearance in wear.

Run-resist fabric consists of groups of slack and tight stitches. The tight stitches combined with tuck stitches form locked stitches. These locked stitches are arranged in a staggered formation and they provide fabric of great strength. In run-resist fabric any broken threads are contained in a small area. A small hole will form but the fabric has virtually no tendency to ladder in either direction.

Tights and pantee-hose are usually, but not necessarily exclusively, ordinary circular knit stockings joined at the welt to nylon panties. The body part is often reinforced and in some ranges the elastic waist band is knitted into the garment instead of being sewn on afterwards.

Circular knit nylons are knitted tubularly all in one. They can be permanently set to shape to make them fit and they can have a mock seam added to make them look like fully-fashioned stockings although this is rarely done nowadays.

Fully-fashioned nylons are more expensive to produce and are unpopular in any case. They are knitted flat to the shape of the leg and then they are sewn up with a back seam afterwards. The difference can be seen by the welt of a circular knit stocking which is completely joined all the way up while a fully-fashioned welt always has a small opening at the back.

Nylon stockings and tights should always be the correct size. If too big they will wear unevenly and wrinkle and if too small they will cramp the toes and hole or ladder quickly. To find the correct size measure the foot in inches from the back of the heel to the tip of the large toe.

Pressing

While ironing is done with a backwards and forwards stroke, 'pressing' needs weight and a moderately hot iron, which must be lifted every time it is moved. With pressing as with ironing, the heat of the iron must be considered and it should always be tested first. Rayons and man-made fibres should be pressed with a medium iron and wool with a warm iron.

All pressing is done on the wrong side; silk and other delicate fabrics are pressed with muslin between the iron and the garment. Dampness from the wet pressing cloth prevents shine on the surface but may shrink the fabric. If the garment has to be stretched, heat only is required so pressing should be over a dry cloth.

It is possible now to buy a silicone pressing cloth which is placed over the garment and then ironed in the usual way. These cloths can be used over and over again.

Without a special pressing cloth, use a piece of cotton, flannel or linen to press lightweight materials. Wring it out lightly and place on the wrong side of the material before pressing until the cloth is nearly dry. Use a moderately hot iron.

Heavy materials are best pressed sandwiched between flannel. Place flannel on the ironing board, put the garment next, another piece of flannel and finally a damp muslin cloth. This avoids the flat 'ironed' appearance that amateur pressing often has.

Remember to place a thick pad under the bust of a suit jacket, coat or frock before pressing. If the bustline of a heavy garment is ironed flat, the shape will be spoiled.

When pressing a suit, flatten the *revers* out before pressing and then quickly hit the pressed area with the back of a clothes brush so that the steam is knocked back into the material. Do not press *revers* into their final position on the suit, simply roll them back.

Tacking threads should be removed before pressing, except where pleats and facings have to be kept in position. These parts will need a second light pressing to remove tack marks. Press darts from the bottom upwards.

Raincoats and mackintoshes

Allow mud stains to dry thoroughly, then brush off with a firm clean brush. If any slight stain remains, sponge off with a cloth wrung out in warm soapy water and then in clear warm water.

Most slight stains can be removed by light sponging with a cloth which is damp but is not wet enough to soak through the garment. A clean cloth moistened with methylated spirit will often remove an isolated stain also.

A 'proofed' raincoat which is badly stained may be sponged with a cleaning fluid providing the surface only is damped very lightly. Most types of proofed winter raincoats should not be washed, and need dry-cleaning. However, there are now many showerproofed coats on the market which can be washed and, indeed, many are labelled as machine-washable. These are usually provided with adequate washing instructions. One point: thorough rinsing is essential or showerproofing may be destroyed.

A rubberized mackintosh must never be sponged with a grease solvent but a paste made from french chalk and water may be spread thickly over any stains and left to dry, or dry french chalk may be rubbed on to the mackintosh and left overnight.

Alternatively a rubberized mackintosh may be sponged with the lather made from soapflakes and warm water. Wring out a cloth or dip a nailbrush in the lather and go over the mackintosh with this, then repeat twice in clear warm water to rinse. Hang in a cool place to dry and ease out any creases while the garment is still damp. On no account press or iron.

For more information on washing a lightweight summer raincoat, see in chapter on 'Laundering' under Coats on page 145.

To rainproof a leaky spot on the shoulders of a raincoat, rub with beeswax, cover with brown paper, then iron gently with a warm iron.

Do not use a grease solvent or spotting fluid on a plastics mackintosh. To clean, sponge with soapy water, rinse and dry in the open air or away from heat.

A *nylon* raincoat can be washed in warm suds. Rinse thoroughly and drip dry. If it is creased, a nylon raincoat can be ironed but a warm iron only must be used.

Shine

Shine usually occurs on fabrics when the fluffiness has been rubbed off the fibres, leaving them thin and worn. If the material is very thin, no treatment will be completely satisfactory although there are several methods which may help, depending upon the amount of wear and shine and the fabric concerned.

Most light materials and serges can be sponged with hot water containing a tablespoonful of household ammonia to each pint. Brush the garment thoroughly first to remove loose dust, then sponge and finally rinse with a clean cloth wrung out in warm water. Press on the wrong side, then reverse and press on the right side over a damp cloth, knocking the steam back into the material (see Pressing on page 197 for details).

Warm blue water or a solution of vinegar and water are also good for removing shine from suits and other clothes, but again these solutions are most effective on dark materials.

Sponge a shiny coat collar with a cloth dipped in vinegar or ammonia but remove grease marks first with a cloth moistened in carbon tetrachloride.

Shoe brushes

If a shoe brush is sticky and clogged with stale polish, soak it in turpentine substitute overnight and next morning wash in hot synthetic detergent suds. Rinse thoroughly in warm then in cold water and leave to dry with the handle uppermost.

Shoe polish

Shoe polish which has become caked and hard or lumpy in the tin can be softened with a few drops of paraffin, olive oil or turpentine. An alternative is to place the tin in a warm oven for 2 or 3 minutes.

Furniture cream makes a good substitute for polish for any shoes or a few drops of milk can be used when cleaning brown shoes. Banana is also effective on brown shoes; for details see under Shoes below.

Shoes

Shoes and boots repay good care and attention by looking better and lasting longer. The thicker the leather, the more thoroughly it should be cleaned so that the wax in the polish can feed the leather right down to the base of the skin.

Where there is a cleaner specifically designed for a certain kind of shoe material, use this if possible. Otherwise use a good paste polish. Newest polishes are smooth and soft and don't harden in the tin. They are made so that it is possible to apply, polish and finish the whole cleaning operation with one brush in one minute.

With leather boots, the polish should be applied to the feather line

—this is the part where the upper meets the sole—and to the welts in order to keep the boots watertight. Remove surface mud from boots with a damp rag. Do not rub, as grit will damage the leather. To help keep boots rain-resistant, use a double-purpose, shine-and-waterproof spray such as Water Stop.

Shoes should not be *stored* near any heat nor even where fumes from gas stoves, boilers or geysers can penetrate. If possible store in a dry dark cupboard or at least away from sunlight, especially with light kid shoes.

Where possible, use well-fitting shoe trees or improvise these, using a pad of paper at heel and toe kept in position with a piece of pliable cane. The cane should be a little longer than the shoe and require bending slightly to fit. Some shoe stores keep canes in shoes while in stock and will usually give them with new shoes if asked.

To avoid slipping when wearing *new shoes* rub the soles with a piece of coarse emery paper.

Soaking the soles of *new shoes* in castor oil overnight is supposed to make them waterproof. An alternative which is thorough but will affect the polish is to coat the entire shoes—soles and uppers—with dubbin or a special waterproof oil.

Children's shoes can be made to last 2 or 3 times as long between repairs. Simply paint the soles with gum copal varnish, repeating with further coats as each one dries into the leather. When the pores are completely filled and the soles are dark and shiny, allow to dry.

Squeaking shoes can often be remedied by standing the shoes in a flat tin containing melted lard, linseed or castor oil. The oil should cover the soles but not reach the uppers and the shoes should be left to soak in a warm place overnight.

To walk firmly without slipping in icy weather, rub the soles and heels of shoes with methylated spirit.

Dry *damp shoes* by padding them with warm newspaper and then standing them by an open window or in a draught to dry—never near heat. If the damp makes the shoes dry hard and stiff, soften them again by rubbing with Vaseline well into the leather with a warm duster. Leave overnight, then polish when completely dry.

If damp shoes will not shine, moisten the shoe brush or cloth with paraffin and then apply polish, or rub with the inside of a used lemon, dry and polish.

It is possible to *waterproof* leather shoes by working paste shoe polish well into the side seams, welts, and feather line and on the soles as well. This should be done before wearing the shoes or boots if possible or after they have dried out completely if they have been worn in damp weather. Waxes are the preservative ingredient of shoe polish.

If shoes have been wet and have dried out with a white tidemark, dry the shoes very slowly—padding them with paper or trees to keep them straight—then when completely dry, polish with a paste polish in a colour as near the shoes as possible. Don't be tempted to polish while the shoes are still slightly damp or the tidemark will reappear when the water evaporates and brings out the sweat salts.

An old hot-water bottle, cut to the correct shape and size makes excellent soles and heels for leather shoes. Use a rubber or all-purpose adhesive to stick them in place.

Metal tacks, toe pieces and protectors should be dipped in water before being nailed into the soles of shoes. If this is done the wet prongs will rust into the leather and stay in position until completely worn away.

If leather shoes are soiled and dirty, give an occasional wash with leather or saddle soap, rinse and dry in the fresh air, then polish well.

If shoes have been worn on a country walk or in the garden and are *caked with mud,* wash as soon as possible with warm water and a soft brush, using leather or saddle soap if possible. Use plenty of soap but very little water, rub the leather well, then rinse off and dry out of doors or near an open window but away from heat. Any grease stains that remain once the shoes are dry should be sponged off with a soft clean cloth moistened in carbon tetrachloride or stain-removing fluid.

Aniline-dyed shoes need special care to keep them looking smart. After every wearing, wipe them with a soft sponge or cotton wool dipped in soapy water (not synthetic detergent suds) then rinse off the soap with a cloth wrung out in clear warm water, dry and polish with good shoe polish or with the special polish made for aniline-dyed shoes.

Boots tend to develop a concertina mark around the ankles with wear and in time the leather cracks. There is no way of preventing this although care can delay wear. Use ordinary good quality shoe polish on leather boots; clean them frequently and rub well after applying polish. Saddle soap tends to make side seams sticky so is not recommended.

If *brown shoes* become badly stained but are in good condition, rub the leather with a cloth moistened with turpentine. Leave overnight and polish next morning with a light shoe polish—preferably one containing silicones to protect against future marks.

Brown shoes which have become shabby at the toes can be given a new lease of life if the leather is painted with several coats of iodine. Allow each coat to dry before applying the next and finally allow to dry thoroughly and polish. Another way of reviving shabby brown shoes is to sponge them with a mixture of milk and turpentine. Better still, use one of the modern proprietary liquids designed to camouflage scuffs.

The inside of a banana skin is excellent for cleaning *brown shoes*; it will remove stains and also improve the colour. Brush the shoes first to remove any mud and dust, then rub the inside of the banana skin all over the leather, leave to dry, then polish with a soft pad.

Light brown leather shoes can be darkened evenly by wiping them over with a damp cloth dipped in soapy lather to remove the old polish, followed by sponging with ammonia. Finally brush with brown polish.

With *calf shoes* brush off all dust and mud after every wearing, paying particular attention to the welts, then use a good cream or wax polish and buff well. A good polish on calf shoes will protect the leather and make it waterproof.

Calf which has become hard and stiff, possibly through drying near heat, can be softened if a mixture of milk and water is rubbed well into the leather. Leave the shoes in a cool place on trees or stuff with newspaper and when completely dry, polish in the usual way.

Canvas shoes should be brushed with an ordinary clothes brush, unless they are white when a special dressing for canvas shoes should be used. White canvas dressing with an applicator makes cleaning quick and easy. Remove spots from canvas shoes with a proprietary dry cleaning fluid applied with a cloth.

Clean *coloured leather shoes* with a special polish in the same shade as the shoes if possible. Failing a tinted cream, use a white polish except on pastel shades where the white cream may bleach out some of the delicate colouring. It is important to use a thin film only, as a blob of polish may stain the leather.

Pastel-coloured shoes should be wiped with damp, soapy cotton wool after every wearing. This should remove kick marks and odd stains. Rinse by wiping with a cloth wrung out in clear warm water, then dry and polish.

Children's coloured shoes soon become black or brown across the toes where the dye has worn off. When coloured shoe polish is ineffective, treat the toe-pieces with a proprietary scuff-concealing preparation according to directions. Or use ordinary cellulose paint or enamel. Clean off any grease and dirt with a cloth wrung out in synthetic detergent suds. Allow to dry thoroughly, then dip a cloth into paint as near as possible to the colour of the shoes and rub on the worn leather. Leave to dry, then polish.

With *fabric shoes* brush off surface dust with a clean, soft brush after every wearing. Remove marks and stains with a clean cloth dipped in cleaning fluid starting outside the mark and working inwards.

If *fabric shoes* are generally soiled and dirty, make a rich lather with a pint of warm water and a teaspoonful of soapflakes or mild soap powder. Whisk thoroughly, then dip a nailbrush into the foam and gently scrub the fabric. Wring out a cloth in clear warm water and rinse off the soap, then wipe the inside of the shoes first with a soapy cloth and then with a clean one. Leave the shoes to dry in a cool place stretched on shoe trees or stuffed with paper.

Use a soft clean brush to remove surface dust from *satin shoes*. Remove stains or kick marks by rubbing lightly with a clean cloth dipped in petrol, methylated spirit or benzine. When not in use, store well wrapped up to avoid dust settling on the satin.

Grubby marks can usually be removed fairly easily from *white satin shoes* if clean cotton wool is moistened in surgical spirit and rubbed lightly across each shoe. When the marks disappear, go over each shoe again with fresh cotton wool dipped in the spirit.

Clean *white buckskin shoes* by brushing off surplus dust and by applying a proprietary white cleaner according to instructions. If the shoes are very dirty, the surface may be lightly washed with warm soapy water before the cleaner is applied.

Neglected or badly marked buckskin shoes can be given a new surface if they are gently rubbed with very fine sandpaper after they have been washed and dried. Begin with heels and toes and use a circular movement, then treat the rest of the shoes in the same way. Next clean the shoes with cotton wool dipped in spirit cleaner and leave them to dry for an hour or so—in the fresh air if possible.

Finish by using proprietary white buckskin cleaner or else sprinkle the shoes generously with french chalk and rub this well into the surface with dry cotton wool. Leave in the fresh air again for 1 or 2 hours, then remove surplus powder with a clean soft brush.

Place *skin shoes* on shoe trees immediately after each wearing and while the shoes are still warm to prevent cracks and creases in the skin. Brush off surface dust and rub with a little matching or white shoe cream for all skins except python and natural lizard which do not need polishing. Have skin shoes repaired frequently and see that the heels do not run down or wear low enough to damage the leather.

Crocodile shoes can be sponged with a cloth dipped in warm, soapy water if the shoes are dirty or greasy but take care not to saturate the leather. Rub the shoes after each wearing with a soft cloth and occasionally give an application of white shoe cream. With these shoes, see that heels are repaired as soon as this becomes necessary.

Natural lizard-skin shoes do not need polishing. They should be placed on trees directly they are removed and be brushed after every wearing to remove dust and particles. The skin may be rubbed with a soft clean duster and this should be sufficient to keep the shoes in good condition as polishing is unnecessary. Watch particularly for signs of wear on lizard-skin shoes and have heels repaired before they are worn low enough to mark the leather.

If *lizard-skin shoes* do become stained and marked, clean by wiping with a cloth dipped in hydrogen peroxide. Allow to dry in the fresh air and then polish with a soft, clean duster.

Place *python-skin shoes* on trees directly after they are removed from the feet and while they are still warm. Dust after every wearing. Brush off any surface mud and rub with a soft clean duster. Polishing with ordinary shoe creams or liquids is unnecessary.

Patent leather was the name originally given to leather with a high gloss finish based on linseed oil. The word 'patent' is a term used to describe a shoe material which is particularly smooth and shiny.

Nowadays patent leather is produced by coating leather with a polyurethane-based lacquer, or by laminating a thick layer of PVC to the surface. Clean real patent leather by wiping with a damp rag and applying Patent Leather Dressing in black or neutral.

Dust patent leather after every wearing and place shoes on trees immediately after use to avoid cracking. Scratches on patent leather can often be disguised by a light application of colourless nail varnish. Leave to dry completely then rub with a soft duster. In cold weather or when patent leather shoes have not been worn for some time, warm them slightly before wearing to soften the leather.

If you have no Patent Leather Dressing, time-old remedies can be used to soften and feed patent leather. Among these are sweet oil, a few drops of milk or beaten egg-white. A few drops of turpentine can also be used to revive dull-looking patent leather.

Coloured patent leather should be treated in the same way as black, using a patent leather cleaner. There are no coloured patent leather cleaners so either black or neutral should be used depending on the colour of the shoes.

Plastic shoes resembling leather are not so much a substitute today as materials accepted in their own right. When shiny PVC is laminated to fabric, the result is known in the trade as 'vinyl patent'. This should be wiped over with a damp cloth when dirty, dusted with a soft dry cloth after each wearing and occasionally given an application of patent shoe cleaner.

Poromeric shoes are those made in the new plastics materials such as Corfam, Clarino and Porvair. These materials recover their shape rather than adapting to the foot so they cannot be 'broken-in' as with ordinary shoes. This means that shoes should fit comfortably when they are bought since they will still be exactly the same size and shape after wearing as they are when new.

Poromeric shoes have the ability to absorb and disperse foot moisture. They are immune to fungus growths or other microbiological attack. This means that the material is suitable for those with fungus foot problems—such as athlete's foot. On the other hand some people find that with these shoes, their feet are hot on warm days and cold on chilly days. This is because the rate of transfer of heat is not the same as with leather.

Shoes made of materials such as Clarino are easy to care for and if they are muddy they can be washed or even held under a running tap. To clean, wipe with a damp cloth. The material cannot stain or fade.

Some poromeric shoes tend to show scuff marks on the uppers if they are carelessly treated. Best way to deal with these is to use a paste polish or shoe cream of a similar colour to the shoes. Meltonian, for instance, produce over twenty shades of shoe cream so this should not be difficult.

Pigskin should be brushed well with a wire brush after each wearing. Regular brushing helps to keep the nap dull. A pigskin or suède cleaner should be used occasionally to keep the colour and the pigskin in good condition. It is possible to buy a liquid or aerosol cleaner for suède or pigskin shoes. Of the two, the aerosol is quicker and also better. Side seams of shoes should be polished in the normal way.

Clean *silver and gilt evening shoes* and remove dust and odd kick marks with cotton wool dipped in soapy water. If the shoes appear shabby the silver or gilt can be revived with special creams which add another coating of metal.

Keep silver and gilt shoes wrapped in black tissue paper to prevent tarnish unless the metal thread is Lurex or a similar non-tarnishable thread. If the metal has become tarnished rub it lightly with a silver-cleaning cloth or with a duster dipped in magnesia powder or bicarbonate of soda.

After every wearing brush off mud and dust from *fur-lined boots*. Wash off any thick mud and dry away from heat. Polish regularly and rub up well.

To clean the fur, damp a clean cloth with detergent suds and go over the fur thoroughly with this, changing the position of the cloth as it becomes soiled. Avoid saturating the fur so that the moisture penetrates to the leather backing, as this may make the leather hard and stiff. If the boots are being stored for the summer, allow to dry thoroughly, spray with moth-proofing solution and stuff with newspaper.

Suède boots should be spray-cleaned as soon as they are bought and before they are worn for the first time. Use a special spray-on suède cleaner, allow it to dry and then brush in circular movements with a wire brush to raise the nap. This should be done frequently. Brush boots after every wearing with a wire brush to remove loose dirt and raise nap of suède. Once suède is allowed to become hard and shiny, the original appearance cannot be restored.

Suède winter boots which have been neglected or stored without cleaning during the summer months can be renovated. Stuff them with paper, then brush thoroughly with a clean stiff brush. Next make a paste with turpentine and fuller's earth and spread thickly over the suède. Remove paper and sprinkle talcum powder inside on fur or lining. Next day brush out the powder and brush off the fuller's earth with a clean stiff brush; raise the nap on any shiny parts of the suède with steam or fine sandpaper, then brush with a soft rubber or wire brush.

If *suède shoes* become wet, allow them to dry slowly and thoroughly away from heat, then raise the nap on the suède by 'steaming' over a boiling kettle. Leave to dry, then brush thoroughly. This treatment also helps if suède shoes look shabby.

If suède shoes have been dampened by sea water a white *tidemark* from the salt often remains. These marks are difficult to remove permanently but can be disguised for a time. First, very gently sand-paper them, then use Meltonian's Suède Shampoo followed by an aerosol suède spray in an appropriate colour.

Clean the edges of the soles of *suède shoes* with an old toothbrush so that there is less chance of marking the suède with polish. Very occasionally, rub shiny patches gently with fine glasspaper.

If the colour of suède shoes is faded and dull, this can be revived with a special aerosol liquid or powder suède cleaner applied according to the manufacturer's instructions.

Marks on light suède shoes can be removed by rubbing talcum powder into the stains and leaving overnight. On dark shoes remove grease marks with a preparation such as Propert's Grease Remover.

Proofed suède shoes are dirt resistant and easy to clean but need gentle handling. Brush lightly after every wearing with a soft clothes brush (not an ordinary wire or rubber suède brush). If the shoes are dirty or soiled, sponge gently before brushing. The newer types of suède shoes are very tough and full instructions for their care come with the shoes. Otherwise treat as for Pigskin.

When *old suède shoes* become too shiny or shabby to renovate they can be polished in the same way as calf. Use an ordinary wax shoe polish the same colour or darker than the suède and rub hard. The finished result is fairly good but it takes several applications of wax and a great deal of rubbing to achieve it.

The new 'wet' *look* shoes have a high gloss, synthetic finish which requires little attention. Dust after each wearing, remove dirt with a damp cloth and occasionally treat with a patent leather cleaner in a neutral shade unless the shoes are black when black Patent Leather Dressing is preferable.

Silver embroidery

Clean as for Metallic Embroidery; see page 195.

Skirt

To improve the 'baggy' appearance on the back of a tight skirt, lay it flat on an ironing-board and place a fairly damp cloth over the stretched area. Supporting the whole weight of the iron in the hand and with the iron only just touching the damp cloth, go over the back of the skirt in small circles. Done correctly, the combination of heat and moisture should shrink the cloth back to its original shape and then the whole skirt may be sponged and pressed in the usual way.

If the pleats are not permanent in a skirt, a good way of making them spring back into position is to sew a small piece of soft elastic inside the skirt across the pleats.

To pack a permanently pleated skirt for travelling, cut the foot off an old stocking, concertina the skirt and pull it into the length of the stocking.

Suède jacket

This may be difficult to clean at home as colours are not always fast and may come out or become patchy during cleaning. If the jacket is badly soiled, professional dry-cleaning is recommended but if it is simply 'tired', steaming and brushing with a rubber suède brush should revive it.

Where a cleaning firm will not accept responsibility for a brightly coloured suède jacket, clean it at home with fuller's earth or french chalk, well rubbed in, left for five minutes and then brushed out. Use a special suède or rubber brush and never a wire brush. Avoid liquid spot remover and dry-cleaning solvents as these may affect the dye. Many reputable dry-cleaners now have special suède departments.

Swimsuit

Buy swimsuits in the correct size or constant tugging with finger-nails will snag the fabric. If a swimsuit is of a reputable make, the dye should be good and the colour unaffected by sea water, but most makers recommend that their swimsuits should be rinsed in clear water immediately after every wearing. Hang to dry away from heat and never in a strong sunlight.

Never roll up a wet swimsuit; when carrying a damp swimsuit home, roll it in a towel, so that most of the moisture is absorbed. If a swimsuit is soiled or dirty and always before storing it away for winter, wash it in mild soap suds. For instructions see under 'Laundering' on page 174.

Ties

Silk ties should never be worn day after day but rested between wear. Never wash, always send for dry-cleaning.

Trousers

Trousers will not *bag at the knees* if, when they are new, a piece of lining material is sewn across the front of the trouser leg from one side seam to the other. Allow a good hem on the fabric to prevent it pulling away and once in position, press the trousers with a damp cloth and a hot iron, on the right side.

If the *knees of trousers have become baggy*, shrink the material back to its correct size before pressing in the ordinary way. To shrink the stretched fabric, place a damp cloth lightly over the trouser knees and, holding the entire weight of the hot iron in the hand, lightly glide the soleplate over the cloth, working in small circles. The moisture and heat combined will shrink the material and then the trousers can be pressed normally.

To *press trousers in a hurry*, fold into the correct creases, hold for a moment over a steaming kettle and pass the legs only through a wringer.

To *crease trouser legs* so that the crease is sharp and crisp, turn the trousers inside out and rub hard yellow washing soap—dry—down the inside of the crease; reverse the legs and carefully put the crease in the correct position, wring out a cloth in warm water until it is almost dry and place over the crease, then press with a hot iron. Care must be taken that the cloth is not wet enough to make the soap foam and that the crease is not out of alignment so that 'tramlines' are formed.

An alternative is to use plastics starch. Turn the legs inside out and damp down the inside of the crease with the semi-permanent starch. Reverse the legs, arrange carefully in position and press firmly over a damp cloth.

If the *backs of turn-ups* wear very quickly through rubbing on the backs of shoes, sew a small trouser button inside the back of each trouser leg about half an inch from the bottom. This will take the wear and protect the trousers.

It is possible to *prevent trouser legs fraying* around the hem if a $\frac{1}{2}$-in. strip of kid or other material is sewn around the inside of the new trouser legs in the place where there is most rub on the shoes. A special trouser binding is sold to make the job of forming new turn-ups easier.

Back trouser buttons will not pop off so easily if they are sewn on to elastic and the elastic is then sewn on to the trouser fabric.

Velvet

To remove dust, fluff and hairs quickly from velvet, damp the bristles of a clothes brush with a few drops of surgical or methylated spirit and lightly brush the velvet at once. This method is effective on a dark suit also.

Wellington boots

Wash off the mud and dirt after every use with warm soapy water. Rinse and dry and store in a cool, dark cupboard. When storing Wellington boots away, pack firmly with crumpled newspaper, wrap in large sheets of brown paper without bending the rubber. Shoe polishes, creams and waxes should not be used in any circumstances although it is quite safe to use a water wax emulsion floor polish if a gloss is desired.

If Wellington boots become damp inside, warm one or two newspapers, screw up and push firmly down inside the boots to absorb the moisture.

White woollen stole or shawl

To clean a soiled white stole or shawl without washing it, spread it on a sheet or old tablecloth and powder it generously with powdered starch or magnesia or talcum powder. Rub the powder into the wool with the finger-tips, then fold the shawl, adding more powder to each fold. Wrap in the sheet and leave overnight or for several hours, then knead the roll, take out of doors and shake or brush out all the powder.

Zip

To insert a zip-fastener neatly and easily, sew up the seam opening with tacking stitches. Stitch the closed zip in position over the seam, then remove the tacking stitches.

5

Spots, stains and marks

Stains generally

As far as possible any spot or stain should be treated the moment it occurs. Once a stain has penetrated the fibres of fabric it is difficult to dislodge, but while it is still on the surface quick simple cleansing will usually remove it.

Immediate measures include rinsing non-greasy stains with plain, cold water and dusting grease spots with ordinary talcum powder, or better still using carbon tetrachloride on the dry fabric. Spread salt at once on a fruit or wine stain on a tablecloth; this will not remove the mark but should prevent it spreading. But do not use salt on a carpet—unless fully rinsed away it may cause discoloration later.

Most stains can be divided into three main categories: fat, carbohydrate and protein. Fat, grease, oil and similar stains respond to grease solvents and to hot synthetic detergent suds. Carbohydrate stains are normally removed by laundering in washing powders and detergents containing sodium perborate. This is in heavy duty washing agents and is also in the new biological washing powders although not the enzyme pre-soak powders. Protein stains which were previously difficult to remove—these include stains such as blood, gravy, egg, etc.—can be removed by soaking in cold, lukewarm or hand-hot solutions of enzyme washing powder.

Wool, silk and flame-proof finishes must not be soaked, nor should fabrics which are not colour-fast. These can be laundered in a warm solution of the enzyme powder either by hand or machine, using a short wash on automatics and working quickly through washing, rinsing, drying when laundering by hand. Fabrics which can be soaked should be left overnight or for several hours to give the enzymes in the solution time to break down the stains sufficiently. If

211

stains are long-standing or have been set by hot-water washing previously, they may need more than one soaking to remove every trace of stain.

When removing stains by this method, do not have the water too hot or the enzymes will be destroyed. Do not use chlorine bleach in the water or this too will destroy the enzymes.

Biological washing powders will also deal effectively with some non-protein stains, such as tea, coffee and wine and it is worth trying this simple method on suitable fabrics. The powders are safe on even the most delicate fabrics and colours although obvious precautions should be taken, i.e. don't soak fabrics which should not be soaked (wool and silk) and don't leave non-fast colours in water for longer than absolutely necessary.

With materials which are not normally washed, always begin with the simplest methods first. Very often sponging with clear warm water will be sufficient to remove a fresh, non-greasy stain. Leave chemicals until other methods have failed.

Most stains, and especially thick or greasy marks, should be treated from the wrong side of the material so that stains are pushed out on to a clean thick pad underneath. If cleaning is started from the right side of the fabric the dirt must be pushed right through the fabric before it can be completely removed.

When using a dry-cleaning liquid or solvent, always make a ring with the moist cloth *outside* the stained area, then gradually work in towards the centre of the stain itself. Never start in the centre of a stain and work outwards or a ring may remain after the stain is removed; it also helps to work near an open window so that the cleaning fluid evaporates quickly.

One or two *stain-removing liquids* should always be immediately available and for details of these see chapter 'Chemicals and cleaners'. Have each bottle clearly labelled and keep the cupboard door locked.

Alternatively, it is now posssible to buy many proprietary stain removers. Obviously no one product can be completely all-purpose, but many will deal efficiently with a good number of the stains you meet. There are also the kit-type stain removers—for example, there is a special first-aid kit containing solvents, solutions and everything else necessary for removing over fifty different spots and stains from carpets, clothes and upholstery, etc. Instructions are on a simple dial which can be turned to the type of stain needing attention. No one dry-cleaning or spotting fluid will remove *all* stains, which is why the kit mentioned contains five or six different solutions. The stain-removal methods mentioned in this chapter are suggested as alternatives to using a proprietary product.

Always remove stains before laundering a garment or washing may make them permanent. Remember that several weak applications of a chemical are better than one strong one.

Test all chemicals first on an inside seam or inconspicuous part of the fabric before treating stains. This applies most particularly to rayons, acetates and triacetates, and delicate or coloured materials. Never allow a bleach to dry into the material, and rinse all chemicals out thoroughly or they may weaken the fibres.

Never use acetone or nail-varnish remover on an acetate fabric.

Always test hydrogen peroxide and methylated spirit on rayon before using and never use hydrogen peroxide on nylon.

Never use a grease solvent fluid, such as carbon tetrachloride, on plastics.

Avoid using solvents on foam-covered upholstery and on expanded polystyrene. Most solvents with the possible exception of pure white spirit or pure turpentine will dissolve these.

Never use trichloroethylene on triacetate fabrics. Many proprietary brands of dry-cleaning fluids contain trichlor, so always test a triacetate fabric, such as Tricel, on an inside hem before using on a stain.

Never use oxalic acid on wool or silk. Treat these instead with diluted hydrogen peroxide (1 part peroxide to 10 parts water). Rinse thoroughly, then launder garment.

For *carpets, heavy curtains and upholstery* use the lather of carpet shampoo suds rather than the liquid itself. To make a rich lather, add carpet shampoo in correct proportion to warm water and repeatedly squeeze a sponge in the suds or whisk briskly with an egg-beater until a thick foam of lather is formed. Use the foam on a cloth or brush to treat a grease mark, or allow to dry thoroughly and then treat with carbon tetrachloride.

Unless the cause of a stain and the correct method of removal are known, never use hot water or this may set the mark firmly into the material.

Acids

Neutralize acids by sponging with a solution made by adding 1 teaspoonful of borax to 1 pint of warm water, then rinse in clear water.

If strong acid is spilt on a *carpet*, dissolve as much bicarbonate of soda as a basin of warm water will hold and sponge the stain with this. If bicarbonate of soda is not available, use borax. Do not use ammonia on carpets.

Alcohol

Should alcohol be spilt on a *carpet*, blot up as much fluid as possible with a clean cloth or towel or with clean blotting paper. Sponge immediately with a clean cloth tightly wrung out in clear, warm water and allow to dry, when the stain should have gone. If any remains, mix a mild detergent solution and apply to the stain with a medicine dropper and work in with the finger-tips or scrub lightly with a brush dipped in the lather, then sponge off with a clean damp cloth and allow to dry as quickly as possible.

Rinsing in clear warm water followed by ordinary laundering is usually sufficient to remove stains from *washable materials*. On white linen or cotton tablecloths, table napkins, etc., if a brown stain remains, apply a few drops of hydrogen peroxide followed by photographer's 'hypo' (sodium thiosulphate) dissolved in warm water. For details see page 131 of chapter 'Chemicals and Cleaners'.

Furniture. Perfumes, medicines and drinks containing alcohol can quickly cause damage if spilled over furniture, because alcohol tends to dissolve the finish. So it is important to wipe up the liquid immediately. If the finish has been polished regularly there may be no spot. If there is, one of the following suggestions may help.

(a) Rub with liquid wax polish.

(b) Rub with silver cleaning pad or silver polish on a cloth (often extremely effective). Buff well.

(c) Rub with a mixture of linseed oil and cigarette-ash, or linseed oil alone. Or use camphorated oil if you have any available.

Alternatively, remove alcohol stains from furniture by rubbing carefully into the wood a paste made with powdered pumice and linseed oil. Work the way of the grain and after a few minutes wipe clean and rub with a little linseed oil.

Rings on polished furniture caused by a damp alcohol glass can usually be removed by rubbing with camphorated oil. If the stain is still wet buff dry, dab with linseed oil, leave overnight, and next morning rub hard before polishing in the usual way.

See also under Beer and Wine.

Alkali

A quick way of removing an alkali stain is to rub the mark with a cloth moistened in neat vinegar or vinegar solution. Rinse or wipe with a clean cloth wrung out in clear water and pat dry.

Axle grease

Scrape away as much of the grease as possible, then place a thick absorbent pad underneath and, working on the *wrong* side of the material, sponge with a grease solvent such as benzol or carbon tetrachloride. Change the position of the pad and the cleaning cloth so that as they become soiled a fresh portion is used. If possible, launder stained fabric afterwards in strong detergent suds.

Providing the material is suitable, a quicker method is to immerse the stained fabric in the grease solvent and rub the marks gently with the finger-tips. Follow by washing in hot synthetic detergent suds.

If no grease solvents are to hand it is sometimes possible to remove this type of stain by rubbing lard well into the grease marks and then laundering in very hot soapless detergent suds.

Ball point ink

There are several ways of removing ball point ink and the best is probably to sponge the stain with methylated spirit, then rinse well. If the mark is on a rayon fabric, test first before treating.

Another way is to stretch the stain over a thick absorbent pad, then drip on a solvent with a medicine dropper or glass rod. Use cleaning benzine, carbon tetrachloride, methylated spirit or petroleum ether. When the ink has dissolved rub on and around the stain with a piece of clean rag moistened with the cleaner and leave to dry.

On non-absorbent surfaces and plastic items, ball point ink stains can usually be removed by rubbing with a cloth dipped in a neat liquid detergent then with a clean damp cloth. If this does not remove the marks, rub gently with a damp cloth or wet nail brush dipped in scouring powder or rub lightly with fine glass paper. Either treatment should remove any stains but may remove gloss from paint as well. In this case, rinse, dry and re-polish where necessary with furniture polish.

Stains on vinyl faced wall covering can also be removed by rubbing very lightly with a damp cloth and a small amount of scouring powder. Try ordinary detergent first, dry detergent on a damp cloth. Rinse and dry.

Balsa cement

Sponge gently with a soft cloth dipped in methylated spirit. Test rayon fabrics on an inconspicuous part first.

Beer

Strangely enough, spilt beer rarely leaves a stain. Simply mop up the beer and wipe the wallpaper, upholstery or material with a clean damp cloth and allow to dry.

A considerable quantity of beer spilt on a *carpet* should be blotted up immediately with a clean cloth. Sponge with warm water, following the instructions given for Alcohol on page 214.

For an obstinate beer stain on *washable material*, when laundering has little effect, rewash in 1 pint of warm soapy water containing 1 teaspoonful of ammonia or vinegar. On white fabrics bleach the stain with hydrogen peroxide, then dry in the sun and finally rinse and rewash.

On *heavy unwashable materials* when this method is impracticable sponge the stain with a cloth dipped in methylated spirit, then rub washing soap into the mark with the finger-tips. Leave to dry, then brush out with a clean dry brush.

Bicarbonate of soda

Remove stains in a glass, caused by bicarbonate of soda, by almost filling with lukewarm water and adding 1 teaspoonful of vinegar. Leave overnight, then rinse and wash in warm detergent suds.

Bicycle grease

To remove oil from silk, cotton, linen or rayon, treat before washing by sponging with a cloth dipped in cleaning benzine or carbon tetrachloride.

Alternatively, rub gently with eucalyptus oil or cover with a thick paste made from fuller's earth or french chalk and cleaning fluid such as carbon tetrachloride. Leave to dry, then brush off with a soft clean brush. This is a good method for unwashable fabrics.

Bird droppings

These are mostly alkaline. But, for instance, a thrush which has been feeding on berries—especially elderberries—will produce a slightly acidic dropping which is strongly coloured due to dye from the berries. Laundering fabric in a fairly strong detergent solution should remove stains with repeated applications of bleach where possible. Where there is little stain ordinary laundering should be sufficient.

Blackberry juice

If this stain is dealt with by careful laundering while it is still moist it should respond immediately but once it has dried hard it may be difficult to remove. As soon as possible after the accident, stretch the stained fabric over a basin and pour on boiling water from a height. If this cannot be done, cover the stain with salt and treat later.

For a bad stain or one that has dried, sprinkle with borax and rub lightly into the material, then pour on boiling water and soak for 10 minutes. Rinse thoroughly before washing in the ordinary way. Do not use soap before neutralizing or diluting the stain or the alkali in the soap may set the stain and change it to a deep blue which will be difficult to remove.

Suitable materials can be boiled or bleached if the stain is persistent or the mark may be moistened with lemon juice and left to dry in the sun. To bleach use 1 teaspoonful 20-vol peroxide, 1 teaspoonful ammonia and 8 teaspoonfuls warm water. Soak until the stain dissolves, then rinse thoroughly and launder.

To remove a fresh, moist stain from heavy fabrics and unwashable materials, sponging with clear warm water should be sufficient. If the stain has dried, rub in a little glycerine to lubricate the stain, leave for a few hours, then sponge off.

Blacklead

If ordinary laundering does not remove the mark from fabric, rub with a clean cloth moistened with turpentine or with carbon tetrachloride and then rewash.

To remove blacklead marks around a fireplace, cover generously with a thick paste made from water and fuller's earth. Leave to dry, then remove with a clean brush.

Blood

Rinse in cold water or cold salt water if the stain is fresh and then wash in the ordinary way. Soak a dried bloodstain in a solution of ammonia in water (1 dessertspoonful to 1 pint) for 1 to 12 hours according to the severity, then wash in warm suds.

White fabrics may be bleached with hydrogen peroxide, well-diluted household bleach or a powder bleach if necessary. Thick fabrics which cannot be soaked can be treated by covering the stain with a paste of starch and cold water. Leave to dry, then brush off.

Both new and old blood stains can be removed from washable fabrics—with the possible exception of wool and silk which should not be soaked—by immersing the stained material in a cold water solution of biological pre-soak or washing powder containing enzymes overnight. Old, set stains, may need to be re-soaked several times to remove every trace.

Blue

Washing blue can usually be removed if the fabric is soaked in a vinegar solution. Soluble blue is a dye and would need to be bleached out.

Brandy

Treat as for Alcohol on page 214.

Bread

It sometimes happens, especially when children are around, that someone drops a piece of bread or a sandwich on the carpet and someone else immediately walks on it. If the bread is dry, sweep up the crumbs with a stiff carpet brush.

For buttered bread dropped wrong side down or a sandwich squashed into the carpet, sweep up the crumbs first, loosen any sticky or greasy pieces with finger-tips, then sponge lightly with warm water and synthetic detergent; avoid soaking the carpet or penetrating the backing. Rinse with a clean cloth wrung out in warm water and dry by rubbing the way of the pile with an old clean towel.

A sandwich dropped on upholstery or accidentally sat upon can be removed in the same way from heavy furnishings. If the stain is very slight, a quick sponge with a grease solvent such as carbon tetrachloride should be sufficient.

Bruise marks

Bruises in furniture can usually be removed with wet blotting paper and a hot iron. Soak the blotting paper so that it is really wet and fold it into several thicknesses; place the blotting paper over the mark and gently hold a hot iron on top for a few minutes but support the weight of the iron and do not rest it on the blotting paper. Give liberal applications of polish afterwards.

Candle wax

If hot candle wax drips on material, scrape away as much wax as possible, then place a sheet of blotting paper under the stain and another on top and press lightly with a warm iron, changing the position of the blotting paper frequently.

Oil-soluble dyestuffs are used in the manufacture of coloured candles so if you remove the wax and are left with a coloured stain treat this with a solvent such as perchloroethylene, trichloroethylene or carbon tetrachloride.

To remove candle wax from furniture, ease off with a thin blunt tool such as a plastics plate scraper, sponge with warm vinegar solution, rub dry immediately and repolish. If the wood has been bleached by the wax, use a scratch cover polish or similar preparation. Where candle drippings are difficult to remove, an ice cube held against the wax often simplifies the task.

See also under Grease and oil on page 231.

Carbon paper

Treatment of the stain depends on the type of carbon paper in question. On black carbon paper, the dye is black pigment in wax-type dispersion. Remove stains with white spirit.

On mauve carbon paper, purple copying ink in wax-type dispersion is used and this is more difficult to remove. Repeated sponging with white spirit may help to carry the dye away but it may take some time. When most of the stain has been removed, launder or if the fabric is white, hang in strong sunlight to help remove final traces of stain.

Car grease

See under Fuel oil on page 229, Grease and oil on page 231 or Tar on page 259.

Cats' urine

See under Urine on page 262.

Caustic pencil

See under Silver Nitrate.

Cellulose adhesives

See under Glue on page 229.

Cellulose lacquers

This would include all types including nitro-cellulose varnish and nail varnishes and lacquers. Remove stains with cellulose thinners, acetone, amyl acetate or nail varnish remover but test these solvents first on acetate fabrics and all synthetic fibre fabrics. These solvents will also attack most paints and varnishes so avoid using them on painted, french-polished or varnished surfaces. Once stain has been removed, wash with liquid detergent and warm water suds or for unwashable fabrics send for dry-cleaning.

Cement

To brighten cement paths and yard, scrub cement with a stiff brush and hot suds. Add domestic bleach if the cement has greenish stains. Odd cement marks on paving stones can sometimes be removed by scrubbing but more usually will need chipping away.

If the cement marks are indoors, on a quarry tiled floor for instance, use a special Jenolite liquid and soak the stains for approximately 20 minutes, then scrub with hot soapy water, scraping any thick patches.

Odd cement stains on floors can sometimes be removed fairly easily by rubbing lightly with moist coarse steel wool.

Chalk

Most chalk marks will brush off and the garment can then be laundered. For indelible chalks see under Crayons on page 223.

Cherry stain

If the stain is on a *cotton garment* or a *tablecloth*, stretch the stained part over a basin, sprinkle with borax and pour boiling water through the mark. Push the stained patch into the solution and leave to soak until the liquid is cool, then rub gently, rinse thoroughly and wash in the usual way.

Remove a cherry stain from *delicate fabric* such as a fine silk blouse or baby's woollen coat by sponging lightly with cold water, then by working a few drops of glycerine gently into the material with the finger-tips. If no glycerine is available, use a few drops of mild soapless hair shampoo instead. Finally moisten the stain with 1 or 2 drops of white vinegar and immediately rinse in clear warm water, then wash in warm soapy water.

Chewing gum

On *washable materials* the easiest way to remove chewing gum is to apply a little egg-white or alternatively carbon tetrachloride, and when the gum is soft, pick off as much as possible and launder in the ordinary way. An alternative is to rub the gum with ice, pick off the loose particles, then wash. On unwashable fabrics sponging with carbon tetrachloride is usually effective.

Chocolate

Scrape away any thick chocolate with a blunt knife and wash in hot suds. If the material is badly stained, sponge with warm borax solution (1 oz. to 1 pint), rinse and launder.

Sponging with warm soapy water containing ammonia often removes a chocolate stain, and another method is to sponge with warm water and then sprinkle with dry borax. Rub the powder into the stain with the finger-tips, leave for half an hour, then rinse and launder.

If chocolate is spilt or trodden into a *carpet*, scrape off as much as possible with a spatula or blunt knife.

If drinking chocolate is spilled, blot up excess with absorbent paper or cloth. Next sponge lightly with a clean cloth wrung out in aerated water (such as soda water) or if this is not available, sponge with clear warm water and leave to dry. This should be sufficient but if any marks remain, mix a mild detergent solution and apply to the stain with a medicine dropper or scrub lightly with a nailbrush dipped in the lather. Rub well into the stain, leave for 15 minutes, then sponge off with a clean damp cloth and dry as quickly as possible.

Occasionally a faint ring will remain after removing a chocolate stain. On washable fabrics laundering will remove this, on heavy materials sponge lightly with methylated spirit, rinse and dry.

Cigarette burns

With most light materials the burn will damage the fibres so that invisible or ordinary mending is necessary. For a light burn treat as for Scorch Marks, page 253.

For a cigarette burn on a carpet, first remove charred fibres by brushing or by rubbing lightly with fine sandpaper. Next mix a mild detergent solution and drip on to the stain: cover with a teaspoonful of dry borax, and rub well in with the finger-tips. Leave for 5 minutes, then sponge off with a clean damp cloth, rinse well and leave to dry. A bad burn can be repaired almost invisibly by a professional carpet firm.

To repair slight burn damage see pages 184 and 253.

Cocoa

With a weak stain, ordinary laundering may be sufficient, otherwise add 1 oz. of borax to 1 pint of warm water and sponge the stain with this. Alternatively sponge with soapy water containing ammonia. With washable materials finish by washing in a mild soapless detergent.

A newer and easier way to remove cocoa stains, whether new or old is to soak the stained fabric in water containing a biological pre-soak or washing powder. These powders contain enzymes which are effective in dealing with cocoa stains. Follow instructions on the packet.

Heavy fabrics can be sponged first with carbon tetrachloride and then with borax solution followed by a weak solution of hydrogen peroxide if necessary.

For a large, strong stain damp the mark with warm water and rub the powdered borax into the stain with the finger-tips. Leave for 30 minutes, then rinse and launder.

Cod-liver oil

Cod-liver oil stains must be dealt with immediately; once dry and hard they are almost impossible to remove. If possible, wash immediately in hot soapless detergent suds. Rubbing with pure glycerine or with soapless shampoo may help. On heavy materials, sponge with carbon tetrachloride. Old stains may have to be bleached out with a solution of hydrogen peroxide after sponging with the grease solvent.

If, as often happens, the cod-liver oil stain is on baby's wool garments, sponge immediately with a grease solvent or with a fairly strong solution of liquid soapless cleanser mixed in warm water. Follow by ordinary washing with warm soapy water.

If cod-liver oil stains are a frequent problem, it is worth considering giving baby the oil or malt at bath time.

Coffee

New coffee stains should be sponged with a cloth dipped in warm water and borax (1 oz. to 1 pint) and then washed in warm soapy water.

Alternatively secure the stained area over a bowl with an elastic band and pour boiling water through the stain from a height, then launder.

Coffee stains will frequently respond to overnight soaking in cold water containing one of the enzyme washing powders. Next day launder in fresh hand-hot suds. Repeat if necessary.

Very often, ordinary sponging will remove a coffee stain but the fat from the milk or cream may leave a mark. This can be removed by sponging lightly with a grease solvent such as carbon tetrachloride.

For heavy or *unwashable fabrics* and carpets, etc., sponge with clear warm water or a mild borax solution, then rinse thoroughly and rub dry. If any mark remains, sponge with a grease solvent.

If coffee is spilt on a *carpet*, as much as possible should be blotted up immediately with paper or a cloth. Next sponge lightly with clear warm water, using just enough to clean the pile without soaking through to the backing. For black coffee this should be sufficient; for white coffee, allow the water to dry thoroughly, then remove any grease remaining from the milk by mixing a mild detergent solution in warm water and dampening the stain with this drop by drop. Work well into the spot, leave for a few minutes, then sponge off with a clean damp cloth. Allow to dry and if any stain remains remove final traces with a dry-cleaning liquid.

Old stains or those on non-washable materials may be sponged with cold water followed by glycerine. Rub the glycerine well into the stain and leave for half an hour to an hour. Rinse with a cloth well wrung out in warm water.

Contact adhesives

Remove stains caused by proprietary contact adhesives by sponging with amyl acetate over an absorbent pad. Finally launder in usual way.

Copying ink

Dab the stains with diluted oleic acid and rub gently into the marks. Leave for 15 minutes, then sponge with ammonia and water or dip stained fabric into the solution. Rub solution into the material with the finger-tips, then rinse and launder in the usual way. Or use a proprietary ink remover.

Crayons

Indelible crayon and chalk marks can usually be removed by

sponging with methylated spirit. On fabrics such as Tricel and acetates use Benzine instead. Sponge over an absorbent pad and finally launder in usual way.

Cream

For *washable materials* soak thoroughly in warm or cold water and later wash in hot detergent suds. Heavy fabrics can be sponged thoroughly with cold or cool water, left to dry and any remaining grease marks removed with a solvent such as carbon tetrachloride or benzol or, if the fabric is not rayon, with acetone.

On *non-washable fabrics* sponge first with the solvent and allow this to dry completely. Then take a clean cloth and sponge the stain with warm water. Finally, rub dry with an old towel.

Cream soup

If possible, rinse off surplus liquid and wash in hot detergent suds immediately. If washing is not possible, place a thick towel under the stain and sponge with hot water. Pat dry and rub lightly with a clean cloth dipped in a grease solvent such as carbon tetrachloride.

Creosote

Place an absorbent pad under the stain against the right side of the fabric, sponge with benzol, eucalyptus oil or carbon tetrachloride, then wash in hot soapless detergent if the material is suitable.

If the stain is severe, immerse the entire stained area in the solvent and rub gently with the finger-tips. When the stain has dissolved, wash in hot suds.

It is sometimes possible to remove an old creosote stain by rubbing glycerine or lard into the marks with the finger-tips to lubricate the stain, followed by thorough washing in hot detergent suds. Repeat the process if necessary.

Crude oil

See under Fuel oil on page 229.

Dandelion

With light staining, the juice from dandelion or other flowers may wash out but if the marks are severe, sponge lightly with a cloth moistened with methylated spirit. (On rayon fabrics test a corner first.) As soon as the methylated spirit dissolves the stain, plunge the garment into warm soapy water and wash normally.

Sometimes dandelion will leave a dark brown stain and if methylated spirit does not remove this, a potassium permanganate solution is effective on most white materials except rayon. For details of treatment see page 128.

Dogs' urine

See under Urine on page 262.

Drip marks

Drip marks in a bath under the taps can be removed by rubbing warm vinegar on the stains followed by thorough rinsing with hot water. The treatment can be repeated daily until the marks disappear but the vinegar should not be left in contact for too long at a time, as it is a corrosive acid.

Another effective way of removing stubborn stains is to rub them with a wedge of lemon dipped in coarse salt. Rinse thoroughly when the marks have disappeared.

For severe brown stains or discoloration under the taps use oxalic acid or salts of lemon solution and rinse thoroughly. See page 127 for details. Or use a non-caustic proprietary cleaner.

Droppings

See under Bird droppings on page 216.

Duplicating ink

This is violet Ormig ink and it is very difficult to remove because it is such a penetrating dye. If it spills on to paintwork, the only solution is to re-paint. On fabrics, if the stain is dealt with immediately it may be possible to remove some or all of it by swamping and blotting with a solvent such as carbon tetrachloride or a similar dry-cleaning solvent such as perchloroethylene. See also Copying ink, page 223.

Dye

Remove a small dye stain by sponging with methylated spirit containing a few drops of ammonia but test first before applying to rayon fabrics and coloured fabrics.

For a dye that has streaked and where the entire colour has to be removed use a special stripper such as Dygon. This will

H

remove ordinary home dyes as well as most permanent colourings.

Egg

White. Dissolve ½ teaspoonful of common salt in ½ pint of warm water and sponge the stain with this. Repeat with clear water and dry. Wash in the ordinary way if necessary and if the fabric is suitable. Do not use hot water first on an egg-white stain or the heat will coagulate the albumen.

Yolk. Dissolve a mild synthetic detergent in warm water and apply the lather only to a heavy non-washable fabric, or the actual liquid suds to other materials. If possible, immerse the garment in the water and wash in the ordinary way. Allow to dry and if any slight stain remains, sponge with carbon tetrachloride.

Whole egg. Sponge first with warm salt water as for egg-white and then launder in hot soapless detergent for washable materials. If the fabric is non-washable, sponge with carbon tetrachloride after scraping off excess.

It is also possible to purchase from some chemists an enzyme digester, used by professional dry-cleaners for removing stains such as egg (and blood) which contain albumen. And of course, enzyme pre-soak powders and enzyme washing powders will remove egg stains if fabric is soaked in the solution for the required length of time and at the correct temperature. Follow manufacturer's instructions exactly.

Emulsion paint

Emulsion paint stains should not be sponged with turpentine. Instead quickly wipe off surplus paint and immediately sponge with cold water or, if fabric permits, leave stained material to soak in cold water, then launder in the usual way. Once these stains have set they may become almost permanent.

Where spots of emulsion paint *have* dried and resist removal you can try sponging with a solution of methylated spirit and water. Test rayon fabrics first.

Remove emulsion paint splashes from a floor with a damp rag while the paint is still wet. Once they have dried, spots may be difficult to remove but should respond to rubbing with fine wire wool dipped in soapy water. Work the way of the grain on wood, use very little water, rinse well and rub dry.

See also under Water-borne paint on page 265.

Enamel paint

This is a slow-drying, highly pigmented gloss varnish so try to remove enamel while it is still wet. Deal with the stain as quickly as possible by sponging gently with a clean cloth dipped in turpentine or turpentine substitute. If the enamel has dried, apply the solvent to both sides of the stain with an absorbent pad underneath. Change the position of the pad and the cleaning cloth frequently so that a clean surface is always in use.

It is important to break down the binder in the enamel and if turpentine or white spirit is not immediately available, use another solvent that may be handy—cellulose thinners, Brushing Belco, amyl acetate, trichlor, C.T.C. or one of the proprietary dry-cleaning fluids. If the stain is obstinate it is worth rinsing out as much of the enamel as possible first with turps or turps substitute and then following with one of the solvents just mentioned, but test these on man-made fibres first. Repeat cleaning until stain moves then wash with soap and water.

Once the stain has dried it will be much more difficult, then use cellulose thinners, Brushing Belco or amyl acetate, but don't use these on acetates nor on upholstery covered foam, or expanded polystyrene.

See also under Paint on page 245.

Eye cosmetics

See under Make-up on page 240.

Fat

See Grease.

Felt pen inks

It usually helps to lubricate these stains first. Use ordinary hard household soap or glycerine, then if the stain is slight, launder in the usual way. For obstinate marks or on unwashable fabrics, sponge with methylated spirit or on Tricel or acetate fabrics use benzine.

Flowers

Treat as given under Dandelion on page 224 or sponge with benzol, then launder in hot synthetic detergent suds.

Fly spots

Easiest way to remove fly spots from electric light bulbs, lampshades and paintwork is to use a weak solution of liquid detergent in warm water. On electrical fittings, switch off electricity and make sure the fittings are dry before switching on again. Fly spots should be removed from metal fittings also because although they don't show so clearly, the spots contain a minute amount of acid which can corrode the metal. Carbon tetrachloride will also remove fly spots and so will methylated spirit.

Food

Food stains very according to the type of food concerned but the new biological washing and soaking powders will deal with most types. Allow to soak for several hours or overnight in cold or warm water (not hot).

French polish

Deal with these stains as given under Spirit varnish on page 258.

Fruit and fruit juice

For a fresh fruit stain on a tablecloth, stretch the patch of material over a basin, secure with an elastic band and pour boiling water through the mark from a height.

If the boiling water method does not quite remove heavy fruit-juice stains from cotton or linen, rub the marks with lemon juice, then launder. Or lubricate stain with glycerine before laundering.

If the stain has dried, soak for 10 minutes in 1 pint of warm water containing 1 teaspoonful of borax. Rub the stain gently with the finger-tips, then rinse and launder in the ordinary way.

Very often obstinate fruit stains from dark fruit such as black-currants will respond to overnight soaking in lukewarm water containing a biological washing powder with enzymes. Follow soaking by machine or hand laundering in the usual way. Do not soak wool or silk fabrics nor those which aren't colour-fast.

Obstinate fruit stains on white fabrics can be bleached with an oxalic acid solution using 1 teaspoonful to $\frac{3}{4}$ pint of water, followed by sponging with ammonia and finally by washing and rinsing thoroughly.

If fruit juice is spilled on coloured fabric, launder immediately. If stain persists, sponge with well-diluted ammonia, then with petrol and finally re-launder. Or try glycerine before laundering. Test rayon fabrics first.

If a fruit-juice stain cannot be dealt with immediately sprinkle salt on the mark to prevent it spreading and treat as soon as possible.

Heavy unwashable fabrics or delicate fabrics such as wool or silk may be sponged first with cold water and then with glycerine. Leave for an hour then sponge lightly with lemon juice or white vinegar and rinse immediately with clear water. Unwashable fabrics can be sponged with a clean damp cloth and dried, other materials laundered in warm soapy water.

Fuel oil

Stains picked up on beaches from fuel oil are crude oil marks. Sponge immediately with a solvent such as ether, white spirit, trichloroethylene, or failing these with methylated spirit, benzine or naphtha. Where possible, follow by laundering with hot detergent suds.

Fuel oil on skin can be removed with special cream made by Ambre Solaire.

See also under Tar on page 259 and Grease and oil on page 231.

Fungus

Some fungi produce an aniline dye which gives a bright pinkish-purple stain, especially on bricks and woodwork. This is difficult to remove but will often respond to a solution of Santobrite and ICI Mould-inhibitor to prevent the spread of the fungus.

Furniture polish

On ordinary materials, washing in hot detergent solution should be sufficient; for heavy fabrics scrape off excess, then sponge with a grease solvent such as carbon tetrachloride or scrub lightly with the lather from a liquid cleaner.

If liquid furniture polish is spilt on a carpet, blot up as much as possible, or with solid polish, scrape up surplus wax. Next sponge with a dry-cleaning fluid to remove grease and allow to dry. Finally mix a mild detergent solution in warm water and drip on to any remaining stains. Work in with finger-tips, leave for 10 minutes and then sponge off with a clean damp cloth and rub dry.

Gin

Treat as for Alcohol on page 214.

Glue

Wash in very hot water containing a little synthetic detergent or if the fabric is suitable and the stain severe, soak in warm vinegar for

1 minute, or boil for 10 minutes. Glue spilt on heavy materials or carpets should be sponged off with hot water or, if severe, sponged with warm vinegar or with a little lemon juice. Place a thick absorbent pad underneath, if possible, rinse with hot clear water, then rub dry.

Some modern adhesives may not respond to simple treatments. In this case try sponging with amyl acetate or acetone but don't use this on acetate fabrics and test first on rayons and man-made fibres especially when there is any doubt about the fibre content. Cellulose adhesives can all be removed with these solvents.

Glycerine

Soak in lukewarm water containing an enzyme powder or liquid detergent then launder in the usual way.

Grapefruit juice

This is sometimes difficult to remove. If possible wash immediately in hot soapy water. If the stains are on white linen or cotton, bleaching may be necessary although hanging the wet material to dry in strong sunlight may be sufficient.

Unwashable materials or heavy fabrics should be sponged with clear warm water or if this is not effective, with a solution of hydrogen peroxide made alkaline by the addition of 1 or 2 drops of ammonia.

Grass

Ordinary laundering in hot suds should remove slight grass stains. For heavy materials or where the staining is severe, soak the fabric in methylated spirit or sponge with a clean cloth dipped in methylated spirit, then rinse in clear warm water and press lightly with a warm iron, placing a thick, clean cloth on both sides of the fabric. Test on rayon materials first.

Two alternative removers are eucalyptus oil and ether; sponge lightly, wipe with a cloth wrung out in clear water and press as above.

Another grass stain remover especially suitable for flannels is made by mixing equal amounts of tartaric acid powder and salt. Rub into the stain with the finger-tips, leave for 10 minutes, then brush off with a clean soft brush.

Obstinate stains will usually respond to a warm mixture of methylated spirit and ammonia. Make this by putting two tablespoons of methylated spirit into a cup; add one tablespoon of ammonia and three tablespoons of very hot (not boiling) water. Sponge stain re-

peatedly. If the solution cools it can be warmed again by standing
the cup in a basin of very hot water.

Grass stains on a carpet should be sponged lightly with methylated spirit or alcohol. Allow to dry, then apply warm detergent
solution to the marks with a medicine dropper. Work into the stain
with the finger-tips, leave for 10 minutes, then sponge off with a clean
cloth wrung out in clear warm water and rub dry.

Gravy

Lightly-stained fabric should be washed immediately in cool
detergent suds and rinsed thoroughly. Where the stain is severe, soak
the garment in cool salt water containing ammonia (1 teaspoonful
to 1 pint), leave for 1 hour, then rinse thoroughly and wash in warm
detergent suds.

Easiest way to remove obstinate stains is to soak the fabric in a
solution of lukewarm water and enzyme pre-soak or washing powder.
Follow instructions on the packet for details of time and temperature
required but do not use hot water.

Gravy stains should not, in any case, be washed in hot water or the
heat may set the protein and make the marks difficult to remove. If
any greasy or oily stains remain after treatment the marks can then
be washed in hot detergent suds or sponged with a grease solvent
such as carbon tetrachloride or benzene. On unwashable fabrics,
place a pad underneath and sponge with the grease solvent.

Grease and oil

On wool, silk, cotton and most *fabrics*, sponge on the wrong side
with carbon tetrachloride or trichlorethylene, but test on rayon first.
Place a thick absorbent pad under the stain and frequently change the
position of this and the cleaning pad so that clean portions are always
in use.

If the stain is caused by black oil such as is found on the beach,
eucalyptus oil is the most effective remedy. If the stain is not too
severe, washable items can be laundered in hot synthetic detergent
suds. A very heavy item such as a *carpet* may be powdered with
french chalk, powdered magnesia, talcum powder, starch, fuller's
earth, or dry bicarbonate of soda. Sprinkle the powder on thickly,
work into the stain with the finger-tips and leave for some hours
before brushing off with a clean brush.

If grease is spilt on *linoleum* or on a wooden floor, immediately
wring out a cloth in hot synthetic detergent suds and mop up the

grease. If hot fat is spilled, immediately splash cold water on to it so that it solidifies and does not soak into the floor. In both cases dry floor well afterwards.

To remove grease marks from *furniture* sponge with a solution made by adding 2 tablespoonfuls of vinegar to 1 pint of warm water. Buff dry immediately with a clean, absorbent duster. To prevent candle wax leaving a heat mark on a polished table, drop cold water quickly on to the hot wax and immediately blot up the liquid, then gently ease up any solid wax with a plastics scraper or blunt spatula. Finally sponge with vinegar solution made by adding 1 tablespoonful of vinegar to $\frac{1}{2}$ pint of warm water, dry and then polish.

French chalk, talcum powder, powdered magnesia, fuller's earth and starch are all effective in removing grease marks from *upholstery* and *wallpaper*. Spread the powder on the stain, replace as it becomes saturated, leave for several hours before brushing off. If the grease stain has dried make the powder into a paste with a few drops of carbon tetrachloride or other cleaning fluid. Spread thickly on to the marks, leave to dry, then brush off. Alternatively, fold clean blotting paper or absorbent brown paper over the stain and press lightly with a warm iron, changing the paper as grease is absorbed into it. Finish by dusting with fresh absorbent powder and brush off with a clean soft brush.

A number of proprietary cleaners will deal effectively with grease stains and one or two effective jelly-type cleaners are sold in tubes. The white powder remaining when the stain has been removed can be brushed away without leaving a ring. Test before using on satin, taffeta and grosgrain.

To remove grease from *leather or fabric shoes*, sponge lightly with a cloth dipped in carbon tetrachloride or proprietary cleaning fluid. Leave to dry, then repolish, brush or wash according to the type of shoe. On leather shoes it is often possible to revive the surface after removing the grease by applying a mixture of two parts of milk to one part of methylated spirit. Allow to dry then polish in the usual way.

On *suède shoes*, use a proprietary grease remover specially made for suède shoes and boots. If the colour is affected, treat the suède afterwards with a suède cleaner the same colour as the shoes. For one odd grease stain, sprinkle with french chalk or talcum powder, leave for as long as possible then brush out with a wire suède brush.

Hair lacquer

Water soluble hair sprays should wash out quite easily. Where shellac has been used and the product is actually lacquer, however, the stains may be difficult. Sponge these with amyl acetate over an absorbent pad and then launder again in the usual way.

Hair oil

For grease stains on upholstery caused by hair oil make a paste with french chalk and carbon tetrachloride or dry-cleaner and spread on to the stains fairly thickly. Allow to dry thoroughly then brush off with a stiff brush. A small mark may be rubbed lightly with a clean cloth moistened with carbon tetrachloride or other cleaning solvent.

Hamster urine

See under Urine on page 262.

Heat marks

On a polished table heat or water marks will often disappear if they are rubbed with a cloth dipped in a linseed and turpentine mixture. To make this, simmer 1 pint of linseed oil for 10 minutes (or buy boiled linseed oil), add ¼ pint of turpentine and bottle. Rub well into the marks, leave overnight, and rub off and polish next day.

On a varnished table, a very little ordinary metal polish rubbed in and around a hot dish mark may remove it. Finish by treating with a scratch remover or with a little brown shoe polish on a soft duster. Camphorated oil can be used in a similar way. If the surface is rough, rub afterwards with very fine-grade steel wool dipped in liquid wax polish.

Yet another remedy for heat marks is to make a paste with salt and olive oil. Spread on the marks, leave overnight, then rub off and polish.

There are several branded products which will remove slight heat or water marks and these scratch removers should be used exactly according to the instructions given.

If a full teapot or hot-water jug is knocked over on a highly polished table or sideboard, mop up the surplus liquid as quickly as possible, then immediately pour on a little milk. Rub well into the stain, dry and polish.

Cigarette ash moistened with linseed or camphorated oil, spread thickly over a heat mark and left overnight will sometimes remove the stain completely. Next morning rub well, brush off the ash and polish.

Another method reputed to remove hot-plate marks from polished furniture is to make a solution of vinegar and warm water and rub the stains well with this. Leave for a few minutes, then polish.

Small heat marks on *french polished furniture* can usually be removed if a little of the polish is dissolved slightly. To do this make a thick absorbent pad and moisten with 1 or at most, 2 drops of methylated spirit. Cover with a piece of thin material and rub lightly on and around the stain. Leave to dry and repolish.

For a heat or burn mark on the side of a *brick fireplace* or on a *brick hearth*, dip a brush in neat vinegar and scrub hard. Rinse by scrubbing with clear warm water and dry.

Honey

If possible soak fabric immediately in warm detergent suds, rub well, then rinse and dry. If the honey stain has dried into the material soak in 1 pint of warm water containing 1 teaspoonful of borax. Leave for half an hour, then rinse thoroughly in cold water and finally wash in the ordinary way.

Ice cream

Soak washable fabrics immediately in hot detergent suds, rub lightly and rinse well. Remove an ice-cream stain on wool by squeezing gently in warm soapy water.

If the ice cream has dried into the material or if there is a doubt about the washability of the fabric, sponge with warm borax solution (1 teaspoonful to $\frac{1}{2}$ pint). Repeat until the stain dissolves, then rinse with a cloth wrung out in clear water and rub dry. If a slight grease mark remains when the fabric is dry, remove with a grease solvent such as carbon tetrachloride, or with methylated spirit providing the fabric is not rayon.

Indelible pencil

Deal with this stain quickly as it is almost impossible to remove once the dye has set into the fabric. If the stain is large, solvent may spread it and professional dry-cleaning is recommended.

For smaller marks, rub gently with methylated spirit or acetone if the material is suitable and sponge any remaining marks with soap and water and launder. Do not use acetone on any type of rayon fabric and test methylated spirit on a hem or seam before using on acetate fabrics.

Where the stain is persistent, white fabrics can be bleached with potassium permanganate. For particulars see page 128 in chapter 'Chemicals and Cleaners'.

On woodwork or paintwork, rub the indelible pencil mark with methylated spirit or with lemon juice and salt, leave to dry, then rinse with clear warm water and rub dry. Very light marks can be rubbed with lemon skin dipped in salt, followed by a damp rag and finally a dry duster.

Indian ink

There are two kinds of indian ink, Galatin which is not very soluble in water and Lac which is often called waterproof drawing ink. With the first kind, home-cleaning is not satisfactory and the stain would need to be dealt with by a professional dry-cleaning firm.

To remove the waterproof drawing or Lac indian ink, blot up any excess immediately with clean blotting paper and then sponge with turpentine or white spirit or, if possible, immerse the stain in fluid and rub gently with the finger-tips. Leave until the ink softens, then clean with fresh solvent and allow to dry. Any remaining stain should be removed with carbon tetrachloride or washed out in hot detergent suds.

Ink stains

For Ball-point, Copying, Indian, Marking and Red Ink see under respective headings. The following details apply principally to ordinary writing or fountain pen inks, and are an alternative to proprietary ink eradicators.

Books. Ink stains can usually be removed from books with special ink remover or by applying a solution of oxalic acid in water with a glass rod.

Carpet. On a light carpet a quick ink-remover is cream of tartar. Spread on to the stain and add a few drops of lemon juice; rub into the stain with a clean cloth and leave for 1 minute only. Brush off with a clean brush and immediately sponge with a cloth wrung out in warm water. Repeat if necessary, but do not leave lemon juice in contact longer than 1 minute each time.

Fresh ink marks can be removed from a carpet with a paste of fuller's earth and water or with milk. Fresh or sour milk should be applied direct to the stain, left for a few minutes, then absorbed with a clean cloth. Finally rub with warm water to which has been added a few drops of ammonia.

Old stains should be soaked in 1 : 4 solution of hydrogen peroxide with few drops vinegar added (but test first for colour fastness). Leave for 15 to 20 minutes, then rinse with clear water.

Delicate or coloured fabrics can be soaked in sour milk and this may be sufficient. Rinse, then re-launder. If the treatment is not effective, apply a permanganate of potash solution ($\frac{1}{2}$ teaspoonful to 1 pint of water) and rinse in cold water.

If a brown stain results from the potash solution remove this by sponging with a mixture made from 1 small teaspoonful of peroxide, $\frac{1}{2}$ teaspoonful of vinegar and 1 tablespoonful of water. Rinse and dry.

Fabrics. If dealt with quickly enough, synthetic detergent suds will remove ink stains from most materials.

Stubborn stains can be removed from white *cotton and linen* if the area is dipped in cold water, stretched over a board and covered with a layer of household salt. Squeeze lemon juice over the salt, cover and leave for an hour or two, then rinse thoroughly and wash in the ordinary way.

Ink stains on white cotton and linen can also be rubbed with lemon dipped in salt followed by boiling water being poured through the mark. Alternatively, spread the stained part over a basin, sprinkle with oxalic acid and then pour boiling water through.

Where it is not possible to launder a tablecloth immediately, spilt ink can often be completely removed by covering the stain immediately with 1 spoonful of made mustard. Leave for an hour or two, then scrape off surplus mustard and wash in the usual way.

Another method is to cover the ink stain with a paste made from dry mustard and vinegar.

Fingers. The inside of banana skin will remove most ink stains from the fingers and rubbing the ink stain with a moistened match head is also effective. Salt, hydrogen peroxide, soapy pumice stone can all be used to remove ink stains from the hands or there are proprietary cleaners such as Peroxchlor or Bantol.

Paint. Ordinary washing with synthetic detergent suds should remove most ink marks from paintwork. If this is not sufficient, try dipping a damp brush or cloth into dry detergent and rubbing the mark with this and if this too fails, use a small amount of scouring powder. This may remove the high gloss from paintwork and if so, rinse, dry and re-polish with furniture cream.

White wood. To remove ink stains from white wood, dip a used lemon rind in salt and rub the marks with this.

Wood generally. Immediately blot up surplus ink and sponge with ½ pint of warm water containing 1 tablespoonful of vinegar.

See also under Red Ink, Printers' Ink, Copying ink, etc.

Iodine

Ordinary washing in warm soapy water containing ammonia is usually effective in removing fresh iodine stains. Once a stain has dried, sponging with a weak ammonia solution often helps, otherwise photographer's 'hypo' should remove the stain easily. For particulars see page 131 in chapter 'Chemicals and Cleaners'.

Iron mould

The best method is to use a proprietary iron mould remover. But here are some alternative remedies. Cover an iron mould stain with salt, squeeze lemon juice over the salt and leave to stand for an hour.

Another method is to spread the stain over a saucepan of boiling water, kept simmering, then squeeze lemon juice on to the stain, let the water continue boiling for a few minutes, then rinse and repeat. This method takes quite a long time but it is quite safe for delicate white cotton lace and most other white materials.

Rhubarb juice or the water in which rhubarb leaves and trimmings have been cooked will sometimes remove obstinate iron mould stains. Dip linen in the liquid and, if possible, boil for a few minutes and then wash in the ordinary way.

Iron mould stains can also be removed from most fabrics, including nylon, with an oxalic acid solution. For details see page 104 in chapter 'Chemicals and Cleaners'. Test coloured fabrics for colour fastness first on an inside seam and do not use on silk, wool or rayon.

See also under Rust on page 252.

Jam

Immediate washing in warm detergent suds should remove the stain, but if this has dried into the material, and persists after washing, soak in 1 pint of warm water containing 1 oz. of borax. Leave for 30 minutes, then rinse thoroughly and wash in warm soapy water.

Soaking overnight in cold or lukewarm water containing one of the enzyme washing powders will often remove the stain from dark fruit jam. Follow soaking by laundering in a hand-hot solution of the washing agent.

Sponging with warm soapy water containing ammonia should also deal effectively with a jam stain on heavy fabrics. If a fruit stain remains after the jam mark has gone, treat stain as for fruit.

Kittens' urine

See under Urine on page 262.

Lacquers

These dry by evaporation of the solvent so deal with stains as quickly as possible. Remove with cellulose thinners, acetone, amyl acetate or nail varnish remover. These may well dissolve cellulose acetate so test first on all rayons and synthetic fibre fabrics. These solvents will also attack most paints and varnish so avoid using on painted, french-polished or varnished surfaces.

Latex adhesive

Latex adhesive accidentally spilled on fabric or carpets is difficult to remove once it is dry. Wiping the stain with a cloth dipped in cold water is often effective if done immediately. Rubbing the dried adhesive with the finger-tips will usually remove it from the hands and from any smooth surface but not from material. The makers of Copydex use a special solvent at their works and they are quite willing to supply this free to anyone bothered by a Copydex stain. Write to the firm at 1 Torquay Street, London, W.2, and enclose 11d. for post and packing.

Lead pencil

On starched or firm materials an ordinary soft pencil eraser will usually remove the marks. If any stain remains, sponge with soap and water, or launder in hot suds.

Pencil marks which resist erasing, sponging or laundering can be bleached from white materials or treated with permanganate of potash. For details see page 128 in chapter 'Chemicals and Cleaners'.

Lemon juice

This can be an obstinate stain if it is allowed to set. Deal with it immediately if possible by pouring boiling water through the stain followed by washing in the ordinary way. White linen and cotton may need to be bleached to remove the final traces of stain. This can be done with diluted hydrogen peroxide or by hanging the wet articles in strong sunlight to dry.

For heavy materials and non-washable fabrics, sponge with clear

warm water followed, if necessary, by a solution of hydrogen peroxide with a few drops of ammonia added. Rinse thoroughly afterwards with clear, warm water.

Lime (slaked)

Do nothing while the stains are wet but when they are completely
dry, brush gently and squeeze lemon juice on to the marks a drop at
a time until the colour in the lemon disappears, then rinse thoroughly
in warm water.

As an alternative, vinegar can be used to neutralize the alkali;
sponge with clear water afterwards to remove any brown mark left
by the vinegar.

On coloured materials, test first on an inside seam and if the acid
removes the colour try to remove the lime stain by sponging repeatedly with clear warm water rubbed in with a piece of material
similar to the stained fabric.

Linseed oil

Sponge with a grease solvent such as benzol or carbon tetrachloride, then launder in hot synthetic detergent if the fabric is washable.
Acetone will also remove linseed oil stains, but this should not be
used on rayon.

Lipstick

Slight stains on ordinary materials can usually be washed away in
hot synthetic detergent suds. For severe stains, on table napkins for
instance, if the lipstick is indelible sponge with cold water and rub
eucalyptus, Vaseline or glycerine well into the material with the
finger-tips before washing. White fabrics can be bleached with
hydrogen peroxide if washing does not remove the stain.

For lipstick stains on non-washable fabrics, rub eucalyptus, Vaseline or glycerine into the marks, then dab on a few drops of ammonia
and rinse well. When dry, finally sponge with carbon tetrachloride.

Liqueur

Most liqueurs contain a great deal of sugar so soaking in lukewarm water is usually the easiest and best solution. Use an enzyme
washing powder in the water and leave for several hours then wash
in the usual way.

Make-up

Brush first to remove any loose particles of powder, then sponge with a grease solvent such as carbon tetrachloride or proprietary dry-cleaner. If the stained material can be soaked, add 1 teaspoonful of ammonia to 1 pint of warm water and soak the fabric for 10 minutes, then rinse well and wash in hot soapless detergent.

When the neckline, collar or bodice only of a garment is marked, sponge with grease solvent, then hang in the fresh air to dry. If the garment is dark, brush with a clean firm brush but a light frock or blouse may be sprinkled with a powder such as calcined magnesia, french chalk or talcum powder if necessary. Hang again in the fresh air for an hour or so, then shake and brush lightly with a soft brush.

Eye make-up can usually be removed in the same way, sponging eyebrow pencil marks with a grease solvent. If any stain remains, moisten some cotton wool with diluted ammonia and wipe the fabric gently, then rinse in clear warm water. Eye-shadow stains should be well moistened with warm water worked into the material with the finger-tips followed by laundering in hot synthetic detergent suds.

The new types of mascara for lashes—known as lash-builders—and the liquid 'eyeliners' are often difficult to remove from the skin. You can buy special cleaning pads for this purpose.

See also under Lipstick, Rouge, etc.

Marking ink

There are two types of marking ink most commonly used—one has an aniline-black dye as a base and the other silver nitrate. The aniline black is very difficult to remove and is frequently immovable once it has completely dried. Dissolve 1 teaspoonful of oxalic acid crystals in $\frac{1}{4}$ pint of hot water and in another container dissolve $\frac{1}{2}$ teaspoonful of permanganate of potash crystals in 1 pint of water. Brush the potash solution on to the stain, leave for a few seconds, then apply the oxalic acid solution and finally rinse. Repeat until the stain dissolves, then rinse thoroughly.

Oxalic acid must not be used on silk or wool and for these fabrics hydrogen peroxide may be used instead. Use 1 teaspoonful of 20-vol. peroxide and $\frac{1}{2}$ teaspoonful of white vinegar to 4 teaspoonfuls of warm water. Use alternately with the permanganate of potash solution, then rinse thoroughly.

If it is known that the marking ink contains silver nitrate, another method is to moisten the stain with one or two drops of tincture of

iodine, then sponge with a damp cloth and finally remove all traces
of iodine by sponging with a solution made by dissolving $\frac{1}{2}$ teaspoonful sodium thiosulphate ('hypo') in $\frac{1}{2}$ cup of water. Rinse thoroughly
and rub dry. On white cotton or linen, javelle water (see page 125)
may be used but the fabric should then be soaked in an ammonia
solution to remove any silver chloride formed.

Mayonnaise

As a mayonnaise stain will probably contain egg or cream as well
as oil and an acid, hot water must not be used first or the protein in
the egg will set and make the stain difficult to remove.

Sponge a mild stain with warm water and then launder in hot
synthetic detergent suds. A severe stain should be moistened with
cool water and sprinkled with bicarbonate of soda; when the soda
has finished effervescing rinse thoroughly and allow to dry. Finally
launder as above or for unwashable fabrics remove the olive-oil
stains with a grease solvent such as carbon tetrachloride or dry-
cleaning fluid.

An alternative way of dealing with a mayonnaise stain on washable
fabrics—other than wool or silk—is to soak the fabric for several
hours in lukewarm water containing one of the proprietary enzyme
washing powders. Leave overnight if possible then wash in a fresh
solution of the washing powder in hand-hot water.

Meat juice

Wash immediately in cool, soapless detergent for a slight mark
or soak in cold water for a large stain, then rinse thoroughly and
wash in the normal way. Heat will set the protein in the meat juice
so do not attempt to wash garment in hot water until the stain has
been treated first with cool or warm water. See also Blood, page 217.

Metallic stain

Apply a few drops of lemon juice or vinegar with a medicine
dropper or glass rod and rub lightly until the stain dissolves. Rinse
thoroughly, launder if possible and dry. Avoid bleaches of any kind
with this type of stain. Remove rusty marks with a proprietary rust
remover.

Metal Polish

Much depends on the product of course but most metal polishes
contain rottenstone, Tripoli powder and abrasives. Usually white

spirit is necessary to remove the oily residue, then allow the stain to dry and brush out the remaining powder with a clean, stiff nylon brush and finally launder or send for dry-cleaning.

Mildew

This should not stain except on leather or fabric and then this is a water stain—the moisture merely carrying the mildew. Launder washable fabrics and bleach where possible. Direct sunlight will also reduce marks. The following details may also help:

Materials. Ordinary laundering should remove mildew stains while they are still fresh enough for the growth to be on the surface of the fabric. Soaking in sour milk and leaving in the sun to dry is often effective as this treatment can be repeated several times. Moistening with lemon juice and salt or rubbing with yellow washing soap or mild toilet soap and then drying in the sun may also often remove mildew stains.

Old mildew stains are very difficult to remove but permanganate of potash is often effective. For details see page 128 in chapter 'Chemicals and Cleaners'.

Obstinate mildew stains can sometimes be removed from white cottons and linens with diluted household bleach or with javelle water, see page 125 in chapter 'Chemicals and Cleaners'. Finish by laundering in the usual way.

Floors. On floors and walls a weak solution of permanganate of potash is often effective ($\frac{1}{4}$ teaspoonful to 1 pint—see page 128 for details). Sponge on to the stain, repeat with diluted peroxide, rinse and dry. Finally rub with a cloth dipped in lavender polish.

Leather. A pine disinfectant oil will often remove mildew from leather. Use 1 teaspoonful to 1 pint of warm water and rub well into the stain, working from the back of the leather if possible. Rub dry and leave in the sunlight or fresh air to dry thoroughly.

Another method which is often successful when the mildew is slight is to rub the leather with Vaseline, working it well into the skin. Leave for short time, then polish gently with a soft chamois leather.

Yet another method of removing mildew from leather is to sprinkle the stain with common salt and rub this well into the leather with an old towel or face cloth; leave for a short while, then brush off the salt and repeat until the stain disappears. Rub in leather polish and leave overnight, polishing next morning.

See also under Fungus on page 229.

Milk

For washable materials rinse thoroughly in cool water, then launder in the usual way. If the stain persists, sprinkle with borax and soapflakes, pour on hot (not boiling) water and rub with finger-tips. Leave for 5 minutes, then rinse thoroughly and launder. Repeat if necessary.

For non-washable fabrics sponge with cool water, and if a grease stain is left when fabric is dry, remove by rubbing lightly with a cloth dipped in a grease solvent such as carbon tetrachloride or, providing the material is not a rayon, with acetone.

For milk spilt on a *carpet*, quickly blot up as much liquid as possible, then wipe with a cloth wrung out in clean water. Allow to dry, then work a solution of mild detergent drop by drop into the mark, or apply the foam only with a nail brush. Leave for 15 min-utes, then sponge off and rub dry, smoothing pile in the right direction. If any stain remains when carpet is dry, wipe with a clean cloth dipped in dry-cleaning fluid.

Modelling clay

Scrape off or brush off as much of the clay as possible and then remove stains with carbon tetrachloride over an absorbent pad. For very small marks, lighter fuel will also remove the stains. Finally launder in the usual way.

Mould

See under Fungus on page 229.

Mud

Do not attempt to remove the stain while the mud is wet. Allow to dry thoroughly, then brush off gently with a stiff brush. Any greasy mark remaining can be removed by sponging with a detergent solution rinsed off with a clean damp cloth. For washable fabrics, launder in detergent suds in the usual way. If a mark is left by the dried mud and this is not greasy, sponge with plain warm water.

On a heavy coat, brush off dried mud with a clean brush, then sponge lightly with a dry-cleaning fluid.

Another method of removing mud stains is very effective but it can be used on black materials only and then only on black silk or a black suit with a smooth, firm weave. Allow the mud to dry, then brush well with a clean firm brush and finally rub on and around the stains with a raw potato cut in half. Allow to dry and then remove the remaining film of starch with a clean, dry brush.

For mud stains on shoes see page 201.

Mustard

For a new moist stain, wash the material in warm soapy water and rinse well. An old mustard stain can be rubbed with warm glycerine and left to stand overnight. Next day launder in the usual way.

Nail varnish

First mop up excess. Then sponge stain with acetone or nail-varnish remover.

When treating viscose rayons or synthetic fabrics test acetone or nail-varnish remover first on an inside seam but if the fabric is an acetate or triacetate do not in any circumstances use these chemicals. If there is any doubt about the nature of the material or the colour fastness of the fabric, sponge with amyl acetate instead. If the acetone does not remove all the varnish colour, wash in a warm detergent or dab with a clean cloth moistened with methylated spirit. (Again, test first for rayons.)

If the nail-lacquer stains have dried, dampen first with a little carbon tetrachloride to soften them, then drop amyl acetate on to the marks and wipe off with a soft cloth. If it is certain that the fabric is not an acetate, then acetone or nail-varnish remover containing acetone may be used and so may cellulose thinners.

See also under Cellulose lacquers on page 220.

Newsprint

Stains resulting from newsprint from newspapers rubbing off on to fabrics can usually be removed fairly easily with white spirit.

Nicotine

Launder in the ordinary way or sponge with methylated spirit. If the stain is on a rayon fabric, test in an inconspicuous place before applying the methylated spirit.

Nicotine on fingers may be removed with cut lemon, or with scouring powder which incorporates a bleach. This is drastic treatment for drastic discoloration, so use plenty of hand cream afterwards.

Nitro-cellulose varnish

Deal with these stains as given under Cellulose lacquers on page 220.

Oil

See under Grease and Oil on page 231.

Orange juice

Dissolve 1 oz. of borax in 1 pint of warm water and sponge the stain with the solution. If the orange juice is concentrated or the stain is severe, immerse the marked area in the borax solution. Rinse thoroughly, then launder in synthetic detergent suds.

Paint

Decide first if paint spilt is water-borne or solvent-borne. Water-borne paints include emulsions and distempers and details of removing these will be found on page 265.

Solvent-borne paints include oil paints, primers, undercoats, resin paints, enamels, varnishes and paints containing polyurethane. Damping and rubbing won't do anything to remove these paints. It is important first to break down the binder in the paint.

For oil paints use a cellulose thinner to break down the binder or a product such as Brushing Belco or amyl acetate which is similar. For varnishes and enamels use white spirit or turpentine or a dry-cleaning fluid such as trichloroethylene, perchloroethylene, carbon tetrachloride or a proprietary dry-cleaning fluid. Whichever solvent you use, try to apply it quickly before the paint dries and sets. Rinse out as much of the paint as possible with white spirit or turpentine or turps substitute first, then continue with one of the other solvents suggested and keep on until the stain moves, then finish by laundering with soap and water.

Bear in mind that trichloroethylene must not be used on triacetate fabrics—such as Tricel—and that if the stain is small, the solvent should be tested first on an unconspicuous part of the garment. Nylon and PVC are easily stained by strong blue and red pigments and will need much more effort to remove the stains.

If paint stains are stubborn or have been allowed to dry then the paint should be softened first. Do this with cellulose thinners, a proprietary product such as Brushing Belco or amyl acetate. Do not use amyl acetate on expanded polystyrene. Once the paint has softened, remove as much of it as possible with a suitable solvent then clean with soap and water or send for dry-cleaning if unwashable.

Try to deal with paint stains the moment they happen. Wipe off surplus paint, then sponge *oil paint* stains with turpentine, turpentine substitute or benzol, applying solvent to both sides of stain.

Old paint stains can sometimes be removed if they are first softened by thoroughly rubbing with lard, butter, glycerine or an oil followed by washing in hot soapy water. A stale but not too old paint stain will often react to sponging with diluted ammonia followed by a sprinkling of turpentine. Roll up the garment for anything from half an hour to 2 hours, then wash in warm soapy water and rinse well. If necessary, wash again in hot synthetic detergent suds. Hardened stains can be removed from clothing by saturating the marked areas with a solution made from equal quantities of ammonia and turpentine.

Another treatment (but not for delicate materials) is to dissolve 3 tablespoonfuls of washing soda in 1 gal. of water and boil the stained material in this. For painters' overalls or other badly stained cotton or linen, cover with a thick layer of hard household soap. Leave overnight and next morning scrub in hot synthetic detergent suds.

Paint spilt on a *carpet* usually presents additional problems as even if the stain is removed it almost always leaves a large clean patch so that the area around must be cleaned also and quite often the entire carpet. Much the same applies to upholstery.

If a large amount of paint is spilt and particularly if it has not been cleaned up immediately, then it is best to send the carpet for professional cleaning.

Deal with a paint stain on a *carpet* immediately before it has time to dry and set. Use a brush rather than your fingers for applying a solvent. Isolate the patch stained over a tin, plate or bowl if possible, then pour the solvent through into the receptacle beneath. Make a dent in the carpet or fabric and then pour the solvent into the dent, working it into the pile with a brush or your finger-tips if no brush is available. Continue until most of stain is removed then finish with detergent suds, rinse and rub dry with a clean towel.

If paint has dried really hard into a carpet, a solvent type of paint remover should soften it. Work the solution into the paint stain with brush or finger-tips and once it has softened, treat as stated.

If paint is spilt on *linoleum*, as much as possible should be scooped up immediately—the quickest way is with a handy paint brush—and any residue mopped up with newspaper or rag. Immediately rub over the floor with a cloth dipped in paraffin or in turpentine and there should be no trace left. The paint collected from the *floor* can be strained and used.

Solid wood floors should be covered up whilst decorating to avoid the risks of accidents. Use newspaper and adhesive tape. On *waxed floors*, odd, dry splashes of paint shouldn't adhere and a flat knife will scrape them off easily.

On a *stone, quarry tile* or *brick floor*—and this means real bricks, of course—paint can be removed fairly easily especially if it is dealt with immediately. Remove the paint quickly with plenty of solvent and then rinse off thoroughly to prevent pigment seeping through. If the paint has set, allow it to dry out thoroughly and then scrape it off with a knife and then use a weak solvent solution.

Paint spilt on *thermoplastic flooring*, including vinyl can be difficult especially with oil paints. Wipe up the spills immediately as some types of flooring can be softened by the solvent in the paint. For this reason it is not easy to choose a solvent to deal with the stain. White spirit is usually the safest on most types of flooring but even this will affect some bitumen-backed tiles. These are sensitive to paint, white spirit, in fact almost any solvent. For these tiles, remove surplus paint quickly and wash. Only if necessary use solvent and then dilute it so that it is as weak as possible. Apply it only to the actual paint stain and then remove quickly with a damp cloth. Repeat until paint has faded then wash with detergent, rinse and dry.

When a whole tin of paint is spilt on a *stone* or *wood floor* quickly pick up as much paint as possible with a brush, spatula, spoon or newspaper. Then throw dry sand or garden earth on to the stain and scrub hard with a stiff yard broom or carpet brush. On a stone floor rub in all directions; on a wooden floor brush the way of the grain only. Sweep up the earth or sand and the stains should have gone; if any remain wash with hot soda water. The paint removed first can be strained through an old nylon stocking and used in the ordinary way.

Paint spilt on a *floor* and which has become dry and hard will need softening. Do this as above or mix 2 parts ammonia to 1 part turpentine or paraffin and rub on to the marks. Next rub with a cloth dipped in turpentine or paraffin or if necessary rub lightly with steel wool or a wire brush moistened with the turpentine. Strong soda water may also remove a dried stain, especially on a stone floor.

If paint is spilt on expanded polystyrene—such as tiles or Kotina for walls there is little that can be done. Most solvents which will dissolve paint will also dissolve the polystyrene and for this reason too, it cannot be painted. The easiest way out of the problem is to cover the splashes with emulsion paint which is water-borne and does not therefore contain the damaging solvents.

Old paint splashes on *windows* and hard floors can be removed by rubbing with a cloth dipped in hot vinegar, or they can be eased off without scratching the surface with a razor blade. Choose a blade with one rigid side or use a razor blade holder.

For details of removing cellulose lacquer see page 220; emulsion paint see page 226; enamel paint see page 227; varnish stains see page 263. Water borne paints, see page 265.

Paraffin

Light washable materials can be treated by immersing immediately in hot detergent suds, rinsing and rewashing. It may be necessary to repeat the treatment several times for severe staining.

Another method is to sandwich the stain between blotting or thick brown paper and press with a warm iron, changing the position of the absorbent paper repeatedly. Sponge any remaining stain with benzol, petrol or carbon tetrachloride.

Paraffin spilt on a *carpet* should be mopped up immediately with clean rag or newspaper and the area should then be shampooed with carpet shampoo or a hot detergent solution. Rinse thoroughly, unless using a no-rinse shampoo, and dry. The treatment may need to be repeated several times and the underfelt may need treating also. In each case dry the carpet as quickly as possible after rinsing. For severe staining, professional cleaning will be necessary.

Peach juice

This stain is very easy to remove with boiling or warm water while it is still fresh and moist but it is often extremely difficult to remove once it has dried. If possible, stretch the material over a basin immediately and pour boiling water on the stain from a height. For a bad stain sprinkle borax on to the mark before pouring on the water. Rinse thoroughly, then launder. For a heavy fabric, sponge with warm water or borax solution, then rinse and dry.

A peach stain would be set by some washing products, so avoid soap until most of the acid in the juice has been neutralized or washed out.

Pear juice

As with peach juice, this is one of the most difficult stains to remove once it has dried. While it is still fresh and moist, treat with boiling water and borax as for a peach stain but once the stain has dried into the material a different method is necessary. Sponge with cold water, then rub glycerine into the mark, leave for a time and then launder.

Perfume

Immediate washing should remove a fresh moist perfume stain from fabric but if it has dried into the material, rub glycerine well into the mark and then wash. On a non-washable fabric, rub in the glycerine thoroughly, leave for a short time, then sponge lightly with a cloth wrung out in clear warm water.

Stains caused by a wet perfume bottle on french polished furniture can sometimes be removed with methylated spirit, using the method given on page 233.

Silver polish may remove perfume stains from lacquered or cellulose furniture. Put a few drops on a piece of cotton wool and rub well over and around the stain. Finish by polishing in the usual way. If this is not sufficient, the methylated spirit method may be tried but use no more than 2 drops, or you may ruin the surface.

If the marks are obstinate or remain after treatment, rub surface with a stain remover such as Teal's Scratch Cover Polish.

Perspiration

Until the advent of enzyme soaking and washing agents, this was difficult to remove as perspiration stains often affect colour. This can sometimes be revived by sponging the garment with weak vinegar or ammonia before laundering. Test fabric before soaking rayon or if colours may not be fast. Do not soak wool or silk. Follow instructions for soaking in biological washing powder.

If the perspiration leaves a stain on white fabrics, soak in cool enzyme detergent or bleach with a solution of hydrogen peroxide, rinse and dry out of doors.

Heavy unwashable garments—other than rayon—may be sponged lightly with methylated spirit to remove a perspiration stain. Rub gently with a clean dry cloth until the spirit has dried. Alternatively, sponge with well-diluted vinegar.

To remove perspiration odour, soak the soiled parts in 1 pint of warm water containing 1 teaspoonful of borax, then wash in warm soapy water containing a few drops of ammonia. Rinse thoroughly. Alternatively, try washing the usual way in hand-hot suds then rinse well in warm water containing a little vinegar. Finally, rinse in clear water and dry out of doors.

Plasticine

Treat as for Modelling clay on page 243.

Plastics starch

If too much plastics stiffener is used during laundering, this cannot be washed out although it will wear out in time. To remove plastics starch soak the article in methylated spirit—test rayons first as some are damaged by this solvent. For slight over-starching, soaking in the spirit will be sufficient but in most cases it will be necessary to rub the fabric between the finger-tips during soaking so that the methylated spirit can penetrate the surface of the material and so dissolve the starch. When the starch is removed, rinse very thoroughly and if possible re-launder.

Port

Treat as for Wine on page 266.

Potassium permanganate

To remove a permanganate of potash stain from fine materials, dilute 1 spoonful of hydrogen peroxide in 5 spoonfuls of water and add a few drops of vinegar. Sponge with this until the stain disappears, then rinse thoroughly and launder.

On materials other than light fabrics oxalic acid will almost always remove the stain. Dissolve 1 teaspoonful of oxalic acid crystals in $\frac{1}{2}$ pint of water and apply to the stain. Repeat if necessary until the stain disappears, then rinse very thoroughly.

Printing ink

Cheap printing ink is light-sensitive so that a mild peroxide of hydrogen solution or hanging in direct sunshine should be sufficient following by laundering. For expensive printing ink stains which are likely to be more durable, treat black stains as for solvent-borne paint, page 245. Red printing ink is more difficult as it is a more penetrating dye. Wipe off surplus then treat stain with white spirit taking care not to spread the stain. On white fabrics try bleaching with peroxide of hydrogen.

Puppies' urine

See under Urine on page 262.

Rain spots

A hat, velvet collar or similar fabric marked with rain spots can usually be cleaned by steaming. With any fabric other than velvet, move the stained area about close to the spout of a fast-boiling kettle, brushing gently with a clean, soft brush, then leave to dry. With velvet, hang the garment over a steaming bath or in gentle steam for 20 to 30 minutes. On a coat, any mud patches should be removed before the rain spots are treated.

Red ink

On table linen, freshly made mustard spread thickly over the mark and left for half an hour should remove the stain. Sponge off and wash article.

Old red ink stains may need sponging with a fairly strong solution of borax or methylated spirit with a little vinegar added, to remove the marks.

For a really obstinate red ink stain, sponge with a solution made from adding 1 teaspoonful of oxalic acid to 2 pints of warm water. Leave for 1 minute, then rinse very thoroughly.

On carpets, red ink will usually disappear if the mark is sponged with clear water and pressed with blotting paper but the treatment may have to be repeated several times.

Another method of removing red ink from a carpet is to blot up excess ink with clean blotting paper, then sponge lightly with methylated spirit. Allow to dry, then if any stain remains, sponge lightly with a mixture of methylated spirit and vinegar, followed by sponging with detergent solution. Wipe with a clean damp cloth and allow to dry as quickly as possible.

If red ink is spilt in bulk on paintwork then it will be impossible to remove and the only solution is repainting. On small areas, it should be possible to deal with the stains by rubbing with a damp cloth or brush dipped in scouring powder. Rinse, dry and re-polish if this removes the gloss surface.

Resins

Sponge with a solvent such as benzol, carbon tetrachloride, turpentine or turpentine substitute, methylated spirit, ether or petrol until the resinous substance dissolves. Place a thick absorbent pad under the stain and sponge the wrong side of the material so that the mark is pushed out of the fabric.

Rhubarb

It should be possible to remove rhubarb stains fairly easily from washable fabrics, using an enzyme detergent. To deal with a rhubarb stain on a floor, try a strong detergent solution first. This may not be successful on some surfaces such as terrazzo or tiles. In this case, try a mild bleach solution, testing for colour reaction first in an out of sight corner. If the bleach is harmless to the surface but has little effect on the stain, increase the strength of the bleach and sponge stains repeatedly with solution.

Rouge

Sponge lightly with carbon tetrachloride and then with methylated spirit. Washable items can be laundered in fairly hot water containing a synthetic detergent.

Rust

Weak phosphoric acid solutions will remove many rust and iron mould stains. These are sold at hardware shops as de-rusting solutions under proprietary names. They can be used on wood, and on baths and washbasins to remove brown rust stains under taps. The following alternative suggestions may also help.

Bath. Remove rust marks on a bath or wash basin by rubbing hard with a cloth dipped in neat vinegar. Or use proprietary bath stain remover.

Carpets. Castors and silent domes often leave rust marks on a carpet especially if water has been splashed during cleaning. The quickest method of removing the stain is to add 1 teaspoonful of salts of lemon to 1 pint of warm water and sponge the stains with this. Leave for 2 minutes, then rinse off and dry. Repeat if necessary but rinse quickly each time. Alternatively, use a proprietary rust stain remover.

Concrete. Slabs and cement can become rust-stained by gates and metal posts. Remove marks with a chemical cleaner or rust-remover available from hardware stores.

Fabric. Add 1 teaspoonful of oxalic acid to 1 pint of hot water and sponge rust stains with this. After a minute or two rinse thoroughly in clear water and, if necessary, launder in the usual way. Or use a proprietary rust stain remover.

Metal. Soak with paraffin, leave for 3 or 4 hours or overnight, then rub with fine steel wool or emery cloth. For chromium plate use a special chrome cleaner applied on fine steel wool if the rusting is severe. If other metals are severely rusted, special rust-removing fluids can be bought.

Oxidized metals should be rubbed well with a cloth dipped in olive or almond oil. Leave overnight, then rub off and polish.

Kitchen utensils frequently collect a light film of rust from remaining in a steamy atmosphere. This can be removed quickly and easily by rubbing the metal lightly with a hard typing rubber, or with fine steel wool. Coating kitchen utensils with a light film of olive or other oil helps to prevent rust from forming.

Salad dressing

Stains from salad dressing can be treated in a similar way as those from mayonnaise, see page 241.

Sauces

Much will depend upon the ingredients in the sauce, of course, but most stains should respond to overnight soaking in cold water containing an enzyme pre-soak or washing powder. Do not soak wool or silk or colours which may not be fast.

Scorch marks

Materials. A light scorch mark can be removed from most fabrics if the marked area is soaked in cold milk immediately.

If the fibres of the material are completely burnt little can be done, but for light scorching a gentle brushing followed by sponging or washing in warm soapy water and borax often helps. Rinse thoroughly to remove all traces of borax afterwards.

On unwashable materials, repeated sponging with hot borax solution is usually effective. Dissolve 2 teaspoonfuls of borax in a pint of hot water. Wring out a cloth in the solution and rub the scorched area well with the damp cloth. Repeat several times, then sponge with a cloth wrung out in clear water and press under a cloth.

A borax paste will sometimes remove fairly severe scorch marks as long as the fibres are not badly damaged. Make a paste with borax and glycerine and spread thickly over the mark. Leave overnight, then rinse thoroughly and wash in the ordinary way. Stains remaining on white materials should be carefully bleached with a peroxide solution.

A very good way of removing light scorch marks from *white material* is to damp a clean white cloth with hydrogen peroxide and place this over the stained area. Cover the cloth with a clean dry cloth (to protect the iron, or stains might result) and press slightly with a warm iron. If the hydrogen peroxide soaks through the protecting cloth immediately replace it with another clean dry cloth.

Another way to remove scorch marks from *white fabrics* is to moisten the fabric with lemon juice and leave in strong sunlight to dry. Moisten repeatedly and as the sun dries the material it will bleach the stain.

A new scorch mark on *linen* will often come out if it is rubbed with a freshly cut onion and then soaked in cold water.

Carpets. Very light scorch marks can be lightly damped, rubbed with powdered borax and left to dry. Brush off the powder and sponge gently with a damp soapy cloth and then with one wrung out in clear water. If the scorch marks have damaged the fibres of the carpet, this can sometimes be disguised by hard brushing to remove the singed pile followed by gentle circular rubbing with fine sandpaper or a wire suède brush. A carpet firm may be able to retuft the damaged portion.

A solution which can be made up and kept ready to deal with scorch marks is effective on linens, carpets, upholstery and most fabrics. To make it, peel and slice a small onion in a pan, add 1 oz. of soda, 1 oz. of fuller's earth and ¼ pint of vinegar. Bring slowly to the boil and simmer for 10 to 15 minutes, then strain and bottle and cap tightly. Spread liquid over scorch marks and leave to dry. When quite dry, brush off with a clean brush and repeat if any stain remains.

Plates. Dip a large bottle cork in water and then in coarse salt and rub hard on the scorched places.

Sealing wax

Scrape off the surplus wax, sandwich article between clean blotting paper and press with a warm iron. Finally sponge with methylated spirit, rinse and launder. If the wax stain is on rayon, test the material first. On unwashable fabrics, sponge with methylated spirit and quickly rub dry with a clean cloth. Again test rayons first.

Sea water

Fabrics. Brush well to remove loose salt, then sponge repeatedly with warm water or soak garment in warm water until all the salt has been dissolved. Finally launder in the usual way. Old sea-water stains are difficult to remove and may need repeated treatments or even professional dry-cleaning.

Shoes. Dissolve ½ oz. of soda in 4 tablespoonfuls of hot milk and apply to the leather with a sponge or cloth. Let the solution dry thoroughly into the leather, then polish.

Another method suitable only on black or brown shoes is to add 2 teaspoonfuls of methylated spirit to 1 dessertspoonful of milk. Moisten a rag with this mixture and wipe over shoes. Leave to dry and then repolish.

Seaweed

Treat generally in the same way as grass stains by rubbing immediately with cotton wool dipped in methylated spirit. If the stain persists on white fabric, bleach with 1 part of 20 volume peroxide to 3 parts water plus a few drops of ammonia. Leave to soak for half an hour, then launder in warm suds.

Shellac

Deal with shellac stains as given under Spirit varnish on page 258.

Sherry

Treat as for Wine on page 266.

Ship's oil (black oil found on beaches)

Sponging with eucalyptus oil should prove the most effective method. Alternatives are carbon tetrachloride and paraffin.

Shoe polish

This is usually made from pigmented paraffin wax so the treatment would be to wipe the mark first with white spirit or naphtha to remove the wax and then launder to remove pigments. On carpets, sponge with white spirit to remove the worst of the mark then mix up rich suds with detergent and work foam into stain, rinse and dry. White spirit is unlikely to affect the colour but test first if doubtful.

For a slight mark, wash in water and synthetic detergent plus a little ammonia, or sponge with methylated spirit, unless on rayon. A more severe stain should be rubbed with Vaseline, then sponged with turpentine substitute, benzol or carbon tetrachloride. Next wash cotton or linen in synthetic detergent suds, and sponge other fabrics with methylated spirit and rinse in clear water. On rayon materials rinse with a clean rag dipped in turpentine or carbon tetrachloride and then in clear water.

White shoe dressings can usually be removed quite easily by sponging thoroughly with warm water and allowing to dry. When the stain is quite dry, brush with a clean firm brush in the direction of the weave, or rub the material—still in the direction of the weave—with another piece of material of similar texture.

On paintwork or light furniture, shoe polish marks can usually be rubbed off with a light furniture cream. Use fine steel wool dipped in liquid wax polish or turpentine for stubborn stains on woodwork. Rub the way of the grain.

Silver nitrate

Caustic pencils used to remove warts cause these stains. Although the pencils look white they turn warts black and can cause a difficult black stain on fabrics. These are not easy to remove and require two or three stages and possibly several separate treatments. It is important to change the silver nitrate into silver iodide first as this can then be more easily removed. Do this by sponging the stain with a solution of tincture of iodine or with a 10 per cent solution of potassium or sodium iodide. Use boiled water for the solution and then leave this on the stain for at least 8 to 10 hours.

The next step is to make a solution with ammonia in three parts of boiled water or a 10 per cent photographic fixing hypo solution in water. Finally rinse then launder in the usual way.

Sodium chlorate

This is a weedkiller used to remove weeds from crazy paving and garden paths. It should not stain clothes badly but it does make them very flammable and it is therefore important to remove spots as soon as possible. Soak clothes in cold or lukewarm water, rinse thoroughly and launder in the usual way.

Soft drinks

Soft-drink stains will usually wash out during laundering but where the fabric is heavy or unwashable, absorb excess moisture, then sponge with clear warm water and dry.

On a carpet blot up excess liquid immediately, then sponge with a damp cloth wrung out in clear warm water. Allow to dry and if any stain remains sponge lightly with a mild detergent solution, rinse with a clean damp cloth and dry quickly.

If the stain has dried into the carpet, whisk some mild detergent suds and a little glycerine in some warm water. Splash the suds a drop at a time on to the stain, work in, then leave for 5 minutes, then rinse and dry firmly. Try to avoid saturating the carpet or soaking through to the backing.

Soot

This is very fine carbon black and it is one of the finest pigments available. It is important to brush, blow or suction off the soot with a vacuum cleaner as soon as possible. Once it has been trodden into a floor or carpet, it is very difficult to remove and professional all-over cleaning will almost certainly be required. After suctioning off surplus soot, wash out thoroughly if possible to irrigate the pigment then wash in normal way with detergent suds, rinse and dry. Try to avoid saturating backing of carpet. The following may also help.

Carpet. For a small mark, remove surplus soot with a vacuum cleaner or by shaking. Moisten a clean cloth with carbon tetrachloride and rub lightly, turning the cloth as it becomes soiled. For a larger area, vacuum clean or sweep off surplus soot, make a rich lather with a strong synthetic detergent and fairly hot water and scrub lightly with a small brush, using the lather only. Rinse by dabbing with a clean damp cloth and rub dry. Or use an electric or push-along shampoo applicator.

If you wish to avoid dampening the carpet, sprinkle an absorbent powder thickly on and around the soot working it into the mark until the powder becomes dirty, then brush off lightly and apply fresh powder. For this purpose, french chalk, fuller's earth, starch or talcum powder can be used. Do not try using salt. It does, in fact, absorb well but it is apt to leave traces behind and these later absorb damp and leave a dark patch on the carpet in wet weather.

It is also possible to combine two or three of these methods. Remove surplus soot first, then apply powder, brush off and sponge with solvent and if necessary wash with detergent.

Fabric. Sponge with carbon tetrachloride or other grease solvent or immerse in hot synthetic detergent suds and rub lightly.

I

Wallpaper. If soot is smeared on *wallpaper* do not brush but suck off soot with a vacuum cleaner or blow it off with bellows or a bicycle pump. Then brush lightly with a soft brush. If a mark remains, follow method on page 231 for removing grease marks from walls. Or try using an ordinary pencil rubber.

Soup

Wash article immediately in warm suds, rinse thoroughly and hang to dry. If immediate washing is not possible, place a towel underneath the stain and sponge with clear warm water and pat dry. See also under Cream soups.

Spirit varnish

Stains from the shellac type varnish can be removed with methylated spirit. Swamp area with spirit and rub with finger-tips or brush over a cup or basin. Finish by washing with liquid detergent and warm water. Send unwashable articles for dry-cleaning as soon as possible.

Squash

See under Soft drinks on page 256.

Starch

Damp starch stains on the soleplate of an *iron* can be removed by rubbing the iron with a damp cloth while it is still warm after each use. If the stains are long standing or severe use a silver plate polish and rub fairly hard.

Sun tan oil

Remove by sponging the material with carbon tetrachloride or other grease solvent over a thick absorbent pad. If the sun tan oil has left a colour stain, next soak the garment in warm water and borax and finally wash in hot detergent suds and rinse well. Bleach only if fabric is suitable.

Sweets

Stains caused by sticky sweets, toffees, bon-bons, etc. can be removed from most materials by ordinary laundering in warm soapless detergent suds or soap powder. For heavy materials sponge with clear warm water and blot dry.

Syrup

Where possible treat immediately by soaking stained fabric in hot detergent suds while the syrup is still moist. Rub well, then rinse thoroughly and dry. If the syrup has dried into the fabric soak in a warm borax solution for 15 minutes, then rinse thoroughly and launder.

Tannin

Remove tannin stains from china or glass with a damp cloth dipped in bicarbonate of soda; rinse thoroughly and wash normally.

Tannin stains on table-ware made from melamine may respond to the above method, or toothpaste rubbed on may be effective. Better still, buy the special safe bleaching powder recommended by the manufacturers. Never use harsh scouring powders.

Tar

Immediately scrape off excess tar and as quickly as possible rub the mark with a cloth moistened with carbon tetrachloride, benzol, turpentine or eucalyptus oil—preferably the latter. If the fabric is not too delicate it is more satisfactory to immerse the stained area in the solvent and rub gently. When the mark has dissolved rinse in warm water and if the fabric permits, wash in hot detergent suds. If a brown sulphur stain remains, sponge with a solution of oleic acid and carbon disulphide. A chemist will mix this in the proportions 75 per cent oleic acid to 25 per cent carbon disulphide. Rinse thoroughly afterwards.

For old dried stains a fairly satisfactory method is to rub warm lard or oil thoroughly into the stains, leave for a short time and then sponge with eucalyptus oil or turpentine and finally wash in hot synthetic detergent suds. Repeat if necessary, softening more tar each time with oil before washing.

It is also possible to buy proprietary tar-removing liquids which are quick and efficient and tar-removing creams for use on the beach. These are made by sun-tan product firms such as Ambre Solaire. Butter will also remove tar from skin and from clothes and it has the advantage of not spreading the stain. Garments must be well laundered afterwards of course to remove grease.

If tar is trodden into a carpet, scrape off excess with a blunt knife, then use one of the above remedies with discretion. If the tar has dried into the carpet soften it first by rubbing with warm olive oil and when the tar is thoroughly soft wash as above. Rinse with a cloth wrung out in clear water and pat dry with a clean towel. Remove any residue of oil with a grease solvent. Shampoo whole area if necessary.

Tea

A quick way of dealing with a tea stain on *linen* or *cotton* the moment it happens is to pour boiling water through the stain from a height. Follow by ordinary washing and boiling or bleaching if necessary.

For an old obstinate stain on white cotton or linen, you can use proprietary bleaches, but natural bleaching is often quite successful. Moisten with lemon juice, then hang fabric in strong sunlight to dry and repeat for 2 or 3 days or until the stain has disappeared.

Another bleach suitable for white fabric is potassium permanganate and again this sometimes succeeds where other methods fail. For details see page 128 in 'Chemicals and cleaners'. Rinse thoroughly and launder in the usual way.

Tea stains on *coloured fabrics* should be sponged with 1 pint of warm water containing 1 oz. of borax. Rub the stain hard, then rinse thoroughly and wash in warm suds.

Very often, obstinate tea stains on coloured fabrics will respond to overnight soaking in cold or lukewarm water containing a biological washing powder with enzymes. Next day launder in fresh hand-hot suds. Repeat the process if necessary.

If tea is spilt on a *blanket*, the stains should be removed immediately; steep the area of blanket marked in warm water and this should remove the stain almost at once. If the stain has dried into the blanket, steep the soiled area in a warm solution of hydrogen peroxide. Use 1 part of 10-volume peroxide to 5 parts of warm water. When the stain is out wash the entire blanket if necessary. Otherwise rinse well and pat dry with towels.

Wash *silk or rayon fabrics* in warm soapy water if the stain is fresh and bleach with hydrogen peroxide (1 part to 6 parts water) if necessary. For old tea stains wet, then rub with glycerine and leave overnight. Next day stretch fabric over a bowl, sprinkle powdered borax over the area and pour warm water through the stain once or twice. Soak the stained patch in the borax solution, rub with the finger-tips, rinse and wash in the ordinary way.

If tea is spilt on a *carpet*, blot as much of the liquid up as possible immediately. Next sponge lightly with a clean cloth wrung out in clear warm water and allow to dry. For tea straight from the pot this should be sufficient. If the tea contained milk, it may be necessary to remove any grease with a mild detergent solution dripped on to the stain with a medicine dropper. Sponge off with a clean damp cloth and dry as quickly as possible.

To remove stains from *plastics teacups*, see under Tannin stains, page 259. Tea should be emptied out of plastics teacups immediately after use to avoid staining.

Tea stains on *china cups* can be removed by rubbing the marks with a damp cloth or cork dipped in coarse salt or bicarbonate of soda.

Tobacco

Ordinary washing in warm detergent suds may remove slight stains, otherwise sponge with methylated spirit unless the fabric is rayon when it should first be tested in an inconspicuous place.

A brown stain from a tobacco pipe may be sponged with a solvent such as methylated spirit or carbon tetrachloride, then rinsed and allowed to dry. Any remaining stain may be moistened with lemon juice and left to dry in the sun.

Very old or severe stains may need a solution of permanganate of potash. For details see page 128 in 'Chemicals and cleaners'. Rinse thoroughly and launder in the usual way.

Tomato

Soak stained material in 1 pint of water containing 1 teaspoonful of borax. Rinse well, then wash in the ordinary way.

Tomato vine

The green stains from a tomato vine may be sponged with methylated spirit, then washed or laundered in the usual way, or moistened with lemon juice and left to dry in the sun for several days. Remaining brown stains may be bleached with a powder bleach or with permanganate of potash crystals (1 teaspoonful to pint).

Transfers

Providing the material is not made of rayon, sponge the transfer stain with a clean cloth dipped in methylated spirit, then wash in the usual way. On rayons test first on an inside hem. With white linen or cotton, transfer marks can usually be removed by ordinary washing, by boiling, or with a weak solution of bleach followed by ordinary laundering.

Urine

In the ordinary way normal human urine is acid and so is that of domestic pets; the urine of herbivorous animals is mostly alkali. If this were invariable, acid urine could be neutralized by sponging with an ammonia or soda bicarbonate solution and alkaline urine stains could be removed by sponging with a mild acid such as vinegar, lemon juice or acetic acid.

In actual practice, urine varies so much in composition that it is difficult to suggest any one stain remover. Usually immediate thorough laundering, or sponging with warm salt water will help preserve the colour of the material stained, and quite often a little hydrogen peroxide added to the salt water helps to remove any remaining stain. Where possible, rinse thoroughly and launder.

Urine stains from puppies depends quite a lot on the sex of the animal and the diet it is being fed. Male puppies' urine tends to be more alkaline than females and if the animal is on a diet of raw meat this will putrefy fairly quickly so the area needs thorough washing.

Urine from cats does not normally stain especially if dealt with quickly by ordinary washing. The urine will, however, stain oak flooring if it is left, so on this type of flooring, wash up immediately, using detergent suds plus a little household bleach or peroxide of hydrogen.

Stains from human urine should be mopped up, rinsed and then the area washed thoroughly, again as quickly as possible after the accident has happened. Dealt with quickly there should be no stain at all but human urine breaks down with time and this is when, due to uric acid, a yellow stain develops.

Urine stains from a hamster are usually very slight, especially if they are dealt with straight away. Wash with ordinary detergent suds, rinse and dry. Stains may develop if the urine is left, especially if the hamster has been in contact with sawdust.

Carpets. Urine stains made by babies or pets on carpets need immediate attention. This is because the colour may move if left for any length of time. The sooner the stain is dealt with the less chance of any stain remaining. Generally quick ordinary washing with detergent mixed to a rich foam with warm water is sufficient. Make up about a pint of detergent suds and add 1 teaspoonful of peroxide of hydrogen. Work the foam into the stain then rinse with clear water and rub dry.

Alternatively, absorb as much of the urine as possible with absorbent paper or a cloth, then sponge thoroughly with clear warm water, making sure the liquid does not penetrate to the backing. Next make a solution with 1 tablespoonful of white vinegar, 3 tablespoonfuls of warm water and 1 teaspoonful of detergent. Drip this on to the stain, work in well, and leave for 15 to 20 minutes. Rinse off with clear water and pat dry.

Old urine stains frequently dye or bleach the carpet and are very difficult to remove. Sponging with $\frac{1}{2}$ pint of cold water containing 2 teaspoonfuls of ammonia will often lessen the stain and revive the original carpet colours but test on an inconspicuous part first for colour-fastness and avoid saturating the carpet.

Floors. Urine stains from pets very often remove the colour from linoleum and wood floors. To avoid this, deal with the trouble as quickly as possible. It is possible to buy a special liquid called Savvy Pet Lotion to add to the washing water. This removes odour and prevents bleaching of the floor.

Varnish

Furniture. Stains caused by standing a wet varnish tin in the wrong place or by drips from varnish during decorating, can be removed by gentle rubbing with a cloth or fine steel wool dipped in methylated spirit followed immediately by more rubbing with a clean dry rag. For a fresh stain, one treatment may be enough; for an old stain, repeat several times. Do not apply the methylated spirit to a polished surface—it may do far more damage than the original varnish stain.

Fabric. Sponge a varnish stain lightly with a cloth dipped in methylated spirit, turpentine or turpentine substitute. On a rayon fabric test first before using methylated spirit and if in any doubt use one of the other solvents.

Obstinate varnish stains often respond to equal quantities of benzol and turpentine mixed and sponged on to both sides of the stain. As soon as the paint or varnish is soft, rinse thoroughly and then launder in hot suds. See also under Paint on pages 220, 227 and 245.

Vaseline

For a very slight mark, wash in hot synthetic detergent. If the stains are fairly new, sponge lightly with turpentine and then launder in hot detergent. Old stains which have been washed unsuccessfully should be soaked in turpentine or turpentine substitute and then re-laundered in hot detergent suds.

Vegetable

Soak the stained fabric for 10 to 15 minutes in warm water containing borax or ammonia or suspend over a basin, sprinkle with borax and pour boiling water through the stain from a height.

For a severe stain, push the stained fabric down into the borax solution after pouring on the boiling water, leave to soak for 15 minutes, then rinse and launder. If this fails, white cottons and linens may be gently bleached.

Obstinate vegetable or fruit stains on the *hands* can usually be removed with well-soaped pumice stone but if this is not effective a commercial preparation such as Handjoy, Bantol or Peroxchlor, can be used.

Verdigris

Copper. Dissolve $\frac{1}{2}$ oz. of citric acid in 1 pint of warm water and stir thoroughly. Brush generously on to the copper, then rinse well under running water or wash in warm suds, rinse and polish. If the verdigris is very slight, a mixture of vinegar and salt rubbed on to the stains may be sufficient to remove all traces. Rinse thoroughly and dry after cleaning.

Silver. Remove verdigris from silver by rubbing hard with silver plate polish, repeating until deposit is dissolved.

Brass. A hot strong solution of ordinary washing soda is usually effective in removing verdigris from brass. If the brass is badly stained and the article is suitable, the brass can be boiled in the soda solution and then scrubbed. If this treatment is still not sufficient use a cleaning solution of hydrochloric acid as described on page 301.

Vinegar

To remove a vinegar stain from material, dissolve 1 teaspoonful of ammonia in 1 pint of warm water and sponge or soak the stain in this. Leave for a few minutes, then rinse thoroughly and if necessary launder in the usual way.

Vomit

Remove most of the vomit by rinsing under cold running water then put the articles to soak overnight in cold water containing a biological washing powder. Launder in fresh hand-hot suds.

On unwashable fabrics, sponge with lukewarm water containing a little ammonia then pat dry with a clean cloth.

Water

Fabric. Water stains on rayon—often caused by sprinkling a dry garment before ironing—can be removed by sponging the whole garment with warm water or dipping it in water, wrapping in a towel to absorb excess moisture and ironing while still damp. Some water stains can be removed by holding the material in the steam from a boiling kettle until fabric is damp. Shake frequently while steaming, then press with a warm iron while still damp.

Carpet. For severe stains on a carpet caused by flooding, a leak, overflowing basin, etc. mop up as much water as possible straight away, using clean towels. It is important to deal with this trouble quickly before the carpet becomes saturated and the backing damaged. Prop a stool, chair or box under the carpet to support the wetted area above floor level.

If possible place a fan or electric convector near to circulate air and dry the carpet as quickly as possible to prevent rot and mildew. Once dry, any small stain can be dealt with by dripping on a mild detergent solution and wiping off with a clean damp cloth.

Severe saturation and staining will need professional cleaning immediately. A badly-saturated carpet will probably shrink, so if it is fitted and has to be taken up for treatment it may not fit when you come to re-lay it. In this case call in a carpet layer. He may be able to re-stretch the carpet for you.

Furniture. On furniture, water stains can often be removed by rubbing Vaseline into the marks repeatedly until they disappear.

A treatment which sometimes removes the white stain left by spilt water is to heat an iron and hold it a few inches above the polished surface. Alternatively, place brown paper over the mark and hold a hot iron an inch or so above the paper. In neither case let the iron touch the furniture or paper.

For further ways of removing water stains from furniture see under the heading Heat marks on page 233.

Water-borne paints

These are emulsions, including P.V.A. or acrylic paints, distempers and water paints. Deal with stains as soon as possible and do not allow them to dry. Wipe up small amounts immediately with a wet rag.

Soften paints with warm liquid detergent/water solution. On carpets and upholstery, rub in, rinse with plenty of clear water. For washable fabrics, launder.

Water-borne paint stains can sometimes be softened with cellulose thinners but this must not be used on rayons or acetates. Some types of paint can be moved if they have dried, using methylated spirit. This should be safe on any fabric but test on hidden area first and dilute spirit with water if doubtful.

Whisky

Treat as for Alcohol on page 214.

White sauce

For washable materials rinse off excess liquid in warm water, then launder in the usual way.

An alternative method is to soak the stained articles overnight in cold or lukewarm water containing one of the biological washing powders with enzymes. Launder next day in a fresh solution of the powder in hand-hot water.

For heavy fabrics or unwashable materials, blot up as much liquid as possible, then gently wipe with a cloth wrung out in clear warm water. If any stain remains, sponge with a grease solvent.

Whitewash

If dealt with immediately, whitewash and washable distemper stains should come out during laundering.

For dried or more severe stains, sponge with vinegar and warm water before laundering.

See also under Water-borne paints, above.

Wine

Treat a wine stain immediately whenever possible, or pour salt on the stain the moment it happens, to stop it spreading.

To remove a wine stain stretch the material over a basin and pour boiling water through the stain at a height until it fades. Finish by washing in the ordinary way and by boiling or bleaching if necessary for white linen or cotton. For a fresh stain on white wool, silk or rayon, soak in a cupful of warm water containing 1 tablespoonful of peroxide. Wash in the ordinary way or rinse thoroughly and dry.

Another way of dealing with a fresh wine stain is to dissolve 1 oz. of borax in 1 pint of hot water and either soak the stained area in the solution or sponge it on to the fabric. Leave for half an hour, then wash in warm soapy water and rinse thoroughly.

For a wine stain that has dried and become fixed in the material, stretch over a basin and sprinkle thickly with powdered borax. Pour boiling water through at a height, then push the stained fabric into the solution and leave to soak. Follow this by washing or by bleaching in peroxide for white materials, then by a thorough rinsing.

If borax is not available, sprinkle a wine stain on a tablecloth with powdered starch and leave for 2 or 3 hours. Shake off powder, wash the cloth thoroughly in cold water and finally launder in the usual way.

Very often wine stains can be removed—especially red wine stains —by soaking the stained fabric overnight in cool water containing one of the enzyme washing powders. Machine or hand wash in the usual way and rinse well.

If wine is spilled on *upholstery* blot up excess immediately and sponge with warm water, then sprinkle with an absorbent powder such as french chalk, fuller's earth or talcum powder. As the powder becomes sticky brush it off and apply fresh absorbent. For a severe stain, sponge with warm water, then rub glycerine into the mark, leave for half an hour and then sponge with warm detergent suds, rinse and rub dry.

Plastics

Introduction

Nowadays a very wide range of materials is to be found in and around the home that are all classed together under the term *plastics*.

These materials are largely synthetic in nature, and are often highly contrasting in their properties. Some are flexible, others rigid; some are tough, others brittle; some are transparent, others opaque; some soften easily with heat; others will withstand sterilizing. Most are light and pleasant to handle and can be bought in a variety of colours. Most, at some stage of their manufacture, have been shaped by flow, usually using the influence of heat and pressure.

There are two distinct groups of families of plastics. Thermoplastics (see page 282) will resoften if heated sufficiently, whereas thermoset plastics (see page 282) remain rigid.

Technically it is correct to use the word plastics, always with the final 's' (i.e. don't say plastic unless you mean 'soft'). The point is covered by the authority of the British Standard Institution, in their publication: 'B.S. 1755, Glossary of Terms Used in the Plastics Industry'. However, common usage is leaning towards the word plastic when one specific material is in mind.

ABS plastics

Such plastics are very tough materials similar in some ways to toughened polystryrene (see page 277) but much superior in their mechanical properties. ABS is now commonly used for telephones and items such as vacuum cleaners and mixers. Common trade names include Abstrene and Cycolac.

Acetals

Plastics moulding materials similar to nylon in having good resistance to most chemicals (except strong acids and a few organic solvents), and in being strong and tough. Two major trade names are Delrin and Kematal.

Acrylics

These are usually colourless, odourless, tasteless thermoplastics materials which are insoluble in water, but easily dissolved in common organic solvents such as carbon tetrachloride, etc. In emulsion form they are used in specialized emulsion paints, washable wallpapers, stoving enamels and leather finishes.

Most acrylics commonly encountered are really a class of material more correctly known as methacrylates. As plastics materials, methacrylates come in two forms, one being sheet which is shaped by bending, pressing or blowing while hot, and the other being granules or powder which are shaped by moulding.

As hard, lightweight plastics, resembling glass, acrylics are used to make dentures, food covers, table-ware, contact lenses, some surgical instruments. Trade names include Diakon, Perspex and Plexiglass.

Clean with hand-hot soapy water but avoid abrasives of any kind as these plastics scratch easily; slight surface scratches may be removed by rubbing lightly with metal polish. Most acrylics soften slightly in boiling water but a special grade can be made to withstand sterilizing; they can be damaged by dropping from a height.

See also under Perspex on page 275.

Akulon

The trade name for a Dutch nylon known as Type 6. For further details, see Nylon (moulded) page 275.

Alkathene

The trade name for a brand of polythene.

Bakelite

The trade name for a variety of plastics materials. The first Bakelite plastics were phenolic moulding materials familiar for their use in telephones, ash-trays, etc. Over the years the company has widened its interests to include other plastics such as polythene but a number of these are still known under the Bakelite trade name.

Breon

The trade name for a brand of polyvinyl chloride (PVC) and other vinyl raw materials made by B.P. Chemicals.

Casein

This protein plastics known as Lactoid, Erinoid, etc. is made principally from the casein derived from milk. It can be brightly coloured and highly polished and is used to make coloured buttons, knitting needles and various fancy goods. Its biggest disadvantage is that it absorbs water; buttons made from this material should therefore be removed before laundering although this may be left on if the garment is to be dry-cleaned; other items made from casein plastic should be polished with a dry duster or, if very soiled, wiped quickly with a slightly damp cloth and then dried immediately.

Catalin

A trade name for cast phenol-formaldehyde; a hard rigid plastics material used to make bag handles, umbrella knobs, etc. Clean with plain hot water or if a cleaner is preferred avoid one containing soda.

Celluloid

See Cellulose nitrate.

Cellulose acetate

A tough, resilient plastic which is similar in appearance to cellulose nitrate (celluloid) but is less flammable. Trade names include Bexoid, Clarifoil, Utilex, Celastoid, etc. It is used to make brush and mirror handles, lipstick cases, lampshades, hair slides, etc. Small colourless packages used to hold toothbrushes, confectionery and hardware items are usually made from thin transparent cellulose acetate sheet.

Wash articles made from cellulose acetate in clear warm water or in mild suds but never with any cleaner containing alkalis or strong acids. This plastic resists weak acids and also salt water and abrasives will not normally harm it. Chemical solvents should be avoided and items should not be placed near heat nor in boiling water nor should they be left to soak in hot water.

Cellulose nitrate

Often known as Celluloid or Xylonite, this is used almost exclusively to make table tennis balls and it can be an extremely tough plastics material resistant to most chemicals. It is moulded to make tool, brush and cutlery handles and cheap articles such as toothbrushes which are not meant to last. A knife with this type of handle should not be used when cooking, as cellulose nitrate—which can often be recognized by its slight camphor smell—is highly flammable. Do not place near a naked flame nor in strong heat, and avoid contact with chemical solvents. As it may shrink and soften in hot water, wash in warm suds only.

Cobex

A trade name for rigid polyvinyl chloride sheet (see page 279). The sheeting is available in plain or corrugated form and in a variety of colours. It is hard wearing, impervious to water and is non-flammable. It can be washed with warm soapy water, but abrasives should be avoided.

Co-polymer emulsions

This is a general term for acrylic emulsions. See page 269.

Darvic

A trade name for rigid polyvinyl sheeting.

Delrin

The trade name for a plastics moulding material made from acetals which is similar to nylon. It is strong, tough and resistant to most chemicals with the exception of strong acids and a few organic solvents.

Diakon

The trade name for an acrylic plastic in granule or powder form.

Diakon is used to make cutlery handles, hair dryers, domestic electrical appliances and car rear-light covers (because it does not craze in contact with petroleum vapours, as do many plastics). It is resistant to most domestic solvents and cleaning materials but Diakon should not be allowed to come into contact with methylated spirit, oil of cloves, oil of wintergreen, amyl acetate or trichlorethylene.

See also under Acrylic on page 269.

Distrene

A trade name for polystryene made by Dow Chemicals.

Dunlofoam

The trade name for Dunlop's polyether foam. Used for mattresses and pillows.

Dunlopillo

The trade name for Dunlop's latex foam. Used for mattresses and pillows.

Epoxides

These are resins used among other things in special adhesives, such as Bostik No. 7 and Araldite, and in the manufacture of laminated and reinforced plastics.

Ethyl cellulose

A very strong, tough thermoplastics material little used in this country. It is resistant to acids and alkalis but alcohol and petrol should be avoided and also any fatty substances, as the plastics is slightly sensitive to oil and grease.

Expanded plastics

See Foam plastics, page 272.

Expanded polystyrene

See Polystyrene foam, page 278.

Fablon

The trade name for a printed, embossed or plain PVC sheeting used for curtaining, tablecloths and, coated with self-adhesive, for covering tables, wall and working surfaces. Clean with a damp cloth.

Fibreglass

See Polyester bonded glass fibre.

Fluon

A trade name for Polytetrafluoroethylene made by ICI Ltd. See P.T.F.E. on page 280.

Foam plastics

A variety of plastics materials are used in the foamed or expanded state. These include polyurethane (page 279), polyvinyl chloride (page 279) and polystyrene (page 277). Depending on their nature, such foams or 'expanded plastics' are used for insulation, padding, upholstery, packaging, in clothing and for toys. See further details under appropriate names.

Formica

The trade name for a laminated plastics material, surfaced with melamine, and used to make kitchen working surfaces, counters, wall panelling, trays, etc. Resistant to most mild chemicals and alcohol, it is very hard-wearing and cannot crack, craze or burn under normal usage.

For further details see under Laminated plastics below.

Hardec

The trade name for a melamine-faced hardboard; it is hard-wearing, scratch-resistant, etc. and has a finish similar to laminated plastics.

Kematal

The trade name for acetal copolymers sold by ICI. Items moulded from Kematal include hot and cold water taps, shower fittings, sprung hinges, machine parts and electrical components. The material is strong and tough and resistant to most chemicals with the exception of strong acids and a few organic solvents.

Laminated plastics

Laminated plastics are used for kitchen tabletops, splashbacks, trays and for shop counters and bars; there are various kinds and much depends on the types of material used. Trade names include Formica, Warerite and Perstorp.

The materials are bonded together into a solid mass with resins and look alike but while some, such as those mentioned, will resist wear indefinitely, others may scratch, chip, crack or blister.

Most laminated surfaces are resistant to chemicals; they will resist heat up to about 300 deg. F. and are not harmed by hot teapots or coffee-pots, although hot baking-dishes and pans—and especially those with heavy, ground aluminium bases—should never be placed directly on the surface but always on top of a protecting mat. Avoid clamping mincing or other machines tightly to the surface or the plastics may crush or mark in the same way that enamel or wood might do under similar conditions. Most laminates may also scratch or mark if used for chopping meat or for cutting bread.

Wash in hot soapy water or wipe with a cloth wrung out in mild suds, rinse and dry. An occasional rub with silicone polish will help protect the surface and add gloss. A liquid polish should be used, as a paste wax is not absorbed and tends to collect dust and dirt.

Lustrex

A trade name for polystyrene moulding compounds.

Maranyl

The trade name for nylon manufactured by ICI. See further details under Nylon (moulded), page 275.

Marlex

The American name for a rigid type of polythene (known in this country as Rigidex) which may be safely sterilized as it retains its shape in boiling water.

Melamine formaldehyde

This is a special type of rigid, almost unbreakable plastics used frequently to make table-ware and picnic items as it looks and feels rather like china. Melamine is similar to urea—the older and cheaper plastics used for picnic-ware—but it is stronger, more highly glazed and does not stain so easily, although it is important that cups are drained immediately after use and washed as soon as possible. To clean picnic or other ware made from melamine, wash in hot soapy water and if necessary use special cleaners recommended by the manufacturerers to remove tea or other stains; abrasives should be avoided.

Melamine has many other uses and there is scarcely any sphere of life in which it is not met. It is used in the manufacture of laminated plastics such as Formica and Warerite; paper towels and handker-chief tissues are treated with melamine resin to give them wet strength and white leather is obtained by using a tanning agent based on melamine. The paints and enamel finishes on refrigerators and cars frequently contain melamine to give them extra hardness and gloss, and materials are often treated with it to give permanent gloss, crease-resistance and to make them flame-proof. (Proban is a mela-mine flame-proof finish used on many garments and materials.)

Melinex

The trade name for a brand of tough transparent flexible film chemically the same as Terylene which is the trade name for a filament and fibre form of the material. Melinex has outstanding chemical, electrical and physical properties, is very strong and hard to wear or tear and is unaffected by high or low temperatures. It is resistant to water, oil, fat and most solvents and chemicals. As well as being used in industry, it is used frequently for bookbinding, packaging, map-making and metallic yarns such as Lurex threads. Clean with a damp, soapy cloth.

Nylon (moulded)

Moulded nylon looks like many other plastics. It is translucent and can be rigid or flexible but it is very tough and also expensive. Articles made from nylon are almost completely unbreakable and can be boiled and sterilized if necessary; they are resistant to most chemicals and solvents except bleach and will burn with difficulty only if actually placed and kept in a flame. Items made from nylon include babies' bottles, tufting for brushes and brooms, pot scourers, beakers, cupboard-door catches, curtain rails, cog-wheels, garden-hose connectors and various parts for mixers and washing machines, etc. Wash in hot suds but avoid abrasives and bleach. Do not place in oven or near strong heat and do not store near hot-water pipes. Trade names include Akulon, Maranyl, Ralsin.

Perspex

The trade name for an acrylic material known technically as polymethyl methacrylate. Made in all colours as well as in transparent, translucent and opaque varieties, it is lightweight, and keeps its crystal appearance indefinitely. Perspex is used to make sinks, door panels, food covers, lighting fittings, etc., and baths are also shaped from the material.

Wash in hot (not boiling) soapy water and if very dirty, clean with caustic soda. Slight surface scratches can be removed by rubbing lightly with metal polish or with special Perspex polish, but avoid abrasives and paint removers.

Further details are included under Acrylic on page 269.

Phenol-formaldehyde

A strong though rather brittle thermoset plastics known as Bakelite, Nestorite, Rockite, Catalin, etc. It is resistant to heat, water, mild alkalis and organic solvents and is used to make buttons, boxes, costume jewellery, clock cases, door furniture, lavatory seats, electric switches, pen handles, ash-trays, and telephones, etc. Articles can be cleaned with plain water (hot or cold) and this is usually sufficient, although household cleaners may be used providing they do not contain an alkali such as soda.

Plasticized PVC

Polyvinyl chloride or PVC (see page 279) can be used in rigid or in flexible forms. The latter are obtained by incorporation of plasticizers with the polyvinyl chloride, whence the material is described as being plasticized. The flexibility conferred by the presence of added 'plasticizers' may be lost if such forms of PVC are exposed for long periods to soapy water or exposed to heat. This is especially so with thin PVC sheeting or film.

Plastics

See Introduction on page 268.

Plexiglass

The trade name for an acrylic material similar in properties to Perspex. It may be treated in the same way. For details see page 275 or under Acrylic on page 269.

Polycarbonate

This is a very tough clear thermoplastics material made in Germany and sold under the trade name Makrolon. Certain quality products such as beakers and dishes are available in polycarbonate. They can be washed quite safely in very hot water but contact with solvents should be avoided.

Polyester bonded glass fibre

This is glass fibre reinforced and impregnated with resin. Mouldings made with glass fibre and polyester resins are very strong, and lighting, sink units and basins made from this material will not chip or crack and are easily cleaned with warm soapy water. There are many other uses for glass fibre and the tubs of some washing machines as well as boats, car bodies and corrugated roof lighting are made from this type of plastics.

Polyether foam
See Polyurethane, page 279.

Polymethyl methacrylate
A hard plastics often referred to by the simpler name of Acrylic. Trade names for polymethyl methacrylate include Diakon, Perspex and Plexiglass. For further details see under Acrylic on page 220 or under trade names.

Polypropylene
This thermoplastics is somewhat similar to polythene (see page 278). But although even lighter, it is more rigid, has a better wearing surface and at the same time, it can be sterilized as it will withstand the action of boiling water. Polypropylene is resistant to acids, alkalis, solvents and will not stain. It is used for many domestic mouldings and especially for some washing-machine parts, also for picnic-ware, mixing spoons and bowls. Propathene is a common trade name.

Polystyrene
A highly-polished, rigid, slightly brittle plastics which gives a ringing, metallic sound when lightly tapped. Trade names include Styron, Distrene and Lustrex. Polystyrene is used to make picnic ware, powder bowls and compacts, electrical fitments, brush mono-filaments, etc. Articles made from polystyrene may break easily if dropped or banged and they may be damaged by bleaches, cleaning fluids, petrol and orange or lemon skins and fruit; abrasives will mark polystyrene articles and heat may cause them to soften. Wash in warm water and mild suds and avoid high temperatures including very hot water.

There are also varieties of toughened polystyrene known as High Impact Polystyrene, Super Impact Polystyrene, etc. These are not so highly polished and are less brittle than ordinary polystyrene; they are more opaque and much stronger. This kind of polystyrene is used to make bread bins, refrigerator interiors and door liners, dish drainers, toys, etc. Wash in hand-hot soap suds or mild detergent; do not use abrasives, boiling water or place near heat.

Polystyrene often becomes electrostatically charged with electricity and tends to attract dust particles. To overcome this, many polystyrene articles are now lacquered but if plastics equipment collects dust this can be prevented by wiping the articles with a damp cloth dipped in any synthetic detergent solution or an anti-static detergent such as Stergene. Allow the detergent to dry on the plastics without rinsing or drying it with a cloth. Alternatively, use a silicone cream polish containing an anti-static ingredient.

Polystyrene foam

Also known as expanded polystyrene, this material is widely used for insulation purposes—in the loft, or as ceiling tiles and as wall linings. It is also used in refrigerators and in packing. The main trade names in use include: Styropor; Styrocell; Marleycell; Polyzote; Styrotherm. Expanded polystyrene can be washed with warm soapy water. However, it should not be exposed to heat nor to any solvents.

Polytetrafluoroethylene

See under P.T.F.E.

Polythene

Sometimes known as Polyethylene, this is a wax-like and flexible plastics, resistant to water, some acids and most solvents except perhaps vegetable and other oils left in contact for any length of time. Trade names include Alkathene and Visqueen film, which is semi-rigid corrugated plastics used for lampshades. Polythene is used to make bowls, waste bins, buckets, sink tidies, cold-water pipes, lunch boxes and so on. It is also made in film form and then it is used to make storage bags, transparent sheeting, lampshades, etc. Polythene is tasteless, almost unbreakable and very strong.

Polythene becomes temporarily more flexible when hot and softens slightly at boiling point. Items made from it may be washed in hot, or even boiling water but should not be sterilized by boiling unless manufacturers' instructions are to the contrary. Hot saucepans should not be placed in an empty polythene bowl. The material is easily scratched by an abrasive such as scouring powder or when creaming sugar and fat together; it can also be easily scratched with a sharp knife.

There is also a high density polythene sometimes known as low pressure polythene, trade names Hostalen and Rigidex, and this is more rigid, will stand a temperature above 250 deg. F. and may be sterilized. This form of polythene is used to make colanders, some mugs, baby utensils, etc. but abrasives and excessive heat must still be avoided. For example, it is quite safe to strain boiling vegetables through a plastics colander but the colander may be permanently damaged if it is then placed on the hot saucepan as is usual with a metal colander.

Polyurethane

This plastics material is best known in its foamed form. The soft foams are also known as polyether foams, plastic foams and polyester foams. It is used for personal and domestic sponges, cushion fillings, mattress covers, padding, etc. but there is a rigid foam which is used for heat and sound insulation. Trade names include Dunlopreme, Kayfoam, etc. See also Foam plastics on page 272.

Polyvinyl acetate

Often referred to as PVA, this is a colourless, odourless, tasteless thermoplastics material which is insoluble in water but easily dissolved in common organic solvents such as carbon tetrachloride, etc. It is used as an adhesive for binding books, is one of the bonding agents in Staflex and is used in the manufacture of many emulsion paints. It is also the base for synthetic starch and some hair sprays.

Polyvinyl chloride

This is usually known as PVC (or P.V.C.) and it is most easily recognized in flexible sheet form although rigid forms are now widely used for guttering and curtain rails. Trade names include Cobex, Vybak, Fablon, Storella, Con-Tact, Velbex, Darvic, Vynide, Welvic, B.X. and Breon PVC.

Polyvinyl chloride is made basically from coke, limestone and salt although nowadays an increasingly large amount is being produced from petroleum sources. PVC is produced in the form of fine white powder or silky fluid which is then processed into long-playing records, floor-covering tiles, etc.

It can be welded and is used to make coat fabrics as well as for the manufacture of plastics raincoats, food and clothing storage bags, curtain materials, cushion covers, waterproof aprons and adhesive shelf and wall coverings. It is also used very widely to make floor covering and upholstery leathercloths.

Resistant to water and most liquids and solvents, PVC tends to stiffen in cold weather and to become flexible again and creaseless if warmed. It is normally non-flammable. Its disadvantage when used in the form of a thin film is that it tears easily if handled carelessly. Wash in warm suds or wipe with a cloth wrung out in soapy water.

Avoid abrasives and do not iron or place near heat. If used on a floor, guard against hot cinders. When using PVC tablecloth *never* place it directly on to a highly polished table but always over a cover.

PVC can be painted but a special paint should be used. This is generally available at garages and motor accessory stockists.

Polyvinylidene chloride

See under woven vinyl filament on page 284.

Propathene

The trade name for ICI's brand of polypropylene, used to make bowls, colanders and similar household items and picnic ware as well as items such as agitators for washing machines. Propathene withstands boiling water, is resistant to acids and alkalis and does not stain. See also, page 277.

Protein plastics

Articles made from protein plastics contain in their composition, as their name suggests, some form of protein such as that derived from milk. See also Casein on page 270.

P.T.F.E.

The full name for this plastics material is polytetrafluoroethylene. The material can be used to coat oven tins, frying-pans and skis to provide a non-stick surface. Trade names for P.T.F.E. include Fluon, Teflon, etc. It is resistant to all common chemicals and solvents and it will withstand high temperatures. Wash in hot water with a soft cloth. Avoid scouring or scratching.

Rigidex

The trade name for a brand of high density polythene which does not soften in boiling water and can be sterilized. Used for baby feeding bottles, measuring jugs, laundry baskets, etc.

For fuller details see under Polythene on page 278.

Rilsan

A special type of nylon (Type 11) made in France. The nylon can be woven into fabric, moulded or processed in other ways.

See also under Nylon (moulded) on page 275 and in 'Fibres and fabrics' chapter on page 73.

Rockite

The trade name for phenol-formaldehyde moulding materials. It is used to make telephone cases and electrical switches, etc. It is shock-resisting and can be made resistant to water, heat, acid and alkalis. To clean, wipe with a cloth wrung out in soapless detergent suds. Wipe with a second cloth wrung out in clear water and dry. As this material is already polished, further polishing is unnecessary.

See also under phenol-formaldehyde, page 275.

Saran

The trade name for a plastics yarn made from polyvinylidene chloride. As well as being used to make pan scourers, dolls' hair and wigs, plastics fabric such as Tygan, is woven from it.

See also under Woven vinyl filament on page 284.

Staflex

The trade name for cotton fabric coated with polyvinyl acetate or other thermoplastics and used for stiffening garments. There are two kinds, one suitable for home laundering and the other for dry-cleaning.

Storella

A trade name for PVC sheeting used for curtains, tablecloths, upholstery, etc. Printed and plain self-adhesive PVC sheeting is made by the same firm and sold under the trade name of Con-Tact.

Styron

This is a trade name for a type of polystyrene. It is a tough, rigid plastics used to make moulded items such as powder bowls, refrigerator and food containers, compacts, toilet seats, soap dishes, wall tiles, etc. To clean, wipe with a soapy cloth or (if the item permits) immerse in moderately hot suds and scrub with a soft brush. Rinse thoroughly and dry on a soft cloth. Odd stains on large items can be wiped off with a damp cloth dipped in soapless detergent suds.

For further details see under Polystyrene, page 277

Teflon

The trade name for an American polytetrafluoroethylene resin finish used to coat glass fibres, iron, aluminium, brass, copper, etc. and various surfaces to make them non-stick. It is also used in the manufacture of glue-pots, rolling-pins, biscuit cutters, baking-tins, funnels, etc. for the same reason.

See also under P.T.F.E.

Thermoplastics

Articles made from thermoplastics can be made to soften by the application of heat, and they can be softened and remoulded simply by applying the right degree of heat and pressure. Cellulose acetate, polythene, Perspex, polystyrene and PVC all come into this category and nowadays a very wide variety of domestic items made of thermoplastics are in daily use. Wash in fairly hot suds but never boil, unless manufacturer's instructions allow this, nor place near a strong heat.

Thermo-setting plastics

Phenol-formaldehyde and urea-formaldehyde belong to the group of materials described as thermo-setting plastics. Articles are formed by intense pressure and heat and once the plastics has set hard it cannot be softened or remoulded. The only way the shape can be changed is by cutting, sawing or drilling. Articles made from thermo-setting plastics include, radio, clock and camera cases, ash-trays, vacuum flask caps, electrical appliances, bottle caps, toilet seats, decorative laminates and door furniture, etc.

Tygan

The trade name for a plastics fabric woven from Saran. It is used for car and furniture upholstery, for radio frets and deck-chair coverings, etc. Clean with soap and water. Tygan is resistant to most chemicals but ammonia must not be used or this will damage the material.

See Woven vinyl filament, page 284.

Urea-formaldehyde

Trade names for this hard, thermo-setting plastics material are Beetle, Scarab, etc. It is rigid and resists most stains as well as grease, alcohol, and diluted acids and alkalis.

As it is odourless and tasteless, urea-formaldehyde is often used for picnic-ware, trays, measuring spoons and cups, beakers, baby-ware and condiment sets, but it may crack if dropped and may be affected by abrasives and bleach. Wash with hot soapy water and use soap powder on a damp cloth to remove tea or other stains. Although this plastics will resist boiling water for a short time, it should never be left soaking in hot water for any length of time.

Velbex

The trade name for a coloured PVC sheeting made in a number of thicknesses and suitable for handbags, curtains, toilet bags, hanging wardrobes, etc. It drapes easily and can be cleaned by sponging down with a soapy sponge followed by a wipe with a damp cloth. Bleaching agents or ammonia should not damage the sheet but dry-cleaning solvents will soften it and make it tacky. When sewing Velbex use stitches as large as possible (about 10 to an inch) and stop sewing about $\frac{1}{4}$ in. before the end of the seam. Parts subject to strain where hooks or fastenings are to be sewn should be reinforced with fabric or tape. With curtains no bottom seam is necessary.

Vinyl plastics

A term often used to refer to one or other forms of polyvinyl chloride or related plastics (see page 279).

Visqueen

The trade name for a polythene film and lay-flat tubing used for bags, sacks, etc.

Vynair

The trade name for a heavy PVC-coated fabric suitable for furniture upholstery. The advantage of Vynair is that it 'breathes' and air vents are not necessary if sprung or foam fillings are used. To clean Vynair wipe with a damp cloth and never use polish of any kind.

Vynide

The trade name for a PVC-coated fabric used for furniture and motor-car upholstery. It is tough and will not crack or become sticky. To clean, wash with a damp soapy rag and dry with a clean duster. Do not use polish of any kind. If really dirty, scrub lightly with a soft brush. Vynide is resistant to most stains.

Vynolay

This is often used as a generic term but it is in fact the trade name for a flooring manufactured by Dunlop. Details are on page 413.

Warerite

The trade name for a hard-wearing decorative plastics laminate used for table-tops, panelling, etc. It is resistant to alcohol and most mild chemicals and will not crack or craze under normal usage. A special cigarette-proof grade is also available.

For further details see under Laminated plastics on page 273.

Welvic

The trade name for all types of PVC compound made by Imperial Chemical Industries Ltd.

Woven vinyl filament

This is a type of PVC known technically as polyvinylidene chloride. It is spun in the form of threads and is then woven into strong, lustrous fabric which is heat- and damp-proof and unaffected by strong sunlight. For this reason it is used for garden furniture and deck-chairs, etc. Trade names include Saran and Tygan.

7

Around the house

Adhesives

Modern adhesives do not claim to work miracles, but if you choose the right adhesive for the job the results can be impressive and very long-lasting.

Remember that the reason you need different adhesives to stick different materials is that the properties of glass, metal, wood and so on vary so much.

There are basically two ways in which materials can be made to adhere together. If the two pieces are both porous—like carpet and binding tape, or wood and wood—you can stick them together with an adhesive of a compatible type which soaks into the pores of both pieces and then sets hard. The hardened adhesive locks the two pieces together.

Non-porous materials, on the other hand, like metal or glass, have to be locked together in a different way. An adhesive must be chosen which has a molecular affinity with the pieces which are being joined together.

Many modern adhesives are extra-effective because they work by not only filling the pores of the materials and solidifying, but also they have this molecular affinity with the materials being joined.

For any repair to be successful it is important that the item should be mended as soon as possible. Where repairs must be delayed, pieces of wood, china, glass, etc. should be kept in a sealed polythene bag to protect them from dust and grease. No repair will be effective unless the surfaces to be joined are clean, dry and free from dust.

Follow manufacturer's instructions exactly and support the article carefully during drying. Strapping the join with self-adhesive cellulose tape, adhesive tape, rubber bands or string is usually sufficient.

Allow adequate time for the adhesive to dry and harden. This will vary according to the adhesive and the article being mended.

There is no all-purpose adhesive which will cope with all materials. With some repairs, strength must be the first consideration. With others, resistance to water and heat are equally important. Here is a summary of the main types available.

Animal and fish glues. These are cheap to buy and convenient to use, though not waterproof. They are suitable for sticking wood joints, as long as the article is not going to be used in a humid atmosphere. They have other uses too, of course. For example, they can be used for sticking china ornaments that will not be washed, and also for sticking polyurethane foam to wood.

These glues dry pale brown.

Excess glue can be wiped off with water if tackled immediately.

Casein adhesive. Although cheap, these have obvious disadvantages and have now been widely replaced.

The adhesive dries a transparent yellow.

Excess glue can be cleaned off with water if tackled immediately.

Cellulose adhesives. These are of the china cement type. They were popular for repairs to china but have now been mainly replaced by synthetic rubber adhesives and epoxy resins. See below for details. Cellulose adhesives dry transparent. Excess can be removed with nail varnish remover or acetone.

Contact adhesives. These give an immediate bond, and though the various makes differ, the main uses are for sticking hardboard, sticking laminated plastics surfaces in position, fixing fabric to wood, sticking rubber soles on to shoes and sticking plastics fabrics and polyurethane foam. The sealing strips on car doors can also be fixed back in position with some types of contact adhesive.

Most types dry opaque, although one or two types do dry transparent, which could be an advantage on some gluing jobs.

Clean off adhesive with nail-varnish remover or acetone. Carbon tetrachloride will also be effective on most types of contact adhesives. One manufacturer sells a special cleaning solvent for their contact adhesive.

Epoxy adhesives. These will stick almost anything where the flexibility of the joint is not important—they will even stick metal to metal. In fact they are the nearest thing to an all-round adhesive obtainable. Epoxy adhesives have two ingredients which come in separate packs and must be mixed before use. They are slow-drying and would be expensive to use except in small quantities. They are excellent for mending glass, china which you will subsequently wish to wash, wood, and for sticking PVC accessories such as door pulls and sliding door channels to wood.

Some types dry white, some a transparent yellow. This may be a small disadvantage where you are joining pieces of glass.

Use epoxy adhesives with care—they may cause skin irritation—and clean off spilled adhesive immediately with methylated spirit, then hot soapy water.

Wash off splashes and excess gum as soon as possible with warm soapy water.

Gums and pastes. Useful for gluing paper.

Sometimes the cork or stopper used to seal a bottle or tube of glue becomes firmly stuck. Dip the cork or stopper in glycerine before replacing it, and it can easily be removed at any time. For a screw-cap jar, smear Vaseline or silicone polish lightly inside the cap.

Many manufacturers nowadays coat glue-bottle stoppers with plastic resins which prevent sticking.

See also under Sealants on page 368.

Latex adhesives. Ideal for binding and repairing carpets and rugs, repairing fabrics and upholstery, trimming lampshades, sticking on rubber soles, and sticking braid on to upholstered furniture. May also be used for sticking paper.

Rub off any spilled latex adhesive before it sets, or it may be impossible to remove from fabrics and carpets without a special cleaning solvent. Copydex, who make one latex adhesive, will supply a solvent if you pay the postage (11d.) (address on Copydex packets). Alternatively, turpentine or lighter fuel may successfully loosen a small stain.

Latex on the fingers is easy to remove—let it set and then rub the fingers together.

PVA adhesives. These are not affected by damp heat and need no preparation, but do not remain strong for any length of time. They stick wood, polyurethane foam, carpets, etc. and also china and glass, although the joint may not stand up to washing.

PVA adhesives dry transparent.

Clean off marks with methylated spirit.

PVC (polyvinyl chloride) adhesive. Used for sticking sheet plastics and PVC, repairing torn plastics macs, tablecloths, etc. The adhesive dries white.

Marks and excess adhesive can be removed with nail-varnish remover or acetone, or carbon tetrachloride, if tackled immediately.

Polystyrene cement. Polystyrene cement is best for sticking polystyrene—for example, picnic boxes and refrigerator trays. It dries transparent.

Clean off with nail-varnish remover, acetone or carbon tetra-chloride.

Rubber adhesives. One type is used for sticking paper of all types —it is used widely in newspaper and magazine offices for pasting proofs, and the gum has the advantage that pictures already stuck down can be lifted and replaced in another position. It is a good adhesive to use for scrapbooks and albums. This dries transparent-to-pale-yellow.

Another type of rubber adhesive is available in tube form and dries black. This is specially formulated for heavy sticking jobs on cars and for outdoor repairs where great strength and weather-resistance are required. It will join rubber, metal, glass, wood, cork, linoleum, roofing-felt, asbestos to such surfaces as concrete, stone, plaster, etc.

A white version of this adhesive is also available and this is ideal for fixing all glazed tiles to surfaces in the bathroom, kitchen, etc.

This also is available in tubes and is proof against water, steam and heat.

Rubber adhesives can be cleaned off with turpentine or lighter fuel.

Spray adhesive. Available in 'regular' and 'heavy duty' strengths, spray adhesive is especially handy for gluing large areas of paper, though perhaps wasteful for a small job, bearing in mind the higher cost. The adhesive dries transparent.

Excess adhesive and stray marks can be cleaned away with nail-varnish remover or acetone.

Synthetic rubber adhesives. These are excellent general-purpose adhesives of which the dried film is virtually colourless and non-staining. They give strong bonds which have good chemical and temperature resistance. They are particularly useful for repairing toys, leather goods, furniture, up-holstery, jewellry and plastics ware with the exception of polythene. One popular type is sold in tubes with a spreader cap.

Excess glue can be cleaned away with nail varnish remover or acetone.

Urea adhesive. Not an instant adhesive: in one make you mix contents of two packs and apply separately. Another make is simply mixed with water.

Used for wood joints, and particularly good where there is damp heat and ordinary glues are unsatisfactory. They will even stick a joint with a gap. The content of the adhesive will react if left in contact with some metals—iron nails or screws may cause a red stain.

Remove excess adhesive with hot soapy water. Do not allow in contact with the skin. Wear rubber gloves and wash off splashes immediately.

Knowing which adhesive sticks a particular substance to something quite different is more than half the battle in mending successfully. The following chart may help. The figures alongside the items refer to the type of adhesive necessary and these are listed below:

Indoors:

Beading—1
Billiard cue tips—1
Bookbinding—1
Braid—1
Brocade—1
Brooches, mending—1, 7
Broom handles, to head—2
Camera repairs—1
Canvas—1, 8
Card—1, 8
Carpets—8
Chair legs—7
Chair seats—1
China—7
Clay floor tiles—2
Cloth—1
Copper—1
Cork tiles—2, 8
Crockery—7
Dart feathers—1
Dolls—1
Dolls' house—1
Draught strip—PVC—1
Draught strip—rubber—2
Earrings—1, 7
Earthenware—2, 7
Fabrics—1, 8
Felt—1
Finger plates—1

Foam plastics (not polystyrene)
    —1
Foam rubber—2, 3
Formica and other laminated
    plastics—3
Frames, picture—1
Glass—1, 7
Glazed tiles—4
Gloves—1
Handbags—1
Hardboard panels—3
Jewellery—1, 7
Lampshades—1
Leather—1, 8
Linoleum—2
Mackintoshes (PVC)—1
Marquetry—1
Melamine sheeting—3
Metals—1, 2, 7
Mosaic—1
Oilcloth—3
Ornaments—1
Paper—1, 8
Parchment—1
Photographs and albums—1
Picture frames—1, 7, 8
Plastic—1
Plastic-faced board—3
Plastic laminates—3

Seat covering—1   Upholstery—1

Boats:

Buoyancy bags (rubber)—2, 3   Decking materials—1, 2
Buoyancy bags (PVC)—1   Racing flag—1
Burgee—1   Rubber decking—2, 3
Canvas decking—2   Rubber strip—2
Centreboard slot rubbers—2   Sails, temporary repairs—1
Chocks padding—2   Trailer padding—2
Cross tree sail protector—2

Key to numbers:

1. Synthetic rubber adhesives, clear and transparent, used as a contact or wet-stick adhesive. This type has fairly good petrol and oil resistance. Example—Bostik 1 Clear Adhesive.
2. Natural rubber adhesives. Generally black in colour, used as a contact or wet-stick adhesive. This type has good water resistance. Example—Bostik Outdoor Adhesive.
3. Synthetic rubber adhesives. Generally buff in colour, particularly suitable for wood and plastic-laminates. Commonly called 'contact-adhesives' or 'impact adhesives' but may be used as a wet-stick in certain circumstances. Examples are Evo-Stick Impact Adhesive and Bostik Contact Adhesive.
4. Natural rubber adhesives, generally white in colour and rather viscous. Used as wet-sticks for bonding tiles to wall surfaces, etc. Example—Bostik Wall Tile Adhesive.
5. Preformed sealing strip, rather like plasticine. This type of sealant does not harden appreciably. It may be moulded to any shape or size in the hands. Example—Bostik White Sealing Strip.
6. Natural rubber sealing compound, generally black in colour, rather viscous. This type of sealant has good water resistance. Example—Bostik Outdoor Sealant.
7. Epoxy two-part adhesives. This type of adhesive gives very strong bonds in shear and tensile but has poor resistance to flexing and peel. Setting of the adhesive is by chemical reaction between the two parts which are mixed immediately before use. As they contain no solvents, no drying-times are necessary and they will set in an enclosed space. Examples—Ciba Araldite Epoxy Adhesive, Bostik 7 Epoxy Adhesive.
8. PVA Emulsion adhesives. These adhesives are particularly

useful for wood-to-wood joints. They are clean to use, are colourless when dry and tools, etc. may be cleaned with water. Examples—Unibond, Dufix, Bostik Bond PVA Adhesive.

9. Polystyrene cement. This is for making and repairing polystyrene articles, models, toys, etc. but not polystyrene foam. Example—Humbrol 77 Polystyrene Adhesive.

10. White sealers. These are synthetic rubber sealing compounds used for sealing round baths, bowls, sinks, tiles, etc. in bathrooms and kitchens. Example—Bostik White Seal.

Alabaster

If very dirty, first wash in warm soapy water, rinse and dry immediately. Rub in a little olive oil, then buff with a clean duster.

Stains can be removed before buffing by moistening a rag in turpentine and dipping this in powdered pumice; rub the marks hard, then wash in warm water containing borax, rinse and dry. Lemon juice might also remove very bad discoloration, but again follow this by washing in water containing borax.

Aluminium

A spoonful of vinegar added to the water when steaming a pudding, preserving fruit or boiling eggs will prevent black stains forming in an aluminium saucepan. The stains are not in any case harmful and stewing apple trimmings in the pan will remove them easily. Despite popular belief, there is no need to keep a special aluminium saucepan for boiling eggs.

Scrambling eggs in an aluminium saucepan also often leaves a black deposit. This is due to the sulphur in the eggs combining with the traces of iron in the aluminium. The iron sulphide leaves a black stain but is quite harmless.

Discoloured aluminium pans can be cleaned by boiling apple or rhubarb trimmings in them. To clean a discoloured saucepan when no trimmings are available, add a teaspoonful of cream of tartar to a pint of water, bring to the boil and simmer for a few minutes. Some housewives like to season a new aluminium saucepan in this way.

To clean aluminium ordinarily, use very fine steel wool and soap or one of the excellent pan cleaners now on the market. Or use a special aluminium cleaner or pads. It should not be necessary to use scouring powder but if it is, check that it is non-alkaline. Any alkali (even plain soda or salted water) will discolour aluminium although a mild acid or boiling apples in the pan will remove the tarnish.

Always dry an aluminium pan after washing it.

Clean a *burned aluminium saucepan* by filling it with water; add an onion, then boil until the burnt particles rise to the surface. A more drastic method is to boil neat bleach in the pan. Be careful, and rinse well. Boiling rhubarb leaves will often serve the same purpose.

It sometimes happens that a pan—for instance a frying-pan—or a preserving-pan—becomes badly burned and stained both inside and out and as cleaning is so difficult, the job is continually left.

For a badly neglected pan of this kind when ordinary cleaning is insufficient or has no effect, place the pan in a metal bucket or bath and add 2 or 3 tablespoonfuls of synthetic detergent, and if wished, a tablespoon of ammonia. Add sufficient cold water to cover the pan and place on a low heat.

Bring slowly to the boil and stir to produce a good lather, adding more detergent if necessary. When the water reaches boiling point simmer for 15 to 20 minutes, remove from the heat and allow the suds to cool to hand-heat. Scour the softened deposits with steel wool, a stiff brush or an efficient pan cleaner. Wash in fresh suds, rinse thoroughly and dry. Repeat the treatment if necessary until the pan is clean and shining, then scour after each use.

Frying-pan. Season a new aluminium frying-pan by melting a small piece of fat in pan. Remove the pan from the heat and sprinkle generously with kitchen salt. Rub vigorously with kitchen paper or tissue, then empty the salt away and wipe with a clean paper towel or cloth. This treatment should not need to be repeated unless the pan is to be used for general frying and is then wanted for pancakes or omelettes. Either may stick to the pan if it is not 'proved' first.

Teapot. To clean an aluminium teapot fill it with water and add 2 tablespoonfuls of borax. Boil, then wash in the ordinary way.

Mild stains should wash off in detergent suds or with a mild abrasive. Even with severe stains soda alone should not be used in an aluminium teapot but always with a proportion of sodium silicate (waterglass). Almost fill the teapot with hot water, add a tablespoonful of washing soda and $\frac{1}{2}$ teaspoonful of sodium silicate. Leave to stand overnight and wash teapot thoroughly next morning in hot soapy water.

American cloth

Dust regularly, and when dirty wipe with a cloth wrung out in hot soapy water or a synthetic detergent, rinse and dry well. Grease may make the fabric deteriorate, so do not use a wax polish.

Angora

The fluff from angora comes off on chairs, clothes and any rough surface. A rubber brush with sponge rosettes in place of bristles will remove the fluff but after several washings the garment should stop shedding hairs. Wearing an angora jumper with a skirt or coat of the same colour makes the fluff less noticeable.

Asbestos sheeting

If this is glazed it can be washed in soapy water and then in clear rinsing water. Unglazed asbestos sheeting can be dusted or wiped over with a damp soapy cloth.

Baby

High chair. If baby repeatedly flings himself back and hits his head against the back of his high chair, buy a cheap plastics-covered tea-cosy and fit this over the top of the chair back. The padding will protect his head and the plastics can be easily wiped clean.

Meals. Use an ordinary triple egg-poacher for serving baby's meals. The poaching-dishes will hold three small portions of different foods and they can be warmed quickly or kept hot if the poacher is left over a low heat. Another advantage: you can sterilize the poaching-dishes.

Snapshots. To take a photograph of a baby who won't stay still, take a tip from the film photographers who stick a tiny piece of cellulose tape on the baby's palm. Baby is so interested in removing the tape and sticking it somewhere else that it is usually possible to get a really natural-looking photograph in a moment.

Bamboo

Either wash with soap and water and polish with a silicone furniture cream or liquid, or clean with salt water, dry and polish with linseed oil.

Baskets

The cane will not dry out and split if shopping, flower and other baskets are occasionally given a thorough soaking in cold water.

Bath cleaning

Manufacturers of bathroom equipment implore housewives not to use harsh scouring powders to clean their baths. The faint scratching which occurs will be very nearly invisible, but eventually the bath surface will deteriorate and staining will occur more and more.

For routine cleaning, buy the special cleaning powder marketed by the manufacturer of your bath—most builders' merchants can supply this. It will gently scour the surface but is formulated to do it harmlessly. The makers even advise that very fine glasspaper, used in conjunction with this special powder, will remove small stubborn marks without causing damage.

For day-to-day cleaning, soap scum or grease on a bath can be removed quickly with a cloth well wrung out in hot water and sprinkled with a synthetic detergent. (Keep a packet by the bath which everybody can use when they have finished bathing.) Rinse with hot water and dry, not forgetting the taps.

A dingy bath or basin can also be brightened by rubbing on a thick paste made by mixing together cream of tartar and hydrogen peroxide. Leave to dry, then rinse off. Marks beneath taps can often be removed with neat vinegar, but be sure to rinse off immediately or damage may occur.

After cleaning a bath, rinse and dry and rub on a little liquid silicone polish to prevent marks forming in future.

For stains on the bath, see page 225.

Bathroom

If a bathroom becomes dense with steam every time a bath is drawn, this can be avoided by fixing a piece of rubber tubing to the hot-water tap. Rest the other end of the tube on the bottom of the bath and add sufficient cold water to cover the opening, then turn on the hot-water tap and fill the bath in the usual way.

Keep a pair of cheap tweezers in the bathroom so that hairs, strands from face cloths and bristles from the cleaning brush can be removed easily from the waste-pipe outlets.

Beads

Ideally nylon should be used for threading a necklace as it is so strong and easy to use, but thread can be used instead. If there isn't a needle small enough to pass through the eye of a bead or pearl for restringing, twist the end of the thread and dip it in nail varnish or melted candle or sealing wax. Shape the end to a fine point between the forefinger and thumb, leave it to dry and it will slide easily through a tiny bead.

To strengthen the thread and to make it firm, dip it in egg-white, then dry it before threading the pearls or beads.

Bed linen

Sheets. When buying sheets remember that if they are even a little too small for the size of the bed they will be very uncomfortable to sleep in, and will wear out very much more quickly. Do not ask for 'single' or 'double' bed sheets but actually measure the length and width and thickness of the mattress and add another 8 in. all round for a good tuck-in at bottom and sides and for a sufficient turnover at the top.

Whether single or double, a bed usually needs sheets at least 108 in. long. Children can manage with shorter ones because they don't reach the full length of the bed. On average a 3-ft. bed sheet needs to measure 70 in. by 108 in. and a 4-ft. 6-in. bed sheet, 90 in. to 100 in. by 108 in.

If a bottom sheet is not long enough to tuck in properly at both ends of the bed, it will remain in position if the top is securely tucked in first and then any surplus is tucked in at the foot of the bed.

As linen can be imitated, it is as well, if you are intent on real linen sheets, to test apparent linen before buying. Held to the light, linen will appear uneven and thicker in places than in others, while non-linen yarns will be uniform. If you break a linen thread, it will give a distinctive snap and have straight wiry ends while cotton or rayon will break softly and have soft, fluffy ends.

The same thing will apply if a lighted match is held to a strand of linen. It will burn easily but have a rounded and blunt end when the flame is put out; cotton, on the other hand, burns freely, has an odd smell rather like paper burning and leaves a white ash; also it remains tufted, even after burning. Nylon will melt and the strands will fuse together.

To give good value for money, sheets need changing at least once a week and, unless there is a real shortage of linen, change BOTH sheets at the same time. Half the delight of a freshly-made clean-sheeted bed is missing if sheets are changed top to bottom and only one at a time.

Sheets last longer if they are given a rest between each use and laundering. To allow for this, every bed should have at least six sheets or, if possible, eight.

If the letters are outlined in pencil before initialling or dating linen with *marking ink*, the ink has less tendency to run. If a special marking pencil is used, it must be kept sharpened to a fine point or the letters will 'run' on the damp material.

Incidentally, it is a good idea to mark sheets 's' (single) or 'D' (double) in one corner. This saves time when taking sheets from the linen cupboard.

Almost always, the middle of a sheet wears out first, leaving sides quite new. When sheets are showing signs of wear but before they become too thin or in holes, cut them down the middle, join the two outside edges together (with a *flat* seam), hem the new edges and the life of the sheets will be doubled.

Storage. If best sheets are used on rare occasions only, they will stay white if stored in blue paper or acid-free tissue paper with further sheets of paper inserted between folds. Alternatively they may be well wrapped in thick brown paper.

Do not store linens in a heated airing cupboard, in a cedar-lined drawer or chest, or near any form of heat, or they may become yellow.

If yellowing does occur through bad storing or washing, re-launder and dry in sunlight once or twice. Bleaching should not be necessary, but if it is, use a mild powdered bleach or hydrogen peroxide rather than a household chlorine bleach, which used in excess would rot the fibres.

For washing instructions, see page 140.

Pillows. Pillows vary tremendously in size and one should not simply ask for 'a pair of pillow-cases' when new ones are needed. If the cases are too small, the pillows will be hard and uncomfortable, and if they are too large, the bed will look sloppy and untidy.

Measure pillows with a tape measure and buy cases at least 2 in. longer and 1 in. wider than the actual pillows. As with sheets, pillow-cases last longer if they rest between each wearing, so allow a minimum of three cases to a pillow.

Hairpins and curlers wear out pillow-cases twice as quickly as normal sleeping does, so if hair is set at night a scarf should be worn over the pins to protect the pillows.

For washing instructions see page 164.

Beds

Bedding will last longer if springs on a metal bedstead are protected with a mattress pad. To prevent springs from rusting, rub them lightly with an oily cloth.

On a really cold night, add an extra blanket *under* the bottom sheet for more warmth.

When going away on holiday or leaving beds unaired for any time, spread a large blanket completely over the bed. Any damp in the room will be absorbed by the blanket and the bed underneath should remain quite dry.

To test a bed for dampness, place a hot-water bottle between the sheets for a short time, then hold a hand mirror in the bed. Any dampness present will show as a mist on the mirror.

Blankets

When buying new blankets measure the length, width and depth of the mattress, then allow at least an extra 6 to 8 in. at each side for a tuck-in and the same amount at the top and bottom.

Blankets do not need to be as long as sheets as there is no need for a wide turn-over at the top. Generally, *minimum* sizes need to be 60 in. by 80 in. for a 2-ft. 6-in. bed; 60 in. by 90 in. for a 3-ft. size; 80 in. or 90 in. by 100 in. for a 4-ft. 6-in. double bed and larger still —say 100 in. by 108 in. for extra comfort. A 5-ft. wide bed will, of course, need the largest size.

Remember that if a tall person is sleeping in a *single* bed he will certainly need a blanket longer than 80 in. A length of 100 in. or more is preferable.

Fine Merino wool blankets are usually warmest and lightest, with ordinary pure wool or Acrilan blankets coming next. Acrilan blankets are moth-proof, easily washed and quickly dried; they will not shrink or felt. Blankets made with a blend of wool and rayon are not so warm and do not wear as well but they feel pleasant and comfortable; those made from wool blended with cotton are hard-wearing although they have less warmth and are inclined to be heavy.

As with sheets, blankets usually wear first down the middle but they cannot be turned sides-to-middle so well. When a blanket wears thin, cut out the worn part, join up the edges again and use it for a child's bed or cot or as a foot or shoulder blanket.

If a blanket is too short to tuck in properly, attach a length of old blanket or a piece of flannel and tuck this portion under the mattress at the foot of the bed.

Books

Whenever a book is borrowed or lent, it is a useful plan to put a brown paper cover on the book and write on the outside the name and address of the owner and the date it was borrowed or lent. This not only keeps the book clean but reminds the borrower to return it promptly.

If the cover of a book breaks away from the spine it can be repaired fairly easily. Damp the insides of the covers and peel off the paper, then ease off the remaining cotton fabric or gauze from the covers but not from the spine. Trim off any loose ends of gauze and leave the book to dry thoroughly, then cut a piece of strong gauze bandage as long as the book and about 2 in. wider than the spine. Glue the bandage to the spine with strong clear adhesive and glue the extra inch on either side to the covers. Leave to dry completely and then paste to each inside cover ordinary writing paper cut to size so that half of the sheet forms a new fly leaf.

Preserve leather bindings on books by polishing occasionally with colourless liquid wax and then buffing with a soft cloth. Where books are old and neglected, the leather may become dry and powdery. In this case, treat with a little soft white handbag, shoe or furniture cream. Allow the cream to soak into the leather then finish with a soft duster. Repeat if necessary until the leather is soft and supple and is no longer flaking.

Bottles and decanters

If a bottle top refuses to turn and no bottle-opener is handy, hold the bottle firmly and tap the top sideways sharply with the wooden handle of a kitchen knife or tool. An alternative is to hold the cap of the bottle under hot water for a few seconds.

A glass stopper which has stuck can usually be removed if the decanter or bottle is held gently and the stopper gripped with a piece of rubber or a rubber glove. If this fails to move the stopper, a little warm olive oil dripped on to the sides of the stopper and left overnight will usually do the trick.

Remove odour from medicine, spirit or other bottles by half-filling with cold water and then adding a tablespoonful of dry mustard. Cork and shake well, then remove the cork and leave to stand overnight. Shake again, empty and wash in hot soapy water, then rinse thoroughly.

Narrow-necked glass bottles and decanters which have become discoloured can be cleaned with egg-shell. Break the shell into tiny pieces and place in the bottle with a little warm water. Shake well, leave to stand overnight, then shake again and wash in warm detergent suds.

An alternative is to use an ammonia solution. Pour some ammonia and warm water into the bottle and leave overnight. Shake thoroughly, wash in warm soapy water and rinse.

Remove a wine or other stain from inside a decanter by pouring an inch or two of vinegar into the bottom; add a teaspoonful of scouring powder and fill the decanter with fairly hot water. Shake well, leave overnight, then shake again, empty and wash in warm detergent suds. Rinse in warm water and dry.

Salt and vinegar are also effective; with this method use a tablespoonful of cooking salt to a ¼ pint of vinegar and leave in the decanter overnight. Shake occasionally, then wash thoroughly in warm detergent suds and rinse.

Brass

Brass can be kept clean by regular treatment with a metal polish but the easiest method is to use a Long Term Brass polish. The exception to this is lacquered brass (more and more items are being marketed already lacquered), which should never be cleaned with metal polish or the lacquer will be damaged. Occasional applications of silicone polish, however, will do no harm, and will provide extra protection for brass which is out of doors.

A soft sheen can also be maintained on lacquered or unlacquered brass by rubbing with a warm duster lightly moistened with olive oil.

There are many ways of dealing with unlacquered brass which has become dirty, discoloured or stained. It can, if simply dirty, be washed in warm soapy water, dried and then polished with metal polish in the ordinary way.

A weak acid such as lemon juice or vinegar plus a little coarse salt or sugar should clean brass which is tarnished and stained but not too badly neglected. Dip half a lemon into salt or sugar and rub. Remove immediately by rinsing thoroughly with clear warm water, then wash in hot soapy water, dry and polish.

To clean brass when the metal polish tin is empty, dip a brush into some ammonia poured into a saucer and scrub the brassware. Rinse well in clear water, wipe dry, then polish hard with a warm, soft duster.

A hot strong solution of ordinary washing soda is usually effective in removing *verdigris* from brass. If the brass is badly stained and the article is suitable, the brass object can be boiled in the soda solution and then scrubbed. Rinse well afterwards.

Ordinary apple-peel rubbed hard on brass will also often remove slight traces of verdigris.

Badly tarnished and neglected brass can also be cleaned with a solution made by diluting 1 part spirits of salts with 6 parts clear water; follow by rinsing thoroughly under running water, then by washing in soapy water and finally by drying and polishing. Note that spirits of salts is extremely poisonous.

Another very drastic method ideal for badly tarnished and neglected brass is to use oxalic acid, but oldest clothes and protective gloves should be worn for the job. *Oxalic acid is very strong and poisonous.* Mix about $\frac{1}{2}$ oz. of oxalic acid crystals with 2 pints of warm water. When the solution has been well rubbed into the brass, leave for 2 or 3 minutes, then rinse off thoroughly. Wash in hot soapy water, dry and polish.

Whether you use spirits of salts or oxalic acid, mix it with a wooden stick and apply it with an old dish mop or with a rag wrapped round one end of a stick.

When *brass is fitted to leather*, try copying the method used in the Royal Mews. There they use charcoal ash, but bonfire ash would do just as well. Dip a cloth in the ash and rub the brass hard. Finish with a soft dry cloth or brush. This method of cleaning does not discolour the leather and is effective.

A *brass fender* will often stay cleaner for longer if it is cleaned regularly with silicone furniture cream rather than with metal polish. Better still, of course, lacquer the brass and simply rub it with a soft dry duster daily.

Lacquer is suitable for many brass items. It is easy to apply and saves endless cleaning. One coat should last about six months out of doors and up to a year to eighteen months in the house. Clean the metal first, then wipe it over with methylated spirit and apply the colourless lacquer. This is cheap and obtainable in small bottles or in aerosol sprays.

For cleaning brass door fittings, see page 318.

Brass pans

Preserving and other pans made from brass should be kept gleaming and free from verdigris. Thorough soaking after cooking should remove jam or other food particles and this should be followed with hot soapless detergent suds using a soft steel wool pad if necessary.

Metal polish should never be used on the inside of a brass pan which is used for cooking, but the metal can be brightened with lemon juice or vinegar and coarse salt. Rub the inside of the pan with the salt and lemon or vinegar, then quickly rinse off very thoroughly under running water. Finally wash in hot soapy water, rinse and dry completely on a warm, dry cloth.

Bread board

Whiten a wooden board by rubbing it with a squeezed-out lemon skin, then wash in cold water.

Bronze

Regular dusting should be sufficient cleaning for bronze, plus occasional rubbing with oil. Leave oil for five minutes, then remove with a clean duster. Bronze can also be cleaned and protected with Long Term Brass and Copper Polish.

If the bronze is soiled, pour very hot—almost boiling—water into a bowl, add a synthetic detergent and then add the bronze ornaments. Clean with a soft brush, then remove, rinse well and dry, and finally rub on a little oil or silicone cream or use polish as above.

Brooms

Keep a broom cupboard tidy and lengthen the lives of brooms by hanging them upside down after use. An efficient broom holder can be easily made with two empty cotton-reels; screw or nail them to the wall about 4 in. apart and high enough for the broom handle to clear the floor.

New bristle brooms will sweep cleaner and last longer if the fibres are soaked in cold salt water before the broom is used for the first time. This does not, however, apply to nylon and plastics mono-filament brooms.

No matter how tightly a broom handle is screwed into the head, it almost invariably works loose in time. This problem can be solved by painting the inside of the socket of the broom head and by screwing in the handle while the paint is still wet. The broom should not be used again until the paint is completely dry.

If a broom has a plain handle which does not screw into the head, bore a small hole through both handle and broom head at an angle and insert a long thin screw. Never fix a broom handle in position with a nail.

Alternatively you can buy quite cheaply a special gadget for fixing on the broom head.

Cleaning brooms. Whatever the filling, brooms and brushes should be washed regularly in warm synthetic suds. Rinse thoroughly in lukewarm water and finally in cold water. Hang to dry with the handle uppermost. Stiff brooms and brushes, such as yard brooms and carpet brushes, should be washed in the same way but given a final rinse in cold salt water. (A dessertspoonful to a pint.)

Brooms and brushes filled with nylon or plastic monofilaments should be washed very frequently. Swish in hand-hot synthetic detergent suds, rinse in clear warm water and shake to remove excess moisture.

Buckram

Odd stains can be cleaned from buckram with a clean cloth moistened with a spirit dry-cleaner such as carbon tetrachloride. In the case of a lampshade, clean lace or trimming by gentle rubbing with cotton wool dipped in the cleaner. Cleaning with soap and water is not advisable as the moisture may affect the stiffening from the buckram and spoil the shape of the shade.

Another way of cleaning a buckram lampshade is to rub powdered magnesia into the shade and the lace or other trimmings. If possible, wrap in a cloth or paper and leave for several hours, then brush out the dust and powder with a clean brush. This will remove general grubbiness but not grease or other stains.

Buckskin

Brush off surplus dust and use a proprietary white cleaner. If very dirty wash with warm soapy water first.

For cleaning buckskin shoes, see under Shoes in Chapter 4 Valeting on page 199.

Cake-tins

To rustproof a new cake-tin wash and dry it, then coat it with lard and bake in a moderate oven for half an hour.

Next time you buy a cake-tin look for a non-rusting one. Non-stick types are worth the extra cost. See also Baking tins, page 380.

Candles

Both candles and candlesticks vary in size but it is possible to make the two match so that the candles fit and remain upright by dipping the base of the candles in an inch of very hot water for a few minutes before placing them in the candlesticks.

Candles and tapers last longer if they are chilled in a refrigerator for twenty-four hours or so before being used.

An ordinary candle can be turned into a steady night-light by piling a teaspoonful of salt up the wick until only about a quarter of an inch projects.

When a candle stump is too small to burn a wick, use it to rub over ink-written addresses on parcels and on garden labels to prevent the ink from smearing in rain.

Cane

Wash in lukewarm soapy water containing salt and rub gently with a soft cloth. Give a final rinse with cold salt water, absorb surplus moisture with an old towel and leave in the fresh air to dry.

The *cane seats* of bedroom chairs often sag untidily without wearing thin. To remedy this, wring out a cloth in hot soda water and sponge both sides of the seat. When the cane is damp, push upwards from underneath so that any sag is uppermost, wipe off surplus moisture and place in the fresh air to dry.

Castors

Castors on heavy furniture will not so easily mark linoleum if the floor under and around the furniture is rubbed with beeswax. Make sure, too, that castors are moving freely. A spot of oil occasionally will prevent jamming.

Another way to prevent marks is to use specially shaped plastics cups into which the castors fit easily. The cups, which are sold by chain stores, will slide across linoleum or carpet without effort and they are ideal for piano legs and other heavy furniture.

An alternative is to replace the castors with domes of silence or with specially shaped plastics feet. The feet—called furniture rests—are fitted with two springed prongs which fit securely into the base or legs of furniture. Heavy furniture can be moved easily once the feet are in position and they will not mark carpets or linoleum.

Ordinary furniture castors should be oiled lightly from time to time. Protect carpet under the castors with paper or foil before oiling. If a carpet is being shampooed, furniture should be removed from the room and should not be replaced until the carpet is quite dry. If the furniture is too awkward or heavy to remove, place waxed paper or pads of aluminium foil under the castors during shampooing and leave in position until the carpet is dry. If this is not done, the castors may become damp and rust, and thus stain the carpet.

Cats

Easiest way to deter cats from porches and gates and to keep them from damaging plants and flowers is to use a special cat and dog deterrent aerosol. Alternatively, spray with a nicotine solution using 1 oz. of nicotine solution to 5 gallons of water. Don't use in stronger solution as nicotine is a dangerous poison. Both items are available from horticulturists.

Cellulosed furniture

A television set, radiogram or other furniture with a glossy cellulose finish requires little more than daily dusting. A hard, protective film can be put on the finish with the occasional use of a liquid silicone polish. This should also prevent finger-marking.

Furniture with a matt cellulose finish should not be polished or the special matt finish would be spoiled. Daily dusting should be sufficient but if the surface becomes sticky and soiled it may be wiped gently and evenly with a damp chamois leather and buffed with a soft cloth.

A dressing-table with a matt cellulose finish should be protected from cosmetics and perfumes by a sheet of glass. A dining-table with this finish must be well protected from hot plates and dishes with heat-proof mats.

If the matt cellulose finish is damaged by spilt liquids, heat or by being polished it can only be restored by professional treatment.

Chamois leather

After use, wash in warm water, adding a squeeze of washing-up liquid if the leather is dirty. This will not cause smears later, whereas ordinary washing powder may. Rinse well. Do not use hot water, or rub. If the leather is hard, add a tablespoonful of olive or castor oil to the washing water. Dry away from heat and knead well when almost dry.

Chamois leather should be stored quite dry, *not* damp in a jar.

Chest of drawers

Most chests of drawers have hollow bases so there is no need to move the furniture to clean underneath. Simply remove the bottom drawer and use a long-handled broom or vacuum-cleaner attachment to remove all the dust and dirt on the floor inside the base surround.

Children's drawing books

Buy rolls of wallpaper lining instead of drawing books: children find this economy idea fun. For splendidly satisfying self-expression, give them felt-tipped water-colour pens too.

Children's paints

If the children's paints become hard and brittle through being stored away at the back of the cupboard for too long, they can be softened by brushing them with one or two drops of glycerine.

Children's pyjamas

If children suffer from chilblains and cold feet in winter, it is a good plan to tack a pair of woollen socks, a size or two larger than usual, to the legs of their pyjamas.

Chimneys

See under Fires, page 326.

China

The word china is often used casually to mean any type of domestic crockery although there is, in fact, a basic difference between china and earthenware.

Earthenware is opaque and is produced from a mixture of ball clay, china clay, ground stone and ground flint. Colours and decorations are usually fixed into the glaze at a very high temperature so that they are completely permanent. Although it appears to be stronger, earthenware is less resistant to chipping and breaking than china and, under the glaze, it is porous.

Although bone china is stronger than earthenware, the decorations, on the other hand, may not be so resistant. With pottery—and some china—decorations are *under* the glaze or fused into it and these are virtually indestructible. Many of the brighter colours and lustres, on china, however, are applied on top of the glaze and these *can* be damaged by harsh treatment.

Bone china is made from china clay, china stone and up to 50 per cent of calcined bone ash. It is fine, pure white, not porous, and although it looks delicate and fragile it is the strongest and toughest tableware yet invented. When held to the light, bone china is translucent and the shadow of a hand placed behind the china can be seen quite clearly. It is the bone ash constituent which gives the china its clear whiteness, translucency and strength.

Until recently the test of translucency distinguished bone china from earthenware and no other type of English domestic pottery was available. Now, however, after many years of research, Royal Doulton have produced an entirely new type of china. This felspathic china is called 'English Translucent China' and it is intended to provide real china for everyday use for those who cannot afford *expensive* bone china.

China decorating. Plain white or uninteresting china can be decorated quite easily. Wash the china thoroughly, then dry it and wipe each piece with a cloth dipped in methylated spirit. Use enamel, lacquer or special ball-point tubes of paint and either design a simple pattern or dab on clear bright spots about the size of a farthing. Leave to dry for 2 or 3 days and avoid using soda or very hot water when washing up.

To make the designs permanent it is necessary to bake the china, but this can be done at home in an ordinary cooking oven. Place the painted articles in a cold oven, decorated side up for flat articles, and set the oven at Regulo 2 for gas or 250 deg. to 270 deg. F. for electricity. Bake for 20 minutes, turn off heat and leave china until the oven is quite cold.

China care. Pottery of any kind should be heated gradually and never submitted to extremes of heat and cold. Heat alone should not cause cracking as the china has already been submitted to extremely high temperatures (far above boiling point) during manufacture. But sudden heat or sudden cold may, indeed, cause pottery to crack.

To warm plates, teapots, dishes, etc. stand them on a plate-rack above the cooker or place them in a bowl of warm water and gradually add hot (not boiling) water to the bowl. If china or earthenware is put into an oven to warm, the oven should be cool when the ware is put in and the heat should be increased gradually.

The most frequent cause of broken and chipped china is careless stacking during clearing the table, washing-up or storing away. Avoid piling plates too high during clearing away and never be tempted to carry fine porcelain cups to the kitchen one inside the other. For further details see under Washing-up on page 387.

Because hard china will scratch a similar surface, fine porcelain should never be stored one plate on top of the next but always with a pad between each piece. Pads can be made from pieces of fabric, or ordinary paper kitchen towels are ideal.

If everyday china is stored one piece on top of the other, never slide out a plate but always lift the pile until the piece wanted is on top.

Very fine or old china used for display only can be given an extra lustre if it is polished gently with a little liquid silicone polish.

China teapot

To remove tannin stains from a china teapot use a cloth dipped in bicarbonate of soda, then wash in hot synthetic detergent suds. Or put washing soda in pot, fill up with very hot but not boiling water and leave overnight. Next morning brush inside spout with a bottle brush, then rinse out pot with plenty of changes of clear hot water.

Christmas

Christmas-tree foliage is highly flammable but it is possible to treat it so that it will not burn so readily. To treat a Christmas tree, mix 4 oz. of boric acid powder with 12 oz. of borax and dissolve this in a gallon of water. Ideally the tree should be dipped in the solution and left to dry but if this is not possible, the tree can be sprayed out of doors with the solution, using a high-pressure garden spray if available.

Artificial snow can be very messy as it tends to fall easily whenever the tree is touched; much more effective and quite clean is artificial snow made from soap powder.

To make it, empty a small carton of white soap powder or flakes into a bowl and add very little water. Whip the mixture with a fork or egg-beater until the suds look like whipped cream, then spread newspaper on the floor under the tree and, starting at the top, spread the 'snow' on each branch with a spoon or flat knife. Leave the suds overnight to dry thoroughly before decorating the tree, and the snow will remain in position until Twelfth Night.

On Twelfth Night when decorations are taken down and the tree is stripped, give the birds *their* Christmas. Plant the tree in the garden in view of the house windows and decorate it with sprays of millet, pieces of fat, stale bread crusts, a coconut shell and peanuts threaded on a piece of cord or wire.

Chromium plate

Polish with a soft duster. If very dirty, wash with soapy water or hot soapless detergent suds, rinse, dry and rub with a soft cloth. Finish by polishing lightly with silicone cream. Rust or other marks can be removed with a special chrome cleaner sold by most garages.

If the chrome cleaner has run out, ammonia can also be used to clean discoloured chromium plate; moisten a soft cloth with ammonia, rub the chrome, then polish with a soft duster.

Alternatively, silver paper, screwed into a smooth ball and soaked in water, is sometimes used to clean stained chromium plate. Squeeze surplus water out of the paper and rub the stains gently.

Very badly neglected chrome—such as on car radiators—should respond to rubbing with specially impregnated steel wool or a fine steel wool pad dipped in the chrome cleaner.

If chrome is badly worn or chipped it is possible to build up a new finish by applying a special chrome powder on a damp cloth. The powder can be applied to metals other than chrome and it will give a chromium plating to brass, steel and copper.

Chromium teapot

Frequent thorough washing should prevent tannin stains forming inside a chromium-plated teapot. Soda should not be used but if the pot is badly stained it can be cleaned by moistening a cloth in vinegar, dipping it in salt and rubbing the stain with this. Rinse the pot immediately in boiling water, then wash thoroughly and rinse once or twice with boiling water before using.

Clocks

Although the mechanism of ordinary clocks or watches allows the hands to be moved backwards or forwards, the hands of a striking clock should never be turned backwards, and even when turned forwards this must be done slowly enough for the clock to strike at the correct times.

Ordinary clocks and watches should be wound by the same person at the same time each day and eight-day clocks should be wound regularly on the same day each week.

An alarm clock will ring at *exactly* the time desired if the clock hands are first set to the exact time required. Wind the alarm once or twice, then slowly revolve the alarm hand until the bell rings. Reset the clock hands to the correct time and wind the alarm spring fully.

Coal

Large pieces of coal can be broken easily along the way of the grain if a pointed hammer is used. Coal should not be placed one lump on top of another when it is being broken. You'll produce more coal dust that way. A large piece of coal will burn longer if it is placed on the fire with the grain running across the grate.

For instructions for making coal balls, bricks and briquettes from coal dust, see page 461.

Coal scuttle

Sprinkle the base with borax to prevent rusting.

Coconut matting

When it is very dirty, coconut matting should be scrubbed with hot soapy water or soapless detergent. Rinse thoroughly, adding a handful of salt to the final rinsing water. Finish by drying in the fresh air or by an open window but away from direct heat.

Coffee percolator

Wash the percolator thoroughly after every use and rinse with hot water. To clean the percolator when it is stained place a spoonful of detergent powder or soapflakes and a spoonful of borax into the coffee-holder and fill with hot water. Heat the percolator and bring to the boil as though making coffee. Leave for 5 or 10 minutes, then wash thoroughly and finally rinse well under running water.

Condensation

An old towel or tea cloth hung over the cooker will absorb steam from boiling saucepans and kettles and stop the walls from becoming streaky and stained.

You can now buy special strips of sponge to fit along window-sills. These are designed to absorb any condensation, and are especially good for steamy bathrooms and kitchens.

Cooker

Cleaning the cooker. A public opinion poll would probably reveal cleaning the oven on Sundays as Housework Hate No. 1. But need it really be such a chore? Modern cookers have cut cleaning to a minimum. And, with any cooker, there are ways to prevent the oven getting dirty including using a spray which coats the oven and prevents grease sticking. Here are eight easy-care tips from the Electric Cooker Information Centre, but they would just as easily apply to gas cooking.

If you are looking for a new cooker:

Tip No. 1: First consider a cooker with a self-cleaning oven. If this is too expensive, try for a cooker with the oven lining easy to get at: a big 'plus' of electric ovens is that they nearly always have removable side panels and often a removable roof and floor tray—even a lift-off door. Some have an all-in-one lining that comes out in one piece. This means that you can get at any burnt marks in comfort and, if necessary, soak them off.

Tip No. 2: Has the oven an electric light so that you can see into the corners?

Having installed your cooker—or having vowed never to let your old one get into such a state again—how do you keep it looking beautiful?

Tip No. 3: Try roasting meat longer at a lower temperature: many gourmets prefer the flavour, and it doesn't reduce the meat so much. Too many cooks go for a high temperature which makes the fat splash and spit.

Tip No. 4: Don't use too large a meat tin. So often a 2-lb. chicken is roasted in a tin intended for a 28-lb. turkey. The fat spreads thinly over the uncovered surface of the tin, gets too hot and splashes.

Tip No. 5: Roast at the bottom of the oven: the even heat of an electric oven means that you can use the floor or the first runner for the joint (see instruction book to find out which is correct for your cooker), and then the roof is less likely to be splashed.

Tip No. 6: You can enclose your joint. If you haven't got a covered roasting-pan you can use aluminium foil. The meat does not always get brown this way so you can uncover it for the last twenty minutes or so.

Tip No. 7: If you sit your joint on, say, the perforated metal rack that comes with your pressure cooker, the grease will trickle over it into the pan and there be shielded from the heat by the rack. This means it won't burn and splash. (Some electric cookers come with a special roasting-tin which achieves this result even more effectively.)

Tip No. 8: This sounds like one of those counsel-of-perfection rules straight out of a textbook. But of all our eight tips, it is the one to be engraved on every cook's heart: wipe the oven while it is still warm. Just that. With damp cloth, kitchen paper or sponge, everything then wipes off at the first touch.

Last resort: This is for the ones who have ignored tips Nos. 1–8:

One of the quickest and easiest ways to clean a dirty oven is with one of the modern non-caustic cleaners. Aerosol types are sprayed on the inside of a cold oven, left a few minutes, then wiped off with a soft wire wool pad. Or there is a cream sold in a tube and this is applied on a damp cloth; the oven is then wiped down with a wet cloth and finally dried. There is also a special oven cleaning stick.

A method which some housewives prefer when cleaning a dirty, greasy oven is to place a small piece of rag in an old dish, containing about a tablespoonful of ammonia, and stand this in the oven overnight. Next morning remove the ammonia and wash out the oven with hot synthetic detergent suds. All the grease and dirt should come off easily.

Gas cooker. Regular cleaning of jets, rings and burners on a cooker allows complete combustion of gas and therefore more heat for the money spent.

Before cleaning a cooker turn off gas, remove all burners, frets and oven shelves, etc. and leave these to soak in a sinkful of really hot soapless detergent suds with soda added. Clean the oven—with a stick or spray cleaner, a non-caustic cream or with hot strong soapless detergent—rinse and dry.

Deal next with the top and outside of the cooker and by then most of the dirt should have soaked off the loose parts.

Use a stiff oven brush when cleaning the burners and deal carefully with the air inlet holes underneath; if these are clogged, use a pipe cleaner to clear them. For oven shelves stained with burnt fruit juices or other marks, use fine steel wool dipped in scouring powder to clean them thoroughly. Rinse, dry and replace.

A white enamel cooker often becomes fumed and yellow after a time. It is almost impossible to remove these yellow fume stains once they have set. The stains can be avoided if the enamel parts of the cooker (and of other equipment in the kitchen) are polished with a white emulsion wax such as Mello. This puts a hard protective gloss on the enamel. The polish contains a cleaner and may help whiten yellowed enamel if the stains are not of too long standing.

Cookery old wives' tales

Do you put tablespoons of water in the roasting-tin 'to stop the meat drying'? Does your kitchen fill with steam whenever you boil greens because 'to put the lid on spoils the colour'? Myths like these are handed down from mother to daughter and fossilize, taking no note of changes in cooking equipment and techniques. The 'water in the roast' for instance is a legacy from the last century and has never been necessary in an electric oven.

One habit still very widespread is to cook the roast at a high temperature for the first few minutes before lowering the controls to the normal roasting figure. This is done to 'seal in the juices' but, in fact, simply causes splashing and a dirty oven: there is no difference in appearance or taste between a roast started from cold and one that has been treated like this.

'Wait for the blue haze before you put the chips in' is another old maxim, not only out of date but dangerous if the pan is full of oil instead of lard or dripping. Oil has a much higher boiling-point and may froth over and catch fire if left until it smokes.

Not only the cooking but the cooker has its folk-lore. Some people still believe, for instance, that anyone buying a new electric cooker will have to buy new saucepans to go with it, wait hours for it to heat up, and pay enormous electricity bills. Before the war there was truth in all of these, but nowadays there is none. Any type of saucepan with a reasonably flat base can be used, whether on the radiant rings or the lightweight sealed ones. Modern electric cookers are just as fast as any other type—some even faster—while costs as well as time have gone down over the years. A fair average today would be one unit of electricity per person per day for a family of four—at the highest rates, not more than 8d. a day.

There is one tip, however, that the experts say *does* work; a little drop of cold water raised to steaming pitch in the milk saucepan before you put the milk in, will make pan much easier to clean afterwards. (Of course, you could use a non-stick pan!)

Cooking smells

Remove the fishy odour from a saucepan after cooking kippers by emptying tea-leaves into the pan. Cover with water, leave for 5 to 10 minutes, rinse and then wash in the ordinary way.

A damp cloth hung over the gas cooker will absorb most of the odour when frying fish.

Add a spoonful of mustard to the washing-up water to remove an odour of fish from silverware, or a piece of lemon peel or a teaspoonful of vinegar to remove a fish or onion smell from china.

An ordinary chlorophyll tablet can be added to the water when washing-up. The tablet will effectively deodorize smells.

Copper

Easiest way to clean tarnished copper is to use a Long Term Brass and Copper Polish occasionally. Or clean frequently with ordinary metal polish and shine with a soft duster.

Badly stained and neglected copper may need more drastic treatment. Rub with a mixture of 1 part spirits of salts to 6 parts water, using an old dish-mop. This acid is poisonous and corrosive and must be rinsed off thoroughly under running water, and the copper should then be washed in hot suds and rinsed again before being dried thoroughly and polished. Flush away surplus acid down the lavatory, and throw away any container used for the operation.

It is possible to buy a specially impregnated cloth which will keep copper clean and shining once it is clean. It should be used on average once a week in summer and twice a week in damp weather.

Proud of a copper kettle? Then boil some water in it and while it is still warm clean the outside with a cloth dipped in sour milk, or to keep it shining for weeks use the Long Term polish mentioned above.

Copper pans

A copper saucepan or preserving pan should be carefully looked after, as veridgris, which quickly develops on neglected copper, is poisonous. It is because of this that copper pans must be dried very thoroughly after cleaning (see above). Remove any verdigris with a mixture of salt and vinegar, then rinse thoroughly and dry well. After cooking, clean a copper pan with very hot detergent suds and fine steel wool or one of the modern highly efficient pan cleaners, such as Scotchbrite.

Food should not be left standing in a copper pan for any length of time after it is cooked. When possible, avoid preparing dishes containing vinegar in a copper saucepan.

Cork table mats

Food stains should be wiped from cork table mats with a damp cloth as soon as the table is cleared. If the mats are generally soiled and grubby either rub them gently with fine sandpaper or damp them one at a time and rub lightly over the surface with wet pumice stone. Wipe with a damp cloth to remove loose powder, then pat dry.

When cork mats are old and shabby they can be given a new lease of life by covering them with self-adhesive plastics. Allow a slight over-lap, as the material often shrinks, and smooth out all air bubbles.

Curtain fittings

Dust curtain tracks thoroughly, then moisten a cloth with paraffin, olive oil or lubricating oil and rub the tracks hard with this. If the curtain track is clogged or rough, clean it with a cloth dipped in turpentine or white spirit and then rub it with fine steel wool. Wipe with a dry duster to remove dirt particles, then rub with silicone polish.

Plastics or nylon tracks should be dusted or, if dirty, wiped with a damp soapy cloth.

If *curtain rings* will not slip easily along a rod, remove the curtains and rub the rod briskly with a cloth dipped in paraffin. Leave for a short time, then polish with a warm duster and replace.

By the sea where damp salt air often rusts old metal curtain fittings, or in a bedroom where quiet is essential, tracks and runners made from nylon or plastics are better, especially for light curtains. In houses where there is a great deal of dust, tubular curtain tracks, completely enclosed, are a help.

Old curtain hooks and rings which are rusty and discoloured can often be cleaned and given a new lease of life if they are boiled in vinegar and water for a few minutes, drained, then dried in a duster.

Another way to clean the rust from old curtain hooks is to let them soak in cloudy ammonia for half an hour or so. Swish them round in the ammonia, then dry on an old duster.

An even better alternative is to buy modern non-rusting hooks and rings.

It is important with very long curtains to have sufficient curtain hooks and runners, and one every three to four inches should be allowed.

Curtains

Heavy opaque plastics material is suitable for kitchen and bath-room where there is steam and condensation. Just as practical and much more luxurious-looking is fibreglass curtaining which always keeps its crispness. As an alternative, choose material such as towel-ling which will absorb moisture without looking limp and crumpled. Coloured terry-towelling and gaily printed linen roller towelling also both make excellent bathroom and kitchen curtains.

Making curtains. Allow $1\frac{1}{2}$ to $1\frac{3}{4}$ times the width of the window for ordinary curtains and at least twice the width for net curtains. Where one or two widths of material must be joined to make each curtain, the design in each width—as well as in each curtain—must match and if the pattern is large, quite an amount of material will inevitably, be wasted and must be allowed for. When calculating the amount of material needed for curtains with a fairly large design, measure a complete pattern and work out how many repeats will be needed in each length of curtain, adding 6 to 9 in. for hems.

Long rayon curtains sometimes tend to drop in the middle and to shorten at the seams. This trouble can often be avoided if the selve-edges of the material are snipped every three or four inches throughout the length. Sewing weights in the corners of hems also helps to hold seams taut.

When using velvet, have the pile running upwards for a richer effect; on pastel shades, however, the pile sloping downwards will make the colour appear more delicate. Whichever way the pile slopes it must be in the same direction on each curtain.

Lining curtains gives them protection against strong sunlight and makes them hang better and appear more luxurious. Cut linings 2 in. shorter than the curtain fabric and 1 in. narrower. Machine linings only to the top of the curtain, leave the lower hem loose and slip stitch the sides. Remove linings before laundering if curtains are heavy.

To repair a tear or rip in a curtain quickly, hold the edges together and stick a piece of transparent adhesive tape on the right side. Next choose the nearest colour in special adhesive mending tape, stick to the wrong side of the material and gently iron until the adhesive melts and bonds in with the fabric. Finally remove the transparent tape.

Pelmets. Gummed buckram can be used to make a straightforward pelmet providing the curtain material is fairly firm. Cut fabric, lining and buckram to the shape and size required, allowing an inch extra on the fabric and lining for turnings. Use a fairly hot iron and press the lining on to the damped buckram, turning the hem over. Press the curtain material on to the unused side of the damped buckram, again turning in hem to other side of buckram.

To make curtains flame-resistant see under Flame-proofing on page 328.

Cutlery

To keep knives, forks and spoons in good condition, the Cutlery

Research Council recommends that cutlery should be washed and dried as soon as possible after use.

Spoons and forks in particular should not be left unwashed for a long time, otherwise stains may be caused by eggs, condiments, etc.

If knives are left undried or immersed in water for a long time, slight corrosion may occur on the blades.

Liquid bleaches should not be used in washing-up water.

If powdered detergents are used they must be thoroughly dissolved before cutlery is placed in the hot water because some undissolved detergents can cause staining or pitting of the surface.

Ordinary salt is very corrosive and, if allowed to come into contact with cutlery in very hot water, may cause pitting of the stainless steel blades.

Undissolved salt from dirty plates may cause dark spots to appear very rapidly on silver or silver plate which is immersed in hot solutions of certain powdered detergents. So always rinse away salt, and use a washing-up liquid in preference to washing powder.

Some liquids, used to remove tarnish from silver without rubbing, discolour steel blades. Knives should not be cleaned with these liquids unless the maker's instructions state that they have no harmful effect on steel.

Never put plastics or wood handles in boiling water. If it is too hot for your hands it is too hot for the handles.

Cutlery which is *kept stored* except for special occasions will stay bright and shining if a little olive oil is rubbed on before it is packed away.

If cutlery has *wooden handles*, keep dry and rubbed up with a soft duster; rub with fine steel wool dipped in wax polish if the handles become rough.

Remove *egg stains* from spoons and forks by rubbing with a damp cloth dipped in ordinary salt. Wash immediately in clear water, then in hot water to which you have added washing-up liquid.

See also under Silver on pages 372 and 467.

See page 342 for particulars on Knives.

Darning stretch-nylon socks

Darn stretch-nylon socks diagonally. Darns then give with the sock.

Distemper

Oil-based distempers are frequently described as 'washable'. In fact they contain only a small proportion of oil and are very absorbent.

The surface can be washed but only with a damp cloth wrung out in liquid paint cleaner or liquid detergent and wiped over the distemper. Use a light stroke as hard rubbing may destroy the surface completely. Wash, rinse and pat dry, working on a small area at a time, overlapping each patch and working from the bottom of the wall upwards.

Water distempers must be treated like whitewash. For details see page 437.

Dog repellent

Avoid the problem of dogs fouling gates and porches by spraying with a special aerosol spray available from horticulturists and household stores. The spray can be used around plants and will also repel cats.

Door furniture

To protect the surrounding woodwork when cleaning a brass doorhandle, letterbox or knocker on the front door, cut a protecting plate from cardboard to fit the brassware. Make the cardboard shields large enough to slip over and just clear the edges of the knocker or doorknob, etc. Keep the shields in the polish cupboard for each occasion when you polish.

The easiest way to keep brass door furniture shining is to polish it until it gleams, wash it in hot soapy water and dry it thoroughly, then wipe it over with a cloth dipped in methylated spirit and finally coat the entire brasswork with clear lacquer. Choose a fine dry day for the job and avoid breathing on the brass. There are a number of proprietary brands of lacquer on sale, all cheap and easy to apply. Once the brasswork is lacquered, metal polish must not be used, but cream or paste wax polish will do no harm.

See also section on Brass, page 300.

Doorstep

A doorstep can be kept white during the winter by using plaster of Paris in place of whitening.

A useful tip when applying whitening or red ochre to a doorstep is to use a very thin starch in place of water. It takes less time and withstands rain better.

It is not advisable to apply red tile seal to a red quarry tiled doorstep. The seal soon wears off in patches with the heavy traffic. Best treatment is regular applications of red tile polish.

Draining-board

Daily scrubbing with cold salt water will whiten a discoloured wooden draining-board.

A plastics draining-board needs daily washing with synthetic detergent; rinse with clear water and dry with a soft cloth. Do not polish: wipe off any grease stains as soon as they occur.

A hinged or movable draining-board which leaves a space at the back and sides can be made leak-proof if a little cellulose rubber or plastic foam is stuck along the edge with waterproof adhesive.

Any other leaks in a draining-board can be made waterproof by using a special sealer along the underneath.

Drawers

A drawer which sticks and jams every time it is opened or closed should be emptied, removed and turned upside down on a table. First check to make sure that nails or screws have not worked loose and replace if necessary. Look for a rough surface or fine sawdust indicating that a piece of wood is jutting slightly and catching every time the drawer is moved; if this is evident, smooth the jutting edge with sandpaper or a wood-smoothing tool.

If no cause can be found for the drawer sticking, rub the rubbers and the bearers it glides on with dry household soap, with the edge of a candle or with a wax silicone polish. Any one of these should provide a thin, slippery surface for the drawer to run on.

Line *dressing-table make-up drawers* with blotting paper to absorb any liquids which spill or run down bottles and jars. A length of elastic, fastened to the drawer sides at intervals with drawing-pins will hold small bottles of nail varnish and make-up tidily.

Silverware drawer. Try keeping camphor block in the silverware drawer to absorb moisture and prevent the silver from tarnishing. The camphor also helps if placed in a damp drawer.

Dustbin

Sprinkle the dustbin with a disinfectant powder daily to deter flies and decay; or, if this is not available, try sprinkling the dustbin with powdered borax instead; it is effective even in hot weather.

During warm weather, paint the inside of the dustbin lid with creosote. This will keep the dustbin clean and deter flies and blue-bottles from hovering around.

A deodorant block, specially made to be stuck to the inside of the dustbin lid, can be used to prevent unpleasant odours. It should be replaced when it has finally worn away.

Another way of freshening a dustbin is to burn a sheet of newspaper in it once or twice a week.

Dusting

On ordinary furniture, and especially if it is highly polished, an impregnated mop—such as those used on cars—makes dusting much easier and quicker and leaves a light film of polish behind. Mops can be washed and re-impregnated with a special inexpensive liquid.

For fragile ornaments, glass animals, etc. a lightweight nylon dusting brush is easier and safer. The brush can be washed frequently and will last indefinitely.

It is often difficult to remove fluff, dust, dog hairs, etc. from a velvet suite or from cushions and rugs with an ordinary brush. If this is the case try using a rubber rosette brush, such as that recommended for removing angora fluff. A damp chamois leather is also frequently effective.

Eiderdowns

See under Quilt on page 363.

Electric blanket

It is very important to use an electric blanket correctly so be sure to buy the type you need. If you are a particularly chilly person and want to keep a blanket switched on when you are in bed, buy an overblanket. An ordinary electric blanket which you lie on should *always* be switched off before you get into bed. Never use any type of electric blanket folded, creased or rucked. Make sure you flatten it completely each time you make the bed.

Never switch on an electric blanket if there is any chance that it might be damp. Don't wash it unless the manufacturer's instructions state that this is permissible. Some blankets are home washable and some may even be laundered in a washing machine but if you are in any doubt send it back to the manufacturer's for cleaning. In any case, send your blanket back for regular servicing. At least every third year—during the summer months.

Never buy a secondhand electric blanket and when you buy a new one, preferably buy one approved by the British Electrical Approvals Board. These are distinguished by a yellow and blue label. Secure your new underblanket to the mattress or bed by the four corners.

This helps to keep it taut and free from wrinkles. Never stick pins in your electric blanket. On children's beds, don't just switch off the blanket before putting the child to bed but disconnect at the plug also, for extra safety.

Electric flex

Lamp flex trailing around the floor is dangerous. Always use the shortest possible flex on any electrical appliance and always use a single unbroken length between plug and appliance. Never join up separate lengths to make a longer lead and never patch up flex with insulating tape—always replace the worn flex with a new length. Frayed flex is one of the most obvious dangers in a home and yet it is very common. Replace flex as soon as it becomes frayed or shorten it to remove the frayed part entirely. Sometimes fraying is caused by too long a flex. Never run flexes under carpets or rugs.

Electric lamps

Fly marks and dust can be removed from electric lamps and fittings with a cloth lightly moistened with methylated spirit. Leave for a few minutes, then rub hard with a clean dry duster. Avoid switching on the electricity until the lamps are dry.

Electric plugs

The familiar plug which brings power to each electrical appliance is a simple, robust device but it can be the cause of—possibly serious —trouble if it is neglected or incorrectly wired.

If a plug gets warm, there is probably a loose connection or a bad electrical contact in the socket. Have it checked by an expert. If a plug becomes cracked or chipped, replace it. Plugs which are subject to heavy use or are frequently dropped—such as those on vacuum cleaners for example—should be made of rubber rather than plastic. These smashproof resilient plugs (marked BS 1363a) cost very little more and last a very long time even when subjected to heavy wear.

The most widely used plug today is the ring-circuit plug, some-times called a 13-amp plug. There are, however, a number of older non-standard plugs still in use. These have round pins and there are three sizes in the three-pin types. There is only one size in the flat pin 13-amp type but they can have fuses of different ratings. The plugs should be marked BS 1363 and the fuses 1362.

Fuse ratings are 13 amp (coloured brown) and 3 amp (coloured blue). It is important to use the right fuse. A 13-amp fuse will not give protection if it serves a lamp or an appliance under 750 watts. So use a 3-amp fuse for anything below 750 watts; a 13-amp fuse for anything over 750 watts and up to 3 kilowatts.

Wiring a plug is fairly easy and straightforward but if you are in any doubt, have it done by a skilled person. The domestic wiring system is made up of three wires: the live wire—which carries the electricity from the generator; the neutral wire—which carries it back; and the earth wire—so called because electricity seeks the shortest path back to earth. This is the safety wire and it should always be connected. A three-core flex should never be connected to a two-pin plug.

Until recently, the three wires in electrical flexes have been identified by the three colours red (for live), black (for neutral) and green (for earth). Now an international agreement has been made and we are changing the colours of three-core flexes so that Britain will conform to an international colour coding. This is much safer especially as many of the electrical aids we use are of foreign origin.

The new colours are brown (for live), blue (for neutral) and green and yellow stripes (for earth).

When you are wiring a plug, the green or the green and yellow lead (the earth) goes to the largest of the three pins usually marked E or with a sign showing a vertical line above three progressively smaller horizontal lines. The red or brown lead goes to the pin marked L (for live) or R (for red) and the black or light blue to the pin marked N (for neutral) or B (for black).

Before screwing the cover on to the plug after connecting the wires, make sure that there are no stray whiskers of bar wire and that the nuts or screws holding the wires are hard down and not just finger-tight. Make sure that the flex is firmly gripped under the clamp where the lead enters the plug. This prevents the wires pulling away from the terminals. There should be no looseness or rattling of any kind when you have finished and all screws or nuts holding the plug together should be firmly tightened.

Some appliances are double insulated and they are fitted with a flex which has only two wires—live and neutral but no earth. It is quite safe to fix these two-core flexes to a three-pin plug leaving the larger earth pin unconnected. But the reverse does not apply and a three-wire flex should never be fitted to a two-pin plug.

If you should buy a foreign appliance with colours other than those mentioned above, always consult a qualified electrician or your electrical shop or showroom before attempting to fit a plug. If you are in any doubt how to fit an electric plug properly, ask at your electrical showroom, at an electrical shop or a qualified electrician. They will be happy to show you how to wire a plug correctly.

See also pages 321 and 453.

Emulsion paint

To clean emulsion paint, see page 424.

Enamel

Enamel saucepans should be left to soak if food is burnt or stuck in them and if some leverage is necessary to loosen the particles, a blunt clothes-peg is useful. A non-scratchy scourer or mild abrasive should be safe but in most cases really hot synthetic suds are sufficient.

In fact, soap and water is the only really safe way of cleaning enamel. Abrasive and scratchy scourers are likely to mar the fine surface and a knife will almost certainly do so. Soda may attack some kinds of enamel and weaken it.

A damp cloth, or better still a *good* pan scourer sprinkled with salt, will usually remove burnt particles of food from an enamel plate or dish, while soaking in a strong borax and water solution will usually remove scorch marks.

Fabric scrapbook

For home dressmakers a fabric and button scrapbook is worth a lot more than the time it takes to make it. Buy or make a cheap scrapbook and use one page for every garment made. On the page make a note of the date, measurements, etc. and stick in a piece of spare material and any odd buttons; keep fabric and buttons in place with self-adhesive tape. If an extra button is needed or a patch has to be made, it takes only a moment to find the correct page in the scrapbook.

Face flannel

To clean a slimy face cloth see under Sponges on page 376.

If you have children and like to keep a flannel in the kitchen for sticky fingers, sew an elastic loop to the flannel and screw a plastic-covered cup hook near to the sink to hold it. The wooden window-frame is often a good place to screw the hook.

Fat fires

A fat fire can start suddenly and become serious very quickly unless it is dealt with promptly and correctly. Turn off gas or electricity immediately, then cover the fat in the pan with a close-fitting lid or with a baking-tin or similar item which will exclude air; and close doors and windows quickly.

If the fat continues to burn, pour salt on to it or bicarbonate of soda or sand. To remove the flaming pan out of the kitchen, wrap a damp cloth around one hand and arm, hold the handle of the pan with this out to one side—never in front of the body. Open the door with the uncovered hand, still keeping the pan to one side. Douse flames with *salt, bicarbonate of soda, sand* or *earth. Never* throw water on it or it will spread over a larger area; do not pour flour on it as this may easily explode.

Feather-proofing

Special feather-proof ticking should be used for pillows or cushion-covers but ordinary material can be treated to close the pores of the fabric so that feathers cannot penetrate. Waterglass (similar to that for preserving eggs) can be used, or ordinary laundry starch will do just as well. Make up a strong solution, dip the material or covers in this, drip dry and iron while still damp. Another method is simply to rub the wrong side of the fabric thoroughly with wax or hard washing soap or with a light solution of plastics starch and then press with a warm iron.

Feathers

Before being used as filling for cushions and eiderdowns, newly-plucked feathers must be cleaned properly. Remove any particularly soiled feathers and any with sharp quills, then pack loosely in muslin or nylon washbags. You can make these from old curtains. Wash in warm water and synthetic detergent, rinse thoroughly, drain and dry. Feathers can be washed, rinsed, then dried in the bag in sunlight, but shake frequently.

Animal oil can be removed by steeping new feathers in lime water. To make this add 1 lb. of lime to a gallon of water. Remove any lime residue, then pour in the feathers and stir thoroughly. Leave for several hours before pouring off the lime water and rinsing with clear running water.

Fibre doormat

The fibres often break and fall out of doormats if they are dry and brittle. To avoid this, damp a new doormat well and occasionally soak it in cold salt water—especially in hot, dry weather. Dry the mat before replacing it on the floor.

Finger-plates

An attractive idea is to use clear glass or transparent plastic finger-plates, and back them with wallpaper. Choose paper to match the contrasting or main wallpaper in the room and cut the design accurately by placing the finger-plate over the paper and cutting round the glass with a sharp razor-blade.

Fireplace

Brick fireplace. Bricks are very absorbent so that soap, soda, soap powders and even soapless detergents should not be used for cleaning, otherwise even in spite of careful rinsing a certain amount of white deposit almost always remains.

Usually scrubbing the bricks with a firm brush and clear warm water is sufficient to clean them safely. If the bricks have not been specially faced, light rubbing with a wire brush removes surface dirt but this treatment is quite drastic and causes a certain amount of powdering. Red bricks are often brightened by rubbing with another red brick after scrubbing.

For specially faced bricks which are very soiled and which cannot be brushed, protect hands, clothes and floor, then make a solution of 1 part hydrochloric acid (spirits of salts) to 6 parts water and brush this on to the brickwork, avoiding the cement entirely or it will crumble. Rinse immediately with plenty of clear water.

If ordinary brushing will not remove a fire-burn mark from a brick fireplace, rub lightly with neat vinegar, rinse off and leave to dry.

Slate fireplace. To restore the colour and surface of a slate fireplace, buy some boiled linseed oil and mix equal parts of white spirit and boiled linseed oil. Dip a soft cloth in the mixture and rub well into the slates. Polish with a clean soft cloth. Repeat occasionally.

Stone fireplace. Avoid using soap, soap powders or ordinary scouring powders as these may affect the colour of the stone. If the fireplace is soiled, scrub it with a stiff wire brush and clear warm water. Clean any really dirty patches in the same way but dip the brush in powdered pumice first.

Redecorating a fireplace. If a brick fireplace is dull, the colour can be changed with plastic emulsion paint. Clean the bricks first with wet pumice stone, rinse and leave to dry. Then fill in any gaps or repair cracks with a filler such as Alabastine, Polyfilla, Celofil, etc. and allow to dry. Pour into a can half as much paint as it is estimated will be needed, add the same quantity of water and paint this solution on to the bricks. Allow to dry thoroughly, then paint again, this time with ordinary full-strength emulsion paint.

Dingy chipped tiles in a fire surround can be painted to tone in with the rest of the room. Clean thoroughly and wipe down with a rag dipped in white spirit, then paint carefully with a heat-proof paint.

Fires

To light a fire quickly and easily, leave a few cinders soaking in a couple of teaspoonfuls of paraffin in a small tin. Lay the fire in the usual way but add the cinders before the pieces of coal. When the grate is cleared, put a few more cinders back into the tin ready for the next day. Keep a lid on the tin (an empty cocoa tin is ideal) and store away from the fire. Easiest method of fire lighting is to use a proprietary fire lighter block.

Split logs give a cheerful fire and if they are placed on the fire bark side down, the sparks will not fly into the room. To draw up a fire quickly, place all logs in the same direction and not crossing.

A dull and neglected fire can be brightened by burning a few pieces of dried orange or lemon peel. This will quickly draw up the fire but it crackles rather noisily in the process. Dried orange peel will also help a new fire to light quickly, being used in the place of wood.

Potato peelings, dried until crisp in a cooling oven, can also be used in place of wood for fire lighting.

When a slow-burning stove or kitchen boiler has been filled with fuel, insert the poker and riddle it slightly so that there is a direct outlet from the fire to the front or top of the stove. If this is done, any trapped gas will escape instead of being closed into a pocket and finally causing a miniature explosion.

If a fireplace has not been used for some time, burn a crumpled sheet of newspaper in the grate before laying the first fire so that any damp or stagnant air collected in the chimney can be driven out.

If rubbish is burned on a fire the chimney will need sweeping more frequently. Any refuse burned should always be rolled tightly in newspaper and placed at the back of the fire. Damp refuse should not be burned regularly—the reason is explained below under Chimneys.

Loose coal dust can be shovelled into paper bags and wrapped in a newspaper. One of these 'parcels' placed on the fire will cake together and burn like coal so long as it is not poked or disturbed.

For details of making Coal Eggs, Briquettes, etc., see page 461. See also heading 'Coal' on page 309.

Chimneys. Most chimneys need to be swept every six months, or more frequently with boiler chimneys where rubbish is regularly burnt. In practice wet rubbish should not be burnt. If wet rubbish is burnt on a boiler—particularly where anthracite is being used— the sulphur in the fuel will combine with the moisture from the rubbish and form sulphuric acid. It is quite common for the sulphuric acid formed to attack the mortar between the bricks and, given sufficient time, the chimney will crack and could even collapse.

Industrial firms and large concerns frequently use a soot-dispersing powder such as Stopsoot and this is available to the public. The powder is sprinkled on to the red-hot coals every seven to ten days and no professional sweeping is necessary.

Smoky chimneys are often a result of too-efficient draught-proofing of doors and windows. The problem can be overcome by fitting special floor ventilators on either side of the fireplace. Alternatively, drill several small holes about the size of a penny by the side of the hearth. For a good finish the holes can be covered with a special type of adjustable grid ventilator obtainable from ironmongers.

Where there is a solid floor and this method of ventilation is out of the question, the next best thing is to fit a ventilator in the outside wall of the room just above the skirting, although frequently drilling a hole in the skirting board and fitting a ventilator over it is sufficient.

If the smoky chimney is caused by downdraught this usually means that a tall building, the roof of another house, a tree, or perhaps a hill is higher than the chimney, causing air to be deflected down the chimney. The remedy is to fit a special cowl or chimney-pot or to make the chimney higher.

Fish odours

See Cooking smells, page 313.

Flags

Most flags or bunting can be washed, although the colours will not invariably be fast. Wash as quickly as possible in a rich lather made with warm water and mild soapflakes. Swish in the suds, keeping the flags under water and moving so that any loose colour runs into the water and not on to the rest of the flag. Rinse quickly in warm water, spin dry or roll in a thick towel or pass through a wringer, and hang immediately to dry in a breeze if possible. In no circumstances leave flags or bunting lying rolled up or bundled together whilst wet and do not dry near heat.

Flame-proofing

Where there are children, old people or invalids, it is a good plan to fire-proof curtains and rugs each time they are washed. It takes only a few minutes and does not affect the fabric in any way.

Mix 5 oz. of borax with 4 oz. of boric acid and dissolve this in $\frac{1}{2}$ gal. of hot water. Stir thoroughly, then immerse the washed curtains or rugs, squeeze out surplus moisture and leave to dry. Curtains can be spin dried or wrung and ironed in the usual way according to the fabric.

It is preferable to buy garments and material treated with Proban permanent anti-flame finish (see page 17) and to buy flare-free nylon net.

To fire-proof a Christmas tree see page 308.

Fleece quilts

These are filled with fleecy lambs' wool instead of the more usual down or down-and-feather blend. The quilts are warm and are often recommended for persons suffering from an allergy or from chronic bronchial or asthmatic troubles as are those with synthetic fibre fillings.

Flour

Keep a large new powder puff—the kind used with a drum of talcum powder is ideal—in the flour canister. The puff makes it much easier to coat a rolling-pin or pastry board quickly and evenly and with the right amount of flour.

Flowers

Cut fresh flowers in the early morning or late evening and cut the stems on as big a slant as possible. If the stems become slimy, hold them under water and recut on the slant, then place the flowers immediately in a vase of water.

Various methods are used for keeping flowers fresh including aspirin dissolved in the water, a copper coin placed in the vase, a few drops of bleach added to keep the water fresh. This last is particularly useful for flowers such as dahlias and marigolds where stems often become odorous in water fairly quickly.

Florists usually keep flowers fresh by changing the water daily and by snipping a fraction off the stem each time, re-bruising hard stems.

It is possible to keep flowers fresh for special occasions by placing them—head first—in a large plastic bag and fastening the end very loosely with a rubber band so that air can get in. Put in the crisper or salad drawer of the refrigerator or if this is not possible, on a shelf in the fridge but with the temperature raised a little so that it isn't too cold. A bouquet, spray or posy of flowers should keep fresh this way for at least 48 hours.

Daffodils last very much longer if, as soon as they are cut, they are placed in 1 in. of very cold water and left in a cool place for half an hour. When they are arranged in a vase, only 1 or 2 in. of water should be used.

Tulips, on the other hand, need to be soaked for several hours, or overnight, in deep cold water as soon as they are brought into the house. If the tulips are put into water without this preliminary soaking, they may droop considerably. The only solution to this is to remove them from the vase and roll each tulip separately in newspaper so that it is encased from the base of the stem to the head. Stand the rolled flowers in very deep cool water for an hour or two until they remain straight when unwrapped and then rearrange them in the vase.

Some flowers last longer if the stems are dipped into boiling water for 1 or 2 minutes before they are arranged in a vase; this opens the pores of the stems so that more water is absorbed. Flowers which respond to the boiling-water treatment include iris, lilies of the valley, primroses, forget-me-nots, roses and cherry blossom.

To make *mimosa* last as long as possible, dip the stems in boiling water before arranging the flowers in a vase and sprinkle or spray the blossom with cold water last thing each night.

Woody-stemmed flowers do not absorb water easily and the ends of the stems should be crushed or slit or else burned to form carbon, which is porous.

Lilac droops fairly quickly and it should never be placed in a draught or air current, whether warm or cold. Cut lilac cleanly with a sharp knife or secateurs but break the ends roughly before immersing the branches in deep cold water. Leave for 1 hour, then arrange properly in vases. Leafy stems can be pulled (with a sharp downward pull) but the stems must be slit before they are placed in the deep water with the lilac flowers.

Hollow-stemmed flowers such as lupins last longer if their stalks are filled with water first. To do this, hold the flower upside down and fill with water, then block the opening with your thumb and immediately plunge the flower into a vase of water.

Chrysanthemum leaves will not turn brown and wilt so quickly if a spoonful of sugar is dissolved in a little warm water, allowed to cool and then added to the vase of flowers. Sugar added to the water also stops larkspur dropping.

Most flowers, and especially *violets*, absorb a certain amount of water through their petals and leaves and these should be sprinkled daily when water is changed or more water is added. Not all flowers like a complete change of water and most prefer extra water added to that already in the vase. The exceptions are flowers which foul the water quickly. Never leave flowers of any sort in a draught or in the fumes from gas.

Preserving roses. If the roses in the garden are exceptionally good, preserve some for winter. Snip the rosebuds in the late evening and dip the ends of the stems into cool melted candle wax or melt a little sealing wax and wrap this around the end of each stem. As soon as the wax sets, wrap each rose separately in aluminium foil, greaseproof paper or tissue paper and pack loosely in an air-tight box. Seal the box and store in a cool place. When roses are wanted, unpack them, cut off the waxed ends of the stems, then stand them in water until next day, when they will look as if they have just bloomed.

To preserve leaves see page 346.

Fly marks

Remove fly marks from glass and hard-surfaced materials (except plastics) with methylated spirit.

Fly-marking on materials—for example on lampshades—is more of a problem. Try using a solution of detergent and warm water applied on a soft brush. Remember, however, that the whole lampshade should be treated, not just the marked areas, otherwise a patchy effect may be achieved. Rinse with clear warm water and pat dry with a towel. Leave to dry slowly.

A word of warning: some lampshades will not take kindly to this treatment, and dry-cleaning is preferable. For example, the adhesive may be softened by warm water, or the colours may be loose, or the fabric may shrink with wetting.

Foot-scraper

To prevent dirt being trodden into the kitchen from the garden, make an efficient foot-scraper by fastening an old scrubbing-brush upside down just outside the back door. To fix the brush, screw it to a board.

French-polished furniture

Polish with a warm dry duster and occasionally with silicone furniture cream. Woodwork can be wiped with a cloth wrung out in warm soapy water if it becomes sticky and soiled but it should be dried immediately with warm dry dusters and then polished.

Front door

If strong sunlight shines directly on to a front door, blistering the paintwork, once every 2 or 3 weeks moisten a cloth with olive oil and rub the door thoroughly with this. Leave for a few minutes, then polish with a clean dry duster to remove surplus oil.

An alternative is to use a sun blind or curtain.

Frozen pipes

There are several ways of thawing frozen pipes and the quickest (though perhaps not the safest) is probably to light a screwed-up newspaper and pass this slowly along the pipe. If the freeze-up is in one particular spot, a hot-water bottle or a stove placed reasonably near should thaw the ice. Another method is to wrap several layers of cloth around the pipe and then pour on boiling water. Turn the taps on before thawing frozen pipes and if the water is frozen in several places, work along the pipe with heat, starting from the tap.

It is easier to prevent frozen pipes than to thaw them. Special insulated pipe wrap which will keep out the cold and store heat is inexpensive to buy and prevents freeze-ups and burst pipes. It is possible to buy white plastic bandage to bind over hessian wrapping if the appearance is important or to keep the wrapping clean.

Frying-pan

Before using an aluminium frying-pan for the first time, season it by melting a nut of fat in the bottom. As soon as the fat runs, remove the pan from the heat, sprinkle generously with salt and rub hard with paper. Wash and dry.

Prevent a lightweight frying-pan from warping by wiping it with a hot wet cloth and allowing to dry completely. Then pour in melted fat to cover the bottom and let this boil gently for a few minutes; pour off fat and dry with kitchen paper.

Clean a greasy frying-pan by pouring in hot water and a little soapless detergent and boiling for a few minutes. Rinse well.

A really dirty frying-pan can usually be cleaned by soaking it in ammonia and water for 10 minutes, followed by ordinary washing.

See also under Aluminium on page 292.

Non-stick frypan. A frying-pan which has been treated with silicones or coated with polytetrafluoroethylene (PTFE) to prevent food sticking needs careful handling. Use half the heat normally required; lift or turn food with a wooden spatula slice or a specially treated metal slice—never with a fork or knife; avoid scratching the base of the pan in any way and never use a scourer or abrasive of any kind. Wash the pan *immediately* after use with a soft cloth and hot water.

Some non-stick frypans become very discoloured even though they still function satisfactorily. Never use scourers to remove the discoloration—instead use a mild solution of household bleach, leaving the pan to soak overnight. This will not harm the non-stick property of the pan.

If the non-stick surface has begun to wear, the pan can still be used with no harmful effects. But some manufacturers will undertake to re-coat pans for a reasonable charge. Larger stores will give advice on where to send them.

Furniture

Most furniture cleaned regularly with silicone or wax polishes needs no more than a light daily dusting.

To remove old polish from furniture rub with a cloth wrung out in vinegar diluted with a little hot water, or in turpentine or turpentine substitute.

Heavily carved furniture sometimes presents a cleaning problem. The easiest method is to use a clear liquid silicone polish and apply it with a soft brush. Work the bristles of the brush into crevices and angles and leave the polish to dry. A faint haze forms as the liquid dries and this can be removed with a duster, using a clean soft brush to burnish the intricate carving.

Bloom. To prevent bloom on furniture, keep furniture in a dry, well-aired room and away from direct sunshine.

Bloom on furniture is usually caused by moisture in the polish film, present through faulty polishing or because of dampness in the room. By polishing over a damp surface, moisture is trapped between two layers of polish; it is more evident in sunlight because the warmth draws out any dampness which may be there. The answer is to remove the top layer of polish first. Add a tablespoonful of vinegar to a pint of warm water, wring out a cloth in the solution and rub the surface hard. Dry with a warm soft duster and buff thoroughly. Alternatively, remove the polish layer with a soft cloth dipped in turpentine or white spirit. (Caution: test surface first.) Buff immediately and thoroughly.

Once the polish is removed, the surface should be allowed to dry thoroughly and then it should be repolished. If the furniture is finished with a high-gloss varnish, cellulose or french polish, use a liquid silicone polish. Where the furniture has an ordinary wax finish, use silicone furniture cream. The use of a silicone polish helps, as this has a resistance to bloom.

Moving furniture. Heavy furniture which is difficult to move on a polished floor can be slid easily if soft dusters are placed under the legs. To move a sideboard or flat-bottomed wardrobe, ease up one side and roll a piece of broom-handle underneath; it should then move without too much effort.

(See under Oak, Mahogany, French-polished Furniture, etc. for details of specialized woods.)

Galvanized iron

Wash with hot water and a soapless detergent to remove any grease, rinse and dry thoroughly. A galvanized bucket can usually be cleaned easily by wiping it thoroughly with a cloth dipped in paraffin.

Gilt frames

To clean gilt when ordinary dusting is not sufficient, stand a bottle of turpentine substitute in a bowl of hot water. Moisten a cloth with the warmed turpentine and rub over the picture or mirror frame.

A slightly soiled gilt frame can be cleaned by rubbing the surface with half a raw onion. Then rinse the juice off immediately with clear warm water and rub with a dry cloth. When dry restore gloss and protect the gilt by polishing with a silicone cream.

The water in which onions have been cooked can also be used for cleaning gilt, or it is possible to use a solution of vinegar and water applied with a clean brush. In both cases rinse off thoroughly, dry and polish.

Glass figurines

Wash frequently in warm water with washing-up liquid added; rinse in clear hot water and drain on a thick towel.

Glassware

If two glasses become jammed one inside the other, pour some cold water into the inner glass and stand the outer one in very warm water. Leave for a few moments and they should separate easily.

To make glassware sparkle, wash it in suds with washing-up liquid added, then rinse in hot water containing a few drops of cloudy ammonia, some ordinary washing blue or a little borax.

Bear in mind that crystal scratches crystal; this means that fine glasses should be washed one at a time, that they should never be stacked one inside the other and that they should be carefully stored side by side and not touching.

Glass when broken

The splinters and fine fragments of broken glass can be picked up easily with wet cotton wool or with a damp cloth. The cotton wool must, of course, be thrown away immediately but the cloth can be shaken over a dustbin and then hung to dry when any remaining glass particles can be brushed off.

Gold

Remove marks on clothes and skin caused by gold jewellery by washing with lukewarm soapy water. Prevent marks by lacquering jewellery with colourless nail varnish.

Grates

Not so many years ago, old-fashioned cast-iron grates needed to be blackleaded regularly. Most of these grates have now been re-placed with hard-wearing enamel-finished fires but for a grate that remains, the easiest way is to paint it with a black fire-proof liquid. This will give a fairly good finish which can be wiped clean, although the liquid will need renewing from time to time.

Hair brushes

Hair-brush bristles which have become limp and useless after frequent washing in hot water can be revived by dipping them in a solution made by dissolving powdered alum in hot water.

Handwriting

If an old recipe is too faded to read, brush over the writing with a solution of sulphide of ammonia. This won't be permanent but it will last long enough for the original writing to be inked over or for a copy to be made.

Hearth

Small pieces of rubber or strips of plastics foam draught sealer fixed to the ends of a hearth curb will prevent scratches and marks on a polished wooden surround.

Heat-resisting glassware

Although oven glassware is tough and heat-resistant, it needs just as much careful handling as fine glass. Do not for instance, take a glass casserole dish out of the oven and stand it on a cold or wet surface or drop it into cold water or it may easily crack. Do not do the reverse either; and that means do not put a cold glass ovenware dish into a very hot oven or on a hotplate or gas-ring.

Heat-resisting glass should be safe in the hottest oven but it must be put into a slow or moderately hot oven and the heat gradually increased or else the dish should be warmed first in hot water.

Warm heat-resisting plates in hot water, on the bottom shelf of an oven or in a plate-warmer but do not hold them over a naked flame or stand them on a hotplate.

The exception to these precautionary warnings is Pyrocil, a more recent introduction in heat-resisting tableware. It can quite literally be taken from the refrigerator and put straight on the hotplate, without fear of breakage. Similarly, it can be plunged into cold water while still hot.

If the food becomes burnt on to a dish of heat-resisting glass, leave it to soak for an hour or more until the particles are soft, then dip fine steel wool or a fine pan cleaner in salt or a mild abrasive and rub off the remaining food.

Transparent heat-resisting glass should remain clear and if it becomes cloudy after use this may be due to insufficient rinsing after washing. Wash plates and dishes in hot water with washing-up liquid added, then rinse thoroughly before draining dry.

Hide furniture

Hide furniture (which is made from cow-skin) needs dusting and an occasional rub with special hide food or a liquid silicone polish, but if it is dirty or sticky it may be washed with warm water and soapless detergent. Do not use ordinary furniture wax for polishing leather upholstery as this may make it sticky.

Really shabby and neglected hide can be treated occasionally. To do this mix 2 teaspoonsful of vinegar with ½ teaspoonful of household ammonia and add a pint of water. Apply to the leather with a soft cloth and allow to dry before rubbing with a cloth moistened with castor oil. When completely dry, polish with silicone cream.

Another way to treat soiled hide furniture is to clean it with a cloth dipped in a 50 per cent solution of vinegar and warm water, then leave to dry before rubbing linseed oil thoroughly into the leather. Leave overnight and next day, using clean dusters, rub the leather well until the oil has completely disappeared and there is no feeling of stickiness. Give a final polish with a white silicone cream.

Hinges

Creaking hinges should be attended to quickly to avoid damage to the hinge metal. Either use oil, or rub the squeaking hinge with a soft pencil lead to provide graphite—an excellent lubricant for locks and hinges.

For details of oiling see page 355.

Hot fat

If hot fat is spilled on floor or wooden surface during cooking, pour cold water on to the fat immediately so that it will quickly harden without soaking into the surface. As soon as it is hard, the fat can easily be scraped up. Wash away any remaining stain with hot soapless detergent suds.

See also Fat Fires on page 323.

Ivory

Dust with a soft cloth or brush and expose to daylight and sunlight as much as possible. Clean discoloured ivory by soaking it in diluted peroxide of hydrogen for an hour if the article is suitable, or by rubbing it with methylated spirit or with lemon juice and salt.

Soiled ivory can be washed with a damp cloth dipped in synthetic detergent suds or rubbed with a mild abrasive if badly stained. Whichever method is used, rinse thoroughly and dry in sunlight if possible.

If the ivory cannot be moistened—as with a book-binding, for instance, make a paste with finely powdered whitening and lemon juice, apply and leave to dry. Then brush off and rub in a little white silicone polish.

For ivory piano keys, see page 359.

Jewellery

Sparkling colour is the first thing most people think of when they talk of gems. But they usually associate a single colour with each stone, such as yellow with topaz and blue with sapphire.

Many stones, however, are to be found in a much wider range of colours. The topaz, for instance, can be white, pink or blue as well as its several shades of gold, from palest yellow to deep tawny. The sapphire has yellow-red, yellow, green, mauve and pink in its repertoire.

Another stone of great versatility is the garnet, which, besides its traditional deep, glowing red, occurs as green, orange, purple and reddish brown.

Pearls are sometimes pink or black, instead of milky white, and yellow diamonds are high fashion. Diamonds have a surprisingly long list of possible colours, including brown, green, pink, red, mauve, black and blue, as well as the favourite clear white.

This variety works in another direction too. A shopper who wants to buy a stone of a particular colour, say yellow, has a wide selection open to her. She can choose between topaz, citrine, beryl or tourmaline, and if the colour is to be red or rose, there are tourmaline and beryl again, together with spinel and rose quartz, as well as the fabulous ruby.

The aquamarine is not the only stone to have a blue-green sparkle. The zircon and the tourmaline have it as well and the blue of the sapphire appears again in the blue spinel.

If the popularity of its name is anything to go by, the ruby may well be one of the most sought after of gems. Red spinels are called, romantically but incorrectly, 'spinel rubies'; pink spinels 'Balas rubies', and pink topaz 'Brazilian rubies'. In the same way, the red tourmaline is sometimes called the 'Siberian Ruby'; the violet-red garnet the 'Ceylon Ruby', and the crimson garnet the 'Cape Ruby'.

Most jewellery—except turquoise, pearls and opals—can be cleaned by soaking for a few minutes in eau-de-Cologne, methylated spirit or a special cleaning fluid. Brush lightly with a soft brush to clean crevices, then shake off excess fluid and rub gently with a soft cloth or brush to polish.

An old extra-soft toothbrush with the bristles trimmed down makes an excellent brush for ring-cleaning.

Only stones with a claw or open setting—where the back of the stone can be seen—should be actually immersed in a solution. Stones which have an enclosed back are almost certainly held in place with glue or special cement and the liquid might dissolve this.

Where stones are stuck into the setting, clean by dipping a soft brush, first into methylated spirit and then into powdered whitening and gently brush the jewellery with this. The whitening should remove any ingrained dirt and dust and there will not be sufficient fluid to loosen the cement. If powdered whitening is not readily available, jeweller's rouge or plate-cleaning powder may be used instead.

More specific advice on cleaning jewellery is given below:

Aquamarine. Clean aquamarine by brushing gently with a soft brush dipped in lukewarm soapy water. Rinse in clear lukewarm water and dry on a soft cloth.

These stones are delicate and crack easily. As they may crack in hot water an aquamarine ring should always be removed before washing up.

Cameos. When they are dirty, brooches and rings set with cameos often look dull and lifeless, but they are easily cleaned. Dip a soft brush into hot soapy water and gently scrub the cameo, making sure that the brush gets into all the crevices. Cameos are rarely stuck into the setting and it is usually safe to immerse them in the suds. The water can be very hot but should not be boiling. Rinse thoroughly to remove all traces of soap and dry on a tissue.

Diamanté. See under Paste Jewellery, page 340.

Diamonds. In case someone wants to test a diamond for its genuineness, this is supposed to be an easy way; drop the diamond into a glass of water and if the facets are blended in with the stone and are almost indistinguishable, it is false; while if the facets stand out clearly, it is real.

When diamond jewellery is not being worn, each item should be separately wrapped. Diamonds are so hard that if they are jumbled in a jewel box without being wrapped they can scratch and damage other stones as well as other diamonds.

Cleaning diamonds. Although they are usually fairly small, diamonds collect a surprising amount of dust, dirt and grease, possibly because the oils in cosmetics coat them and then powder and dust stick to the oils; soap usually dries on the underside of a diamond ring and cakes hard. To clean, soak the diamond jewellery in a solution made with hot water and synthetic detergent, then brush the stone lightly on top and underneath with a soft-bristled toothbrush. Rinse in hot water and then dip the diamonds in alcohol and dry on a handkerchief tissue or soft cloth. Wrap when not in use.

Emeralds. These stones must be kept clean if they are to show to best advantage. They are, however, delicate and need to be handled carefully. To clean an emerald, swish in lukewarm soapy water and then brush lightly with a soft brush. Rinse in clear lukewarm water and dry on a tissue. Always remove an emerald ring before immersing the hands in hot water.

Garnet. Deep velvety red stone—clean as for emeralds.

Gilt jewellery. A quick rub with a soft duster or with an impregnated spectacle cloth should be sufficient but if the jewellery becomes soiled it can be washed in warm suds and dried thoroughly on a soft duster.

Gold. Bracelets, necklets, etc. can be washed in warm soapy water and, if necessary, scrubbed lightly with a soft brush so that crevices and links can be cleaned. Where washing is not suitable clean with jeweller's rouge on a soft cloth or rub with a specially impregnated cloth sold by jewellers. Where possible, send gold to a jeweller for cleaning and buffing. See also page 334.

Marcasite. If the jewellery is very dirty and ingrained with dust, brush gently with a soft brush dipped in plate-cleaning powder. For ordinary day-to-day cleaning, rub with an impregnated silver cloth.

Do not let marcasites get near a fire. Heat can dull their sparkle.

Opal. White with flecks of colour. The superstition that opals are unlucky for those not October-born is rapidly fading into limbo. But opals need cherishing, because being very porous and inclined to be soft and brittle, the lack of moisture in the air in countries that are hot and dry can cause them to crack open and split. In this country there is no danger of this happening, but even here, and certainly when taking opals to the tropics, the wearer should take care not to immerse them in water—when washing-up for instance—and they should be checked professionally every now and again to see that the setting is quite firm.

Paste jewellery. Paste and diamanté stones are usually stuck into their setting and they may be easily dislodged or the glue dissolved. For this reason, paste or diamanté jewellery should not be dropped or knocked and it should be cleaned gently without immersing it in any cleaning fluid. The only safe method is to brush the jewellery lightly with a brush or impregnated cloth or to send it to a jeweller for professional cleaning.

Pearls. To clean dirty or discoloured pearls, place in a small tin and cover completely with powdered magnesia. Replace the lid, shake gently and leave until next day. Then shake again and remove, brushing off any surplus powder with a soft cloth or brush.

If the pearls are stained and discoloured, it is sometimes possible to whiten them at home by 'washing' them in a mixture of powdered blue and starch. As an alternative try starch and ground rice. Finish by polishing lightly with a soft warm duster.

Real pearls can be washed in lukewarm soapy water but they should not be immersed for any time as wetting the thread sometimes weakens it. If there is any doubt about the thread, wring out a cloth in the suds and gently wipe each pearl.

The moisture will not harm the pearls and many jewellers, when pearls are sent for restringing, wash them in boiling detergent suds. Although this is quite safe for the pearls, it may damage the thread and the method isn't recommended for home cleaning unless the pearls are being restrung.

It is said that to give real pearls a beauty treatment you should wear them as much as possible—even in bed. They gain colour and lustre by absorbing the skin's natural oils.

Imitation pearls are more delicate and need to be cleaned carefully or the thin pearly coating may peel off. Remove dust and dirt by rubbing lightly with a damp chamois leather. If the pearl finish does peel off, paint lightly with pearlescent nail lacquer.

Rubies. These stones are not as hard as they appear. A ruby ring should always be removed before washing up or before immersing the hands in hot water. Wash by swishing in warm soapy water; rinse in clear warm water and dry on a tissue.

Sapphires. These beautiful stones are very delicate and even hand-hot water may crack them. Clean by brushing gently with a soft brush in warm suds and rinse in water of the same temperature. Drain dry on a soft tissue or cloth. Remove a sapphire ring before immersing the hands in water.

Turquoise. These stones may be washed or cleaned in spirit solution but are better cleaned with a dry powder. For further details see under Pearls on opposite page.

Kerb

Clean a *wooden kerb* by rubbing the way of the grain with fine steel wool dipped in turpentine, dry and polish.

A *marble hearth kerb* can be cleaned with hot synthetic detergent suds or, if it is badly stained or marked, make a paste with ½ oz. of whitening and 1 oz. of crushed soda: add a little boiling water to make a thick paste, spread on the stains, leave overnight and finally wash off, dry and polish with a white silicone cream.

Kettles

Always switch off or remove the plug from the connector of an electric kettle before filling the kettle or pouring out the water.

A child's marble, cleaned and left in a kettle, will prevent scale collecting, or a special shell can be bought for the purpose. This must be discarded when it is covered with fur.

Remove fur from a kettle with one of the special de-scaling fluids. Alternatively fill the kettle with cold water, add 1 level dessertspoon of borax and bring to the boil. Pour away water, rub softened deposit with soft scourer and rinse. Repeat if necessary.

For electric kettles this may be considered too drastic by the kettle manufacturer. In this case a very effective but gentle method of de-scaling is to add a few tablespoonfuls of Calgon water softener to the filled kettle and bring to the boil. Leave until cold, then rinse out. Repeat until all scale has been loosened.

Daily scouring with a nylon scourer will clean fur from the inside of a kettle but this is only possible with an electric or other kettle fitted with a large lid.

An iron kettle can be freed from fur by filling with water, adding a tablespoonful of sal ammoniac and boiling for a few minutes. Empty and place over heat when the fur will peel away. Refill, add soda and boil again for a few minutes, then rinse thoroughly with cold water.

A picnic kettle will not rust between uses if it is dried thoroughly over heat and then stored with two lumps of sugar inside.

If the lid of a kettle is hot to touch replace the knob with the cork from a medicine bottle, screwed in from underneath.

To clean a copper kettle, see page 314.

Kitchen surfaces

According to statistics, a pound of grease is vaporized on to kitchen surfaces every day. This means that enamel, plastics, chrome, tiles and paintwork gradually become dulled with a film of grease and dirt and this applies particularly to white and pastel surfaces.

Hot synthetic detergent suds will remove the grease and a white silicone cream or wax will protect the surfaces afterwards. Alternatively use a combination cleaner-polish such as Mello. This will dissolve grease and dust and leave a film of wax behind. Apply it with a damp cloth, rub gently and then wipe off.

Kitchen tools

When a kitchen is redecorated, it is quite a simple matter to change the colours of the handles of kitchen tools so that they match the new colour scheme. Wash the handles first in synthetic detergent to remove any grease, allow to dry and then rub lightly with fine glasspaper to remove gloss. A strong heat-resisting enamel is the best choice for kitchen tools and this is easy to apply and will dry quickly. Let the tools dry thoroughly before using them and avoid very hot strong detergents until the enamel is well hardened.

Knitting

If a proper wool-holder is not to hand, knitting wool can be kept clean by placing the ball in a large envelope. Pull the wool through one corner at the top and seal the envelope.

An angora wool garment will cost much less to make if each alternate row is knitted with ordinary two-ply wool in the same colour.

Home-knitted socks won't shrink or 'felt' if the skeins of wool are plunged into really hot water. Leave the wool to soak for about a minute, squeeze gently, hang to dry and then wind into balls for knitting.

Another way of pre-shrinking wool before knitting is to place the skeins in a paper bag and hang this over a steaming kettle for five minutes or so.

Knives

The blade of a knife should never be used for odd jobs—for cutting string, opening a lighter screw, prising off a lid, etc. Keep cooking-knives separate from dining-knives and never leave a knife standing on the side of the cooker.

Knives should not be jumbled together in a drawer. Plastics *knife racks* are inexpensive and it takes only a moment to place each knife in a separate slot.

It is important to hold a knife at the correct angle when *sharpening* it; a too narrow angle will not sharpen sufficiently and a too-wide angle will dull the blade. Ideally, a knife should be held at a 20-deg. angle on the oil stone or special knife steel.

To keep *knife handles white* and to prevent them yellowing do not allow them to become wet. Directly after use, stand the knife blades in a jar or jug of warm soapy water, leave for 5 minutes (no longer), then rinse thoroughly and dry on a soft cloth. If the knives are reasonably clean, wash them one at a time in clean soapy water, holding the handle so that it does not become wet. Dry immediately.

Stainless steel knives should always be washed as quickly as possible after a meal and they should not be left with particles of food stuck to them or in contact with salt.

Bicarbonate of soda will usually deal with the *stains on knife blades*, while a damp cloth dipped in table salt will remove most stains from the *handles*, but rinse thoroughly.

If the *stains* are long standing and resist treatment, another method is to squeeze the juice of half a lemon and mix this with enough Spanish whitening to make a thin paste. Spread the paste over the stained handles and leave for 20 minutes to half an hour, then rinse thoroughly in warm water, rub dry and polish.

Knife handles which are not badly stained but simply *yellowing* can be treated with lemon juice and whitening paste once every 3 or 4 weeks. An alternative is to use a paste made from lemon juice and french chalk; this can be left on for half an hour to an hour and then rinsed off.

A quick way to *whiten knife handles* at home is to dip half a lemon in salt and rub the handles briskly, then rinse thoroughly in warm water, dry on a soft duster and polish with white silicone furniture cream.

Bone knife handles which have become yellowed can be whitened by rubbing them with a cloth dipped in diluted hydrogen peroxide.

Yellowed knife handles can be whitened professionally, and many jewellers will undertake this work, or if knife handles are very shabby while the blades are still good, it is often possible to send them back to the makers to have *new handles* fitted. The jeweller should be able to advise. The job is usually impossible, however, if the shanks or tangs of the knives are broken.

For one odd *loose handle*, pull out the shank and with a skewer or knitting-needle clean out all the old fixative from the hollow of the handle. Remove any fixative from the metal tang of the knife and coat with a strong adhesive such as Bostik or Durofix. Squeeze a little adhesive into the hole in the handle, leave for the required time, then insert the shank, push it in place, wipe off any surplus adhesive and leave to set hard before using. If a knife tang is held in place with a rivet, this method is not suitable and the knife will need to be expertly mended.

Another method of repairing a *loose knife handle* is to pull the blade out and clean the handle and tang thoroughly, then fill the hole in the handle with finely powdered resin and add a tiny blob of candle wax or beeswax. Rub the tang of the knife (the shank which goes into the handle) with coarse sandpaper to roughen it, then heat it thoroughly and press it securely into the knife handle as far as it will go. Immerse the whole knife in warm water and leave it for a few min-minutes, then trim off any surplus resin and leave for 24 hours before using.

To *remove smells* from a knife after peeling onions and preparing fish, plunge the blade into fresh earth. Rust marks can often be removed in the same way. Alternatively, rub the knife blade with dry mustard on a damp cloth.

Lacquer

To remove old lacquer from metal, rub with methylated spirit, then rinse repeatedly with clear water. Nail varnish remover can also be used to remove old lacquer.

To re-lacquer metal, remove old lacquer then clean with metal polish or chrome cleaner until highly polished. Wipe with a clean cloth moistened with methylated spirit and then spray or brush on the lacquer. Allow to dry and apply a second coat. When spraying on lacquer, mask cellulose or other finishes to protect from lacquer and avoid breathing on surface being treated.

Once chrome, brass and copper have been lacquered they must not be cleaned with metal polish. Special colourless lacquers are cheap to buy and should preserve metal from 6 to 18 months before re-lacquering is necessary.

Lampshades

If a lampshade made of *fabric* is not sewn but stuck, remove grease or surface dust marks with a cloth moistened with carbon tetra-chloride or cleaning solvent.

If the material is sewn, the entire lampshade may be swished in a bowl of warm soapy water, rinsed in lukewarm clear water and left to drip dry. Remove first any coloured trimmings which might 'run'. Finish drying by replacing shade and switching on electric light.

If there is any doubt about the washability of a sewn shade or if the fabric is very delicate, dry-clean as described above instead of washing.

Nylon shades can usually be washed as above.

To clean a *buckram* lampshade, see page 303.

Plastics or *Crinothene* lampshades should be sponged with warm detergent suds, rinsed and dried with a soft cloth. Do not polish.

To clean a *parchment* shade, see page 357.

A *lace* lampshade is apt to collect dust rather quickly and frequently dry cleaners will not accept responsibility for such a delicate article. An odd stain may be lightly sponged off with carbon tetrachloride but general grubbiness is more easily removed by gently rubbing powdered magnesia into the lace and silk. Use a soft baby brush or powder brush or cotton wool to rub the powder well into the fabric and leave for an hour or so to absorb any grease. Finally brush out the powder gently with a soft brush.

A *white lace* lampshade often becomes slightly yellow or discoloured due to the heat from the lamp but unfortunately this stain cannot be removed.

To dry-clean a lampshade other than lace when there is doubt about the advisability of washing or sponging, dip a clean cotton-wool pad in fine oatmeal and rub this over the whole shade. Leave for 5 or 10 minutes, then rub lightly with a clean cloth or fresh pad. Remove any actual grease stains gently with a grease solvent.

Latex foam

Most latex foam pillows and mattresses are stitched inside a cover which keeps the rubber clean and protects it from light (direct sunlight causes deterioration in some cases). In the case of a cot mattress or an invalid's pillow, however, staining sometimes penetrates the protective covering. In this case remove the cover and launder, then make up a lather with warm water and mild soap flakes. Wring out a cloth in the warm soapy water and sponge the latex foam with this, then rinse each part two or three times with a clean cloth wrung out in clear warm water. Wipe as dry as possible with an old clean towel and leave to dry out thoroughly by an open window but away from sunlight or any form of heat.

Replace the cover and restitch when the rubber is quite dry—possibly 2 or 3 days for a pillow and up to a week for a heavy mattress.

Lavatory pan

Brush daily, and once a week clean with hot strong detergent or soda water containing disinfectant. Wash the outside of the pan with the suds first, rinse, dry and then clean the inside.

A neglected lavatory pan can be cleaned with a proprietary brand of powder or with liquid bleach or with 1 part of spirits of salt diluted with 6 parts of water. Rub quickly with an old brush or mop and immediately flush the pan several times.

Leather

Stains can often be removed from leather by rubbing it lightly with a cloth dipped in eucalpytus oil. This is a volatile oil, so all traces disappear with, it is to be hoped, the stain. Grease marks will often respond to gentle rubbing with a cloth dipped in carbon tetrachloride and frequently a liquid wax will clean and polish leather.

Suitcases, golf bags and other leather luggage can be protected and fed by regular polishing with any good quality paste wax or a special leather polish. A wax furniture polish is quite suitable but should be well buffed.

For detailed treatment of various kinds of leather see under *Hide Furniture* on page 336 for treating leather upholstery and also under *Handbags* and *Shoes* in Valeting chapter, pages 189 and 199.

Leathercloth

Dust regularly, and if further cleaning is necessary wipe with a damp cloth, or with a cloth wrung out in soapy water if the leathercloth is sticky. Rinse with a cloth wrung out in clear warm water and rub dry. There should be no need for any further treatment although if a polish is preferred, an emulsion floor polish could be used without harm. Furniture polishes must not be used as they usually contain paraffin or turpentine which may dissolve any rubber present in the leathercloth.

Pram hoods and aprons made from leathercloth should be cleaned regularly by the above method.

Leaves

An easy way to preserve leaves—and especially red or attractively coloured ones—is to use ordinary cleaned builder's sand. About

3 bowlfuls are needed and a box large enough to take the leaves easily. Spread 2 bowlfuls of the clean sand on the bottom of the box and carefully smooth it flat, then arrange the leafy branches on this, using ordinary hairpins to keep them flat. Gently heat 1 bowlful of sand until it is just hot, then immediately sift this over the leaves until they are completely but evenly covered and store until required.

To preserve roses, see page 330.

Lighting

Adequate lighting costs very little and a well-lit home is a safer home. Use electric lighting not only for convenience but also for safety. Two-way switches can be fitted at the top and bottom of stairs to avoid the danger of groping about in the dark. In addition, it adds to the convenience of a home to have extra lights installed to brighten up gloomy landings and unexpected steps. Metal standard lamps and table lamps must always be earthed. Buy all light fittings from a registered electrical contractor and take his advice about safety.

There are two main types of lamp for use in home lighting—filament and fluorescent. Filament lamps are most common and can be either clear or pearl. The clear lamps are intended for totally enclosed fittings and the pearl—which give a softer glow—are for ordinary fittings. There are also silica-coated lamps for fittings where the lamps show and you want to cut down glare as much as possible. These give even diffused light. Filament lamps are mushroom or pear shaped usually. The mushroom shaped kind are smaller and neater to handle. Twice coiled filament lamps—called coiled coil—give off more light than a single coil and they are therefore slightly more expensive.

Care must be taken with the mushroom-shaped lamps not to use a higher wattage filament lamp than the wattage recommended. Because the lamps are smaller by comparison than the pear-shaped lamps it is tempting to use a higher wattage. The correct wattage should be marked on the light fitting and this size should be used. Too powerful a lamp can damage the shade of the fitting by overheating.

Fluorescent lamps are glass tubes coated inside with a special powder which, when electrically activated, gives off light. Baffles and diffusers can disguise the tube and spread the light. Tubes are in lengths from 6 in. (4 watts) to 8 ft. (125 watts) and slim tubes are now available for concealed fittings.

The general rule for choosing fluorescent lamps is 1 watt for every square foot to be lit. A single ceiling-mounted tube may be sufficient for the average kitchen but two 5 ft. tubes in a fitting—which can be mounted flush—may be needed in larger rooms.

Sometimes a fitting has a barely audible hum which can be irritating. One cure is to get the electrician to remove the choke from the fitting and fix away from the tube, possibly on a ceiling joist in a suitable enclosure. Instant start fittings eliminate the flickering effect as they are switched on.

Lighting costs very little: 2d. worth of electricity will light a 60-watt lamp for 17 hours, a 100-watt lamp for 11 hours, 1 150-watt lamp for 7½ hours and a 5 ft. (80-watt) tube for 12 hours. The 80-watt tube gives three times as much light as the 100-watt lamp. Further details of running costs of electricity are given on page 453.

The average operating life of a normal filament lamp is about 1,000 hours but long-life lamps which have a life of about 2,000 hours are available. They cost about 20 per cent more than normal lamps and have a slightly lower light output (about 7½ per cent less light) for the same electricity consumption. They do not need changing so often so are ideal for situation where a lighting fitting is installed in an inaccessible position.

See also page 321.

Light oak

See under Oak, page 354.

Limed oak

Furniture with this finish needs regular dusting and occasional polishing with a silicone cream to protect the surface, but unfortunately, even with care the white streaks which typify limed-oak furniture often wear away, leaving the woodwork with a shabby appearance.

There are several ways of restoring the whitish streaks on furniture with a limed-oak finish but if the woodwork is varnished or polished it must first be stripped with a paint or varnish stripper. Then rub the woodwork with a cloth dipped in linseed oil and while it is still moist sprinkle french chalk over the surface; cover a block of wood with a piece of velvet or other soft material and rub the chalk into the grain of the oak. Leave to dry and then repeat two or three times more with oil and french chalk until the linseed oil has penetrated the wood and the surface is satisfactory.

For an odd patch of limed oak which needs restoring, pour some metal polish into a dish, leave it to evaporate and then rub the resulting white powder into the grain of the wood.

Plaster of Paris mixed with a zinc paste can be used in a similar way and white powder distemper is also used. To use this mix the distemper with a little water to make a thin milk-like liquid; brush this over the wood and leave to dry; lightly sandpaper the surface so that the oak grain only retains the distemper, and coat with clear cellulose or white shellac.

To remove the liming from oak, wash or scrub the woodwork (going the way of the grain) with steel wool, soap and water. It may be necessary to repeat the washing several times before all the lime is removed from the grain but it should all come away eventually. If any parts are particularly resistant, leave the wood to dry out completely, then rub the marks with very fine steel wool dipped in vinegar, still working the way of the grain. Rinse well.

If the oak is preferred a little darker than it appears when the liming is removed, rub linseed oil into the wood with a soft muslin cloth and leave for 2 or 3 days for the wood to absorb the oil. Finally rub with a clean cloth to remove any surplus oil, then polish with a white wax or silicone cream polish, leave overnight and buff the next day.

Linen

See under Bed linen, page 296.

Locks

If a lock jams and the key will not turn, try smearing the key with grease of any kind—Vaseline is ideal. Place the key in the lock, pull the door towards you hard, lift the key very slightly and it will usually turn. Alternatively, locks can be treated with powdered graphite, which can be bought in a puffer pack. Unlike oil, graphite lubricates without clogging. Ordinary lead pencil may be grated with a sharp knife to produce graphite suitable for this purpose.

Loofah

If a loofah becomes limp and soggy, soak it in a basin of warm salt water and leave overnight. Next morning remove it from the water and leave it to dry out in the open air or sunshine.

Loose-covers

It is sometimes difficult to keep loose-covers neatly in place on a hide suite. There are two methods which may help to anchor the covers. If they are loose with plenty of material to spare, tuck the surplus down between the seat and the sides and back of the chair, then roll whole newspapers tightly and wedge these down also as far as possible. The wedges will shape themselves to the chair and keep the covers from riding up.

Smoothly tailored loose-covers cannot be treated in this way and with these, the easiest method is to sew two long tapes to each corner of the covers and tightly tie the two sides together and the back and front together underneath the furniture.

For laundering instructions, see page 162.

Mahogany

Clean mahogany with vinegar and warm water or with warm beer or strained warm tea, then dry and polish.

Prevent bloom marks by regularly polishing well with a silicone wax polish. To remove bloom marks, see page 333.

If wet, sticky glasses have marked a mahogany table, clean with a cloth well wrung out in warm soapy water, rinse immediately and dry thoroughly before repolishing.

Odd white stains or marks on mahogany can often be removed if the surface is covered with a fairly thick coating of Vaseline. Leave the Vaseline for 2 or 3 days if possible, then wipe off with a soft warm duster and polish. White heat marks may disappear if you rub the wood with metal polish. See also under Furniture, page 332.

Mantelpiece

Polish a wooden mantelpiece and surround, using wax polish or silicone cream. Alternatively, prepare the surface and then seal the wood with a special polyurethane furniture seal or a wood seal such as that used for wood floors.

To clean a marble mantelpiece see following entry.

Marble

Clean by washing with soap and water, then polish with silicone cream. Synthetic detergent suds or neat washing-up liquid should dissolve grease marks and a mild abrasive should remove stains but if any are obstinate a little lemon juice or vinegar can be rubbed on. It must, however, be rinsed off immediately. Rinse several times, then dry and polish.

If the marble is very dull, clean it thoroughly, then moisten a cloth with turpentine and wipe this over the surface. Leave it for a few minutes, then polish with a clean duster. Treat carved marble in the same way but apply turpentine with a brush.

A discoloured marble mantelpiece can be whitened by making a paste of whitening and washing soda plus some chalk if available. Mix to a paste with hot water, allow to cool, then rub on to the marble and leave to dry. Finally wash the surface and rinse in clear cold water.

Mattresses

An ordinary flock, feather or hair mattress needs turning daily from end to end and from side to side occasionally; an inner spring mattress does not need turning more than once in every 2 or 3 weeks, turning from end to end and side to side alternately. Turn these mattresses carefully by the handles and avoid rolling the mattress in any way. Latex foam and polyether foam mattresses do not need turning.

All mattresses need regular cleaning according to their type. A stiff brush or the dusting attachment of a vacuum cleaner is ideal for the job, paying particular attention to the area round and beneath the leather, cloth or plastics 'buttons'.

However thoroughly they are cleaned, all mattresses except latex or polyether foam types collect dirt and dust inside, and experts reckon that after 3 or 4 years' use a hair or wool mattress collects as much as 12 to 20 lb. of dust inside it. This is removed when the mattress is remade. Ideally every mattress (except a foam type) needs remaking every few years, though in practice many bedding manufacturers say that remaking is only worth while with the higher priced mattresses.

The wire spring forming the base of an ordinary bed needs regular dusting with a soft long-haired brush. If a wire bed base creaks, check that the springs are all securely fastened to the framework, because the bed will be noisy if even one spring becomes unhooked.

Medicine

If medicine has an unpleasant taste, give the patient an ice cube to suck for a few seconds first.

For a child who finds it impossible to swallow a pill or tablet, break or crush the pill and mix it in a spoonful of jelly or jam and follow this with a drink of water. Powders can be given in the same way.

Oily medicines are sometimes unpalatable but this is easily overcome if a china cup is heated, a little lemon juice is poured into the
bottom, the oil added and then more lemon juice is poured on top.
It is important not to let the oil run down the side of the cup as it is
poured in; a little lemon juice smeared round the rim of the cup will
also disguise the oil.

In place of lemon juice, orange, hot milk, brandy or black coffee
may be used. Instruct the patient to hold his breath as he swallows
the medicine in one gulp. If it is still difficult offer him a slice of
lemon to suck before giving the medicine and again afterwards.

Metal polish

Try using old, clean powder puffs for applying metal polish and
for rubbing up afterwards. They are soft, easily washed and they
give a good shine.

To economize on polish, damp the cloth slightly before moistening
it with metal polish.

Mica

Avoid using soap or water for cleaning mica. If it is discoloured,
clean by rubbing gently with a cloth moistened with a little metal
polish or with a damp cloth dipped in vinegar. The vinegar should
not be allowed to touch any of the enamel parts of the stove.

Milk bottles

To get the last drain of milk out of a bottle, pour the milk into a
jug and leave the empty bottle lying on its side for a few minutes.
Any remaining milk will collect in a pool in one place near the neck
of the bottle and this can immediately be poured out, leaving the
bottle completely empty.

Milk contains protein and protein congeals in heat. Anything
which has held milk, therefore, should be rinsed in cold water before
being washed in warm soapy water.

The quickest way to wash a milk bottle is to fill it with cold water
the moment it is emptied; cover the opening and shake the bottle
well; empty, refill with cold water, empty again and drain or swish
in suds and then rinse and drain.

Mincer

To oil a mincing machine use a few drops of glycerine; it will not
flavour the food.

To clean a mincing machine of fat and grease, grind pieces of dry bread through it after each use.

Mirrors

Rub the bathroom mirror with a cloth dipped in glycerine or in equal amounts of glycerine and methylated spirit. Polish off with a clean duster and the mirror will not steam over every time someone runs a hot bath.

Alternatives are to use an impregnated de-misting cloth or one of the de-misting liquids such as those used on car windscreens.

See also under Windows on page 390.

Mixing bowl

If a mixing bowl slides about on the kitchen table instead of remaining firm and still during beating or whisking, anchor the bowl by standing it on a damp cloth or on a piece of plastic foam.

Morocco furniture

Dust daily and polish occasionally with a silicone cream. If the leather is marked by sticky fingers or spilt liquids, wash with warm water containing a little washing-up liquid. Wipe with a cloth wrung out in clean water, dry and polish.

Damp spots on morocco leather can be removed by rubbing gently with a cloth dipped in methylated spirit. Allow to dry and repeat if necessary.

Mother-of-pearl

Clean by making a paste with water and precipitated whitening, rub on and allow to dry. Polish off the whitening with a clean cloth, then wash in lukewarm soapy water, rinse and rub dry.

Needleloom carpet

This carpet is made from a type of felt with a rubber backing, but as it has a much shorter life than a pile carpet it needs to be handled more carefully. Clean by gentle sweeping with a stiff broom or with a vacuum cleaner. Stains can be removed with synthetic detergent and warm water, but rub gently. Rinse and pat dry.

Net curtains

Net curtains will have a longer life if tops and bottoms are made alike, each with a double row of stitching. After every laundering, reverse the curtains so that the rod is put through the opposite end.

Terylene 'Rufflette' tape is now available. This is suitable for fine net curtains and allows hooks or rings to be used in place of rods. Where this method of hanging is employed, there is less wear on the curtain fabric, although some housewives may feel this advantage is outweighed by the fact that hooks or rings should be removed before laundering.

Notes

For cooking reminders, shopping needs and other odd notes in the kitchen, use a child's slate or miniature blackboard. Fix it to the wall, add a small groove or box for chalk and keep a pretty duster hanging beneath. It looks efficient, cannot get lost and it is easier to make a note of something with chalk when in the midst of cooking or washing-up than it is to use pencil and paper.

Nylon ribbons

Stop the ends of nylon hair ribbon from fraying by holding them in the flame of a lighted match for a second or two.

Oak

Dust frequently and occasionally polish with white wax or silicone wax furniture cream, using clean dusters or rag every time to avoid darkening the wood.

If the wood is greasy or discoloured through over-polishing or an accumulation of wax, moisten a clean cloth or cotton wool with turpentine and rub the furniture with this. If the finish will stand it, apply the turpentine with very fine-grade steel wool. Buff well, then finish with a light even coat of liquid wax and buff.

Alternatively, grease spots on oak furniture can usually be removed by rubbing the stains with a cloth dipped in warm beer. Dregs left in an empty beer bottle will do. Or remove built-up marks with metal polish, removing every trace afterwards.

Oak furniture which is smoky and soiled may be cleaned by wiping it with a cloth wrung out in a 50 per cent vinegar and warm water solution. Clean the entire surface once or twice, then wipe dry and polish.

Oak panelling

Regular wax polishing is essential to preserve the oak but if the panelling has been neglected or there is a build-up of discoloured polish, rub panelling thoroughly first with a medium grade of steel wool dipped in turpentine, working with the way of the grain. Dust off and give a thorough polish with silicone wax.

Oil

An occasional trip throughout the entire house with a small oil can will often save jammed locks and squeaky noises at inconvenient times, but do not use oil indiscriminately. Usually one or two drops of oil—seldom more—are needed where two pieces of metal move against one another or where there are springs. If oil is used in places where it is not needed, it will collect dust and may cause clogging.

Castors on chairs, settees, trolleys, etc. need one drop of oil close to the middle of the wheel so that the oil runs down to the spindle. Furniture usually needs to be turned first on one side and then on the other for this to be done, and it is wise to protect a carpet with folded newspapers.

Hinges on doors, gates, french windows, cupboards, etc. should have a drop or two of oil placed on the top of the hinge; it will gradually trickle down between the two surfaces of metal where it is needed.

Locks can usually be oiled most easily if a little oil or Vaseline is placed on the key; insert the moist key into the lock and turn it several times. Add a few drops of oil to the tongue of the latch and turn the door handle until it moves smoothly.

Another excellent lubricant for locks is powdered graphite, available in a puffer pack. You can make your own supply of powdered graphite if you scrape an ordinary pencil lead. Graphite has the advantage that it will not clog.

Pulleys of clothes-lines and ceiling airers, etc. work more easily when they are oiled and the pulley should have a drop or two of oil dripped in the centre so that it trickles and lubricates the spindle.

Oilcloth

Oilcloth should not be cleaned by scrubbing with soap and water unless very soiled. An emulsion polish applied occasionally and allowed to dry completely will keep oilcloth clean and also preserve it. If the floor is very dirty, wipe with a soapy cloth, rinse, dry and polish as above.

Oil paintings

Valuable paintings should, of course, be cleaned by an expert but an ordinary oil painting can be cleaned at home. Wash gently with cotton wool dipped in mineral oil (from any chemist). Alternatively, rub the canvas lightly with a freshly-cut potato dipped in cold water. Wipe off the potato with a clean damp cloth, then rinse with a fresh cloth wrung out in warm water. Dry the painting with a piece of silk if possible and finally rub lightly with a cloth dipped in linseed oil. An alternative is to use a special picture cleaner available from art shops.

It is possible to protect a canvas against dust and grime by giving it a coat of clear varnish, but this treatment should not be applied to a valuable painting. See also page 360.

Onions

See Cooking Smells on page 313 for particulars of removing onion smells from china and cutlery.

Ormolu

Dust with a soft brush or soft chamois leather and apply a very little silicone liquid polish occasionally to protect the finish. If ormolu handles are sticky or soiled they may be washed with warm soapy water containing a spoonful of vinegar. Rinse, dry and polish but never use metal polish or lacquer.

Ornaments

Clean and treat according to the type of material—bronze, copper, etc. China ornaments should be washed piece by piece in warm water with washing-up liquid added, rinsed in hand-hot water and dried. China ornaments which have been broken and then mended should be wiped, not washed. A light rub with liquid silicone polish will protect against finger and fly marks.

Oven

See under Cooker, page 310.

Oven glass

See Heat-resisting glassware on page 335.

Oxidized metal

Dust or rub with a soft cloth and occasionally apply a little silicone furniture cream or oil. If the metal becomes very dirty or sticky, wash in warm soapy water, rinse, dry and rub in a little polish. Never use metal polishes or abrasives.

Paintwork

To clean paintwork, see page 430.

Paraffin lamps and stoves

When inserting a new wick into a paraffin appliance, follow manufacturer's instructions and then leave the appliance to stand for about an hour before lighting it for the first time. This ensures that the capillary action of the wick is not impaired by lighting it before it is fully impregnated with paraffin.

Do not use salt, vinegar or any other additive in a modern paraffin appliance as this may do irreparable harm. Salt will not improve the flame and may eat through the brass container.

Parcels

Make parcels more secure by wetting the string before tying up the parcel; it will become firm and taut as it dries.

If the parcel is addressed in ink, avoid the risk of the ink running in rainy weather by rubbing an old candle-stump over the writing or by sticking transparent adhesive tape over the address.

To send china safely by post, pack it in several layers of damp paper. As the paper slowly dries, it forms a protective wrapping for the china.

Parchment

A dull parchment or vellum lampshade, firescreen, writing-case, etc. can be brightened by wiping the entire surface with a clean cloth moistened with olive oil.

Remove odd stains by rubbing lightly from the outside inwards with a cloth dipped in a grease solvent such as carbon tetrachloride. If the whole shade is soiled it may be rubbed with paper cleaner which can be bought from an art shop. This will remove general grubbiness but not actual grease stains.

Another way of cleaning parchment is to dissolve a teaspoonful of soapflakes in a little warm water. Stir well, then add 2 or 3 teaspoonfuls of methylated spirit and stir again. Sponge this on to the shade with a clean soft cloth, wipe off any lather and go over the entire shade again with a second cloth dipped in pure methylated spirit. Leave to dry, then polish with a soft, dry duster.

Pastry board

A pastry board and rolling-pin can be cleaned quickly if they are sprinkled with coarse salt and then rubbed hard with a damp cloth.

Occasionally scrub both pastry board and rolling-pin with hot soapy water going the way of the grain, but remove meat and vegetable stains first with cold salt water. Rinse thoroughly in warm and then in cold water and stand in the fresh air or by an open window to dry.

Patterns

It is sometimes difficult to cut out thin material from a pattern as the fabric slips easily; this can be avoided by laying the paper pattern on to the material and pressing the two together lightly with a warm iron. The heat will make the paper and fabric cling together so that cutting out is easier.

Petit point

Fine petit point is frequently protected with transparent plastics or glass but where the needlework is exposed it should be dusted regularly with a soft brush. Stains should be removed immediately with clean linen moistened with a dry-cleaning fluid such as carbon tetrachloride. Repeat the spotting with a fresh cloth dipped in clean fluid.

When petit point backs a dressing-table set, care should be taken that it is not marked by polish when the silver or other backing is cleaned or by water when the brushes are washed.

An easy way to protect brush backs from splashes during washing or cleaning is to slip a plastics jug or basin cover over the back; the elastic will hold it in place but the brush should not be immersed in water; simply swish the bristles in warm suds and clean them with a small brush or with the finger-tips.

Pets' dish

If a dog's or cat's dish tends to slip about on the floor during feeding, a rubber ring from a pickle jar glued to the bottom should anchor it. An alternative is to stick pieces of self-adhesive foam draught-excluder under the dish.

Pewter

Where only a soft gleam is required, polish pewter simply by rubbing it frequently with a soft duster. If a polish and gloss is preferred, then a special pewter polish is available.

Modern pewter tarnishes very slowly and a little pewter polish soon restores its shine. Antique pewter, however, becomes coated with a stubborn tarnish fairly quickly. If the pewter has been neglected for a short time only, then the tarnish can usually be removed by rubbing the metal with ordinary brass polish followed by pewter polish.

Where antique pewter has been neglected for a long time, however, fairly drastic treatment is needed to remove the tarnish and for this purpose hydrochloric acid or caustic soda are necessary. *Both are corrosive chemicals and should be handled with care.* It is preferable to wear rubber or plastics gloves and to use an old dish mop for the actual cleaning.

One method is to wash the pewter in hot soapy water containing soda and then to paint the surface with a 50 per cent solution of hydrochloric acid. Leave for a few minutes, then clean off with very fine emery paper and water. Wash again in hot, soapy water, dry and polish. Repeat if necessary.

Another way of removing obstinate tarnish from antique pewter is to dissolve $\frac{1}{2}$ lb. caustic soda (in a vitreous enamel pan if possible) in 2 gal. of warm water. Immerse the pewter in the solution, place over heat and boil for 2 or 3 hours. Finally remove the loosened tarnish with a coarse polishing powder, wash in hot suds and then rub with brass polish and finally with special pewter polish.

Once the tarnish has been removed, regular applications of pewter polish should keep it in a good condition.

Piano

Do not stand a piano against an outside wall or near a window and avoid placing ornaments, pictures or vases on top. A piano should be kept closed when not in use and should be tuned regularly (some experts say every 3 months) whether used or not.

Piano keys

Diluted hydrogen peroxide, methylated spirit, eau-de-Cologne, lemon juice, alcohol and metal polish will all whiten ivory piano keys to a certain extent.

Badly-stained ivory piano keys can usually be whitened with a paste made from a solution of potash and enough whitening to make a putty-like mixture. Spread on and leave for 24 hours, then brush off and polish.

A similar method is to use whitening mixed to a paste with hydrogen peroxide or milk. Alternatively use a paste made from benzine and french chalk. In both cases leave to dry, then wipe off and polish.

Modern plastics piano keys can be cleaned by wiping with a damp cloth.

When cleaning piano keys take care that no powder, paste or liquid falls between the piano keys. Polish each key separately and always avoid running a duster along the entire keyboard in one movement.

Pictures

To protect them properly, oil paintings need a waterproof canvas backing but in any case pictures should never be hung on damp walls and this applies most particularly to water-colours which are liable to be affected by the damp. Pictures should not be hung over a fire-place either, unless they are protected by glass. No matter how often an uncovered painting is dusted, the dirt and smoke from the fire are almost certain to ruin the painting. In a centrally-heated house avoid hanging a picture above a radiator, to avoid discoloration.

Generally, pictures should be hung on eye-level but glazed pictures should not be hung opposite a window or the reflection of light only will be seen. A very heavy picture needs two separate chains for hanging and only a light frame should be hung on brass wire as this can corrode and break suddenly.

If the paper backing on a picture is torn and needs replacing, damp the brown paper first, then apply the adhesive and stick the paper in place while it is still moist so that it dries taut and firm.

Two pieces of cork stuck to the lower corners of a picture will keep the frame away from the wall. Even easier to apply and quite unnoticeable in use are ordinary corn plasters; they are felt-backed, thick enough for the job and easily replaced. Yet another solution is self-adhesive draught-proofing strip or special felt pads.

Repair chipped frames by moulding on plastic wood and then stain or gild the patches.

Cleaning

The glass protecting pictures can be cleaned with methylated spirit, with a specially impregnated cloth or proprietary window-cleaning agent. Water should not be used as it may trickle inside the glass and damage the picture, but a cloth or leather well wrung out to remove excess moisture is quite satisfactory.

See also page 355 for oil paintings.

Pillows

Buying new pillows can be quite a task because of the wide number of filling materials available. Down (from the breast of ducks and geese) is the most expensive and the softest but if this and possibly latex foam are too expensive, then water-fowl feathers or Polyether foam are the next best choice. Duck and geese feathers have a natural springiness and buoyancy and a long life.

A too-soft pillow can be just as uncomfortable as one that is too hard. To test a pillow, lay it flat and press the centre with the hand; a good pillow will quickly spring back to its original shape. Next try holding the pillow on outstretched hand, when it should retain its shape. If it droops at the ends it is probably worn out, has lost most of its filling or is of very poor quality. The average life-expectancy of a latex or polyether foam pillow is about five to seven years but this can vary considerably depending on usage and care.

A guide when buying new pillows is the British Standards kite-mark (No. B.S. 1877). This governs the quality, weight and cleanliness of the filling, the quality of the covering fabric and even the closeness of the stitching. It also requires that the manufacturer labels the pillow accurately with details of the filling.

All pillows—except latex and polyether foam—need shaking daily. Pat them into shape and occasionally give them an airing out of doors in sunshine if possible or, failing this, in an airing cupboard.

To wash latex and polyether foam pillows, see page 164.

Pillow-cases

See page 297, under Bed linen.

Plaster items

Ornaments and statuettes made from plaster can usually be cleaned sufficiently by dusting. If they are dirty, a starch paste may help and this can be made by mixing a tablespoonful of starch with a little warm water to make a thick paste. Spread this on to the plaster ornaments with a brush or cloth and leave to dry overnight **away** from any heat or current of air. As it dries, the starch will fall away from the ornament, leaving it cleaner.

Plastics teacups

Tea often leaves a stain in plastics teacups and vacuum-flask tops, especially if they are not washed up immediately after use.

Rubbing with a damp cloth dipped in bicarbonate of soda or toothpaste will often remove the marks, but if they are obstinate, buy a proprietary powder bleach containing sodium perborate. It is sold especially for plastics tableware. Use according to directions. Never use ordinary chlorine bleach or scouring powders, or the surface will be impaired and staining will occur increasingly.

Plastics laminated working surfaces

Use neat detergent—liquid or powder—to remove marks from plastics laminated working surfaces. If this does not work, use a paste cleaner, rinse well. Do not use ordinary scouring powders, or the surface may be finely scratched and staining will occur increasingly. A steel wool pad in a very fine grade should remove bad staining, but do not repeat often—it is fairly drastic.

Plastics upholstery

Wash with water mixed to a lather with a mild soapless detergent or soapflakes. Heavy plastics can be lightly scrubbed to remove dirt, but do not use chemicals, soda, strong soap powders or polish. There is a special cleanser for plastics which cleans and polishes at the same time.

Repair PVC plastics upholstery with PVC adhesive, cutting a patch larger than the damaged area and pasting it neatly down.

Plates

To heat plates, hold them under a running hot-water tap or dip in a bowl of hot (not boiling) water. Heating plates in a hot oven may cause them to become crazed and discoloured, and possibly to crack.

Playing cards

Do not clean with an ordinary pencil rubber. Most stains can be removed if the surface of the cards is lightly rubbed with precipitated whitening or with stale bread-crumbs. Or rub with the inside of a white loaf. Some packs of playing-cards have a special wipe-clean finish.

Plush upholstery

Keep plush upholstery free of dust by brushing it regularly with a hand vacuum cleaner or with the upholstery brush attachment of an ordinary vacuum cleaner. Brushing with a stiff brush should remove dust from the plush but will scatter it on to other furniture.

To remove soil marks from plush, take the chair or settee out of doors or near a window and wipe a small patch at a time with a cloth dipped in carbon tetrachloride, trichlorethylene or other cleaning solvent. Overlap each area and then sponge the entire furniture lightly with a clean cloth freshly moistened in the cleaner. Allow to dry, then brush with a clean brush.

Polish

See page 465 for home-made polishes.

Polyether foam

Plastics foam used for mattresses and pillows. For washing instructions, see under Pillows on page 164.

Porridge saucepan

Many people believe that filling a porridge saucepan with cold water makes for easier cleaning but in fact it is quicker to fill the pan with boiling or hot water, leave for a few minutes, empty and then fill with cold water when the oatmeal will come away from the sides of the pan easily.

If a double saucepan is used to make porridge, place a jar lid or a marble in the lower pan and if the water boils low the lid or marble will rattle as a reminder.

Preserving pan

See under Aluminium, Brass or Copper for cleaning instructions.

Quilt

Although used in this book, the word 'eiderdown' is dying out and the words 'down quilt' are taking its place. Stores and shops are largely responsible for this change because, under present law, if they advertise or sell 'eiderdowns' and these are filled with anything other than the down of eider duck, they render themselves liable to prosecution.

Although most good quilts contain pure China-duck down or

goose-feather down, not all down quilts are made from pure down. The majority of quilts probably contain a mixture of down and feather blended together. The better the quilt, the lighter it is and the more down it contains so that lightness is a fairly good indication of quality.

If a quilt has a 'stalky' feel when the corners are squeezed this invariably indicates the presence of feathers. The spines of large feathers would work through even very tough material in time so that any quilt containing a large proportion of feathers is poor economy.

When buying a quilt, check that the filling goes right into the corners and that the outer panels are not too wide. To check the fullness of the filling, press the centre of the quilt rather than the panels which are usually well padded.

An eiderdown should go on top of all the other bed-clothes; it needs a very gentle shaking occasionally but no other attention. A hot-water bottle placed in the bed will restore the buoyancy of the quilt if it appears flat.

Do not sit on a quilt or stand a case or any other heavy item on it. If the top of the eiderdown has quilted embroidery, this is probably delicate and there for decoration, and the quilt should be handled only by its sateen backing.

If woven bedcovers with matching curtains or other furnishings are used, it is often preferred to place the quilt under the bedcover; in this case a special type of quilt called a comforter is needed rather than an eiderdown. A comforter is almost as warm but not as attractive as a down quilt and it will not spoil by having a bedspread placed on top of it.

To stop an eiderdown slipping off the bed at night, sew a piece of plain material—to match it if possible—to one end of the quilt and tuck this under the mattress. An alternative is to sew two fairly long strips of material—about 6 in. is wide enough—one at each side at the foot end. Leave these under the eiderdown during the day and tuck them under the mattress at night. When sewing fabric to the quilt, care must be taken to avoid sewing through the lining or down will later work through.

See also under Fleece quilts on page 328.

Raffia

Although raffia is not absorbent, it can be softened by over-wetting and this should be borne in mind when cleaning raffia table mats, plaited raffia, etc. Make a lather with a mild soapless detergent, then either wring out a cloth, or dip a nailbrush in the lather and gently clean the entire raffia surface. Wring out a second cloth in clear lukewarm water and rinse the mats with this. Rub dry with a soft towel and leave to finish drying, away from heat but so that air can circulate around the raffia. For small table mats and the like, a wire cake tray is ideal as a drying rack.

Razor blades

Razor blades will not blunt so easily if the entire razor is placed in a borax solution every morning after use. Dissolve a teaspoonful of borax in half a mug of water and keep the razor standing in this between uses. The borax prevents a fine film of rust and soap forming on the blade edge.

Records

Old 78 r.p.m. discs need to be dusted with a soft cloth or brush but they must not be dampened.

Long-playing records should be wiped with a very fine plastics sponge lightly moistened with water or, better still, with an anti-static liquid or a specially impregnated cloth sold specially for this purpose. Do not use paraffin for cleaning or this may clog the fine grooves.

Refrigerator

Keep the *door* tightly closed when the refrigerator is in use, open when it is not and do not put hot or warm food into the cabinet.

A *gas refrigerator* should not be placed in a confined space such as a pantry.

The *coldest place* in a refrigerator is just underneath the freezing unit; the least cold place is the top left-hand corner if the freezing unit is on the top, or top right if the position is reversed.

Most *foods* are best stored in polythene bags or plastic boxes. Any foods which tend to absorb odours easily—such as those containing fats (milk, butter, cheese, etc.)—should be kept covered or wrapped.

To make *ice cubes* fill ice-trays with fresh cold water until they are three-quarters full then dry the outside of the trays thoroughly and place in the freezing unit.

To prevent metal ice trays freezing hard to the refrigerator shelves, dry the base of the trays thoroughly after filling, then smear them and the shelves lightly with glycerine.

For *cocktails*, add a cherry, a piece of lemon peel or orange or a sprig of parsley to the water to make each cube attractive; for *fruit drinks* colour the water with fruit juice or vegetable colouring.

If *cubes are difficult to remove*, run the tray under cold water for a moment. Large ice cubes can easily be broken if they are pierced with a strong pin.

Defrost a refrigerator when ice on the freezing compartment is about ¼ in. thick. Unnecessary defrosting may cause corrosion of the flue on some types of refrigerators, while too-infrequent defrosting means the refrigerator operates less efficiently and consumes more fuel.

The amount of frost or ice formed can be kept to a minimum if all liquids in the cabinet are kept covered, and if the refrigerator door is not opened more than necessary.

Defrosting can be carried out more quickly if ice trays are filled with very hot water. Direct heat—from a fire, for instance—should never be used to accelerate defrosting as this may damage the refrigerator lining.

Anything spilled in a refrigerator should be wiped up at once and the whole cabinet, inside and out, should be washed regularly with warm water. Pull out the refrigerator to wash behind it too if possible. Rinse thoroughly with clear warm water containing a teaspoonful of bicarbonate of soda, then dry well. Wash the ice trays with clear warm water only—never with soap.

Rexine

Dust and buff regularly with a warm dry duster. If the rexine becomes dirty or sticky, wipe with a damp cloth wrung out in soapless detergent or washing-up liquid, then rinse with a clean damp cloth and dry thoroughly. Rexine does not need polishing or 'feeding' although a little petroleum jelly may be applied to the surface to prevent cracking is necessary.

Rolling-pin

See under Pastry board on page 358.

Rubber bath mat

If rubber bath mats or kneeling pads become hard and stiff with age, immerse them in a bath of warm water and add more hot water frequently so that the water remains at the same temperature. Leave for an hour or more, then rub dry.

Rubber gloves

Push tiny pads of cotton wool into the finger-tips of washing-up gloves, so that finger-nails will not cut through the rubber.

Rubber gloves used for washing-up should be rinsed thoroughly after each use and hung to dry—this way they will last much longer. Some manufacturers provide free of charge special pegs for hanging their gloves.

Rubber sheeting

Rubber sheeting for cots or for ordinary beds in case of illness should be washed with warm soapy water, rinsed well and dried very thoroughly with an old towel. Keep well away from heat of any kind and finish by dusting with french chalk.

If the rubber sheeting is being stored after use, roll on a broom-handle, cardboard or newspaper and leave in a dry, well-aired cupboard (but not a heated cupboard such as an airing cupboard). In no circumstances fold it or the rubber will perish.

Sardine tins

To open a sardine tin easily, turn the tin upside down, wipe the bottom and cut the whole of the base out with a wheel-type tin-opener. If, on the other hand, the tin has already been partially opened with a sardine key, insert a metal skewer into the handle of the key and use this as a lever; it will generally force the entire top of the tin off as the key is turned.

Saucepans

If a pan handle becomes hot and difficult to hold, bind it with washable self-adhesive PVC tape.

A burnt saucepan can usually be cleaned by filling it with cold water, adding a tablespoonful of vinegar or lemon juice and boiling for 5 minutes. Repeat until the pan is clear. Salt and water can also be used in the same way but may need to simmer longer or to stand overnight after boiling. If the burning is really serious, a drastic method is to pour in neat liquid bleach, add borax, and boil up saucepan for 5 minutes. Beware of splashing, and rinse thoroughly afterwards. Whichever method is used, several treatments may be necessary.

Saucepan warmer. If an enamel or earthenware dish will fit exactly into the top of a saucepan, a meal can be warmed or a piece of fish steamed while vegetables are being cooked. Use the saucepan lid to cover the dish.

See also under Aluminium on page 292.

Scratches

Furniture. Scratches on dark furniture can be removed successfully with a special dispenser or scratch remover. There are excellent scratch-removing liquids on sale at most hardware shops and department stores.

An odd scratch can often be disguised by painting it with iodine. A mixture of equal quantities of linseed oil and turpentine mixed in a bottle and rubbed on the scratches will also often hide them completely.

On natural teak furniture where the surface has not been finished with polish or varnish, light scratches can often be removed by rubbing gently with *fine* steel wool or sandpaper followed by an application of teak oil.

Glass. With thick safety-glass used in doors and car windscreens, etc., scratches can usually be made less obvious by making a paste with jeweller's rouge and methylated spirit and rubbing this into the mark. Leave to dry and then polish well with a soft duster.

For scratches on plastics see under Perspex on page 275.

Scrubbing brushes

After cleaning, rinse scrubbing brushes under cold running water and store them bristle downwards so that water can run off instead of collecting in the bristle ends.

If the bristles of a scrubbing brush have become limp and soft, soak them for a time in cold water containing a handful of salt; remove and leave in the open air to dry, handle uppermost.

Sealants

These are special forms of adhesive which will also seal gaps and cracks. A black version is available in tubes and is used for sealing irregular gaps and cracks on the car, outside the house, on garden sheds, greenhouses, etc.

It provides a strong, permanent seal which is proof against dust, dirt, weather, heat and occasional contact with oil and grease. It can be painted over when dry.

A white version of the sealant is available in strip form which will not crack, shrink or become brittle even after long use. It is proof against weather, oil, water, grease and dust, etc. This too can be painted, once hard.

Sealants can be removed from the hands with lighter fuel or cellulose thinners.

It is important to use the correct sealant for the job in hand. The following list may help. The figures alongside refer to the type of sealant most suitable and details of these are listed below:

Indoors:

Aquaria—2
Bath to wall—1, 3
Coal scuttles—2
Fireplace surrounds—1
Frames, window and door to wall—1
Hand-wash basins to wall—1, 3
Metal frames and fixtures—1

Pipes, frozen; temporary repairs —2
Plaster to wood, metal, etc.—1
Sink to wall—1, 3
Tiled wall to door, surround, etc.—1, 3
Wash basins to wall—1, 3

Outdoors:

Buckets, etc.—2
Chimney cowls, flashing, etc.—2
Cold frames—1
Corrugated iron—2
Drainpipes—2
Earthenware—2
Frames of windows, etc. to wall —2
Galvanized iron—2

Glazing—1
Greenhouses—1, 2
Gutters—2
Leaks in gutters, roofs, etc.—2
Roof tiles—2
Slates—2
Terra-cotta ornaments, etc.—2
Watering cans—2

Car, caravan, etc.:

Dashboards—1
Draughts—2
Guttering—2
Headlights, etc.—1
Leaks—2
Rain channels—2

Rear lights—1
Sunshine roofs—2
Window frames—2
Windscreens—2
Windscreen wiper holes through bonnet—1

Boats:

Centreboard bolt—1
Centreboard slot to keep—2
Decking—2

Keel to hull—6
Leaks—temporary repairs—2
Rubber strake—2

Suction bailers—2
Venturi tube—2

Watertight hatches, temporary sealing—1
Watertight hatches, permanent sealing—2

Key to numbers:

1. Preformed sealing strip similar in appearance to plasticine. This type of sealant does not harden appreciably. It may be moulded to any shape or size in the hands. Example—Bostik White Sealing Strip.
2. Natural rubber sealing compound, generally black in colour, rather viscous. This type of sealant has good water resistance. Example—Bostik Outdoor Sealant.
3. White sealer. This is a synthetic rubber sealing compound used for sealing round baths, bowls, sinks, tiles, etc. in bathrooms and kitchens. Example—Bostik White Seal.

Sewing machine

When using a sewing machine for the first time after oiling it, run a piece of blotting paper through the machine first to absorb excess oil.

Shampoo mitts

For drying hair quickly and easily after a shampoo—and especially for children—cut an old towel into two and make two big mitts. With these slipped over the hand, hair-drying is simple. To make the mitts more attractive, use coloured terry towelling; make two bags, open at the top, and then machine in the shape of a large hand through both thicknesses of towelling in a contrasting colour. Sew tiny rings to one corner for hanging in the bathroom. When the mitts become too old for use in the bathroom, they are ideal for drying down a pet which has been out in the rain.

Sheepskin rugs

Sheepskin rugs—and also pram covers—may be washed, but if the backing is wetted it should be carefully treated or it will harden on drying.

In the Shetland Islands the islanders *do* wet the skins: in fact they wash the raw fleeces in washing machines before treating the backing skins with chemicals.

Here is one recommended method for home washing in a washing machine. (Provided of course the rug is not too big to fit in your washing machine tub.) Make up a mixture of 1 pint water, plenty of soapflakes (say 10 oz.) and 2 to 4 oz. of olive oil, depending on the size of the rug. Boil this mixture in a saucepan, stirring well to emulsify the oil. Then add 1 to 2 oz. of glycerine to feed and soften the leather.

Meanwhile, pre-wash the skin in cold water in the washing machine without soap. Alternatively simply leave the skin tc soak in the tub.

Then spin dry the cold water away, or if you have no spin dryer squeeze the rug with the hands but do not twist or put through a wringer.

If you have an automatic machine, use the pre-wash or rinse programme.

Next, give the rug a warm wash (40 deg. C.) with the above soap mixture added to the machine. Only one rinse is necessary unless the water is very dirty, as it is best to leave a little soap in the skin. If the skin is exceptionally dirty, re-wash the rug with a similar soap solution, and again rinse once.

Spin dry or gently squeeze excess water away, then smooth the skin and put to dry away from direct heat or sunlight. Occasionally beat the back of the sheepskin and shake it hard. When the skin is nearly dry, rub the back with a mixture of oatmeal and flour to restore softness, finishing up with a good brushing with a solid-bristled brush or nylon brush.

If the sheepskin rug has a hessian backing covering the natural skin, do not immerse the rug in water. Instead, wash the wool with the same soap mixture as given above, or use this 'recipe':

Add 2 teaspoonfuls each of borax, olive oil and glycerine to a pint of water. Add 10 oz. of soapflakes. Bring to the boil and boil for 1 minute. Add a pint of cold water, mix well, and when the mixture is cool work the liquid into the wool, treating a small patch at a time.

Wipe off the lather from each patch with a cloth wrung out in clear warm water, then leave the sheepskin to dry out of doors if possible, and away from any heat.

The above method may also be used by those who have no washing machine.

Carpet cleaning solution may also be used to clean a sheepskin rug; try the non-rinse variety.

If, in spite of all your efforts, the back of a sheepskin rug still feels hard and crackly, give occasional repeat treatments by rubbing a mixture of flour and coarse oatmeal into the backing. Work it well with the hands or over a chairback to soften the skin. If *this* does not work, rub in olive oil occasionally.

If washing by any method is inconvenient, use a dry shampoo made for carpets. Or simply sprinkle the carpet all over with powdered magnesia, working it well into the pile with the finger-tips. Roll up the rug and leave overnight, then next morning hang it over a line and beat it, shake it thoroughly or clean with a vacuum-cleaner attachment to remove all powder and dust.

Silver

To clean silver correctly, examine it under a magnifying-glass or under a bright light and look for microscopic scratches running in the same direction; these were made when the silver was originally buffed and polished by the maker. On cutlery the marks usually run lengthwise, on larger pieces such as a teapot or jug the marks are mostly circular. Ideally, polish should always be applied in the same direction as these original marks and then polishing—with a clean, soft, velvety cloth—should be done in the same way.

The quickest way to clean silver is to rub with a specially impregnated silicone cloth or with cotton wool dipped in a liquid silver cleaner.

Small items may be dipped into a liquid dip-type cleaner which is sold in a wide-necked jar, but do not allow this cleaner to touch stainless steel. This cleaner is intended mainly for removing tarnish rather than for polishing. It is quite harmless on any silver but if the silver plate is wearing thin and the liquid touches the base metal underneath, a black stain may result. This stain is also harmless and can easily be removed with ordinary silver polish. It is worth noting, however, that if the silver is immersed in the Silver Dip for only a few seconds and is then rinsed and dried as given in the instructions, no stains will occur.

There are now special silver cleaners such as Long Term which, once used, keep silver items shining for months, without tarnishing. The shine these polishes give is excellent but if it mellows an occasional buff with a Long Term Silver Cloth will quickly restore shine.

To clean small silver—such as cutlery—inexpensively, place a strip of aluminium in an enamel pie dish, add a pint of water and a knob of soda and bring to the boil. Add the cutlery and simmer for a few minutes, then remove and wash in soapy water. Perforated aluminium sheet can be bought for this purpose or ordinary aluminium will do;

it is also possible to add the soda and water to an old aluminium saucepan and immerse the cutlery in this.

A similar method of cleaning silver—probably easier today—is to use aluminium foil and bicarbonate of soda. Cut off about a foot square of foil, place in a saucepan with a rounded tablespoonful of bicarbonate of soda and 3 pints of water. Add the cutlery, bring to the boil and simmer for 5 minutes, then remove the cutlery and wash it in hot soapy water.

Silver ash-trays can be quickly cleaned by rubbing them daily with the ash remaining in the tray after emptying.

Finely precipitated whitening moistened with ammonia or methylated spirit is excellent for cleaning silver, so is jeweller's rouge or plate-cleaning powder moistened in the same way. Apply with a soft cloth or with a brush where the silver is engraved, then wash in hot soapy water, rinse in hot water and dry immediately.

In an emergency, tarnish can be quickly removed by rubbing the stain with a damp cloth dipped in bicarbonate of soda or by steeping it in a pint of hot water containing a dessertspoonful of ammonia. Rub dry on a soft cloth and polish.

If table silver is not in daily use—and use is really the best thing for it as regular handling gives it a soft lustre—then avoid tarnish by cleaning it thoroughly and then wrapping it in tarnish-proof tissue or kitchen foil and keeping it in a polythene bag.

Never jumble silver together when clearing away or laying a table, when washing-up or cleaning the silver. Table silver should be kept in a cutlery box or canteen if possible or, if it is being stored away until the next important occasion, it should be wrapped as already described.

Egg, salt and vinegar will quickly stain any type of silver, so as soon as a meal is finished, rub these and any other food particles off silver cutlery *before* placing them in the washing-up water. In any case do not leave any household silver in contact with food longer than is necessary. Most food and condiments will stain the silver.

Silver salt-cellars should be washed in a fairly strong solution of hot soda water followed by rubbing with a cloth dipped in ammonia.

Dry silver while it is still hot from the washing-up water and polish immediately on a second dry cloth.

Silver articles such as candlesticks which are not washed regularly and are difficult to clean can be lacquered, but unless the item is quite plain, this should be done by a jeweller. Once lacquered, the silver should stay bright for years providing it is dusted only, and not washed or cleaned.

Silver teapot

If a silver tea or coffee pot is used on special occasions only, stop it from becoming musty by placing a sliver of wood across the top so that the lid cannot close.

Alternatively, prevent must in a teapot not in use by leaving two lumps of sugar in the washed and dried pot. Throw away the sugar when the pot is used and replace with fresh sugar when storing again.

Remove tannin stains with hot water and borax. Use about a teaspoonful of borax to a pint of hot water and leave for an hour or two before cleaning with a cloth and a fine brush for the spout. Finish by washing in warm soapy water, then rinse very thoroughly.

Sink

Avoid black scratches on a sink by using a rubber or plastics sink mat and by resting aluminium pans on this when cleaning them.

A sink must fit tightly to the tiles or wall to prevent water dripping down between the two. Any cracks or gaps can be sealed with a special waterproof compound.

Wash the sink each time after washing up and remove stains with hot synthetic detergent suds or a paste cleaner.

Boiling water and strong detergent or soda used weekly should keep the pipes from becoming blocked. However, if a pipe from the sink or bathroom should become clogged, mix together equal amounts of coarse salt and soda (crushed soda or soda crystals). Force the mixture down the outlet hole, add a teaspoonful of strong synthetic detergent, then pour down one or two large kettlefuls of boiling water.

Alternatively, use one of the proprietary drain cleaners from an ironmongers to keep drains clear. Whichever agent is used, when the pipes are clear rinse them thoroughly with hot or cold running water.

A plastics sink plunger or rubber force cup used vigorously will often move an obstruction in a blocked pipe, but the rim of the cup should be greased and a cloth should be held over the overflow vent for the plunger to be completely effective. An emergency force-cup can be made by cutting a piece out of an old rubber ball, placing the hole over the sink outlet and squeezing the ball several times.

If the pipe remains blocked, place a bucket under the U-bend and remove the inspection trap at the bottom of the 'U'. An obstruction can usually be removed with the fingers, with a piece of cane or with flexible metal tubing, which you can buy from an ironmonger. Avoid probing with a sharp metal tool as the inside of the pipe can easily be damaged. Flush the pipe with running water before replacing the nut.

Serious blockages in the sink drain may need attention by one of the firms specializing in such matters.

Acrylic plastics sinks, which are lightweight and not designed for really heavy use, are often fitted in caravans and boats. They can be damaged by hot tins and dishes and by cigarette burns as well as by certain chemicals such as paint stripper.

When cleaning a sink of this type, care must be taken to avoid scratching the surface, although rubbing with metal polish may remove slight surface marks. Wash with hot soapless detergent suds or a mild solution of household bleach.

An *enamel sink* needs care and it should be protected against chipping. Use a plastics washing-up bowl and a ridged polythene or rubber mat on an enamel draining board. Harsh cleansers must be avoided and should not be necessary. Diluted household bleach or a mild paste cleanser should remove even obstinate marks.

Fibreglass sinks vary according to the manufacturers and the quality but, generally, the surface can be easily scratched or damaged with a sharp knife. Avoid harsh cleansers and use hot detergent suds for cleaning.

A *porcelain sink* which is badly stained or neglected should be treated by one of the methods given on page 295, under Bath.

Stainless steel sink. To protect a stainless steel sink or draining board, wash, rinse and wipe dry after each use. This should be sufficient to keep it gleaming. Avoid grease films collecting on the sink—wash off grease as soon as possible, using washing-up liquid. Synthetic detergent powders sometimes mark stainless steel, and here too, after using such a product the sink must be thoroughly rinsed.

Similarly, see that neat disinfectants, chemicals, household bleaches and sterilizing solutions do not splash stainless steel or remain in contact for long. All these things (even as mild a chemical as salt) should be rinsed away as soon as possible.

Marks can be removed from stainless steel sinks with a cleanser made especially for stainless steel, or with a cloth dipped in a mild paste abrasive or whitening.

Never use liquid silver cleaner near a stainless steel sink or draining board, and if silver has been cleaned in this way, give it a final wash in a separate bowl.

Sink tidy

A sink tidy is often too flat to allow proper drainage so that a pool collects in the tidy, making it messy and unpleasant. Deal with this problem by buying a card of kettle knobs from an ironmonger and fix these under the three corners of the tidy. Ordinary corks would also do, if screwed in position with a tiny screw.

Smelling salts

If the moisture has evaporated from a bottle of smelling salts, a few drops of ammonia added to the crystals will revive them a little.

Sponges

The slime on a sponge is due to soap accumulating with lime compounds in the water and in hard-water districts this can be quite a problem.

The best cure is prevention. Wash the sponge in very hot detergent suds every few days—add it to the washing machine load (together with all face flannels in the house) whenever you are doing a hot wash. This way sponges will never go slimy, especially if a soapless detergent is used.

For those without a washing machine, boiling the sponge for 10 minutes in vinegar and water is a quick remedy, and this method is also very effective in dealing with a slimy face cloth. Finish by rinsing in clear water containing a few drops of ammonia.

A simple alternative is to wash the sponge in hot synthetic detergent suds, working the lather into the sponge with the finger-tips. Rinse thoroughly afterwards.

Steel

Old-fashioned steel fire-irons, etc., which are not stainless steel, should be regularly cleaned and burnished with steel wool. Fine steel wool should remove slight rust marks but severe stains may need a special rust-removing fluid. After cleaning rub with silicone furniture cream to protect the steel.

Steel wool

This is sold in many grades. A guide to their use is given below:

Grade 000: For use in cabinet-making and similar trades.

Grade 00: Not quite so fine as 000. Used in cabinet making, also for burnishing non-ferrous metals.

Grade 0: Used with soap for cleaning household ware, also dry for burnishing and similar purposes. Used with oil it is ideal for removing rust.

Grade 1: For similar purposes, but with quicker action for more drastic cleaning.

Grade 2: Used dry for smoothing wood, or with oil for removing heavier rust deposits.

Grade 3: A sharp, quick-cutting grade for heavier cleaning and for preparing floors.

Sticking plaster

Remove the ugly black marks left by sticking plaster with cotton wool dipped in surgical or methylated spirit or with ordinary nail-varnish remover.

Suède

Ordinary suède belts, handbags, jackets, etc., can be cleaned and freshened by sponging lightly with a gauze and cotton-wool pad moistened with a grease solvent such as cleaning benzine or carbon tetrachloride.

When cleaning a suède handbag, brush the inside first to remove dust and sponge with a grease solvent if necessary. After cleaning the outside and when the solvent has completely dried, hold the bag in the steam of a boiling kettle. Allow to dry, then gently brush any shiny patches with a wire suède brush, a piece of sandpaper or a manicure emery board.

Tables

A sheet of plate glass over a highly polished coffee table will protect the surface. If the table top is of indifferent quality or badly marked, cover the surface with holiday snaps, coloured views or labels and place the glass on top of these. Transparent adhesive tape will seal the gap between glass and table to prevent dust from seeping in.

A silicone cream polish used regularly on a table top will, to a great extent, prevent glasses and cups from leaving ring and heat marks. If liquid is spilt or a mark is left, it can be removed easily if wiped off at once.

It is also possible to protect a table or other highly polished surface by painting the top with a clear polyurethane seal. This dries by a chemical action and, once dry, the surface has a hard, mirror-like finish and is resistant to heat and solvents. The seal can be used to protect woodwork or to give a finish to hardboard or cork.

To remove heat marks, see page 233.

Tapestry

Sprinkle with powdered magnesia and work it well in with the finger-tips or with a clean cloth. Leave overnight or for several hours, then brush out gently with a soft clean brush.

Odd grease marks or stains can be removed with clean cotton wool moistened with carbon tetrachloride or other cleaning fluid.

Tea-cloths

Tea-cloths and towels will last longer and not tear so easily if elastic loops are sewn on to the ends instead of tape.

If old tea-towels tend to leave fluff on china and glass, give them a final rinse in weak starch.

Teak

Dust daily and occasionally polish with teak oil or teak cream. Ordinary wax polish should not be used on teak. Deal with scratches and marks by rubbing teak oil well into them then oil the entire surface and rub with a soft cloth.

Teapot

See Silver, China, Chrome, etc. for special instructions.

Terra cotta

Wash with warm soapy water, rinse thoroughly and dry. Dirty marks which remain may be rubbed lightly with a mild abrasive or cleaning paste on a cloth or on fine steel wool.

Tin

Wash in hot soapy water, rinse in hot water and dry thoroughly. To avoid rusting, finish drying near heat or in a warm oven. If the tinware is very dirty or greasy, boil in soda water, wash and dry.

To polish tin, wash and dry as above, then rub with powdered whitening and polish.

Tinned food

Make it a habit to date tinned foods immediately they are bought so that they can be used in rotation as far as possible. If this is not done, currently-bought tins are invariably opened first because they are most easily accessible.

Tinned foods keep reasonably well for long periods but the length of time depends on the contents and on the method of storing. The higher the storage temperature, the sooner will noticeable changes appear in the colour and flavour of the product. Canned ham should be stored in a refrigerator and may be kept for up to twelve months.

As a rough guide, evaporated milk and fish in tomato sauce keep well for about a year; fruit canned in syrup for a year to a year and a half; vegetables for 2 years, while meat, sardines or other fish in oil keep for about 5 years.

Under normal conditions, canned fruit will keep for twelve months, after which time, cans containing acid fruits—such as plums—may swell. This is due to the formation of a harmless gas (hydrogen) resulting from the interaction between the fruit acids and the metal of the can. Canned fruit should therefore be consumed before the commencement of the following season.

The gold colour, often found in fruit cans, is a thin film of lacquer. In the case of fruit, lacquer is used to preserve the colour of the fruit and to prevent interaction between the fruit acids and the tinplate. In the case of meat products, lacquer is often used to prevent a blue colour developing on the interior of the can. This arises from the protein in the meat and is quite harmless although unattractive.

Canned shellfish is particularly liable to discolour and, in addition to the lacquer, the can may be lined with parchment paper.

Refuse to buy tinned food if the can is not in good condition and if a tin in the store cupboard has bulged outwards at the ends since purchase, throw it away immediately. Blown cans arise from two causes. One, the food acids attacking the tinplate with a consequent generation of harmless hydrogen gas, or two, bacteria growing in the food and forming a mixture of gases. This does not apply to carbonated beverages such as beer and soft drinks, which naturally have an internal pressure which causes the can to bulge slightly at either end.

Food is not usually harmed by a can being dented. The only exception to this is if the can shows signs of leaking. Cans can only be damaged through careless storing. Damp storage will cause rusting of the outside of the can and this may, in time, cause the can to perforate and thus spoil the contents.

Never open a tin of food without thoroughly cleaning the top of the tin first. Removing the label helps a can opener to work more easily. Puncture or open the end of a corned beef tin before opening with key provided. The meat will then slide out easily.

Once opened, food *can* be kept quite safely in the tin with the exception of fruit, which may change flavour. But it is far better to use small plastic containers with a seal-type lid for all such left-overs.

Always use the liquid in which food has been preserved. If not served with the food it can be used for cooking or for stock, soup, stew, etc. The syrup from canned fruit forms an excellent basis for jellies.

Tins

Clean baking-tins in hot soapy water. Loosen burnt particles by soaking or by boiling in hot soapy water containing soda. A mild abrasive on fine steel wool can be used to make the tinware shine. Rinse the tins and dry very thoroughly first on a cloth and then in a warm oven.

If aluminium tins are very neglected, put them in a large container and boil in a strong solution of soda and water. Rinse well and dry in a warm oven.

To prevent ordinary baking-tins from becoming rusty, cover them with lard when they are new and heat them thoroughly in a hot oven.

Some tins are treated to make them rustproof and so that they will retain their shiny newness. Food does not normally stick to these tins and little or no fat is needed to grease them. To clean them wash in hot soapy water and dry on a cloth.

Store baking- and patty-tins in a warm, dry cupboard. Moisture may penetrate the seams or any weak places and cause rusting.

If baking-tins become rusty, clean with a mild abrasive and fine steel wool and if the tins are not to be used immediately, rub a piece of lard paper over the entire surface to prevent further rusting.

See also under Cake-Tins, page 303.

Tobacco pipes

Strictly a male job this; stale tobacco should be scraped out of the bowl and when it is clear a little alcohol should be poured in, allowed to stand for a moment and then run out through the mouthpiece. Dip pipe cleaner in methylated spirit to clean stem.

Toilet brushes

Hair and other toilet brushes should be washed regularly in warm synthetic detergent suds. Brushes filled with nylon need no special care nor do those with plastics backs.

Ebony and other wooden backed brushes should be protected by smearing the backs and handles with a little petroleum jelly before immersing the bristles only in water. Protect a petit-point or similar back with a plastics basin cover stretched over the back. The elastic should hold it in place but wash the brush carefully to avoid wetting the back.

Brushes filled with pure bristle should be washed in warm suds, then they should be rinsed in clear warm water and finally in plenty of cold water to harden the bristles. If bristles become soft and cold water does not harden them, soak them for half an hour in a little warm water containing a small quantity of alum. Rinse well in cold water, shake off excess moisture and dry out of doors.

For clothes brushes see page 185.

Tortoiseshell

Wash imitation tortoiseshell in warm soapy water, rinse and dry. Real tortoiseshell should be cleaned with a paste made by moistening jeweller's rouge with 1 or 2 drops of olive oil. Apply on a soft rag, leave for a few minutes, then polish with a soft duster.

Towels

When buying new towels avoid asking for 'bath' or 'hand' towels but ask for them by their actual size according to what is needed. A hand towel can be any size from 18 in. by 36 in. to 27 in. by 54 in.; while a bath towel can be anything from 30 in. by 53 in. to sheet size, 4 ft. wide and nearly 7 ft. long.

A small towel is not economical because it becomes soaked too easily, needs washing more often and so wears out more quickly. Men usually prefer a larger size towel than women, even for ordinary hand drying.

It is better to have more towels than are needed so that they can rest between use. Do not try to economize by making towels from terry towelling. This towelling sold by the yard is a much thinner fabric designed for curtains and beachwear and it will not stand up to day-to-day use, nor for bathing.

Trim off any loose or pulled threads with scissors; this will not damage the towel but it *will* stop further threads from un-ravelling.

Wash towels before they are really dirty to make them last and keep their colour, and store clean ones at the bottom of the pile so that they are used in rotation.

For laundering instructions see page 176.

If towels wear thin and tear at the edges, bind all four sides of each towel with tape or brightly coloured binding contrasting with the original colours. At the same time check that rubber towel holders or metal hooks are not worn and tearing the towels. Towels hung on smooth rails do not tear so quickly at the edges.

Instead of sewing tape loops on towels for hanging, sew on elastic loops. These will give if the towel is pulled, without tearing the material.

Toys

Clean plastics toys regularly by washing in hot soapless detergent suds containing a few drops of disinfectant; rinse well and dry. Water should not be allowed to penetrate hollow toys; for these, sponging with a damp cloth wrung out in soapy water is a better method.

White woollen toys need not be washed; make a paste with cold water and starch and spread on to the toy. Leave to dry thoroughly —in the fresh air if possible—then brush off the powder and brush the wool well with a clean brush.

Stuffed toys such as teddy bears can be cleaned with detergent whisked in warm water. Use a nail brush and scrub lightly, using the lather only. Rinse with a sponge wrung out in clear warm water, leave out of doors to dry—in sunlight if possible—and air thoroughly. Finally brush the fur well with a firm, clean brush.

Alternatively, use a carpet shampoo of the non-rinse variety.

Bath time toys scatter quickly and look untidy strewn around the bathroom. Easiest way round the problem is to use a nylon or plastic mesh shopping bag to match the bathroom. All the toys can be put in the mesh bag and hung on a suction hook over the bath to dry. They stay tidy until wanted again and the bright colours look attractive especially against a plain tiled wall.

Transfers

Embroidery transfers should be applied to material—shiny side down—with a hot iron. If the fabric is coarse, flatten it first by pressing it with a steam iron or under a damp cloth.

Upholstery

Choose fabric with a close-textured weave if it is wanted to last a long time, but avoid thick material in pastel or plain shades if you want to avoid frequent cleaning. Fabrics with loose or raised threads are not suitable where there are children, cats or dogs as the threads quickly become pulled. Closely woven weaves in tweedy or medium colours wear well and do not show dirt quickly.

A fitted divan cover should be made of material which will withstand constant handling and pulling without stretching out of shape or pulling away at joins.

Cleaning upholstery. Remove loose dust by sweeping chair, settee or other upholstery, preferably with the upholstery tool on a vacuum cleaner. Use the specially shaped cleaning nozzle to remove dust from the sides of seats and arms in a deep armchair. Remove greasy marks or stains from hair oil by rubbing the stains lightly with a clean cloth dipped in a spirit dry-cleaning solvent such as carbon tetrachloride, trichlorethylene or a commercial product.

General light surface dirt can also be removed with a cloth moistened in the cleaning fluid and rubbed lightly over the upholstery. An alternative is to wring out a cloth tightly in mild synthetic suds and rub over the surface. These treatments are suitable for wool fabrics, tapestry, velveteen and moquette, etc.

Small odd greasy finger-marks or similar stains can be covered with french chalk or fuller's earth and left overnight to absorb the grease. Next morning brush off with a clean brush. If the mark is on the back of the chair and the powder will not stay in place, mix it with a little carbon tetrachloride to form a thick paste and spread this over the stain.

Very badly soiled upholstery will need to be shampooed, but test for colour fastness first on an inconspicuous part of the fabric.

To shampoo upholstery use mild synthetic detergent suds, or if possible, a special upholstery cleaner. Whisk to a good lather and scrub the fabric lightly, using the foam suds on a soft brush. Rinse with a damp sponge, dry with an old towel and overlap each area.

It is also possible to buy a hand cleaner which is filled with a special upholstery shampoo solution. Foam is forced through the sponge head of the cleaner and will effectively treat most types of upholstery and heavy furnishings.

For details of cleaning Plastics Upholstery and Plush Upholstery, see pages 362 and 363.

Vacuum flasks

Clean with hot water containing a teaspoonful of bicarbonate of soda. Leave to soak, then wash thoroughly.

Occasionally remove the glass flask from the metal or plastics container and rinse and dry both thoroughly and carefully.

If a vacuum flask is not in daily use, store with the cup and stopper removed.

When using a vacuum flask for tea, strain the freshly made tea into the flask and add sugar if required. Milk should be carried in a separate bottle and not added to the tea in the flask.

Alternatively, fill the flask with clear boiling water only, and when, later, you are ready for tea, open the flask and pop in two or three tea bags, depending on strength required. Replace lid while tea 'draws'. Carry milk and sugar separately.

After a vacuum flask has been in use for some time it may become tainted and stained but it can be easily cleaned and freshened. Pour a teaspoonful of vinegar into the bottom of the flask and add the broken shell of an egg and half a teacupful of warm water; shake thoroughly, leave to stand as long as possible, then shake again and rinse well.

Vases

If vases are filled with sand when they are being used for table decoration or as ornaments they will be less likely to be knocked over and broken.

To stop dust collecting in narrow, long-necked vases which are difficult to clean, plug the necks with cotton wool, pushed down just far enough to be out of sight. Dust will collect on the top of the wool only. The cotton-wool plugs can be replaced quickly whenever the vases are washed.

A porous vase can be used for flowers if you seal the inside with a special seal sold for tiles, concrete and wood. This can be applied to the inside of the vase with a cloth or brush and a second coat applied when the first is quite dry.

Cleaning vases. Rinse thoroughly, then wash in warm water containing washing-up liquid and a little ammonia.

Badly stained and discoloured glass can usually be cleaned fairly easily by mixing equal amounts of vinegar and silver sand and leaving this to stand in the vase for some hours. Shake frequently, then rub hard with a long-handled brush, rinse and wash in warm detergent.

As an alternative to silver sand, use scouring powder or vinegar and salt well mixed. Leave in the vase overnight, then wash in warm detergent suds using a bottle brush or dish mop to remove the softened stains. Sand and a cleaner such as Jops is also effective—but watch your hands.

Figurines and vases should be washed piece by piece in a plastics or papier-mâché bowl if possible. Use warm water with washing-up liquid added and clean cut or embossed surfaces, crevices and filigree, etc., with a soft brush. Rinse in clear warm water and drain on an old towel.

Where possible, rub china vases after cleaning with a little liquid silicone polish. This will make them shine, and protect against dust and fly-marks.

Vellum

See under Parchment on page 357 for details of cleaning.

Veneer

Dust regularly and protect with a silicone or wax polish. Veneer which has blistered due to damp or to water being spilt on the surface may need to be renewed unless the blistering is slight. For slight blistering, pressing with a hot iron is often effective. Put several layers of blotting or brown paper over the veneer and press lightly with a moderately hot iron for 2 or 3 minutes.

Another way of dealing with veneer which has 'bubbled' is to remove it, reduce it slightly and then replace it. Cut round the bubble with a sharp knife or razor-blade, removing a disc of veneer slightly larger than the blister. Revolve the disc on a piece of garnet paper so that it is evenly reduced, then press it flat and test it for size in the gap. If it fits exactly, clean the back with a cloth dipped in boiling water, dry and re-stick in position with glue. If the disc breaks during handling, it should not matter very much and the two pieces can be stuck back separately. Once the veneer is back in position, cover it with a piece of material after wiping away surplus adhesive; leave a heavy weight on top for several hours, then repolish.

Loose veneer can be repaired in much the same way. Carefully insert a thin knife or a razor-blade under the veneer and lever up or break off the whole of the loose portion. Clean off the old glue and re-stick in position as before.

Broken veneer can usually be refixed in a similar way but missing portions will need to be replaced. Trace over the missing area on paper and make a particular note of the direction of the grain of the wood. The grain is shown by fine marks and channels in the wood, often no thicker than a hair; the figuring on the veneer is not the grain and the two must not be confused. Make a note of the figuring or pattern in the veneer also, and when buying a new piece (from any handicraft or marquetry shop) choose veneer as near as possible to the missing piece.

Place the tracing on to the veneer—with the grain running in the correct direction—and cut round the tracing carefully with sharp scissors. Test it for size and shape and then glue and place in position. Leave overnight with a heavy weight on top, and next day sand the veneer level with fine garnet paper, stain it to match and then polish.

Real wood veneer is now also sold in sheets with a self-adhesive backing.

Wallpaper

To clean wallpaper, see page 436.

Wallplugs

The introduction of the Rawlplug revolutionized the method of holding fixtures to masonry and has, in fact, made it possible to fix a screw into concrete or brickwork and obtain as satisfactory a fixture as one would by driving a screw into timber.

These wallplugs are manufactured from a natural, rotproof material—jute. The jute fibres are bonded together and treated during the course of their manufacture with various preservatives which make them suitable for both indoor and outdoor applications.

Walnut

Clean walnut furniture occasionally with a duster moistened with vinegar and water (one part vinegar, four parts warm water). Or wipe briefly with cloth dipped in turpentine or turpentine substitute, and immediately buff.

Eau de Cologne, perfume and similar stains caused by alcohol are easiest dealt with by using a product such as Furniglass. Follow instructions carefully.

See also Furniture, page 332.

Washbasin

A cracked washbasin can be mended if strips of linen are glued to the outside of the basin and painted over with white enamel or paint.

A better and more permanent way is to use 2-in. wide strong white webbing in place of linen and a lead and size mixture instead of glue. A builders' merchant or ironmonger will make a red and white lead and gold size mixture and this should be painted on the outside of the cracks after cleaning and drying the outside of the basin. Put the webbing in position over the cracks and press firmly, then cover with the mixture and leave to set hard before using the basin.

Better still, have the basin replaced: remember many house insurance policies cover you for accidentally-broken washbasins.

To clean, see under Bath on page 294 and treat in the same way.

For stains on a washbasin see under Drip Marks on page 225.

Washing-up

Expensive china should be washed in warm water with washing-up liquid added. The water should not be too hot. Use a soft cloth or brush for cleaning the china and avoid scourers, abrasives, bleach, soda and hard rubbing if the china is decorated or gold trimmed.

Although the *gilt* and other decorations on good china are hard and resistant to ordinary use, these can be affected by some acids. Never use soda for washing fine china, and if vinegar, lemon juice or pineapple remains on a plate at the end of a meal, rinse the acid off quickly as these may affect the sheen of the colours if they are left too long in contact with the decoration.

If it is not possible to wash-up immediately after a meal, scrape off bits and rinse plates and dishes in cold water. Do not leave decorated china soaking for too long.

A *plate drainer* is essential to protect fine china as it ensures that every piece is drained separately. If plates are drained one on top of the other, the hard back of one plate may scratch the decorated surface of the next piece.

To *protect china* during washing-up, stack carefully in small piles; use a plastics bowl; have rubber washers on the tips of protruding taps; place a draining-mat or cloth on a hard or slippery draining-board; remove plates from the plate-drainer or draining-board before it becomes too full and remember to add the china to the hot suds and not to pour hot water on to china.

Crockery used for milk or egg should be rinsed thoroughly in cold water before being washed in hot suds. A damp cloth dipped in salt will remove egg stains or food burnt on to a china dish or plate, while a damp cloth dipped in bicarbonate of soda will remove tea or coffee stains.

As already mentioned, ideally china should be washed-up in a plastics bowl, each piece separately. Occasionally, however, china is washed-up in an aluminium or metal bowl or an aluminium pan will rub against the china, leaving thin black lines and marks which ordinary washing will not remove immediately. A paste made with bicarbonate of soda and warm water spread on to the marks is usually effective. Leave the paste to dry, then rinse off and wash in the ordinary way. For an old metal mark on china dip a damp cloth in silver plate powder and rub the black hairline with this.

One loofah makes two or three excellent dish-washers. Cut the loofah into pieces, sew a button on to a short loop of tape and stitch the tape to one of the pieces of the loofah. Use the button for scraping off hard bits of food from dishes and the loop for hanging.

See also entries under China, Cutlery, etc.

To remove cooking smells when washing-up, see page 313.

Water pipes

A water pipe which rumbles or whines every time someone turns on a tap can often be corrected if a new washer is fitted to the faulty tap in question. If the faulty tap cannot be located, or if this does not correct the trouble, the local Water Board will send along an expert —often without charge.

If the seating has worn on an old tap so that ordinary washers are not effective in preventing the tap from dripping, it is possible to use a special type of combined tap washer and seating known as a 'Full-Stop'. The unit will fit any standard tap and is made from a special type of nylon. It will withstand boiling water and steam and is impervious to corrosion. Turn water off at the mains before removing the tap head and fitting the new washer and seating.

If a pipe bursts, place a bucket under the leak and wrap a towel tightly around the damaged area. Next, turn off water at the main and turn on all the cold-water taps (not hot taps), then call a plumber. If the plumber cannot attend to the leak immediately, dry the area around the burst, then stick a large adhesive plaster or first-aid dressing over the leak and bind it firmly in position. Turn on the mains tap again very slowly until it is about half-way and this should allow sufficient water through for normal use without causing further damage. A boiler fire must be put out if a burst occurs in a hot-water pipe or if the hot-water system is in any way affected.

It is possible to seal a leak also with gasket cement (obtainable from any garage). Spread the cement on to a piece of rag or bandage, bind this tightly around the leak or faulty joint and when quite dry, paint to match the rest of the pipe.

When painting water pipes, clean them thoroughly first with steel wool, then coat twice with aluminium paint or rust-resisting paint. Ordinary enamel or other paint can be applied on top of the rust-resisting paint if necessary.

Wax polish

All wax polish must be removed from furniture if the wood is to be painted. This can be done with fine steel wool dipped in turpentine substitute.

Wedding dress

To store a white wedding dress, buy plenty of acid-free tissue paper from a good stationery store and carefully place this inside the dress and on the outside of the back. Fold the sleeves and skirt of the dress over more paper and finally fold the bodice, using screwed-up tissue to prevent the fabric from flattening and possibly cracking.

When the dress is carefully folded, pack it to fit into a cardboard box with a well-fitting lid; choose a box which is not too big but just large enough for the folded dress to fit in comfortably without being squashed. Seal the box with transparent adhesive tape and store in a cool, dry, well-ventilated cupboard.

Whitewash

Clean whitewashed or distempered surfaces by dusting lightly with a soft wall brush or with a clean nylon broom, using long light strokes. Grubby marks or stains can be removed with stale bread, art rubber or cleaning dough as given under Wallpaper on page 468.

Ordinary whitewash should not be washed, however lightly, but if a 'washable' kind has been used, then it may be wiped gently with a damp sponge or cloth. On no account wash in the ordinary way.

Wickerwork

Brush to remove surplus dust, then scrub with warm water and synthetic detergent containing a spoonful of borax. Use the lather only, where possible, to avoid overwetting, then rinse in clear warm water, or for white wickerwork, rinse in cold salt water and allow to dry in the fresh air. A little furniture polish or silicone cream can be rubbed into the wickerwork once it is completely dry.

Old grease stains on wickerwork can often be removed with a cloth dipped in methylated spirit.

Windows

Window-panes will not steam over during winter if they are rubbed with a cloth moistened in glycerine, methylated spirit or a mixture of both. It is also possible to buy impregnated anti-mist cloths and liquids, and these are quick and efficient. Yet another method is to stick chemically treated transparent cellophane film to the window.

Ice on windows can be removed quickly by rubbing with a cloth moistened with ammonia or use a de-icing aerosol, sold by motor accessory suppliers for car windscreens.

To make windows opaque without glazing with reeded or similar glass, frost them by dabbing on a paste made with Epsom salt and vinegar.

Window sashcords will last very much longer and work more easily if they are rubbed thoroughly with hard soap or with a silicone and wax polish. This treatment can also be given to blind cords.

Cleaning windows. Choose a warm but dull day for window cleaning if possible. Frost, rain or sun will make the job difficult. If windows must be cleaned in damp weather, methylated spirit is ideal as it evaporates quickly and dries the superfluous moisture too.

There are many proprietary window cleaners. There are creamy solutions, creams in tubes, impregnated pads and cloths and excellent spirit solutions which are sprayed on and wiped off.

Apply the cleanser as directed but use a really large cloth for polishing it off. Keep turning the cloth so that a fresh area is continually exposed and use two cloths on a really dirty window—one for wiping the preparation off and the other for actually polishing.

Probably the quickest method of all is the window-cleaners' way—a damp leather and a dry piece of linen scrim. But it is essential that the leather be a good one, sufficiently large and very clean. You can add a squeeze of washing-up liquid if windows are really dirty, but never use soap or soapless powders or the leather will become slimy and the windows smeary.

Ordinary *paraffin* makes an alternative cleaner for windows, mirrors, etc. It should be applied with an old cloth and polished off with soft absorbent paper such as kitchen paper. Even crumpled news-paper may be used.

If *streaky windows* are a problem, try adding a few drops of vinegar to the cleaning water.

A few drops of ammonia added to the cleaning water gives windows a good shine afterwards.

Wine cask

A new cask should be treated before being used for home-made wine; to do this fill the cask with boiling water and add 4 oz. of common washing soda for each gallon of water, insert the bung and leave to stand for at least 24 hours. Empty, wash thoroughly, then pour in enough wine or cider to cover the bottom of the barrel— about a pint should be sufficient—and swish it around for 30 to 40 minutes so that the wine or cider washes each part of the barrel. The idea of this treatment is to prevent a woody flavour later; if no wine or cider is available, pour a gallon of water into the cask, add ½ oz. of citric acid and swirl this around in the same way, for about half an hour. Empty the cask and wash again thoroughly, then fill to the brim with boiling water, leave to cool, empty and repeat twice more. The cask will then be sterilized and ready for use.

Wood

For wood floorings, see page 415.

For wooden furniture see page 332, or under separate woods: mahogany, oak, etc.

Wood panelling

Dust regularly and polish with a silicone wax polish. If the wood-work is light use a silicone cream applied on a clean cloth. Odd marks can be removed with turpentine substitute or by washing with a cloth wrung out in warm soapy water. Badly soiled or neglected wood panelling may be cleaned by rubbing the way of the grain with very fine steel wool dipped in turpentine. Buff well and apply a wax polish.

See also under Oak panelling on page 354.

Wooden tableware

Wipe clean after use but do not wash. Occasionally rub with a cloth moistened with olive oil or other oil to preserve the wood. If the wood is marked, rub lightly with very fine steel wool moistened with a little oil.

Wooden tableware is sometimes given a special cellulose or other water-resistant finish. Treated wood is almost always labelled with care instructions, but if there is any doubt, advice should be sought when purchasing wooden tableware.

Items which have been specially finished should be wiped clean with a damp cloth and then rubbed dry. They should not be washed or left to soak, and wooden cutlery handles should be kept out of water.

Dishes which come into contact with food will need to be wiped after every use; other items, such as pepper mills, should be oiled only when necessary.

Zinc netting

Scrub with hot synthetic detergent suds, rinse thoroughly and rub dry. A little disinfectant added to the water will discourage flies if the zinc is used for ventilating a larder or meat safe.

8

Flooring

Asphalt flooring

Follow instructions as given for Mastic flooring on page 407.

Bitumastic flooring

Follow instructions as given for Mastic flooring on page 407.

Carpet

Laying a carpet. Always lay a carpet so that the pile lies against the light, that is, so that the pile slopes away from the window. If this is done the carpet will not so easily show tread marks and shading or patches due to unequal wear.

Before *laying a carpet*, remove any old nails or tacks and watch out for loose or uneven floorboards, straying electric flex and a too-low door which rubs; all these will wear out a carpet more quickly.

An *underlay* lengthens the life of a carpet as well as making it look better and feel more expensive to the tread. Use a rubberized underlay where there is damp, likelihood of moths or where the floorboards are uneven.

Joins in an underlay should meet but not overlap; they should never coincide with joins in the carpet. It is not essential to stitch or tape the edges together, although professional carpet layers usually do so.

Unless your carpet is permanently moth-proofed, protect it against *moths* where there is central heating, where food may be dropped, leaving stains, where there are joins and seams in the carpet and where there is furniture which is kept permanently in one place.

A certain amount of fluff usually comes away from a new carpet. This is the result of a shearing process during the final stages of carpet manufacture, which acts rather like a lawn-mower cutting the lawn. Fragments of the fibre are left in the pile, and these come to the surface during the first few months of wear—a fact which can be most irritating for the housewife. This shedding of fluff occurs far less in looped pile or twisted pile (crush-proof) carpets, simply because they are not sheared.

But there is no need to worry about this shedding. It does not mean that your carpet is going to wear thin in a few months; even if you seem to be removing copious amounts of fluff this represents a very small percentage of the pile weight. Take comfort in the fact that the fluff never was attached to the backing, and no amount of treading-in will cause it to take root. It has to come away some time.

From the day it is laid, you can safely vacuum-clean the carpet once or twice a week, using the cleaner smoothly and slowly. Alternatively, use a carpet sweeper or brush gently by hand.

Shampooing a carpet. To shampoo a carpet at home, first vacuum clean or brush thoroughly and, if possible, clean the underlay also. Choose a warm, dry, breezy day and leave windows and doors open so that the carpet can dry as quickly as possible.

The easiest way to shampoo a carpet is with a shampoo applicator (electric or push-along type). Non-rinse shampoo diluted with water is poured into the container and a trigger on the handle releases the fluid in the form of foam. Revolving brushes or a sponge roller work the shampoo foam into the pile without soaking the carpet. When the carpet is covered with a light lather, and well worked in, it is left to dry overnight—or better still for 14 to 16 hours—and then brushed or vacuum-cleaned to remove the suspended dirt.

An alternative is to use a specially shaped hand brush and a carpet cleaning and renovating solution, but with this method—as with ordinary carpet shampoos—the job must be done on the hands and knees. There are also reliable well-known liquid carpet shampoos and special soap-ball carpet cleaners.

For man-made fibre or moth-proofed carpets, most makes are suitable but for untreated wool carpets a moth-proofing shampoo liquid is recommended.

Dilute according to the manufacturer's instructions, then sponge the carpet with a rough cloth or soft brush, using the lather only and working on one patch at a time. Beware of overwetting the carpet. As each patch is washed, rinse it with a damp cloth wrung out in clear water and dry it with a clean dry towel. Avoid treading on the carpet while it is damp and do not replace furniture until the pile is quite dry.

Odd stains can often be removed with a carpet-cleaning powder. This cleaner also contains a pest killer effective in dealing with moths, silver fish, cockroaches and carpet beetle. The powder is sprinkled on to the carpet, left for 8 hours, then brushed out with a vacuum cleaner.

See also Haircord carpet on page 404.

Never sprinkle damp tea leaves, salt or cigarette-ash on a carpet; these do not benefit or clean the carpet but may damage the colours permanently.

Never believe the old wives' tale that adding ammonia when shampooing a carpet will do it good. Ammonia may cause the colours to bleed.

Carpet first aid. Any *odd threads* longer than others on a pile carpet can be snipped off level with scissors but they should not be pulled. With a loop carpet, on the other hand, the threads should not be cut but pulled; almost certainly a long loop indicates a short one nearby. Pull on the short one with a pin until both loops are of equal length.

There are several ways of dealing with *carpet edges which fray.* The quickest method where just a few strands are fraying is to brush on a rubber latex solution such as Copydex underneath. This will dry hard and hold the edges firm. If quite a lot of carpet has frayed and this looks untidy, the edges will need to be bound properly.

This can be done with self-adhesive binding which is simply pressed in position; or with adhesive binding which is ironed on to the carpet ends; or with ordinary carpet binding which must be sewn on by hand, or the latex adhesive already mentioned can be used. The adhesive is in a bottle complete with a brush so that it is easy to use, but the method will depend upon the type of carpet which is being bound.

To bind *Wilton carpet*, trim the edge neatly with scissors and place the carpet, pile downwards, on newspaper. Paste Copydex or other latex adhesive just over an inch wide along the back of the carpet, along the edge and half-way along the pile. Paste 1½ in. binding (in a matching colour preferably) with adhesive, leave for two or three minutes and then place in position along the back of the carpet so that only half an inch of the binding extends over the edge. Turn the half-inch over and press firmly against the pile, then hammer lightly to make the join secure.

Axminster carpet. Simply pull away a few strands of the backing so that a fringe remains. Place the carpet, pile downwards, on newspaper and paste along the back, then press the loose cotton ends back into the adhesive firmly. Hammer well for good results, and even better, cover the edge with carpet tape, fixed in position with latex adhesive. Allow to dry and the edge should be neat and firm.

To bind *coconut matting* use special binding tape 3 in. wide and cut it an inch longer than the matting so that half an inch extends at each end. Apply the adhesive to one side of the matting in a strip about 1½ in. wide and while it is drying, paste half the width of the binding tape. Leave for about 5 minutes to dry and then press the pasted tape to the matting and hammer firmly. Reverse the matting and repeat the process. Paste the two ends of tape, press firmly with the finger-tips to ensure a close join and then hammer the ends. Allow to dry for a quarter of an hour and then cut off the ends flush with the matting.

Worn, torn or burnt patches of carpet can be replaced with new pieces of carpet where these are available. Remove the damaged area, cutting a neat square or oblong shape with a sharp razor or blade and working from the reverse side. Paste the raw edges half-way up with adhesive to prevent fraying. The new patch must be exactly the same size and shape and the pattern should match as far as possible. Paste the edges of the patch and half-way up the pile to prevent fraying and leave to dry.

The easiest way to secure the new patch is to paste a piece of hessian—slightly larger than the damaged area—to the back of the carpet over the hole. This will provide a base for the patch. Place the carpet right way up and apply latex adhesive to the hessian and to the base of the patch. Leave for 3 or 4 minutes, then insert the new piece of carpet carefully and hammer firmly to ensure a sound join.

If the corner of a carpet or rug curls up and won't stay flat, it can be fastened to the floor with a special carpet press stud. Other methods are to stitch pieces of carpet pile down to the undersides of each corner, or coat the back with a thin layer of latex adhesive and leave until dry. It is also possible to use a layer of starch; to do this make a thick starch paste and apply to the under edge of the rug, put a piece of brown paper over the starch and iron with a hot iron until dry. You can also buy special foam plastics to stick to the back of rugs to prevent curling and creeping.

Cement

See under Concrete on page 397.

Composition flooring

Follow instructions as for Thermoplastic tiles on page 412.

Concrete

Synthetic detergent, or better still a special floor-cleaning preparation, may be used for cleaning a cement or concrete floor. If it would be spoiled by smears, however, use plain water, adding soda if the floor is greasy.

You can buy a special floor seal, either transparent or coloured, for concrete. Follow directions given by the manufacturers.

Concrete in a yard often develops a green film which ordinary washing does not remove. Clean by scrubbing with a yard broom dipped in hot water mixed with an equal amount of household bleach. Add soda if the concrete is also muddy.

Cork flooring

In a kitchen where wear is heavy or in a bathroom where water may be frequently spilt it is better to have a sealed cork floor so that grease and water cannot penetrate. Any spills can then be wiped up without harm and if the floor is dirty it may be mopped with a cloth wrung out in warm soapy water.

These days cork floorings are usually sealed by the flooring contractors at the time of laying. You can even have a flooring laid of cork tiles which have a thick glossy coating of PVC plastic. However, you can treat an unsealed floor yourself provided you buy a seal specifically recommended for cork and prepare the flooring carefully according to directions.

Apply one coat of a floor seal suitable for cork with a brush and allow this to dry completely. When dry apply a second coat reasonably liberally. Leave to dry for 48 hours and if a gloss is required a coat of plastic emulsion may be used on top of the seal. Afterwards, no special care need be taken so long as the floor is mopped or swept daily and dirty marks are wiped away with a damp cloth. Stubborn blemishes can be removed by rubbing with fine steel wool.

Never attempt to seal cork flooring which has been subjected to regular wax polishing for long periods. It will be almost impossible to remove the wax residue, which would defeat any attempts to secure a successfully sealed surface.

Unsealed cork flooring is easily damaged by grease or water so that in a kitchen spills should be wiped up at once, and in a bathroom care should be taken that water does not seep between cork tiles. In a bedroom or children's nursery where wear is light, regular polishing with a very little liquid or paste wax about once a fortnight should be sufficient to keep the cork looking bright, especially where an electric polisher is used. It is also possible to buy a special tan paste wax polish intended for cork flooring.

Where the floor is regularly polished the cork will eventually become impregnated with dirt unless the wax is applied very sparingly and is well buffed afterwards. If the wax does become thick and sticky it should be removed with turpentine substitute and a medium grade of steel wool, and the surface should then be lightly rewaxed.

Repairing cork. Repair odd chips and holes in cork flooring by mixing powdered cork to a thick, stiff paste with ordinary glue. Smooth into the hole, pressing hard. Leave to harden and dry, then smooth with sandpaper and polish or seal.

To strip off old polish from floor before applying a dual purpose cleaner or after required number of applications, dissolve half a cup of ordinary household detergent powder in 1 gallon of cold water. Add half a cup of household ammonia. Thoroughly wet floor with the solution and leave to soak for at least 10 to 15 minutes or up to 20 minutes for a heavy build-up of polish. Scrub floor with a stiff brush, dipping it frequently in the detergent solution and all the old polish should be easily removed.

Always sweep the floor to remove grit and dust before applying the product. A product such as Dual Extra is very concentrated so use sparingly, undiluted. Usually twice a week is sufficient to clean and polish a floor, although if a floor has a lot of heavy wear, more frequent applications may be necessary. Between applications, the floor can be cleaned by wiping it with a damp mop or cloth wrung out in clean, warm water.

Dual purpose cleaners

These products are combined detergents and non-slip polish. The detergent loosens the dirt and draws it away from the floor and on to the cleaning mop or cloth. The dirt is removed but a thin layer of polish is left on the floor. The polish is a self-shining one which dries to a gloss by itself. No rubbing or buffing is needed. Dual is a good example of this type of floor cleaner/polisher.

This type of product is recommended for any floors which would normally be washed—linoleum, vinyl, clay tiles, rubber, plastics and cork floors. It can also be used on sealed wood floors but is not recommended for any flooring which is embossed or deeply indented, either through wear or because it was laid unevenly.

Follow manufacturer's instructions for best results with this type of product. Don't expect maximum shine until the third or fourth application. The first and second time, it acts as a sealer for the floor. The first time it is used, start by stripping off old polish. Don't use a worn-out cloth, mop or pad. Don't dilute unless following manufacturer's instructions. Wring your mop or cloth almost dry and keep rinsing it during applications. To keep the floor looking its best, strip off polish after 25–30 applications.

Emulsion polishes

These water-based emulsion polishes are especially suitable for thermoplastic, vinyl, rubber and asphalt floors. They should not be used on unsealed wood floors. If instructions are carefully followed they give a glossy finish and cut down floor maintenance by providing a hard film which prevents dirt penetration. They are not, however, to be confused with real floor seals (though one brand is misleadingly named).

Many housewives become confused—very understandably—by the different terms used in describing water-based emulsion polishes. You may find tins labelled with 'hard-drying (self-shining) liquid emulsion', or 'self-polishing floor dressing', or 'plastic emulsion' or 'water wax emulsion'. To add to the apparent confusion there is a new type of emulsion called 'buffable emulsion.' The easiest way is to realize that emulsion falls into two categories: non-buffable and buffable emulsions.

Non-buffable emulsions. These are self-shining emulsions which are applied to a clean sealed or unsealed floor and left to dry, when a soft, glossy (though not necessarily shiny) appearance will be apparent. Two thin coats are preferable, but emulsion polishes should never be applied thickly because one of their inherent disadvantages is that they gradually 'build up' and may discolour the floor eventually.

This build-up may be removed with medium grade steel wool and hot detergent suds or a special floor cleaner.

Buffable emulsion. The buffable type of emulsion was developed first for industrial and commercial use, since most business premises have electric polishers and found no advantage in self-shining emulsions. Now available for domestic use, a buffable emulsion is *the* emulsion to buy if you have an electric polisher and want to use an emulsion, rather than a wax polish.

An important tip is never to attempt to buff a buffable emulsion with polishing pads which have previously been used for ordinary wax polish. Wax and emulsion won't mix, and produce a smeary, patchy effect.

You can also, of course, buff by hand or by weighted polishing mop if you wish.

The biggest advantage of the burnishable water wax emulsion is that there is no build-up of polish and dirt. And used correctly it does produce excellent results.

Felt

Heavy quality felt, such as that used for bedroom flooring, should be cleaned gently as it will not stand up to rough handling. Brush gently with a stiff brush or use a vacuum cleaner with slow, smooth strokes. The felt may show spill marks easily although wear marks should not show very quickly. To deal with spots and stains sponge lightly with a cloth dipped in warm mild synthetic detergent suds, rinse with a cloth wrung out in clear water and pat dry. Remove greasy marks with carbon tetrachloride.

Floor dressings

One of the newer flooring products is the type of floor dressing which claims to clean and polish in one operation. Though not in general use long enough for a final verdict, this would appear to be a useful answer for many housewives.

Intended for linoleum, vinyl, plastics, rubber and clay tiles, the dressing has a detergent action and lifts light soiling as you apply it. Follow directions to the letter. Spread the liquid with a damp cloth, rinsing out frequently, and a light gloss should be left on the flooring.

Do not expect this type of dressing to clean and polish a really dirty floor. Do not expect it to remove scuff marks either—here fine steel wool would probably be the answer.

Floor seals

Completely permanent seals do not exist. All, in time, will wear off the surface of a floor which is walked over, and obviously heavy traffic areas will wear first. But the protective finish which the seals give lasts a considerable time, especially on lightly-used floors such as a surround where there is little foot tread.

So far, the most permanent of the floor seals is 100 per cent poly-urethane, which is a plastics lacquer. This differs from other types of seal as it can be used to seal almost any floor surface except the thermoplastics, and it can last up to four years.

Oleo-resinous (oil-based) seals or epoxy resins, sometimes con-taining a proportion of polyurethane, may last up to one year. Other plastics lacquers may last up to six months.

Be sure when you buy a floor seal that it is suitable for the floor you wish to treat. Many types of seal are not suitable for rubber, plastics and printed linoleum. (Be sure, too, that you do not confuse floor seals with the emulsion polishes which are intended for the weekly maintenance of the new synthetic floors. See page 399).

With many types of seal, floor areas where wear is particularly heavy can be stripped and resealed without the need to re-treat the whole floor.

A warning. Before you embark on sealing a floor, it is as well to realize that it takes considerable time and effort on your part to do properly (and also some way of keeping the family well away). There are no short cuts, and for established, heavily waxed floorings it is better to go on waxing (buy an electric polisher if you are trying to cut down on elbow-grease!) rather than to attempt to remove the deeply-ingrained wax polish.

Applying the seal. It is important when applying a floor seal to follow the manufacturer's instructions exactly and to make sure that the floor surface is completely clean and dry and free from all wax and grease. Manufacturers generally suggest that existing wax both on polished floors or new linoleum should be removed with turpen-tine or turpentine substitute. (These days turpentine substitute is considered to be cheaper and better.) Although this dissolves the wax on the surface there is usually a proportion of wax in the pores or just below the surface of the floor and it is important that all this is removed, so that after using turpentine or substitute the floor should be well washed with hot water and a strong synthetic deter-gent, using a scrubbing brush or better still steel wool to ensure that every trace of wax residue is removed. Rinse the floor thoroughly after washing and then leave it to dry.

Plenty of air is necessary for drying the floor after washing and also after applying the seal so that doors and windows should be left open to ensure a good draught. Many people make the mistake of applying too much seal when they first treat a floor. Sparing applica-tions put on with a cloth are far more effective, they dry more rapidly and harden and set more easily. If a floor is very absorbent, such as cork, then it will be necessary to give it more than one coat but each coat should be sparing and evenly applied and must be thoroughly dry before the next coat is put on. Allow at least 6 hours before walking on the floor after applying a seal but at least 48 hours before mopping, damping or applying polish to the floor. The 100 per cent polyurethane seals may require even longer drying time initially.

For a glossy surface an emulsion, liquid wax or paste wax polish may be applied on top of the seal, but not for at least 48 hours.

If the floor remains tacky and appears to have little bumps under the surface after applying the seal this also means that there was wax or grease present on the wood or linoleum and this has delayed drying. Quite often if you open windows and doors and leave the room for a whole day the surface will dry out sufficiently for the bumps to be rubbed down with steel wool and for fresh seal to be applied on the tacky areas. Dry-mop carefully before re-applying the seal, to remove any dust raised by the steel wool.

If a floor seal does not dry even after several days it usually means that there was some wax or grease on the floor which has prevented the seal from drying, or that the seal was applied too thickly. The only thing to do is to remove all the wet seal and wax with white spirit and steel wool and then scrub the floor with hot water and detergent, using a fairly coarse steel wool to dislodge any obstinate particles. Rinse thoroughly, leave the floor to dry out and then re-apply the seal sparingly with a lint-free cloth.

Sometimes a seal floor will *dry patchily* with some areas having a matt surface and others shiny. This is often due to the fact that parts of the floor are more absorbent than others so that the seal was completely drawn into the floor in the dull patches although some of it remained on the surface of the shiny areas. Usually wiping a further very thin coat of seal on to the dull patches and leaving this to dry is sufficient, although the whole floor will need to have a final thin coating when the patches are dry. Don't be tempted to apply the seal lavishly to build up the dull areas and, of course, never apply a further coat until the previous one is completely dry.

Sometimes if polish is applied too soon after the final coat of seal the result is a *dull, smeary floor which is slippery* and unattractive. It is essential to leave at least 48 hours before applying any polish to the surface of a seal. If the floor has been polished too quickly and is smeary, rub over the dull surface with medium grade steel wool to remove most of the polish and then leave for 2 or 3 days so that air can harden the surface, then reapply a plastic emulsion polish, using a very thin coat and putting it on with a clean damp mop or cloth. Leave it to dry and do not buff. If an ordinary paste wax is preferred, again apply sparingly and evenly and do not rub it in while applying. Simply leave it to dry completely and then burnish it quickly and evenly.

White powdery marks. If floor seal has been applied to a surface containing wax or grease residue, even though it may dry, the bonding will be suspect and will result in the surface coatings of seal being easily removed. This will be noticeable as white powdery marks if and when furniture is lightly moved across the surface. If this happens, rub the surface down vigorously with coarse steel wool, remove all dust, and reapply a single coat of floor seal.

Floor stain

An amateur can stain a floor easily but the surface must be properly prepared first to get a good finish. All old stain must be completely removed and to do this it is necessary to scrub hard with hot strong soda water. Hands should be protected and any nails in the floor should be removed first. If any patches of stain resist removal, rub with steel wool and soap or use a special scraper. An easier method of stripping is to use a sanding machine, which you can hire.

When the stain has been removed leave the floor to dry out thoroughly, then fill in the cracks or gaps between the floorboards. Small cracks or holes can be filled with a special wood filler which is quite cheap to buy. For extensive cracks where floorboards have shrunk, a home-made papier-mâché filling would be cheaper. (See page 464.)

Whichever filler is being used, leave it to dry, then rub it down with a scraper or wire wool until it is level with the rest of the floor.

There are a number of floor stains available, or one can be made up at home (see page 463). Varnish stain is easy to apply but it is not recommended unless the floor is in very bad condition and the surface needs to be obscured as much as possible. Varnish stains will colour the surface of the wood only and consequently will soon wear off, particularly in doorways where traffic is heavy. A water stain is just as easy to apply and will stand up to much more wear. After staining, leave the floor for 2 or 3 days and then seal (see page 400) or polish with a wax floor polish.

Instead of staining, many people prefer to use a wood dye which is absorbed into the fibres of the floor. This means that the colouring penetrates into the wood and cannot wear off. Only one application is needed and a pint covers approximately 80 square feet.

Wood dye will take properly only if the floor is clean, bare, dry and quite free from wax, oil or other finishes. Paint or varnish can be removed with a non-caustic paint stripper. Soda must not be used, and the wood must not be sized before applying the dye.

The dye is best applied with a soft cloth, working the way of the grain. Once applied it should be left overnight to dry. If the floor is to be sealed it should be rubbed over with a coarse cloth before applying the seal. For details of sealing see page 400, under Floor Seals.

Haircord carpet

This can be shampooed, but if being done by hand it should be dried out of doors if possible. Whip up warm water and liquid synthetic detergent or soap powder to a thick lather and apply the suds to the carpet with a cloth or soft brush, cleaning a small area at a time. Rinse with a cloth wrung out in clear lukewarm water and overlap each area. Dry as quickly as possible and do not replace on floor or felt until quite dry. If the job must be done indoors, remove any underfelt and sweep the floor underneath the carpet first.

Alternatively, shampoo in position with electric shampoo applicator or push-along shampoo applicator. This makes the job quick and easy.

Hardboard floors

Hardboard floors should always be sealed as soon as they are laid in order to prevent staining by any spilled liquids. Sweep the floor and lightly rub it with a grade '0' steel wool if there is any sign of roughness, then seal, using a cloth pad and rubbing the seal in well. Start at a point farthest from the door, and leave the seal to dry for at least 4 to 6 hours, then apply a second coat of seal with a cloth or with a brush if preferred. Leave the seal to dry for at least 48 hours and then to get a high polish use plastic emulsion polish. This should keep the floor in good condition so that it needs little but daily mopping. Renew the emulsion polish as it wears or in this case ordinary wax polish well buffed can be used if preferred. It is only necessary to reapply polish to wear areas.

Linoleum

It is important that linoleum is properly laid and that the correct gauge is chosen, if the flooring is to last. Ideally, linoleum should be bonded to the existing floor, using special linoleum adhesive.

On a wooden floor, all 'proud' nails should be pulled out or punched in, boards should be planed level and then felt underlay paper should be laid. This should be cut to fit smoothly and neatly and it should be stuck in position with linoleum adhesive or with paperhanger's paste.

Sheet linoleum should be laid at right angles to the paper felt and at right angles to the window so that joins do not show. All joins should meet exactly and not overlap. If the room is shaped so that it is more economical to run the linoleum *across* the room rather than along the length of it, this can be done but it must be remembered that joins running across the light from the main window will tend to show up more.

Linoleum can be bonded to concrete, asphalt or stone in the same way, providing the floor is clean, dry and level. If there is any sign of rising dampness, the floor will need to be treated first and this is really a job for the specialist. To test for dampness in doubtful cases, place a square of linoleum, right side down, on the floor. Place a heavy weight on top and leave in position for 24 hours. Examine the linoleum and the floor where it has been and if neither shows signs of dampness or moisture then the floor should be sufficiently dry for linoleum to be laid.

It is important that the floor is smooth and level and if the concrete is worn, cracked or irregular, it should be screeded first. This can be done with latex-cement or latex-bitumen cement or with bituminous or P.V.A.-based underlays.

To cut linoleum, make a pencil line where the cutting is necessary and score half-way through the top of the sheeting with the point of a knife. Fold the linoleum back so that it splits down the cut and then draw the point of the knife between the two folds to cut the hessian backing.

Linoleum tiles are easier for the amateur to handle and they are also more suitable where the room is awkwardly shaped. They are laid in the same way as sheet linoleum but laying should start from the centre of the room instead of along the outside of the room.

Find the centre of the room by measuring the walls and marking the mid-point of each wall. Chalk a piece of string and fix it at the mid-point of one wall and stretch it across to the mid-point of the opposite wall. 'Twang' the taut string and the chalk will make a line across the floor. Do the same with the two end walls. The point where the two chalk lines cross is the centre of the room.

When laying linoleum tiles to a design, draw a plan first on squared paper, and colour each square with crayons or paint. Mark the position of each tile on the floor by chalking in the first letter of the colour and· as each tile is stuck in position, cross it off the plan.

To patch worn or torn linoleum, match up a square or oblong of linoleum a little larger than the damaged area and carefully tack this in place over the worn part. Using a metal-edged ruler on top of the patch as a guide, cut through to the worn linoleum with a very sharp knife, but do not cut the old hessian backing. Remove the patch, strip the old, worn linoleum away. Then strip the hessian backing from the new patch and smear the linoleum with adhesive and drop the new patch neatly into place. Leave a heavy weight on top until the adhesive is dry.

As an alternative to sticking the new patch in position, leave on the hessian backing and nail down the patch and the edges surrounding the patch with headless linoleum tacks.

For a tiny hole in linoleum caused by a chair castor or something similar, choose a wax crayon of the same colour, melt it gently and press firmly into the hole with the flat blade of a knife. Leave to harden and polish.

A larger hole will need to be filled with plastic filler and this can be coloured with cement colouring or special dye. Press firmly into the hole, leave to dry overnight, then smooth down with sandpaper and seal or polish.

Maintenance of linoleum. Avoid washing unsealed linoleum more than necessary. Hot water and soap tend to open the pores and to remove the oils blended into the linoleum during manufacture so that it becomes increasingly more difficult to clean.

Regular polishing and wiping with a well wrung-out cloth should be sufficient but the linoleum can be effectively and safely cleaned, if necessary, with a cloth dipped in turpentine substitute. This should remove any black marks or old stains, or if the floor is really dirty wash it with a mop or cloth frequently rinsed in clear water, then rub it dry.

Linoleum will stand up to years of this type of washing but not when strong soaps, soda, washing powders or other alkaline cleaning agents are used. If you feel you must use something in the water for washing (in the kitchen for instance) then use a very mild soap or soapless detergent or washing-up liquid. Rinse thoroughly, then rub dry.

Normally when linoleum is polished regularly it will maintain a bright glossy surface if the floor is well mopped every day with a dry or impregnated mop. An electric polisher, used with a paste wax or liquid wax polish, makes light work of maintaining a linoleum floor perfectly.

Another way to maintain a linoleum floor is to seal the surface before polishing. However, this cannot be done if the floor has been regularly waxed for a good many years, as even a strong cleaner will not remove the residue of wax in the pores of the linoleum.

Reasonably new linoleum which has been polished but for not too long a time can be treated before sealing with a special floor cleaner, or it may be washed with a strong household detergent, followed by scouring with a grade '0' steel wool before sealing. New linoleum should also be washed with detergent or floor cleaner before sealing in order to remove the manufacturer's protective wax film.

See page 400 for sealing.
See page 434 for renewing old polish.

Mastic flooring

This is a generic term covering asphalt, bitumastic, pitchmastic and similar flooring materials. Oil and grease may have a damaging effect on these types of flooring, and should be wiped up immediately if spilt. The mastic floorings should not be treated with oil-based seals, nor should solvent-based wax floor polishes be used. Use only emulsion polish or a special asphalt floor dressing, which coats the flooring with a hard waterproof film.

Such polishes should be applied after the surface has been thoroughly washed with hot soapless detergent suds or with a special asphalt cleaning solution, suitably diluted.

Remove any obstinate marks with steel wool grade '0', then mop, rinse clean and allow to dry.

Apply the emulsion with a special applicator or with a cloth, following directions given by the manufacturer.

Afterwards the floor can be kept clean and glossy by sweeping daily, and removing any marks with a damp mop or cloth, moistened with emulsion polish if wished. Rubber footmarks can be removed by rubbing with fine, dry steel wool.

Mildew—to remove from wood floors

A weak solution of permanganate of potash is often effective in removing mildew stains from wood floors. Dissolve ½ teaspoonful of crystals in 1 pint of warm water. Sponge on to the stain, repeat with diluted peroxide, then rinse and dry. Finally rub with a cloth dipped in lavender polish.

Oak strip flooring

See under Wood floors, page 415, and Floor Seals, page 400.

Parquet

See under Wood floors, page 415, and Floor Seals, page 400.

Pitchmastic flooring

See Mastic flooring on page 407.

Plastics floor tiles

For PVC plastics (vinyl) tiles follow instructions on page 413, or for Thermoplastic tiles page 412.

Plastics sheet flooring

This is usually a PVC type flooring. See under Vinyl and Vynolay, pages 413–414.

Polish—to remove

See under Stripping, page 434.

Polyvinyl chloride flooring

See under Vinyl flooring, page 413.

Quarry tiles

Red quarry tiles often tend to fade, so wax polish used to seal and shine the tiles should contain a red pigment to preserve the colour.

There are several non-slip red tile polishes on sale but whichever is used, the wax paste should be applied sparingly and left to harden; it should then be buffed with a floor brush and finally burnished with a cloth under the brush. Between polishes, a light buffing should be sufficient especially if the polish is waterproof.

To remove a white alkaline deposit, clean with a weak solution of oxalic acid (1 in 8), rinse thoroughly, dry and polish.

Neglected red tiles should be cleaned with turpentine substitute, applied with medium/coarse steel wool. Repeat if necessary.

Red quarry tiles may also be treated with special red tile seal.

Rubber flooring

As with most other types of flooring, regular washing with hot soapy water tends to make the surface more porous and cleaning increasingly difficult. When the floor is very dirty and washing is unavoidable use warm soapy water and a cloth (not a brush), rinse well, then dry thoroughly. Preserve a rubber floor by applying emulsion polish regularly until the pores of the rubber are filled and non-absorbent. Solvent-based floor waxes should not be used as these may perish the rubber.

If the rubber is laid in a bathroom and bath-salts are used, wipe up any water splashes quickly to avoid damaging the colour of the flooring. In a kitchen, wipe up grease splashes immediately and protect the floor under a cooker if possible.

There are synthetic rubber floorings available which are much more resistant to splashes and grease marks.

It is important to use only emulsion-type polishes on rubber flooring. Oil-based floor seals should never be used. See page 399.

Rugs

Rugs will not slip on a polished floor if they are backed with a special nonslip material or if pieces of Matgrip—a rubber-threaded webbing sold in 1-yard packets—are sewn across each corner.

Another way to anchor rugs both on a shiny floor or on a carpet is to brush latex adhesive (such as Copydex, Jiffytex, Texweld, etc.) on the edges of the backing. Allow to dry thoroughly and it will form an almost colourless backing that won't slip or creep.

The rubber rings from pickle jars sewn under each corner of a rug will also stop it from sliding on a well-polished floor or thin foam plastics sheeting can be stuck to the back of the rug.

Use a similar method on a 'creeping' hearthrug or sew pieces of carpet with the pile downwards on to the under corners of the rug.

Yet another method, and this is good for large and heavy rugs, is to sew a special type of press fastener to each corner. The lower half of the fastener is screwed into the floor in the correct position.

Contrary to popular belief, a rug should not be hung over a clothes-line nor laid flat on a path and beaten, neither should it be shaken nor banged against a wall. All these methods weaken the backing and the fibres. If a rug *must* be beaten, it should be placed face down on a soft surface such as a lawn and a Rattan beater used rather than a wire one.

Make it a habit to vacuum clean the *backs* of rugs occasionally. When vacuum cleaning the top of a rug, sweep crosswise rather than along the length of the rug and it will not wrinkle so easily.

Shampooing rugs. Shampoo small rugs by scrubbing with a brush dipped in the lather of a carpet cleaning solution as advised for carpets (see page 394), and avoid wetting the backing of the rug. Better still, shampoo with an electric or push-along shampoo applicator. Alternatively, a thin rug can be washed in a large bath in warm soapy water or detergent suds. Rinse very thoroughly in two or three waters, then hang out of doors to drip dry. Brush thoroughly with a stiff brush or vacuum cleaner when dry to raise the pile.

Some modern rugs may be washed in a washing machine and then spin dried. Look for rugs bearing a special washability label.

Semastic flooring

This is the trade name of Dunlop Semtex. For further details see under Mastic flooring on page 407 and treat accordingly.

Slippery floor

Floors which are slippery have usually been allowed to accumulate an excessive build-up of polish—quite often, too, a polish of poor quality. Poor quality polishes provide soft greasy wax films which are easily smeared. Dirt collects on the softened wax and probably much too soon an extra layer of wax is added to the first and so there is what is known as a 'build-up'.

The solution to this problem is to remove all the wax from the floor, using a special cleaner or turpentine substitute and medium/coarse steel wool. On a wood floor rub the way of the grain and mop up the wax as it is softened. Leave the floor for an hour or so to dry. Even after this treatment it is quite possible that there will be sufficient wax left on the floor to produce a good shine if the surface is well buffed with a brush.

Now apply sparingly and evenly a good quality solid paste wax, preferably one containing an anti-slip ingredient. Leave the polish for as long as possible and do not try to rub it into the floor. After several hours buff the floor with a stiff-bristled brush or a polisher to the desired shine.

It is important to buff a polished floor frequently but not to add more polish until it is absolutely necessary. Manufacturers (who after all are anxious to sell their polishes) still maintain that most housewives use too much polish too frequently.

Stair carpet

Stair carpet has to stand up to harder wear than carpet anywhere else in the house so it is important that it should be properly laid and cared for. Soft, thick stair-pads help a great deal but hard, unyielding pads or old worn carpet underneath do no good at all. Make sure the pads completely cover the nosing of each stair, where wear is heaviest.

Allow at least a foot of extra carpet at the top and bottom of the staircase to allow for the carpet being moved to even out wear. Ideally the carpet should be moved twice during the first 6 months and then about twice a year.

Start laying the carpet at the bottom step and work upwards and if there is a bend in the stair, pleat the surplus carpet on the inside of the step, on the upright front of the rise and tack it down firmly.

It is very important that the pile of the carpet should flow from the top of the stairs to the bottom. It is easy to see which way the pile lies if a hand is brushed lightly over the surface.

Clips are adequate on narrow stairs but rods will hold stair carpet more firmly especially on wide stairs, and they will prevent bagginess in the middle of each step where wear is heaviest. 'Invisible' carpet grips are also available.

Professional carpet layers sometimes prefer simply to tack down stair-carpet. Tacks soon become unnoticeable and the firm can return annually to re-position the carpet. Even then, this could work out as cheaply as buying fairly expensive 'invisible' carpet grips.

Stairs

A hand vacuum cleaner is ideal for brushing stair-carpet, or use the special tools from your vacuum cleaner. Without a vacuum cleaner, begin at the top and clean every step separately, collecting the dust into a wide dustpan.

An impregnated hand-dusting mop will quickly remove dust from paintwork and clean between banister rails.

Failing a dusting mop, buy a cheap washing-up mop and stand the head into a jam jar containing paraffin. Leave overnight, then drip dry. Another quick method is to spray the mop with a liquid polish.

An aerosol such as that made by O'Cedar is ideal. Either will quickly absorb dust from around banister rails and stair treads, etc.

Stone flooring

Follow instructions as given for Concrete on page 397.

Terrazzo

Clean with a cloth wrung out in hot water containing soda; dry thoroughly, then polish with a thin film of wax or emulsion polish. Avoid soaps, acids, any abrasive and an excess of polish.

An easy way to maintain this type of flooring is to seal the surface, using a suitable floor seal. Wash the floor first, using detergent or special floor cleaner and allow it to dry thoroughly, then apply seal lightly with a cloth pad, and leave to dry. Only one coat of seal is needed but it should be allowed to dry out for 48 hours. Once the surface is completely dry the floor can be swept daily and any dirty marks or footprints can be wiped away with a damp mop.

Thermoplastic tiles

These and other plastic and composition floors may be cleaned by washing with warm water and a soapless detergent. Very dirty marks can be removed by rubbing with fine steel wool and with any special cleaning agent made by the manufacturers.

Ordinary solvent-based floor polishes should be avoided but many manufacturers make a special polish for their own brand of flooring such as Dunlop Safeshine, Marley Waterwax for Marley tiles and Accogloss for Accotiles. Where possible use this special polish; otherwise use a self-shining or buffable emulsion. See page 399.

To avoid cleaning, seal the floor, using an oil-based seal recommended for this type of flooring. Only one coat should be used and it *must* be sparingly and evenly applied with a cloth. Forty-eight hours after sealing, apply a coat of plastic emulsion and renew this occasionally. The floor should then need little more than damp mopping to remove footmarks and stains. Avoid floor seals which are not specifically recommended for thermoplastic flooring.

Tiles

Avoid abrasives and do not scrub glazed tiles but simply wash with soapy water, rinse and dry thoroughly; polish by rubbing with a soft duster or apply a light film of silicone polish. Unglazed tiles may be scrubbed with hot soapy water, using an abrasive if necessary; soda should not be used. Polish with non-slip tile polish or seal with a suitable floor seal.

Marks on a tile hearth caused by cinders or cigarette-ends can be cleaned off by rubbing with a damp cloth and a mild abrasive powder. If the marks are severe, dip a soap-impregnated fine steel wool pad in the abrasive. Or try metal polish on steel wool. Afterwards polish with a silicone cream.

See page 408 for Quarry tiles; for Thermoplastic tiles see page 412 and below.

Vinyl

The word vinyl is the popular shortening of the plastic polyvinyl chloride, or PVC. There are various types and grades of vinyl flooring. They include solid vinyl in sheet and tile form, vinyl with felt-paper backing in sheet form, and vinyl with felt or foam backing in sheet form. Vinyl asbestos, as the name implies, does contain polyvinyl chloride, but it is reinforced with asbestos fibre.

If the flooring is of the glossy or semi-glossy PVC type, wash with hot soapy water or soapless detergent. Rinse well and dry thoroughly. Severe stains can be removed with fine steel wool or a mild paste abrasive.

Avoid oil-based seals and also strong cleaners, alkaline detergents, solvents such as paraffin, turpentine, etc.

If polish is necessary, use a self-shining or a buffable emulsion, either of which are quite safe and will protect the floor surface. See page 399. Solvent-based polishes such as paste wax and liquid wax should not be used.

Emulsion polishes wear off floors after a time, and usually cleaning the surface with hot detergent suds or with special floor cleaner is sufficient to remove the residue when necessary. Stubborn surface blemishes will need the abrasive action of medium-grade steel wool.

Matt PVC flooring and *vinyl asbestos floorings* can be washed, scrubbed and polished with any type of polish, though emulsion polishes (self-shining or buffable) are still the best.

Felt-backed vinyl flooring should be washed with warm water and very little mild detergent. Avoid solvents and solvent-based polishes. If the flooring is embossed, scrub lightly the way of the grain to remove dirt. Rinse thoroughly, rub dry and give one or two coats of self-shining emulsion to protect the surface.

Details of laying vinyl sheeting, preparing subfloor and care is given under Vynolay below.

Vynolay

The trade name for Dunlop vinyl flooring. It is a sheet flooring which is fairly easy to lay, especially if a narrow width is chosen. Vynolay is in rolls 75 ft. long and 48 in. and 72 in. wide. Once unrolled, it is flexible and almost impossible to tear. It is easier to handle if it is left, in the roll, in a warm room overnight. It can be cut with ordinary kitchen scissors or a Stanley knife and it is easily cut to fit into corners or around fitments.

The subfloor needs no elaborate preparation. It should simply be smooth, even, clean and dry. The only exception is when the subfloor has been treated with a wood preservative. In this case, a non-porous foil lining paper should be used between the floor and the Vynolay, laid with the foil face down.

Although vinyl itself is waterproof and rotproof, it should never be used to seal a damp floor as moisture will collect underneath and cause various complications.

If a wooden floor is uneven, a good solution is to cover it with hardboard before laying the vinyl. It is best to lay the hardboard crossways to avoid joints coinciding. Make sure, too, that a timber subfloor is adequately ventilated from below. Uneven concrete, brick or tile floors may need screeding to make them level.

All vinyl floorings tend to shrink slightly when first laid, so allow for all joints to overlap by at least $\frac{1}{2}$ in. and leave about 1 in. extra all round the edges of the room. After the flooring has settled—that is after about 10 to 14 days—cut through any overlap that remains and finally trim round the skirtings and fittings.

Vynolay lies flat without sticking, although it can be stuck down if preferred. Although light in weight, it is extremely hard-wearing because of the high percentage of tough PVC resin in its manufacture. Tough and durable, it will not chip, crack or tear under normal circumstances. It is also rotproof and flames will not spread on it easily.

Vynolay, like most vinyl sheeting, has its own built-in satin sheen and only needs polishing if a high gloss finish is required. Normal spillages can simply be wiped up with a damp cloth and all-over cleaning can be done with a solution of mild soap or detergent.

To remove a build-up of polish or for more general cleaning, use Dunlop Safeshine Cleaner, carefully diluting it according to the instructions on the bottle. Obstinate marks can be removed by rubbing gently with a little scouring powder—never use bleach or spirit cleaner as these can damage the surface irreparably. The smooth surface is resistant to ingraining dirt but if a high gloss finish is required, use Dunlop Safeshine.

Wax polish

Always buy a good-quality wax polish. Reputable manufacturers take care to incorporate ingredients which will benefit and not do harm to your flooring, and most take the trouble to provide adequate application instructions to guide the housewife through the confusing array of floorings with which she has to cope.

Wax polishes can be divided into paste wax polishes (the type in a round tin, used by housewives for generations but many incorporating newer, effective ingredients too—for example silicones) and liquid wax polishes. Paste wax polishes contain a certain amount of solvent—these days it is usually turpentine substitute. Liquid wax polishes contain much more solvent, and are very useful where it is wished to clean and polish a floor at the same time.

There are also the silicone cream polishes, but these are intended mainly for furniture.

Wood block floors

Wood block floors should not be washed as the wood is inclined to swell when wet; the swollen blocks become uneven and sometimes displaced and this naturally spoils the surface of the floor. Clean by regular polishing or use a wood seal. For details see Wood floors, below, and Floor seals, page 400.

Wood floors

To maintain a wood floor you have two alternatives. One is to use a paste wax or liquid wax polish, the other is to seal the floor and then polish with a wax or emulsion polish. Opinions are divided on the best method: one school of thought supports the view that sealing is the only answer, followed by occasional polishing; the other point of view, often held by professional floor-laying contractors incidentally, is that a wood floor should not be sealed—certainly not for the first year or two at least, until it has had time to settle down. And, they say, there is nothing to beat the natural shine of a well-waxed, well-buffed floor.

Whichever point of view you decide to adopt, follow these general principles:

If waxing only. To obtain a good shine on a wood floor, use a paste wax initially so that it will fill all the tiny pits and cracks in the surface. Then use a good paste wax or liquid wax polish regularly, spreading on evenly. Do not wax the whole floor each time—usually it is enough to wax wear areas only. Leave to dry and then buff.

The secret with a wax polish is to allow it to dry thoroughly, because the longer it dries, the easier it is to polish. When it is dry, buff thoroughly with an electric polisher, or use a floor-polishing brush, finally burnishing the polish by placing a soft cloth under the brush.

Most scratches, stains, marks, dirt and built-up wax polish can be removed from a wood floor by rubbing lightly with a cloth or fine steel wool moistened in turpentine or white spirit (turpentine substitute). Turpentine is not used anything like as frequently as in the past, it being accepted now that white spirit (turpentine substitute) is the cheaper and better solvent to use when you wish to clean off and then repolish a wood floor.

Work the way of the grain, mopping up the wax as it is softened, and finally rub over the whole floor with a liquid wax polish or with a coat of wax polish diluted with a little more turpentine substitute. Wear gloves or protect hands during cleaning by using a special rubber or plastics holder for steel wool. After this go back to your normal polishing routine.

This treatment is quite harmless to wood floors and may be repeated two or three times a year or whenever necessary.

Never let an unsealed wood floor get wet (unless you are scrubbing it in preparation for sealing, and then only sparingly). Water will cause watermarks and may cause the grain of the wood to become raised. In the case of parquet flooring an excess of water could cause the blocks to swell and become uneven and displaced. If water splashes on to a wood floor, wipe up immediately and apply a little polish. If a watermark is left, rub in linseed oil daily until the mark disappears.

If sealing a wood floor. To obviate the hard work of regular and frequent polishing, and to enable you to wipe up spills easily, you may prefer to seal the floor with a special seal. Only apply a floor seal if all traces of wax polish can be thoroughly removed from the surface of, and within, the timber. In most cases it is best to have the floor sanded—you can hire a sanding machine for this purpose.

If you feel there is not too great a build-up of wax, you can clean the floor with turpentine substitute and hot detergent suds, or with a special floor-cleaning preparation. Use medium/coarse steel wool, working the way of the grain and protecting your fingers with a rubber or plastic holder for the steel wool. Make sure that all old waxes and polishes are removed, then rinse well.

When the floor is thoroughly dry (leave overnight, with some heat in the room, if you have scrubbed with detergent suds), apply the seal according to instructions (see page 400) and when dry apply a second—and even a third—thin coat of seal. For a high gloss finish, rub the floor with steel wool grade '0' before applying the final coat of seal. Leave for 48 hours and then apply a coat of paste wax, liquid wax or emulsion polish.

Where traffic is heavy, in a doorway for instance, the seal may show signs of wear after several months. In this case, clean the part thoroughly to remove any wax and then reseal the worn area.

See also Emulsion polishes on page 399 and Floor seals on page 400.

Home Decorating

Alkyd liquid paint

This is a modern alkyd based paint with a range of finishes from high gloss or enamel to eggshell and matt. Alkyd paints tend to dry on the surface overnight but they take up to five days to harden right through. Once quite dry, they are hard, flexible and not easily chipped or cracked. Use recommended undercoat and one or two top coats when starting from a bare or primed surface. Previously painted work in good condition can often be re-coated with a single coat of finish after cleaning. It is important that surfaces are clean, free from any oil or grease and quite dry before commencing painting.

Bath

If the enamel on the bottom of the bath has chipped and cracked the bath can be repainted. Clean it very thoroughly with hot synthetic detergent suds and then with a rag dipped in turpentine substitute; dry well, then paint with a special bath enamel, giving a very thin coat. When the enamel has dried completely, apply a second thin coat and leave this to dry; repeat with a third coat and when this has dried, fill the bath with cold water and leave for 2 or 3 days or a week if possible. After painting a bath, always run cold water in before hot.

Brushes

When 'breaking in' a new paint brush, use it for applying under-coats before painting a top coat with it.

Although a *varnish brush* may be used for painting, a paint brush should never be used for varnish.

When *painting has finished for the day*, wipe out as much paint as possible from the bristles, then stand the brush in cold water. Suspend the brush so that it is not resting on the bristles and don't let the water reach any metal parts. Ideally, bore a small hole in the handle, push a skewer through this, and balance it on the rim of a jam jar half-filled with water. Shake and wipe the brush before beginning painting next day.

When the job is finally completed, remove paint from the bristles by brushing them out on paper, then by wiping with rag and finally by washing in paraffin or turpentine. Work this and any remaining paint out of the bristles on a board, dry and wrap in wax paper or tinfoil.

If the job is not finished but the brush will not be needed for some time, clean it, wash it in warm soda water, rinse thoroughly under a running tap, then moisten the bristles with linseed oil. When stopping work temporarily, leave a *varnish brush* soaking in linseed oil.

Brushes which have been used for *spirit stain* should be cleaned with methylated spirit after the surplus stain has been removed from the bristles with paper or old rag.

Use a proprietary cleansing liquid to clean a brush if the paint will not come out easily.

Equal quantities of turpentine and linseed oil will often soften a *hardened paint brush.* Leave the brush to soak, then wash in warm soda water and when the bristles are dry, gently knead them.

Another way of *cleaning a neglected paint brush* is to soak it in paraffin for a week by suspending it so that the bristles do not rest on the bottom of the jar. Wash in warm soda water or detergent and rinse thoroughly.

Alternatively, neglected paint brushes can often be cleaned by bringing a little vinegar to boiling point, placing the bristles in this and simmering for 30 minutes. Wash well in synthetic detergent, rinse and shake dry.

Ceiling

If the part of the ceiling over a gas cooker or lamp has become soiled and darkened, it can be whitened quickly by applying a thick starch to the patch. When it is quite dry, brush off the surplus.

An alum wash will help correct small particles of whitening which keep falling from a ceiling. Dissolve 1 oz. of alum in 2 pints of water and brush on to the ceiling.

Many people find papering a ceiling for the first time difficult, due to the long lengths of paper which must be supported. The solution is to tear—not cut—the length of paper into two or three shorter pieces which can be easily managed. Made carefully and positioned in the right order, joins should be invisible.

Cellulose

It is difficult to strip a highly polished cellulose finish without damaging the veneer or surface underneath, especially if this has been specially treated. Two or three applications of paint stripper should remove the cellulose but it should be tried on an inconspicuous part first. If the result is satisfactory, apply the stripper until the surface is evenly matt, then rub lightly with very fine glasspaper, going the way of the grain and finally polish with a good wax cream or polish. Remove cellulose from plain woodwork with a cellulose 'thinner'.

Colours

There are only three primary colours—red, yellow and blue. By combining any two together the result is a secondary colour which may be orange, green or violet, depending upon which two primaries are combined. Progress one step further, combine any two of the secondaries and a third colour is produced. This again is one of a group of three, known as tertiaries.

Colours which harmonize, such as violet and pink, contain a colour common to them both, in this instance, red. Colours which contrast, for instance green and red, contain no common colour.

Here are a few of the main colours with those which harmonize with them and the contrasting colour:

Colour	Harmonies	Contrast
Yellow	Lemon, lime green, orange	Magenta
Orange	Geranium, nasturtium	Blue
Nasturtium	Yellow, orange	Violet
Geranium	Red, flame	Sea green
Purple	Violet, magenta	Yellow
Violet	Purple, blue, magenta	Nasturtium
Green	Peacock blue, sea green, lime	Yellow
Blue	Violet, peacock blue	Orange
Red	Geranium, magenta, plum	Green

Red, orange and yellow are warm colours; blue, green and grey are cold colours, so that a room facing north can be made to appear warm and cheerful by choosing any of the first three colours, while if it faces south, it can be made to look cool and peaceful by choosing from green, grey and blue when decorating or furnishing the room.

When redecorating it should be remembered that orange and yellow seem to advance while blue, green and grey appear to withdraw. Therefore, if the end wall of a long narrow room is painted red or yellow the room will appear more square and if the ceiling of a low room is painted pale green or blue, it will appear higher and in better proportion.

White, primrose yellow and mist green reflect most light while golden brown, red and black reflect least. In a dark, dismal hall, therefore, one of the first three colours should be chosen or failing this, the window wall at least should be painted in a good light-reflecting colour to give an appearance of lightness.

Concrete

It is possible to buy special paints for decorating concrete floors. These are in a range of colours, can be easily applied and once dry give a smooth, easy-to-clean surface.

For walls and other cement surfaces a special cement paint, such as Hydramic Waterproof Cement Paint, made in two or three colours is ideal. This is hard-wearing and has an attractive finish.

Condensation

If water vapour in the air condenses on a cold surface it forms beads of moisture which we know as condensation. This occurs more frequently in *kitchens and bathrooms* because there is more water vapour in these rooms and it is more noticeable in winter than in summer because surfaces are more likely to be cold in winter.

While a cold surface will become wet whenever *steam* is produced, a warm surface will remain comparatively dry and this points to the remedy. Either there must be sufficient ventilation and circulation of air to carry moist air away from cold surfaces or the surfaces themselves must be warm so that moisture does not condense.

Emulsion paint will absorb quite a lot of moisture providing it is applied over a suitable surface; applied on top of oil-bound distemper or enamel, for instance, it would quickly flake off. Ordinary distemper and wallpaper will also absorb moisture. High gloss paint will not absorb moisture but it can be wiped down easily and a rubberized paint, ideal for kitchens and bathrooms, will absorb moisture and can be cleaned without damage.

Ideally, when redecorating, walls and ceiling should be cleaned back to the plaster and then a priming coat should be given—preferably one made and recommended by the manufacturer of the paint which is to be applied on top of the primer.

In a well-heated, well-ventilated house, condensation seldom occurs. To increase the circulation of air, a ventilating fan is of considerable help especially if it is let into the window or outside wall above the cooker or bath where steam rises. This means that damp air will be carried away, but it must be replaced with more air and this should, if possible, be warm. The easiest way to introduce warm air is to open an inside door so that the air comes in from a living-room or warm hall or at least passes a heater, fire or stove.

For *pipes, tanks* and various surfaces which show condensation quickly there are also special anti-condensation paints available; some of these contain particles of cork, others are texturized paints which are made up from powder and applied fairly thickly, then stippled to give a rough, or slightly raised surface. In some circumstances *embossed wallpapers* help because of the pockets of air formed behind the raised surfaces.

When a modern all-night burner is in use, dampness will sometimes appear due to condensation in the flue. This happens because the smoke rises so slowly that it becomes cold and condenses before reaching the chimney top; the resulting moisture gradually seeps through walls or ceiling and shows as a damp patch. The trouble can be remedied temporarily by letting the fire out for several days while the dampness dries, then painting the affected area with special waterproofing liquid, with two coats of aluminium primer or with two coats of shellac knotting fluid. Line and decorate over the top. If the dampness has seeped through to the outside also, coat with an invisible silicone liquid according to directions.

Co-polymer liquid emulsion

One of the modern paints produced in a very wide range of colours. It resists grease, splashes and condensation and can be washed without losing colour. Apply with a brush or roller, wash out with water after use. If using a pale shade over a deep tone or over patterned wallpaper, two or three coats may be needed.

Dampness

If there is dampness in a house check for condensation, bad drainage of subsoil, a defective damp-course, crumbled pointing, etc., and remedy these causes. When the dampness is due—as it is in most cases, as almost all building materials are porous—to direct penetration of rain through the walls, then painting with a liquid silicone such as Szerelmey Liquid should remedy the trouble. One coat is usually sufficient and this can be applied to any and every kind of building material. There are different solutions for internal and external walls but both are invisible. Care must be taken, however, not to 'sandwich' dampness in a wall, between two layers of damp-proof solutions.

To damp-proof one odd patch of wall before redecorating, give two coats of waterglass solution, mixed in the same way as for preserving eggs. It makes an excellent substitute for ordinary sealer. Other water-proofing solutions are aluminium primer and shellac knotting; in both cases use two coats.

Old houses built without a damp-course are often affected by rising dampness which shows itself in damp patches on inside walls under certain weather conditions. This really needs expert advice and attention but an old unscientific remedy which is often surprisingly effective is to plant several laurel bushes a short distance from the walls. The thirsty bushes attract any surplus moisture, thus leaving the house walls warm and dry.

Distemper

This is the cheapest wall-covering available; it can be used on recently plastered walls in new houses and it is ideal for ceilings also. Distemper becomes dirty fairly quickly and is usually difficult to clean: on the other hand it is easily removed and quite cheaply replaced with fresh distemper. It can be applied with a brush or roller but the whole room must be done at the same time and because it dries so quickly windows and doors should be kept closed while work is in progress.

Unless walls and ceilings are new, they should be thoroughly washed down before beginning to distemper. New walls do not need cleaning although any odd nibs of plaster should be removed with a stripping knife (not with glasspaper) so that the surface is quite smooth. Give walls and ceilings a coat of size next to stop the distemper from being absorbed and to make work easier but allow sufficient time for the size to dry or harden before starting work.

It is not wise to distemper over wallpaper as the water used for thinning the distemper may easily soften the paste holding the wallpaper so that it comes away from the wall later. Even if the paper resists the water and holds, decorating next time will be twice as much work as stripping will be considerably harder.

A 7-lb. tin of distemper will cover approximately 25 sq. yds. with two coats. A 7-in. wide brush should be used for applying distemper but a paint roller can be used equally well and is probably the easier —and certainly the quicker—method for an amateur. Whether brush or roller is used, care must be taken not to overload it.

Start distempering by the window and work away from the light always; two coats should be sufficient, the first fairly thin and the second of the consistency of thin cream. Clean up any splashes with a damp cloth as they occur, as left to dry they may be difficult to remove.

Emulsion paint

This is a water-based plastics resin which dries as the water in it evaporates. It is porous, allows moisture through and can be used on new walls. It is not suitable on surfaces that flake or might flake later; surfaces can be tested to see if they are loose and might flake by wiping them with a wet cloth.

Two coats of emulsion paint should be used and a quart tin is enough to give 20 sq. yds. two good coats. A brush or roller can be used although the roller is the easier and quicker way for an amateur but neither will show brush marks. It is not necessary to size the surface before using emulsion paint.

Emulsion paint is quite satisfactory in a kitchen or bathroom where there is condensation—providing the walls are completely stripped of any high gloss paint, oil-bound distemper or other finish which may flake. If emulsion paint is to be used where there is steam it is important that it is applied over a suitable surface where there is a certain amount of porosity—as there is with plaster walls.

There is now a type of emulsion paint which kills flies—ideal for kitchens—and another type which is fire-proof.

Emulsion or matt surface paint can be washed with a sponge dipped in a solution of paintwork cleaner or liquid detergent. Start at the bottom of a wall and work upwards, rinsing in clear warm water and drying each patch as it is cleaned, overlapping patches to avoid tide-marks.

See page 434 for removing emulsion paint.

Enamel

When enamel or lacquer is being used for painting in cold weather, it helps to stand the tin in a bowl of hot water for half an hour before starting work. The heat will thin the enamel and make it easier to apply as well as giving a harder and glossier finish.

Floor seals

For details of sealing a floor see page 400.

French polish

To remove french polish in order to give a wax or other finish, mix together equal amounts of household bleach and strong (not household) ammonia. A mask or handkerchief should be worn as a protection from unpleasant fumes, then the mixture should be brushed on to the woodwork. As soon as the polish is stripped off completely, rub the wood with very fine glasspaper working the way of the grain. Finally rub well with wax, beeswax or other preparation and polish.

French polish can also be removed using a non-caustic paint stripper, following the manufacturer's instructions exactly, and this is the easier method if the surface is to be re-french polished afterwards.

There are special polishing kits available to make french polishing easy for amateurs to tackle at home, and Furniglass is a good example. Kits contain all the preparations necessary together with complete instructions for stripping, polishing and finishing and also for giving a heat-resistant surface.

Garden furniture

If garden or other furniture is being painted out of doors, newspaper placed to protect a path or terrace quickly tears in the wind. An easier way is to throw down handfuls of sand or earth over the terrace and then brush this out lightly so that there is an even covering. Paint drips will then be absorbed by the soil or sand and it takes only a few minutes to sweep it up later.

To clean and restore garden furniture, scrub it well with warm water and synthetic detergent; remove any stains by dipping fine steel wool in the suds and rubbing marks with this. Whether scrubbing or using wire wool, always rub the way of the grain and not across it. Rinse the furniture thoroughly with a cloth moistened with cold water and leave it to dry completely. When the wood is really dry, dip a cloth in ordinary raw linseed oil and rub every part of the furniture with this. Leave the oil to penetrate into the wood and then wipe away any surplus with a clean dry cloth before using the furniture.

Jelly emulsion paints

See under Thixotropic, page 435.

Jelly gloss paint

This is a very thick modern paint. It sometimes contains polyure-thane and it has a very hard chip-free surface when dry. It is not so easy to use as some of the other paints.

Knotting

This is a spirit preparation rather like a quick-drying varnish. It is used to seal knots in woodwork so that resin cannot later exude from the knots to spoil the finish of paintwork. A very little knotting goes a long way and in an average household a ¼-pint tin would last a very long time.

Where new wood has been stained with a wood dye, a coat of pale knotting should be applied 24 hours after the dye has dried before varnishing or french polishing the surface.

Linoleum paint

If the linoleum is well worn and needs resurfacing, clean the floor with detergent suds to remove surface dust and dirt, then if the linoleum has odd bumps and rough particles go over it carefully with a medium grade sandpaper. Next wipe the floor very well with a cloth dipped in turpentine substitute to remove any polish and give it a thin coat of linoleum paint. Allow this to dry thoroughly, then give a second coat and do not use the room until the floor has completely dried hard.

Mirrors

If a bathroom is being tiled and it is planned to modernize it by setting mirrors into the walls, it should be remembered that ordinary mirrors will quickly become cloudy and marked. Mirrors must have a lead or copper backing to protect the silver before being fixed into the tiles or a wall surface. This is not expensive and is easily done by a glazing firm.

If the silver on an ordinary mirror does become mottled and cloudy it can be resilvered by an expert. A glazing firm will estimate the cost.

Frameless mirrors crack very easily if the dome-cap screw is over-tightened during fixing. This can be avoided if a tiny blob of putty is placed under the head of the screw. Continue tightening the screw until the putty starts to ooze, then stop and there will be no chance of the glass cracking.

Nail holes

Nail holes in woodwork can be filled in with wood-stopping which can be bought in most colours. For an odd nail hole mix sawdust with a little glue to make a thick paste and press this into the hole. Once dry it will become hard as wood and can be sandpapered and painted. An acrylic filler—such as Celofil or Polyfilla—can also be used and is preferable where nail holes are numerous and where there are plaster walls also. A substitute filler for holes can be made by mixing a little french polish well with ordinary whitening. It dries quickly and becomes very hard.

Nails

To insert a nail in a plaster wall, first place a cross of transparent cellulose tape over the spot so that the double thickness of tape comes where the nail is to be inserted; the adhesive tape will prevent the plaster from chipping and flaking.

If plaster walls are crumbly and will not take the weight of a nail or picture, use a wall plug or scoop out the loose plaster and fill the hole with an acrylic filler or plaster of Paris mixed to a thick paste with water. Gently reinsert the nail and leave to harden.

Avoid using bent nails of any kind but do not discard rusty nails as they will hold better once they are hammered home although they may be more difficult to insert.

There are various types and sizes of nails and it is important to choose the correct nails for the job in hand. The most common nails —round with a large flat head—are french nails, but these are mainly used for rough or unimportant jobs. Some nails are made so that they will penetrate wood easily without splitting it—these are often oval—others are designed to hold fabric in place without tearing it. Protect the head of a decorative nail (when tacking upholstery braiding in place, for instance) by holding a piece of material, rubber or cardboard between the nail head and the hammer.

In any hard wood, it is easier to insert a nail once a small hole has been made; use a bradawl to make the hole, then drive in the nail at a slight angle—not straight. In most cases the weight of the hammer should be enough to drive the nail in and it should not require effort and strength as well.

It is as important to choose the correct type of hammer as nail. Avoid a hammer with an old battered head and one which is out of proportion to the size of the nail. If the hammer has been in constant use for a long time, have the head reground.

When nailing very thin wood which might split, tap the point of the nail very lightly with a hammer: this slightly blunts the point so that it cuts and bursts the fibres of wood instead of splitting them apart.

A piece of cardboard or stiff paper can be used to hold a small nail or tack in place while it is hammered home.

Store nails and screws in small screw-cap jars and bottles but do not use up shelf space; instead screw each cap to the underside of a shelf and screw the jars up into the caps. Nails will be immediately visible but out of the way.

Non-drip emulsion paint

See under Thixotropic, page 435.

Oak

To change the colour of dark oak, strip off the existing stain and varnish, using a liquid paint stripper according to instructions, then remove the surface of the wood by rubbing with sandpaper until the oak is consistently light. Next dip a cloth in linseed oil and rub the wood with this in a circular motion until the oil has completely soaked in. If necessary apply a second or third coat of oil in the same way and when this has been absorbed, polish well with a white wax polish.

Alternatively, remove existing finish with a paint or wax stripper, then apply a wood dye to the surface. Allow to dry thoroughly, then seal or polish.

See also page 434, this chapter, for stripping wood.

Oil-based paint

There are various finishes for oil-based paints. All are suitable for woodwork, plasterwork and smooth metal such as radiators. The surface, once hard, is resistant to stains and knocks and it can be scrubbed or washed and polished also if more gloss is required after cleaning. Use an eggshell or flat paint if the surface is uneven or marred as gloss highlights unevenness. Choose a fine-bristled, pliable brush for this type of paint and clean it with white spirit after use.

Paint

Stretch a thin piece of wire over the top of a paint can and use this for wiping a brush on after every dip; the surplus paint will drip back into the pot. Paint wiped on the side of the can partly solidifies and is wasted.

Always remove any top skin on paint before stirring thoroughly. Storing a paint tin upside down will prevent a skin forming and so will pouring a little turpentine over the top of the paint. Yet another way to prevent skin forming is to cut a disc of aluminium foil fractionally smaller than the tin and float this on top of the paint. Avoid tilting a half-filled paint tin or fresh paint may go over the foil or over skin formed.

To remove any sediment, skin or dust from paint, stretch an old nylon stocking over a can and pour the paint through the nylon. It makes an efficient sieve.

To remove the odour of paint from a room, place a handful of hay in a bowl or bucket of water, stand it in the centre of the room and leave for half an hour.

It is also possible to use an air freshener spray or a weak solution of a chlorophyll liquid such as Amplexol.

To accelerate the drying of oil paints, add about 1 teaspoonful of terabine to each pint of paint. It will dry very much more quickly but this does not apply to emulsion and other modern paints.

Many modern paints are now formulated to dry very quickly. Some even incorporate two-stage drying—they remain liquid long enough to allow you to apply paint easily, then rapidly dry.

When a painting job is finally completed, fill an empty nail-varnish bottle with some of the paint and screw the cap on tightly. Any odd scratches or chips can then be painted out using the tiny brush already in the varnish bottle.

Painting

To obtain a good covering of paint on a fairly broad surface first paint with the strokes all going in one direction (say up and down), then with the same brush and without reloading with paint, cross all the strokes at right angles (from side to side) so that the same area is being painted but now in a different direction. Finally go over once more in the same direction as at first, finishing so lightly at the end of each stroke that no brush marks are left.

Paint will blister if moisture is trapped underneath the paint film. To avoid blistering, the outside of a house should not be painted until knots (which might exude resin) have been sealed; until the morning dew has evaporated; and until any rain has cleared and the surface has completely dried.

Each coat of paint should be thin; thick coats dry slowly and are more likely to form blisters. Make sure each coat is thoroughly dry before applying the next coat and dust the surface before painting.

Paintwork

The best cleaning method is to use a proprietary paint cleaner, which is designed for the job. Ordinary liquid detergent (washing-up liquid) may also be used, but washing powders are not recommended as they contain fluorescers which could in certain circumstances affect the colour of your paint.

Another cleaning agent for paint is sugar soap, but this must be mixed according to directions; a mild solution only is necessary (not more than $\frac{1}{2}$ lb. to 1 gal. of warm water) and it must be completely rinsed off.

When cleaning paint, always begin at the bottom of a wall and work upwards, and have a bowl of soapy water and one of clear warm water to hand with a sponge or absorbent cloth in each. Wash an area of about 2 ft. sq., rinse and dry; clean the next patch, overlapping the first and carry on until the whole surface is clean.

It is also possible to clean paintwork quickly by using a special cream which is wiped on and then off and this is the method used by many large industries. Special paint cleaners are available in small tins, tubes and bottles and are ideal if only a little time can be spared for chores such as paint cleaning.

Alternatively, a special cleaner for small areas can be made at home by mixing powdered whitening with soap jelly and methylated spirit to form a thin paste. Apply with a damp cloth, rinse off, dry and polish.

Remove odd dirty marks from paintwork using a brush rather than a cloth. Dip the brush in soapy water and scrub gently. For stubborn marks, dip the brush into an abrasive powder such as ordinary kitchen scouring powder. The reason for a brush rather than a cloth is that a rag tends to rub the stain into the paintwork rather than removing it; this applies particularly to matt finishes. If the abrasive powder removes the shine from a gloss finish, rinse, dry and re-polish with furniture cream.

Kitchen paintwork often becomes dull and shabby very quickly due to steam, condensation and grease, coupled with frequent cleaning. Revive the painted woodwork by rubbing it briskly with a clean cloth dipped in linseed oil. Rub hard with the linseed oil cloth, leave for a while, then polish off with a warm soft duster.

Obstinate marks on paintwork can often be removed by rubbing very gently with fine steel wool dipped in turpentine.

Yellowing of white paintwork cannot be removed. It is caused by sun and weather attacking the pigments in the paint and the only solution is to repaint.

See also: Emulsion Paint, Distemper, Whitewash, etc.

Plaster

New plaster or cement can be painted with emulsion paint as soon as it has dried out—say in 2 or 3 days. If oil paint or enamel is preferred to emulsion, allow the plaster to dry out, then coat the walls with new plaster primer according to the instructions and finally paint in the ordinary way.

Polyurethane paints

These are modern gloss and eggshell finish paints with a very hard surface once dry. Providing the base is sound, the finish has higher resistance to chips, knocks, scratches and stains than any other type of paint. Either one undercoat plus two coats is necessary or three coats of polyurethane paint.

Putty

When a window is being reglazed the old putty must be removed first by scraping with a chisel or screwdriver. If the putty is very hard and difficult to remove, holding a red-hot poker over it should soften it sufficiently for it to be scraped out. Alternatively, coat the putty generously with paint stripper, leave it to penetrate, then scrape out the putty. Repeat with paint stripper if necessary but avoid touching the surrounding paintwork with stripper or the surface will need to be repainted.

PVA emulsion

This is an emulsion paint based on polyvinyl acetate. It is easy to apply to any porous surface inside or out and it dries in 1 to 2 hours.

One coat is often sufficient but a second can be applied when the first is dry, if required. Use a large brush or roller and wash with clear water after use. If using on a gloss painted surface, flatten first with fine sandpaper. There are various finishes; not all withstand condensation so check if it is for use in a kitchen.

Radiators

Pipes and radiators can be repainted fairly easily but ordinary paint should not be used as it may be affected by the heat. Turn off the heat, then rub down the surfaces to be repainted with wire wool or an emery cloth and if there are any rusted areas, burnish these until all trace of rust has gone and the patch is silver. Use special radiator enamel which is available in silver, gold, bronze and similar colours or use one of the heat-proof enamels which are made in a number of bright and pastel colours. In either case one coat should be sufficient unless the colour of the radiator is being changed to a complete contrast to the original colour.

Rollers

Paint rollers which are usually covered in mohair, lamb's wool or plastics foam are easily used especially if painting or distempering has to be done over a large flat surface. Most amateurs can obtain a more even finish with a roller than with a brush except, perhaps, with the finish of hard, gloss paint, when some rollers may have a faint mottled effect.

It is important to follow the manufacturer's instructions exactly, both for the amount of paint poured into the tray and for the coating of the roller. Whatever the make, rollers must be cleaned after *every* use as they may be permanently damaged if paint dries into them. Clean according to instructions, wiping out all surplus oil paint on newspaper or washing immediately in water if the roller has been used for emulsion paint.

Rubber

Draught excluder, flooring, or other rubber will cut much more easily if the knife blade is wetted first.

Screws

To withdraw a screw which has become too firmly embedded to move, hold a red-hot poker against the head of the screw for a few seconds, taking care not to burn the surrounding woodwork. If this is not successful, drip one or two drops of paraffin round the screw, or use a penetrating oil, let it soak in, then tap the screw-head lightly and the screw should withdraw easily.

Smear screws with a little Vaseline or other grease before inserting them into woodwork and they will always be easy to withdraw in future; to prevent them rusting on the surface, paint screw-heads with clear varnish.

Sizing

Walls and ceilings should be sized before wallpaper, distemper, enamel or hard gloss paints are applied. It is not necessary to size surfaces when using emulsion paint. Size can be obtained from your paint merchant. Before applying to previously painted walls, wash surfaces first with hot water containing mild household detergent. Rinse well with clear hot water then leave to dry before applying size.

Newly-plastered walls should be given a coat of vinegar size to neutralize any active lime in the plaster. Make vinegar size by adding 1 pint of vinegar to 2 pints of cold water. Brush on and leave to dry.

One of the snags when sizing walls or ceiling prior to redecorating is the fact that it is difficult to see which patches have been covered and which missed. The difficulty is easily overcome by adding a few drops of cochineal or some other colouring to the size before starting.

Stain

It is very difficult to apply ordinary paint to woodwork which has previously been stained as the stain almost always penetrates the paint eventually. The only way of avoiding trouble is to seal the stain with a coating of sealer of some kind; aluminium paint, 'knotting' or even a water-proof solution would be adequate. Allow to dry, give a second coat of sealer and then undercoat and finish in the usual way.

It is sometimes difficult when the family must use the stairs and you wish to stain them. To leave a clearway during painting, start at the top of the staircase and paint every other stair. The alternate stairs can be used and when the paint is completely dried, the other steps can be painted or stained.

Alternatively, paint the sides of the stairs only where carpet will cover the centre.

Step-ladder

A household step-ladder will be safer if strips of emery paper are tacked or stuck to each step, especially before spring cleaning. Feet will not slip on the rough surface even if shoes are wet.

An alternative method, ideal if a step-ladder is being repainted, is to sprinkle a little clean dry sand on to each step before the paint dries, to give a firm non-slip surface.

Stripping

To get down to the original woodwork when furniture or other woodwork has been stained and varnished or painted, the various finishes must be stripped off and any stain will need to be bleached out of the wood.

Apply liquid paint stripper according to the directions but do so near a window or in the fresh air and away from any flame. When the varnish or paint is loosened, gently ease it off with a scraper and stop the action of the chemical by brushing on methylated spirit or turpentine.

Oxalic acid will bleach out any remaining stain. Apply it with an old brush and leave to dry, then brush the woodwork with a stiff brush and once more coat with turpentine or spirit. Rub the surface lightly with fine glasspaper working the way of the grain and finally finish with a good wax polish.

It is possible to buy non-caustic stripper to remove french polish, paint and cellulose from wood and metal and many are non-caustic, non-inflammable and are neutralized with water.

Wax can be stripped from woodwork with strong detergent or soda solution but it is probably easier to use a special wax stripper which is inexpensive and quite safe.

For stripping accumulations of wax and polish from floors before sealing or staining, detergents *can* be used but, again, it is easier and quicker to use a special floor cleaner made by floor-polish manufacturers. Alternatively, dissolve about half a cupful of synthetic detergent in a little hot water in a bucket and add half a cupful of ammonia. Half fill the bucket with cold water and stir the solution, then sponge it freely on to the floor. Leave for 10 to 15 minutes then scrub hard to remove loosened polish deposits. Rinse thoroughly with clear water and dry. Re-polish next day.

Thixotropic paint

These are paints and emulsions which are thick and jelly-like so that they don't drip. This means that it takes more energy to apply a thixotropic paint but on the other hand it doesn't drip and run when high walls and ceilings are painted. Quite often one coat will cover effectively and in any case, two coats does a very complete covering job.

Tiles

Before fixing tiles, the surface must be cleaned thoroughly with hot soda water to remove any grease film. Allow to dry, then, if the surface is smooth and shiny, roughen it with sandpaper so that the fixative can grip properly. Use a thin coat of cellulose tile cement and apply it to the tiles and the surface on which they are to be applied.

Plastics tiles can be fixed quite easily by an amateur. They are 4 to 6 in. square and are sold in a variety of colours. Odd tiles to fit corners and awkward places can be cut with scissors. A special adhesive to apply the tiles is made by most manufacturers and full instructions for the various makes are available.

When no fixative is available, odd tiles which have worked loose can be refixed quickly and firmly by using one of the modern adhesives suitable for the job.

It is possible to paint over glazed or unglazed tiles if this is desired. Clean tiles thoroughly with hot detergent suds, rinse well and allow to dry completely. Paint in the usual way using undercoat and a gloss paint thinned 10 per cent, then leave to dry out completely.

Varnish

In cold weather, when varnish is thick, do not thin it but stand the tin in a basin of hot water. When varnishing for the first time, the brush has a tendency to 'pull' and this too can be overcome by heating the varnish in a warm oven or hot water first. Warming the varnish reduces the pulling tendency and makes it easier to apply.

To remove varnish from woodwork use a spirit varnish remover or liquid paint remover. See also under Stripping on page 434.

Clean varnished woodwork with a vinegar solution—1 tablespoonful to 1 pint of warm water. Wring out a clean cloth in the solution, wipe the varnished woodwork, wipe dry with a soft duster and polish. Dull varnish can be brightened by rubbing with a cloth dipped in linseed oil. Cold tea will also revive dull varnished woodwork.

If a wet varnish tin leaves a mark on the floor, wipe it off with a cloth dipped in methylated spirit.

Wallpaper

Protect new or expensive wallpaper with a colourless fluid which is painted on like varnish. The invisible solution will give a protective skin to almost any paper so that jam, sticky finger-marks or other stains can be easily wiped off with a damp cloth.

If wallpaper is stained beyond remedy or scratched and torn, a patch is fairly easy to apply providing a piece of matching paper is available. (Do not paper over a grease mark or the stain will gradually seep through but remove the grease stain first with carbon tetrachloride.)

Match the paper, allowing for a larger piece of paper than the stain, then turn the paper face *downwards* on a table and unevenly tear the approximate size required. Paste in position with a cellulose or other paste, paying particular attention to the edges and carefully matching the design.

It is not a good idea to use distemper or emulsion paint on top of wallpaper as the water used to thin the distemper may soften the wallpaper paste in time, and also next time the room is to be redecorated preparation will be twice as hard. Paper which is matt and highly absorbent, should be stripped first and the paint or distemper applied directly to the bare wall.

It is possible, however, to cover wallpaper with paint, emulsion paint or distemper providing the paper has a glossy or slightly glazed finish.

Professional decorators invariably use cold-water paste for hanging wallpaper but cellulose paste is easier for an amateur to handle as any marks made accidentally on the surface of the paper dry out without leaving a stain. In an emergency, ordinary laundry starch makes an excellent substitute, adheres well and also dries without staining.

If wallpaper has a plastics or other finish and is described as washable, it can be sponged down lightly with the lather from warm soapy water. Use the foam only, and very gentle strokes, and avoid damping the paper more than necessary. Wipe down with a second cloth wrung out in clear warm water and pat dry.

Absorbent paper must not be washed. If it is dusty, an old net or lace curtain tied to the head of a mop or broom makes an excellent cleaner—especially for gilt papers. Or use the dusting brush attachment of a vacuum cleaner.

Grease marks can be removed if dealt with fairly quickly, by making a paste with french chalk or fuller's earth and a few drops of grease solvent. Leave overnight or until dry, then brush off. Another way of removing a grease mark from wallpaper is to put several thicknesses of blotting paper over the stain and press with a hot iron. Dabbing gently (not rubbing) with a grease solvent such as carbon tetrachloride is also effective.

Odd marks can usually be removed by rubbing gently with stale bread or soft art rubber, while for general grime, smokiness and all-over dirt, a cleaning dough is usually the answer. A commercial cleaning dough can be bought fairly cheaply, or it is possible to make one at home, using the recipe on page 468. The dough will quickly remove soot and grime if it is kneaded in the hands, then wiped down the wall, using long firm strokes. It is important to turn the dough continually so that a clean portion is always in use and to overlap each portion of paper so that no part is missed.

Varnished wallpaper can be brightened by rubbing with a cloth moistened with linseed oil. If the paper is soiled, add a tablespoonful of borax to a pint of hot water and wipe the varnished paper with a cloth well wrung out in this. A cloth well wrung out in warm soapy water would probably do no harm but actual washing in suds may dissolve the varnish.

If the varnished paper is really dirty and the borax solution or wiping is not enough, wash with hot water containing paraffin. Avoid making the paper too wet; simply wring out a cloth in the solution and wipe over the paper. Allow to dry and apply a coat of silicone polish or rub with a cloth dipped in linseed oil.

Water-based paint

This has a matt finish and is ideal for walls and ceiling and big areas of new plaster as it adheres firmly and allows it to dry out. Apply with a large brush or a foam roller. Wash either out afterwards in clear water.

Whitewashing

Amateurs usually find a ready-made colourwash is easier to

use and it is certainly less trouble than making it at home with whiting and size. Prepare surface as given under Distemper on page 423.

Windows

Paint spots quickly mark window-panes but there are several solutions to the problem when painting window-frames. One way is to smear the glass with soap, petroleum jelly or metal polish before starting to paint: the splashes cannot stick to the panes and any streaks can easily be wiped off afterwards.

A special paint shield can be bought for protecting the glass, or it is possible to make one from cardboard; an even easier way is to stick a strip of decorator's masking tape down the window beside the frame. As each piece of frame is finished, peel off the tape and stick it in the next place.

If paint does splash window glass, remove it while it is still wet with a cloth dipped in turpentine substitute or, once it has dried, with vinegar. A penny or a razor-blade should remove hard paint marks easily and so should liquid-paint remover.

Woodwork

To protect woodwork with a good grain give two or three coats of special wood seal. The seal has the effect of darkening the wood slightly with each coat applied so that often no other stain is required; if a fairly dark wood is wanted, however, a light coat of suitable stain should be applied before the first coat of wood seal. Allow each coat to dry thoroughly, then rub in a white silicone cream or use an emulsion polish.

Old woodwork which has been neglected can be made to look new and highly polished again by coating it with a french polish preparation made for use by amateurs, or with a plastics coating. Both methods require time and trouble but the ultimate results more than justify the effort involved. The plastics coating gives a surface which is damp- and heat-resistant and it can be used on hardboard as well as on wood.

For details of wood sealing, see page 400, and for further particulars of french polishing, see page 425.

Wrought iron

Wrought iron can be painted, washed and cleaned then protected with wax furniture polish. Black wrought-iron fittings to a front door should be given a coat of varnish to protect them; after this, occasional washing and polishing should be sufficient.

10

Facts and Figures

Decimal currency

The United Kingdom changes to decimal currency on Monday, 15th February 1971 and this is being called Decimal Day or D Day.

The pound (£) stays unchanged. It will be divided into 100 new pence (100p.) each worth 2.4 of our present pence. The lowest value coin will be the new halfpenny, worth 1.2 of our present pence. The symbol for pound will remain £; the new penny will be abbreviated to p. and the new halfpenny to $\frac{1}{2}$p.

Our six £ s. d. coins and the 10s. note will be replaced by six decimal coins but the changes will not all take place at once. The £1, £5 and £10 notes need not be changed.

Cupro-nickel ('silver') coins came into circulation as legal tender on 23rd April 1968. Except for the designs, these coins are identical in value, size, weight and metal content with the shilling and two-shilling piece and completely interchangeable with them.

A seven-sided cupro-nickel ('silver') 50p. coin replaced the 10s. note from 14th October 1969. It has a smooth, non-milled edge and in size and weight is about midway between a two-shilling piece and a half-crown. Its shape is technically known as an equilateral curve heptagon.

There will be three new bronze ('copper') coins: $\frac{1}{2}$p., 1p. and 2p. Two $\frac{1}{2}$p. coins weigh the same as a new penny (1p.) and two 1p. coins weigh the same as one 2p., so weight and value are proportional. A pound's worth (£1) of the new bronze weighs a little over $\frac{3}{4}$ lb. The bronze coins are not legal tender until D Day.

The old halfpenny ceased to be legal tender from 1st August 1969 and the half-crown from 1st January 1970. The present penny, three-penny bit and sixpence will cease to be legal tender at the end of the changeover period and not later than August 1972.

As shown in the chart below in the £p. system there is no payable exact equivalent of any £ s. d. sum which is not a multiple of sixpence. Many £ s. d. amounts can be converted exactly on the basis that 1d.=5/12p. but these are units of calculation and not necessarily payable amounts. This means that calculations such as wholesale unit prices and hourly wage rates can be converted exactly.

All the new decimal coins carry on the obverse, the portrait (by Mr. Arnold Machin, O.B.E., R.A.) of the Queen wearing a diamond tiara, a wedding present from Queen Mary. The reverse designs of the coins are by Mr. Christopher Ironside. The ½p. shows the Royal Crown; the 1p. a portcullis with chains royally crowned, originally a badge of King Henry VII, and for long closely associated with the Palace of Westminster.

The 2p. coin shows the badge of the Prince of Wales. Three ostrich feathers enfiling a coronet of crosses *pattée* and fleurs-de-lis, with the motto 'Ich Dien'. The 5p. shows the badge of Scotland, a thistle royally crowned.

The 10p. coin shows part of the crest of England. A lion *passant guardant* royally crowned. 50p. coins show Britannia seated beside a lion.

The following is the 'new halfpenny' conversion table recommended by the Decimal Currency Board and accepted by the Government. In this table only sixpence, one shilling, ten shillings and £1 have the exact equivalent; all the other prices up to one shilling are rounded up or down. Five are rounded up and five down and the overall effect is that buyers' and sellers' gains even out.

£ s. d.	=	£p.	(Rounding)
1d.	=	½p.	(+ 0·2d.)
2d.	=	1p.	(+ 0·4d.)
3d.	=	1p.	(− 0·6d.)
4d.	=	1½p.	·4d.)
5d.	=	2p.	(− 0·2d.)
6d.	=	2½p.	
7d.	=	3p.	(+ 0·2d.)
8d.	=	3½p.	(+ 0·4d.)
9d.	=	4p.	(+ 0·6d.)
10d.	=	4p.	(− 0·4d.)
11d.	=	4½p.	(− 0·2d.)
1s. 0d.	=	5p.	
10s. 0d.	=	50p.	
£1 0s. 0d.	=	100p.	

Metric equivalents

Most countries in the world use the metric system. Starting in 1970 Britain will begin to adopt metric units and by 1975 it is hoped that every profession, business, craft and trade will use metric units for all measurements—not only length and area, but everything that is measured.

SI Units (Système International d'Unités) have been accepted by international agreement. The system has six basic units:

Length: The Metre. This is equivalent to about 39·37 in. The millimetre will also be used. This is about 1/25th in.

Mass: The Kilogramme. This is equivalent to about 2¼ lb. This unit is composed of 1,000 grammes. One gramme equals about 1/30th oz. The gramme and the tonne (1,000 kilogrammes) will also be used.

Time: The Second. Minutes, hours, days, etc., as now, will be used.

Electric current: The Ampere. As now used in the U.K.

Light: The Candela. This is the measure of light.

For most people this will simply mean learning the metric system with regard to size, volume and weight. This is not difficult because of the consistent relationship between the basic units. Any basic metric unit can be multiplied or divided by 10, 100, 1,000 and upwards to produce larger and smaller units. A prefix is then added to the basic unit to indicate its size.

Some prefixes used in the metric system

micro— means a millionth part of
milli — means a thousandth part of
centi — means a hundredth part of
deci — means a tenth part of
deca — means ten times
hecto— means a hundred times
kilo — means a thousand times
mega— means a million times

Of these prefixes only the first two and the last two will be generally used and the others will be avoided unless absolutely necessary.

Comparisons of some popular units

Length:
1 millimetre (mm.) = 0·03937 in.
This is about 1/25th in.
so 25 mm. = 1 in.
1 centimetre (cm.) = approximately 2/5th in.
so 2½ cm. = 1 in.

1 metre (m.)	=	39·37 in.
	=	3·28 ft.
	=	1·0936 yd.

So a metre is about 39 in.

| 1 kilometre (km.) | = | 3,281 ft. |
| | = | 0·6214 mile |

so a kilometre is about $\frac{5}{8}$ mile
and 8 km. = 5 miles

Capacity:

1 litre	=	1 cubic decimetre (dm³)
	=	1·76 pints
	=	0·22 gallons
1 minim	=	0·059 millilitres or cubic centimetres
1 drachm	=	3·5515 mil. or c.c.
1 fluid ounce	=	28·412 mil. or c.c.
1 gill	=	1·420 decilitres
1 pint	=	0·568 litres
1 quart	=	1·137 litres
1 gallon	=	4·54596 litres

Approximate capacity measure:

1 litre	=	approximately 1¾ pints
1 pint	=	,, ½ litre
2 gills	=	,, ¼ litre
1 gallon	=	,, 4½ litres

1 hectolitre	=	21·9975 gallons
1 litre	=	1·7598 pints
1 decilitre	=	0·176 pints
1 centilitre	=	0·3519 fl. oz.
1 millilitre	=	0·0352 fl. oz. or 16·89408 minims.

See also page 446

Volume

1 cubic metre (m³)	=	35·315 cubic feet
	=	1·308 cubic yards
	=	220 gallons
3 cubic metres	=	approximately 4 cubic yards

Weight:

1 gramme (g.)	=	0·353 oz.
15 grammes	=	approximately ½ oz.
50 grammes	=	,, 1¾ oz.
100 grammes	=	,, 3½ oz.
500 grammes	=	,, 1 lb. 1½ oz.
1 kilogramme (kg.)	=	2·2046 lb. or 35·27 oz.
1,000 kilogrammes	=	1 tonne (t)
1 tonne	=	2,204·6 lb.

Approximate weights:

1 ounce	=	28·4 grammes
		For recipe purposes convert by using 25 grammes
1 pound (lb.)	=	453·59 grammes
		For large quantity recipes, convert by using 500 grammes
2¼ lb.	=	approximately 1 kilogramme
1 cwt.	=	approximately 50 kilogrammes
1 Imperial ton	=	approximately 1 tonne or 1,000 kilogrammes

Temperature:

0° Centigrade	=	32° Fahrenheit
10° C.	=	50° F.
20° C.	=	68° F.
30° C.	=	86° F.
40° C.	=	104° F.
50° C.	=	122° F.
60° C.	=	140° F.
70° C.	=	158° F.
80° C.	=	176° F.
90° C.	=	194° F.
100° C.	=	212° F.

0° C. is the freezing point of water
15° C. is the temperature on a warm spring day
30° C. is the temperature on a very hot summer's day
37° C. is the normal body temperature
100° C. is the boiling-point of water

To obtain tepid water without a thermometer, add 1 part of boiling water to 2 parts of cold water and the approximate temperature of the water should then be 80°F.

An approximate guide for some popular conversions to metric:

1 ounce	=	just over 25 grammes
1 pound	=	just under 500 grammes
1 pint	=	just over ½ litre
1 gallon	=	,, ,, 4½ litres
1 inch	=	,, ,, 25 mm. or 2½ cm.
1 foot	=	,, ,, 30 cm.
1 yard	=	just under 1 metre (which is about 3 in. more)
1 mile	=	just over 1½ km.
5 miles	=	8 km.

Catering

Professional caterers avoid waste by allowing an exact quantity of food or drink for each person. Allowing for a little extra for special general favourites, it is possible to work out more or less accurately how much drink to order and the quantities of food to buy or cook.

Meat, vegetables, etc., are the weight as purchased and before preparation or cooking:

	Allow each person
Artichokes, Globe	— 1
Jerusalem	— 5 oz.
Beetroot	— 1 small
Brains	— 1
Broad beans	— ½ lb.
Brussels sprouts	— 6 oz.
Butter beans	— 2 oz.
Cabbage	— ½ lb.
Carrots	— 4 oz.
Cauliflower	— ½ small
Celery	— ½ small head
Chicory	— 3 leaves
Chop	— 1
Cooked meat	— 3 oz. or 2 slices
Corned beef	— 2 slices
Curly kale	— ½ lb.
Endive	— 1 leaf
Fish with heavy bones	— 5 oz.
Fish with light or no bones	— 4 oz.
Gravy	— ⅛ pint
Ham	— 1 slice
Kidney	— 1½
Lettuce	— ½ small or 2 to 3 large leaves
Liver	— 3 oz.
Macaroni	— 2 oz.

	Allow each person
Meat, on the bone	— 5 oz.
boneless	— 3 oz.
minced	— 4 oz.
Onions	— 6 oz.
Oysters	— 4–5
Parsnips	— 6 oz.
Peas	— ½ lb.
Pork, tinned	— 2 slices
Porridge	— 1½ oz.
Potatoes	— ½ lb.
Pressed beef	— 2 oz. or 1 slice
Rice	— 1½ oz.
Runner beans	— 6 oz.
Sauce	— ⅛ pint
Sausages	— ¼ lb.
Savoy	— 6 oz.
Soup	— ¼ pint
Spaghetti	— 2 oz.
Spinach	— ½ lb.
Spring greens	— ½ lb.
Steak	— ¼ lb.
Stewed fruit	— ½ lb.
Sweetbreads	— 1
Tomatoes	— 1
Tongue	— 2 oz. or 1 slice
Tripe	— ¼ lb.
Turkey	— 2–3 oz.
Turnips	— ½ lb.
Watercress	— 2 oz.

Parties

Bouchée cases	2 each
Bridge rolls	1 each
Cakes: Small cakes	2 per person
Fruit cake	7 in. cake cuts into 8 portions
Wedding cake	2 oz. each
Chicken	1 large bird will serve 7
Cream	½ pint serves 6 portions
Eggs (for mayonnaise)	½ per person
Flan	6–8 servings
Fruit salad	1 pint serves 4
Ice cream	1 pint serves 6
Jellies	1 pint serves 6

Lobster	Made into patties (2 small per person) will serve 18
Lobster mayonnaise	1 will serve 4
Sandwiches	4 per person
Sausage rolls	1 each
Smoked salmon	1½ oz. per person

Liquid measures

8 drachms	=	1 fluid oz.
5 fluid ounces	=	1 gill
1 gill	=	¼ pint
4 gills	=	1 pint
1 pint	=	20 fluid oz.
2 pints	=	1 quart
1 quart	=	40 fluid oz. or 2½ lb. (weight in water)
4 quarts	=	1 gallon
1 gallon	=	160 fluid oz. or 10 lb. (weight in water)

Approximate handy equivalents—liquids

Note: Strictly speaking, small amounts of liquids should be measured in millilitres (mil.) but frequently cubic centimetres (c.c.) are used, especially on cosmetic containers, for instance. For all practical purposes, the two measurements are identical.

1 medicine measuring spoon	=	5 c.c. or 5 mil.
1 thimbleful	=	30 drops
60 drops	=	1 average teaspoonful
1 teaspoon (average)	=	1 drachm or 4 c.c. or mil. or ⅛ fluid oz.
1 dessertspoon ,,	=	2 drachms or 8 mil. or c.c. or ¼ fluid oz.
1 tablespoon ,,	=	4 drachms or ½ fluid oz. or 15 c.c. or mil.
2 tablespoons ,,	=	1 fluid oz. or 8 drachms or 30 c.c. or 30 mil.
10 tablespoons ,,	=	5 fluid oz. or ¼ pint or 1 gill or 150 c.c.
1 wineglass ,,	=	2½ fluid oz. or ½ gill or 75 c.c.
1 teacup ,,	=	1 gill or ¼ pint or 5 fluid oz. or 150 c.c.
1 tumbler ,,	=	½ pint or 10 fluid oz. or 300 c.c.
1 American pint	=	16 fluid oz.
1 American standard cup	=	8 fluid oz. or approximately 1½ gills

Note: Although in most parts of Britain, 1 gill is equal to ¼ pint, in the North of England it is sometimes reckoned as ½ pint.

See also page 443

Note: The following weights refer only to *water*. Other liquids may weigh differently—dense liquids weighing heavier and other liquids, such as spirits, weighing lighter. Temperature also affects weight and at fairly low or moderately high temperatures the weight will be different. These weights of water are at approximately 62° F.

1 fluid ounce of water weighs	1 oz.
1 pint of water weighs	1¼ lb.
1 quart of water weighs	2½ lb.
1 gallon of water weighs	10 lb.

Drinks guide

A cocktail glass hold about ½ gill or ⅛ pint
A sherry glass holds about ½ gill or ⅛ pint
A large wine glass holds almost ¼ pint
A small wine glass holds about 2 fl. oz.
A small jigger holds about 1 fl. oz.
A tumbler holds about ½ pint

Beer	One quart bottle serves 5 glasses (¾ full)
Champagne	One bottle will serve 6 glasses
Cider	One quart bottle serves 5 glasses (¾ full)
Cocktail	One bottle will serve about 20 glasses
Gin	One bottle will make approximately 32 cocktails
Hock	One bottle will serve 6 glasses
Liqueur	One bottle will serve 36 glasses
Madeira	One bottle will serve about 12 glasses
Marsala	One bottle will serve about 12 glasses
Moselle	One bottle will serve 6 glasses
Port	One bottle will serve about 12 glasses or 8 large glasses (¾ full)
Sherry	One bottle will serve about 12–16 glasses or 8 large glasses (¾ full)
Squash	One bottle will serve 15–20 glasses
Whisky	One bottle will make approximately 32 cocktails
Wine	One bottle will serve 6 glasses (¾ full)

Some wines—and most particularly champagne—come in sizes other than the conventional bottle. The various fancy shapes are usually given names and these, above the tregnum size, are for some reason or other, the names of Biblical characters. Occasionally any larger-than-usual bottle of wine is called a magnum but the correct sizes and quantities are as follows:

Baby	is equal to	⅛ bottle of Champagne	
Nip	,, ,, ,,	¼ ,, ,, ,,	
Bottle of Champagne	,, ,, ,,	1.2/5 pints ,, ,,	
Magnum	,, ,, ,,	2 bottles of Champagne	(approx. ⅓ gal.)
Tregnum (sometimes called a Tappit Hen)	,, ,, ,,	3 ,, ,, ,,	(approx. ½ gal.)

Jeroboam (sometimes called a Double Magnum)	is equal to	4	bottles of Champagne	(approx. ¾ gal.)
Rehoboam	,, ,, ,,	6	,, ,, ,,	(approx. 1 gal.)
Methuselah	,, ,, ,,	8	,, ,, ,,	(approx. 1½ gal.)
Salmanazar	,, ,, ,,	12	,, ,, ,,	(approx. 2 gal.)
Balthazar	,, ,, ,,	16	,, ,, ,,	(approx. 3 gal.)
Nebuchadnezzar	,, ,, ,,	20	,, ,, ,,	(equals 3½ gal.)

Beverages

Coffee	1 lb. coffee makes approximately 48 large cupfuls or 96 coffee cupfuls
	1 pint coffee serves 8 or 9 small coffee cups
Milk	1 pint milk makes about 33 cups of tea; or 8 cups coffee
Tea	½ lb. makes about 100 cupfuls

Dry measures

Avoirdupois Weight

16 drams	= 1 ounce
16 ounces	= 1 pound (lb.)
14 pounds	= 1 stone
28 pounds	= 1 quarter
56 pounds	= ½ hundredweight (cwt.)
112 ,,	= 1 ,,
4 quarters	= 1 ,,
8 stone	= 1 ,,
2,240 pounds	= 1 ton
20 cwt.	= 1 ,,

Special measures

(These are customary but not legal measures)

1 stone of butcher's meat	= 8 lb.
1 stone of cheese	= 16 lb.
1 stone of flour	= 14 lb.
1 peck of flour	= 14 lb.
1 barrel of flour	= 1¼ cwt. or 196 lb.
1 peck of potatoes	= 20 lb.
3 bushels of potatoes	= 56 lb.
1 cwt. of potatoes	= 120 lb.
1 sack of potatoes	= 1½ cwt. or 168 lb.
1 carton of plums	= 9 lb.
1 peck of plums	= 18 lb.
1 peck of apples	= 16 lb.
1 peck of broad beans	= 10 lb.
1 peck of gooseberries	= 16 lb.
1 peck of onions	= 16 lb.
1 peck of peas	= 8 lb.
1 peck of pears	= 18 lb.
1 peck of strawberries	= 12 lb.
1 peck of swedes	= 18 lb.

1 peck of turnips	=	16 lb.
1 peck of salt	=	14 lb.
1 drum of Turkey figs	=	24 lb.
1 drum of raisins	=	24 lb.
1 gallon of honey	=	12 lb.
1 sieve of cherries	=	48 lb.
1 talley of cabbage	=	5 dozen
1 talley of lettuce	=	5 dozen
1 baker's dozen	=	13
1 long hundred eggs	=	120
1 score	=	20
1 gross	=	144

Approximate handy equivalents—dry goods

Cupful (unless stated otherwise) means a level British Standard cup or an ordinary large breakfast cup which holds $\frac{1}{2}$ pint of liquid. The following table gives approximate equivalents for dry goods such as flour, custard powder, etc.

1 rounded saltspoonful	weighs approximately		$\frac{1}{8}$ oz.
1 ,, teaspoonful	,,	,,	$\frac{1}{4}$ oz.
1 level dessertspoonful	,,	,,	$\frac{1}{4}$ oz.
1 rounded ,,	,,	,,	$\frac{1}{2}$ oz.
1 level tablespoonful	,,	,,	$\frac{1}{2}$ oz.
1 rounded ,,	,,	,,	1 oz.
1 teacupful	,,	,,	6 oz.
1 breakfastcupful	,,	,,	8 oz.
4 saltspoonfuls	=	1 teaspoonful	
2 teaspoonfuls	=	1 dessertspoonful	
4 teaspoonfuls	=	1 tablespoonful	
2 dessertspoonfuls	=	1 tablespoonful	
6 tablespoonfuls	=	1 teacupful	
2 teacupfuls	=	1 breakfastcupful	

Baking powder	1	rounded tablespoonful	=	1 oz.
Breadcrumbs: dry	2	heaped tablespoonfuls	=	1 oz.
	1	cupful	=	6 oz.
,, fresh	4	heaped tablespoonfuls	=	1 oz.
,,	1	cupful	=	3 oz.
Butter	1	level cupful	=	8 oz.
Cheese	4	tablespoonfuls	=	1 oz.
	1	cupful	=	4 oz.
Cocoa	1	rounded tablespoonful	=	1 oz.
Coffee	1	rounded tablespoonful	=	1 oz.
Cornflour	1	level dessertspoonful	=	$\frac{1}{4}$ oz.
	1	rounded dessertspoonful	=	$\frac{1}{2}$ oz.
	1	level tablespoonful	=	$\frac{1}{2}$ oz.
	1	rounded tablespoonful	=	1 oz.
Custard powder	2	tablespoonfuls	=	1 oz.
	1	cupful	=	5 oz.

Dried fruit	1	cupful	=	6 oz.
Dripping	1	cupful	=	8 oz.
Flour	1	rounded tablespoonful	=	1 oz.
	1	cupful	=	5 oz.
	$1\frac{1}{2}$	cupfuls	=	$\frac{1}{2}$ lb.
Gelatine	1	rounded tablespoonful	=	1 oz.
Honey: cold from cold tin	1	tablespoonful	=	2 oz.
warm, runny from warm tin	1	tablespoonful	=	1 oz.
Jam	1	level tablespoonful	=	1 oz.
	1	cupful	=	12 oz.
Lentils	1	level tablespoonful	=	1 oz.
Margarine	1	level tablespoonful	=	1 oz.
	1	level cupful	=	$\frac{1}{2}$ lb.
Oatmeal	4	level tablespoonfuls	=	1 oz.
Raisins	2	level tablespoonfuls	=	1 oz.
	1	cupful	=	$6\frac{1}{2}$ oz.
Rice	1	level tablespoonful	=	1 oz.
Rolled oats	3	tablespoonfuls	=	1 oz.
	1	cupful	=	5 oz.
Salt	1	level tablespoonful	=	1 oz.
Semolina: ordinary	2	level tablespoonfuls	=	1 oz.
fine	3	level tablespoonfuls	=	1 oz.
Soya flour	1	rounded tablespoonful	=	1 oz.
Sugar: castor	2	level tablespoonfuls	=	1 oz.
	1	cupful	=	8 oz.
demerara	1	level tablespoonful	=	1 oz.
	1	cupful	=	7 oz.
granulated	1	level tablespoonful	=	1 oz.
	1	teacupful	=	6 oz.
	1	breakfastcupful	=	8 oz.
icing	1	heaped tablespoonful	=	1 oz.
	1	cupful, sifted	=	5 oz.
Sultanas	1	tablespoonful	=	$\frac{1}{2}$ oz.
	1	cupful	=	7 oz.
Syrup: cold from cold tin	1	tablespoonful	=	2 oz.
warm, runny from warm tin	1	tablespoonful	=	1 oz.
Treacle: cold from cold tin	1	tablespoonful	=	2 oz.
warm, runny from warm tin	1	tablespoonful	=	1 oz.

Fat: a piece of butter, margarine, etc., the size of a small egg, weighs approximately 1 oz. To measure half a cupful of butter, lard, margarine, etc., half-fill a cup of cold water and add fat until the water rises to the rim of the cup. Drain off the water and half a cupful of fat will remain. If $\frac{1}{3}$ cup of butter is required, fill the cup $\frac{2}{3}$ full of cold water and then add fat.

American equivalents for recipes

American magazines and cookery books often contain interesting and unusual recipes. Ingredients are usually stated differently, however, and this is frequently confusing to anyone used to English weights and measures. This table gives some approximate comparison. All measures are level. One American cup usually holds 8 fl. oz. One American pint is 16 fl. oz. One English pint is 20 fl. oz.

	American measure	English equivalent
Almonds (chopped)	1 cup	1 lb.
Apples	1 quart	$1\frac{1}{2}$ lb.
Apricots (dried)	$3\frac{2}{3}$ cups	1 lb.
Breadcrumbs	1 cup	$2\frac{3}{4}$ oz.
Butter	1 cup	$\frac{1}{2}$ lb.
Butter	1 tablespoon	$\frac{1}{2}$ oz.
Butter beans	1 cup	$\frac{1}{2}$ lb.
Cheese (grated)	1 cup	$\frac{1}{4}$ lb.
Cheese	1 tablespoon	$\frac{1}{4}$ oz.
Cocoa	1 cup	$\frac{1}{4}$ lb.
Cocoa	1 tablespoon	$\frac{1}{2}$ oz.
Cottage cheese	1 cup	$\frac{1}{2}$ lb.
Currants	$2\frac{3}{8}$ cups	1 lb.
Dates	1 cup	$\frac{1}{2}$ lb.
Egg whites	$1\frac{1}{2}$ tablespoons	1
Egg yolks	1 tablespoon	1
Fat	1 cup	$\frac{1}{2}$ lb.
Fat	1 tablespoon	$\frac{1}{2}$ oz.
Figs (chopped)	2 cups	1 lb.
Flour	4 cups	1 lb.
Flour	4 tablespoons	1 oz.
Jam	1 tablespoon	1 oz.
Lard	1 cup	$\frac{1}{2}$ lb.
Macaroni	1 cup	4 oz.
Margarine	1 cup	$\frac{1}{2}$ lb.
Meat (cubed or diced)	1 cup	$\frac{1}{2}$ lb.
Onions (chopped)	1 cup	5 oz.
Raisins	1 cup	$5\frac{1}{4}$ oz.
Rice	1 cup	$\frac{1}{2}$ lb.
Sugar granulated	1 cup	$\frac{1}{2}$ lb.
granulated	1 tablespoon	$\frac{1}{2}$ oz.
brown moist	1 cup	$5\frac{1}{4}$ oz.
Tapioca	1 cup	6 oz.
Treacle or syrup	1 cup	12 oz.
Treacle or syrup	1 tablespoon	$\frac{1}{2}$ oz.
Walnuts (shelled)	1 cup	12 oz.

1 English pint	= 20 fluid oz.
1 American pint	= 16 fluid oz.
1 American measuring cup	= 8 fluid oz.
1 American measuring cup	= $\frac{1}{2}$ lb.
4 level American tablespoons =	1 oz.

English equivalent or substitute for American ingredients or terms

American terms	English equivalent or substitute
Alligator pears	Avocado pears
Angel cake	A light cake made with a considerable number of egg-whites
Baking soda	Bicarbonate of soda
Barcelona nuts	Hazel nuts
Biscuit	A scone
Broil	To grill
Candy	Sweet or chocolate
Chocolate (1 square)	1 oz. chocolate
Clam	A type of cockle found off the Atlantic coasts
Confectioner's sugar	Icing sugar
Cookie	Sweet biscuit
Cornstarch	Cornflour
Crackers	Any plain or dry biscuit
Cream: heavy	Double cream
light	Single cream
Double active baking powder	$1\frac{1}{2}$ times ordinary baking powder
Eggplant	Aubergine
English rabbit	Welsh rarebit
Flapjack	Pancake
Gelatine (1 envelope)	$\frac{1}{3}$ oz. gelatine
Graham crackers	Use crispbreads, unsweetened digestive or wholemeal biscuits
Hominy	Broken or split maize—also used to make popcorn
Lima beans	Butter beans
Molasses	Treacle or golden syrup
Oil	Peanut, maize, corn oil, etc. *Not* olive oil
Pie	Tart
Pumpkin	Similar to vegetable marrow. Available in England as pumpkin
Raisins	Sultanas
Raspings	Ground breadcrumbs for coating, browned
Shortening	Cooking fat
Shortening—sweet	Butter or margarine
Squash	Vegetable marrow
Sugar	Castor sugar—*Not* granulated
Sweet corn	Maize or corn-on-the-cob

American terms	English equivalent or substitute
Sweet potato	A sweet tuber which is no relation to ordinary potato, but obtainable here
Yeast (1 cake)	⅔ oz. fresh yeast or heaped teaspoon dry yeast
Zwiebach crumbs	Rusk crumbs

Electricity

All electricity is supplied under a central nationalized authority although regional boards do vary in the way they arrive at domestic tariffs. One unit of electricity (kilowatt-hour) is 1,000 W. (1 kW.) used continuously for 1 hour. The average cost of running an appliance on the normal domestic tariffs in England and Wales is about 1·8 pence per unit depending on the prices fixed by the Electricity Board in the region. On the special cheap rate tariff or White Meter tariff, 1 unit costs approximately 0·75d.—less than 1 penny.

Some average running costs of appliances on the Normal Domestic Tariff:

Bath: Bath of water heated by electricity costs about 8d.

Blankets: An underblanket will cost less than ¼d. an evening and an overblanket in use all night about 1d.

Can opener: Rated at 115 W. will open 3,500 cans for 1d.

Carving knife: Will slice 3,000 sandwiches for ½d.

Coffee percolator: Will make about 40 cups of fresh coffee for 1d.

Cooker: Costs 2d. per person each day for a family of four.

Deep freeze: About 3½d. per cubic foot per week.

Dishwater: A family's dinner dishes for 2d.

Hair dryer: A portable dryer costs 1d. for about an hour's use.

Iron: More than 2 hours ironing can be done for 2d.

Kettle: Will boil 15 pints of water for 2d.

Light: 2d. worth of electricity will light a 100-W. lamp for 11 hours and a fluorescent tube (80 W.—5 ft.) for 12 hours. It is worth noting that the fluorescent 80-W. tube will give three times as much light as the 100-W. lamp.

Radiant heater: With a loading of 2 kW. costs about 3½d. (2 units) an hour.

Refrigerator: The popular table-top compressor type costs between 2d. and 2½d. a day to run.

Spin dryer: Less than ¼d. for the week's wash.

Tape recorder: 12 hours for 1d.

Television set: 9 hours for 2d.

Tumbler dryer: About 3½d. for an hour.

Vacuum cleaner: Will do nearly 5 hours of continuous cleaning for 2d.

Washing machine: Heating its own water will do an average family wash for about 6d. depending on the type and size of the machine. If using hot water from kitchen supply then it costs much less.

Waste disposer: Costs about 2d. a week.

Note that where appliances—such as irons—are thermostatically controlled, the fact that they are not running full-on for the whole hour should also be taken into account. For example 1 unit of electricity may be sufficient for more than 2 hours' steady ironing although the iron may be rated to use 1 unit of electricity in 1 hour. This is because the temperature is being thermostatically controlled and is switching off when the heat level selected on the dial is reached.

When judging the amount of electricity used by an appliance, the loading (the number of watts or kilowatts) must be taken into account. An electric cooker can be from 3 kW. to 8 kW.; a washing machine with heater 2 kW. or 3kW. and an electric fire anything from ½ kW. to 3 kW. A kilowatt is equal to 1,000 watts.

It is important to buy electrical appliances of the correct voltage for the supply or the equipment will not work properly. Suppose, for instance, the voltage supply is 200 volts; if lamps meant for 230 volts are used, the light will be very much dimmer, but the lamps themselves could last much longer; a 230-volt kettle will take much longer to boil; a vacuum cleaner will work less efficiently and the motor burn out and a fire will give less heat although it will also burn less current and elements could last longer.

If the voltage supply is 230 volts and equipment marked 200 volts is used, then all equipment will draw more current, rapidly fail and could overload the wiring circuit.

Electric–Gas oven temperatures

This comparative oven temperature chart has been agreed upon by both the Electricity and Gas Councils. So if a recipe gives only the cooking temperature or only the gas oven setting, you can still cook it correctly in your own oven, whether gas or electricity.

Electric oven setting	Gas oven settings
200° F.	–
225° F.	$\frac{1}{4}$
250° F.	$\frac{1}{2}$
275° F.	1
300° F.	2
325° F.	3
350° F.	4
375° F.	5
400° F.	6
425° F.	7
450° F.	8
475° F.	9
500° F.	–

Gas

One British Thermal Unit (B.Th.U.) is the amount of heat required to heat 1 lb. of water through 1 deg. Fahrenheit. A therm of gas equals 100,000 British Thermal Units or roughly the heat required to bring 64 gals. of cold water to the boil. It is interesting to note that an ordinary gas burner normally consumes about five times as much air as an adult. One therm of gas will:

Give $\frac{1}{2}$ gal. of hot water from a sink heater 133 times.
Heat water for eight or nine baths.
Boil $2\frac{1}{2}$ lb. of potatoes 40 times.
Cook dinner in the oven for four people 8 times.
Work a small refrigerator continuously 10 days.
Run an average gas fire full on for an hour 6 times.
Cook 60 dinners in a school or canteen.
Boil the water in a school or canteen for 400 cups of tea.
Give sufficient hot water from a sink heater for a family of four for 1 week.

Gas oven temperatures. Most foods will cook in a gas oven just as well from a cold start as they do when the oven is fully heated beforehand. A cold start saves time and also a certain amount of gas.

All gas cookers are required by British Standards to cook the same foods at the same thermostat marks. This does not, however, mean that the temperature represented by the marks are the same for every model. They can vary slightly according to the actual design of the oven.

The chart below will help when deciding on the correct gas mark for a particular recipe or oven heat. The setting relates to the heat at the centre of the oven; the top is rather hotter and the bottom of the oven rather cooler.

Although temperatures in ovens vary, the same results should be obtained from any cooker by using the same thermostat setting. This is because the British Standard for gas cookers provides for tests at specified settings rather than for definite temperatures. One cooker may require a higher temperature than another to obtain the same results so that the thermostat setting is based on results. Therefore any gas oven should, for example, cook a sponge to the same evenness and brownness when set at No. 5 regardless of temperature.

	Thermostat settings	Heat of oven
Fruit bottling	$\frac{1}{4}$	Very cool
Slow stewing	$\frac{1}{2}$	Very cool
Milk puddings	1	Very cool
Casseroles; rich fruit cake	2	Cool
Slow roasting; shortbread; fruit	3	Warm
Madeira and plain fruit cake; biscuits; Victoria sandwich	4	Moderate
Queen cakes; sponges	5	Fairly hot
Plain buns; short pastry	6	Fairly hot
Quick roasting; flaky pastry; scones	7	Hot
Puff pastry	8	Very hot
Small items of puff pastry	9	Very hot

Modern gas cookers have many advantages. Grills need not be pre-heated, for instance, but food must be watched as new grills are usually quicker than the older types. Thermostats have been used in ovens since 1923 and it is now possible to have one fitted to the hot-plate burner as well. They give accurate control avoiding the need to watch a pan.

Other burners have a pre-set simmer position, indicated by a click: no need to judge by the flame size. Grills too can be fitted with three heat intensities—super, fast and normal. This type can be turned lower than most conventional grills without losing the overall even grilling effect.

Wallpapers

There are several ways of calculating the amount of wallpaper needed to paper a room. English papers are usually supplied in rolls (known technically as pieces) 11½ yds. long and 21 in. wide. A simple way of calculating is to measure the height of the wall from picture

rail to skirting and then take a strip of wallpaper, trim the ends and
mark each width along the walls with a pencil.

The area of a roll of wallpaper is 7 sq. yds. so another method is to
measure the height and width of the walls in feet, divide by nine so
that the total is in square yards and divide this by seven to find out
the number of rolls required. As this method works out the paper
accurately an extra roll of paper to each seven rolls should be
added to allow for wastage, cutting and matching the design.

Easier still is to use a chart and on the next two pages are the ones
issued by the Wallpaper Manufacturers Ltd. To use the wallpaper
chart measure the height of the walls from skirting to picture rail
or ceiling in feet then measure round the walls including doors and
windows, etc. The doors and windows obviously do not have to be
papered but the surplus amount allows for wastage in trimming and
for matching the pattern, etc. The figures in the first chart show the
number of rolls of wallpaper needed and in the second chart the
number of rolls of ceiling paper that would be required.

Measurement in feet round walls, including doors and windows

Height in feet from skirting	28	32	36	40	44	48	52	56	60	64	68	72	76	80	84	88	92	96	100
7 and under 7½	4	4	5	5	6	6	7	7	8	8	9	9	9	10	10	11	11	12	12
7½ ,, ,, 8	4	4	5	5	6	6	7	8	8	9	9	10	10	11	11	12	12	13	13
8 ,, ,, 8½	4	5	5	6	6	7	7	8	8	9	9	10	10	11	12	12	13	13	14
8½ ,, ,, 9	4	5	5	6	6	7	8	8	9	9	10	11	11	12	12	13	13	14	14
9 ,, ,, 9½	4	5	6	6	7	7	8	9	9	10	10	11	12	12	13	13	14	15	15
9½ ,, ,, 10	5	5	6	7	7	8	9	9	10	10	11	12	12	13	14	14	15	15	16
10 ,, ,, 10½	5	5	6	7	8	8	9	10	10	11	12	12	13	14	14	15	16	16	17
10½ ,, ,, 11	5	6	7	7	8	9	9	10	11	11	12	13	13	14	15	16	16	17	18
11 ,, ,, 11½	5	6	7	8	8	9	10	10	11	12	12	13	14	15	16	16	17	18	18

CEILING CHART

Measurement round room	Number of rolls required	Measurement round room	Number of rolls required	Measurement round room	Number of rolls required	Measurement round room	Number of rolls required
20 feet	1	40 feet	2	60 feet	5	80 feet	8
24 feet	1	42 feet	3	62 feet	5	82 feet	8
26 feet	1	44 feet	3	64 feet	5	86 feet	9
28 feet	1	46 feet	3	66 feet	5	88 feet	9
30 feet	2	48 feet	3	68 feet	6	90 feet	10
32 feet	2	52 feet	4	70 feet	6	92 feet	10
34 feet	2	54 feet	4	74 feet	7	96 feet	11
36 feet	2	56 feet	4	76 feet	7	98 feet	11
38 feet	2	58 feet	4	78 feet	7	100 feet	12

Make it yourself

For the most part, preparations made by reputable manufacturers are better than those that can be made at home.

Well-established firms have perfected manufacturing conditions and formulae through extensive research, so that the amateur cannot hope to compete.

The directions given here are intended mainly for use in emergency and one or two simply for economy. Occasionally, however, there is the sheer satisfaction of making something at home which is normally bought, and one or two of the items are included for this reason.

There are also instructions intended to put to practical use a surplus of something in the home or garden.

Baking powder

A good baking powder can be made by mixing 4 oz. of bicarbonate of soda with 2 oz. tartaric acid and 8 oz. of ground rice flour. It must be stored in an airtight jar in a dry cupboard and once added to a mixture, the mixture should be cooked almost at once as the powder will start 'working'.

Bath salts

Home-made bath salts can be made quite cheaply. Buy a 7-lb. bag of sodium sesquicarbonate at a chain store chemist (this is sold for water softening and is much cheaper bought this way) and empty into a large warm bowl. Add 3 teaspoonfuls of oil of verbena and 1 teaspoonful of oil of lemon and mix well together with a wooden spoon. Store in large glass jars with screw caps and use 1 or 2 tablespoonfuls to a bath.

Butter

To make butter at home, use best Channel Island (or similar) milk and remove the cream from the milk for several days; place this in a screw-top jar and stand it in a refrigerator or cool larder. The butter can be made by shaking the screw-top jar until the clot of butter forms but it can be made more quickly in a mixer or shaker or with some types of beater. If salted butter is required, put the clot of butter into a basin and work a little salt into it, then pat the butter in muslin or kitchen paper to absorb any surplus moisture and serve.

Clotted cream

Pour 3 or 4 pints of best Channel Island milk into a large shallow pan and leave this to stand in a cool larder for several hours or until the cream has risen and settled on the surface. Place the pan over hot water or on as low a heat as possible and heat it *very* slowly; it should not reach simmering point, and 180 deg. F., is about the temperature to aim at. Keep it at this temperature until the cream forms a thick yellow crust, then remove the pan from the heat carefully and leave to become cold. When the clotted cream is cold, gently cut it with a knife into three or four pieces and lift these out on a fish slice and serve.

Coal briquettes

Mix together 10 parts coal slack with 1 part cement and sufficient water to make a thick paste. Press into a wooden box or flower-pot, turn out and leave to dry. Do not poke the *briquettes* once they are on the fire.

Coal bricks which give off a good heat can also be made from coal dust, sawdust and glue. To make them, dissolve glue crystals or a small tube of glue in boiling water. Mix 1 cupful of sawdust with 2 cupfuls of coal dust and mix to a thick paste with a little of the glue water. Form into an egg or brick shape and leave to dry and harden.

Alternatively you can make *coal balls*. For these, mix 6 parts of coal dust with 1 part of damp clay and roll into small balls.

Another quick way of using up coal dust is to mix it with a little ordinary soil from the garden, pack it firmly into empty sugar packets and leave it out of doors until very hard, then burn the packet on a red fire without poking.

An even quicker way of making coal bricks is to fill up empty sugar cartons with coal dust, leaving just a little space at the top. Last thing at night, or to make a fire last, pour 1 tablespoonful of cold water on to the dust, fold down the flap of the carton so that it is sealed, and place on the hot fire.

See also page 327.

Coal flowers

Coal flowers—a type of coloured fungus really—can be grown from ordinary coal. Fill a glass bowl or vase with small pieces of coal about the size of an apple and pour on a mixture made by mixing together 3 tablespoonfuls of cold water, 3 tablespoonfuls of household ammonia, 2 tablespoonfuls of common salt and 1 tablespoonful each of Prussian blue and red ink. Stir well and pour over the coal, then leave the bowl in a warm place.

Two or three times a week, dissolve 1 teaspoonful of salt in 1 tablespoonful of water and add this gently to the bowl without disturbing the mixture. To vary the colours of the flowers, add a few drops of coloured ink to the salt water.

Cooker cleaner

Dissolve 1 tablespoonful of caustic soda in $\frac{1}{2}$ pint of boiling water; next mix 1 tablespoonful of flour with just enough cold water to make a thin cream and immediately stir in the boiling caustic soda solution. Mix thoroughly and apply to the dirty cooker with a mop or brush. The mixture may be bottled and stored but should be poured into a ridged poison bottle, clearly labelled, and it should be kept on a high shelf or in a locked cupboard if possible.

Cough mixture

A pleasant cough syrup, quite safe for children, can be made by mixing 5 oz. of honey with 4 oz. of treacle and $\frac{1}{2}$ pint of vinegar. Bring to the boil and simmer for a quarter of an hour, then remove from the heat and when almost cool, stir in 3 teaspoonfuls of ipecacuanha wine. The syrup can be taken every 4 hours, 1 tablespoonful for adults and 1 to 2 teaspoonfuls for children.

Doorstep whitening

If you require a doorstep whitening which will not wash off with the first shower of rain, melt $\frac{1}{2}$ lb. of glue in $1\frac{1}{2}$ pints of water and when it has completely dissolved stir in 1 lb. of powdered whitening. Clean the step and brush on.

See also page 318.

Dusting cloth

Soak a clean duster in paraffin and hang to dry. When it is sufficiently dry that no smear is left when the duster is rubbed on a shiny surface it can be used. The duster will collect dirt and dust quickly and needs to be shaken frequently. It will probably need washing and resaturating in paraffin every 4 or 5 weeks. A floor cloth similarly treated will use much less floor polish than ordinary rag. Even better is to impregnate a duster or mop with a liquid polish sold for this purpose. There is also an all-purpose polish in an aerosol which can be sprayed on to a duster or mop.

There is another way to make a special dusting polisher, which will remove surface dust and leave a film of polish behind at the same time. Pour $\frac{1}{4}$ pint of very hot water into a dish, add 1 teaspoonful of silicone furniture cream and stir well. Soak a clean dry duster in the solution and leave it to drip dry. The duster can be used until it is really dirty, then it can be laundered and redipped.

Floor stain

A simple floor stain can be made by dissolving 2 oz. of permanganate of potash in $2\frac{1}{2}$ pints of boiling water. Stir thoroughly, then strain through an old nylon stocking and brush on to the prepared floor with an old brush, a dish mop or with a rag tied on to a stick to form a pad. Leave for 36 hours, then apply wax polish, leave overnight and buff next day.

Another efficient stain can be made just as easily by dissolving 2 oz. of vandyke brown water stain in just enough ammonia to make a thick paste; pour on 1 pint of fast-boiling water, stir thoroughly and apply as for the stain above.

Furniture reviver

Mix together equal quantitites of methylated spirit, vinegar, paraffin and turpentine, and bottle. Shake well and apply with an old rag to remove dirt, stains and grease marks from furniture. Polish off immediately to avoid damage to surface. If in doubt, test first on inconspicuous part of woodwork.

A similar furniture reviver can be made by mixing equal amounts of turpentine, methylated spirit and vinegar. Shake well, then add 1 or 2 drops of linseed oil and shake again until thoroughly mixed. Apply the reviver on a soft cloth, then polish really hard.

Health salts

Home-made health salts are quite pleasant to take and a little cheaper than bought ones. Simply mix together 2 oz. of cream of tartar with 2 oz. of tartaric acid and 2 oz. of bicarbonate of soda. Add 1 oz. of powdered magnesia and 2 oz. of Epsom salt and stir thoroughly until completely blended. Store in a screw-cap jar and add a teaspoonful or more to a glass of warm water.

Instant starch

Make your own instant starch. Make up a strong solution of boiling water starch according to the directions on the packet. Allow to cool and store in an airtight container (for example, one of the round polythene types with a special air-sealed lid) in the refrigerator. When it is required, dilute two or three tablespoonsful of the mixture with hot water.

Jam-pot covers

To make airtight jam-pot covers, dip large rounds of greaseproof paper into hot starch and put over the hot jam jars. Keep in place with elastic bands and the covers will dry like parchment.

Ointment

Ideal for cracked fingers and chapped hands is a simple ointment which can be made only in the early summer. Dissolve the contents of a jar of Vaseline petroleum jelly in a saucepan and gradually stir in as many elderflowers as possible, adding more as they are absorbed. When no more can be added, lower the heat and simmer very gently for 40 to 50 minutes, ensuring that the liquid does not actually boil. Remove from the heat, strain through a sieve or muslin and pour into 2 or 3 small make-up jars.

Papier-mâché

To make papier-mâché suitable for modelling, moulding, etc. tear up about $\frac{1}{2}$ lb. of paper into small pieces and boil in a little water until it is soft and pulpy. In the meantime, dissolve $1\frac{1}{2}$ lb. of glue in 4 to 5 pints of hot water and simmer gently until completely dissolved, then add to the paper pulp. Stir thoroughly and when well mixed, slowly add and mix in powdered whitening until the mixture is thick enough to be moulded. Boil for a few minutes, remove from the heat and leave to cool.

When the papier-mâché is to be used for filling cracks between floorboards, pulp the torn newspaper in boiling water, measure the amount in a jug and for each pint add about an ounce of powdered glue or concentrated size. Stir until the glue or size is completely dissolved and mixed in, then leave to cool. When quite cold, press into the cracks with a palette knife and leave to dry, then sandpaper smooth before staining.

Polishes

Beeswax floor polish. An easy way to use up beeswax is to make floor polish at home. Stand a large jar in boiling water and into it shred 4 oz. of beeswax. Add 1 pint of turpentine, mix well and pour into wide-mouthed jars or tins to set. Turpentine is highly flammable and must not be heated over a flame or stove.

Chrome and paintwork polish. Mix together two parts of paraffin with one part of methylated spirit. Use sparingly on a damp rag on chrome and paintwork. It costs little and goes a long way. Do not use on furniture without first testing.

Furniture polish. Collect $\frac{1}{2}$ pint of rain water to make a furniture polish ideal for old or antique furniture. To make it, put $\frac{1}{2}$ oz. of white wax in an old pan, add 1 oz. of beeswax and then pour on $\frac{1}{4}$ pint of rain water. Bring very slowly to the boil, stirring the whole time with an old wooden spoon or a stick until it is simmering. Remove from heat and leave to cool for 5 or 10 minutes, then add $\frac{1}{2}$ pint of turpentine substitute and stir thoroughly. Pour immediately into jars or bottles, cap or cork tightly and shake well. Leave the polish to become completely cold, shaking frequently as the liquid cools.

Linoleum polish. A non-slip polish can be made at home. Stand a large wide-necked jar or tin in a basin of very hot water away from any heat or flame. Add 1 pint of methylated spirit, then stir in 3 oz. of brown shellac. Stir until dissolved, then cover securely. The linoleum should first be washed and dried and then the polish brushed on and left to dry.

Another linoleum polish which is non-slip and lasts for several months can be made by mixing together $\frac{1}{4}$ pint of vinegar, linseed oil, turpentine substitute and clear varnish. Stir well and bottle. Wash the linoleum with hot soda water to remove any old polish, then rub the new polish into the floor in the usual way.

Try adding white spirit (turpentine substitute) to wax polish when polishing floors. It goes on easily and less is required.

Pewter polish. A polish for badly neglected pewter can be made at home. Dissolve 1 oz. of soft soap in 2 tablespoonfuls of boiling water, add 4 oz. of rottenstone and 4 oz. of turpentine, put in a screw-top jar and shake well. Apply to pewter and leave overnight. Next morning wash the pewter in hot soapy water, rinse and dry on a chamois leather. The polish will keep if stored in a tightly corked bottle. A similar polish can be made quickly by moistening powdered rotten-stone with equal amounts of turpentine and linseed oil.

Potpourri

If a garden is well supplied with rose petals, a potpourri can be made which should keep its fragrance for some years. If it does dry out, simply add a little brandy and stir thoroughly. The potpourri must stay in the one bowl so choose one which will not be needed for something else and one which is attractive as it will be permanently on show.

To make, mix 4 oz. of kitchen salt with 4 lb. of fresh rose petals. Leave for 4 or 5 days, then stir in a mixture made with 2 oz. each of brown sugar, powdered orris, allspice, cloves, salt and a few bay and rosemary leaves if available, or other sweet-scented flowers such as mignonette or heliotrope.

Stir the mixture thoroughly, then add a small handful of lavender and 1 dessertspoonful of verbena or other flower essence and stir again. Cover the bowl and next day add 2 or 3 oz. of brandy and stir again. Cover, leave until next day and the potpourri should be ready.

Another potpourri can be made by drying rose petals from a bush, not fallen petals, in the sun or in an airing cupboard until they are crisp. If available, add bay leaves, clover heads, geranium blossoms, delphinium petals, mock orange blossom flowers, lavender, laurel leaves, red gillyflowers (wallflowers), acacia blossoms, shavings of orange and lemon peel and leaves of mint and let them all dry slowly together. Mix together powdered cinnamon, ground cloves, allspice, mace, kitchen salt and sea salt (bay salt). Powder the flower petals together in the hands and stir, then pour a layer in the bottom of a large screw-cap jar or airtight tin, add a layer of the mixed salt and spices and more petals and continue until the mixtures are used up. Put out a handful of potpourri into a small bowl and keep the remainder tightly stoppered to replace the mixture in the small bowl when the perfume dies.

Scented pillow

Another way of using up rose petals is to make a scented pillow. Not very practical for everyday use but a charming idea for a guest room or for an invalid or anyone who needs an afternoon nap. Dry the rose petals and crumble them, then mix with ordinary cloves crushed with a heavy weight. Add a handful of dried mint, rubbed to a powder between the hands, together with some sweet briar leaves, dried lavender, sweet geranium leaves, lemon verbena and any other sweet-smelling petals. If available, add a little powdered cinnamon, orris, dried grated orange peel and any dried herbs, stir thoroughly and empty into a small dainty cover so that it is stuffed fairly tightly; if there is not quite enough mixture to fill the pillow, empty into a large bowl and add finely chopped chaff, fine bran, hay, etc., stir well, then refill the pillow and sew ends to seal.

Scouring paste

To make an efficient scouring paste mix $\frac{1}{2}$ lb. of silver sand with $\frac{1}{2}$ lb. of whiteneing in an old stone jar. Add $\frac{1}{2}$ lb of soft soap and stir thoroughly.

Scouring powder

A scouring powder for cleaning stained crockery and pans is easily made by mixing $\frac{1}{2}$ lb. of powdered pumice with a packet of soapless detergent.

Setting lotion

To set hair for an important engagement when ordinary setting lotion has been completely used up, water is a very poor substitute. It is possible to make a quick, efficient setting lotion, however, by adding 4 teaspoonfuls of warm water to 1 teaspoonful of raw white of egg. Mix well, comb through hair and set. Sounds odd, but it works! Ordinary pale ale is also good for setting hair after a shampoo.

Silver cleaner

A good silver cleaner can be made quite cheaply if a box of plate powder is mixed with 1 dessertspoonful of ammonia and the same amount of warm water. Mix thoroughly and bottle.

Silver polishing cloth

Make an efficient silver polishing cloth quickly and easily by mixing 1 tablespoonful of ammonia with 1 teaspoonful of plate powder and 1 small teacupful of lukewarm water. Stir thoroughly, then soak a cloth in the solution and leave it to drip dry. Made this way it will not shower white powder each time it is used.

If a cloth is to be used only for polishing silver, dip a piece of old towelling in the solution but a quicker method is to dip a teacloth in the mixture and reserve this for drying cutlery after every washing-up. The teacloth can be washed weekly and any black marks will come out immediately; redipping takes only a few minutes.

Toothpowder

Buy ¼ lb. of precipitated chalk from a chemist, tip it into a dry basin and for flavouring add either a crushed peppermint, dried and powdered orange or tangerine skin, together with a crushed clove or dried sage, powdered and sieved. Add 1 teaspoonful of salt and 1 teaspoonful of bicarbonate of soda; sieve again, stir thoroughly and store in a screw-cap jar.

A cleaning and whitening toothpowder can also be made by mixing a powdered charcoal tablet with precipitated chalk.

Transfer ink

Make transfer ink by mixing equal amounts of sugar and ordinary powdered washing blue with enough lukewarm water to make a thick creamy liquid. Dip a pen in the solution and outline any design on the reverse side of the paper. Allow to dry and press on to the material with a warm iron. The design will appear right way round.

Wallpaper cleaning dough

Put 6 tablespoonfuls of flour in a basin, make a hole in the centre and pour in 3 tablespoonfuls of turpentine substitute. Mix to a thick paste and add 3 tablespoonfuls of lukewarm water. Make into a dough with the hands and knead thoroughly so that the spirit is evenly distributed.

Wipe in long firm strokes down the soiled wallpaper, turning the dough frequently so that a clean portion is always in use. The dough, if not too badly soiled, can be stored for some time in an airtight tin. It must be freshly kneaded before each use so that it is soft and pliable.

Window cleaner

A cheap window cleaner can be made by mixing equal quantities of paraffin, methylated spirit and water. Shake well and rub on glass; allow to dry and polish off.

Another window cleaner that can be made at home is one blending a cupful of water with a cupful of finely powdered whiting. Mix the whiting to a smooth paste with a little of the water. When mixed smooth, add the rest of the water and half a cupful of ammonia. Mix well together, then bottle and shake well before using. This polish can also be used for cleaning metal.

Index

Where an entry appears more than once in the text the main reference is indicated first

Approximate decimal equivalents, 442
Apron, weight, 180
Araldite, 272, 291
Ariel, 112, 119
Arnel, 18
Artificial flowers, to revive, 184
Asbestos sheeting, 294
Asphalt solvent, 114
Aspro Nicholas, 113
Astrakhan, 18
Automatic washing machines, 178
Avisco, 18
Avoirdupois weight, 448
 American equivalents, 451
 approximate equivalents, 449
 metric equivalents, 443
 special measures, 448
Avril, 19, 75
Avron, 19
Axle grease stains, 215
Axminster carpet, 39, 395
Azlon, 78

Baby, 294
 clothes, laundering, 139
 napkins, to launder, 163
 pants, to launder, 139
 woollies, 139
Bakelite, 269, 275
Baking powder, 131
 to make at home, 460
Ball-point pen ink stains, 126, 215
Balsa cement stains, 216
Bamboo, to wash, 294
Bancroft, Joseph & Sons, 19
Ban-Lon, 19, 26
Bantol, 236, 264
Barber & Nicholls Ltd., 11
Baskets, to prevent cane splitting, 294
Bath:
 to clean, 294
 drip marks, 225
 to repaint, 418
 rubber mat, to soften, 366
 rust stains, 252
 salts, to make, 460
 stains, to remove, 127
 towel, weight, 180
Bathroom, to prevent steaming up, 295
Batiste, 19
Beads, to thread, 295
Bedford cord, 19
Bed jacket, 139

Bed linen:
 to launder, 140
 weight, 180
 when buying, 296
Beds, 297
 to test for dampness, 298
Bedspread, weight, 180
Beer:
 glasses to a bottle, 447
 stains, 216
Beeswax, 112
 floor polish, to make, 465
Beetle plastics, 282
Bel-O-Fast, 19
Bemberg, 19
Benzene, 112, 123
Benzine, 112, 123
Benzol, 113
Berets, to wash or clean, 191
Bexoid, 270
Bicarbonate of soda, 113
 stains, 216
Bi-component acrylic fibres, 20, 15, 29, 84
Bicycle oil stains, 122, 216
Big S, 113, 119, 169
Biological washing powders, 113, 119, 163, 169, 211
Biotex, 113, 119, 169
Bird droppings, stains to remove, 216
Blackberry juice stains, 217
Blacklead stains, 217
Blankets, 298
 to darn, 185
 to launder, 141, 181
 sizes, 298
 tea stains, 260
 weight, 180
 yellowing, 141
Bleaches, 113, 124, 125, 128, 129, 130
Bleaching, 141
Blend, 20
Blocked drains, 121
Blood stains, 217, 111, 121, 211
Bloom on furniture, to remove, 333
Blouses, to launder, 142
 weight, 180
Blue C nylon, 65
Blueing, 142
Blue stains, 218
Bobbin net, 51
Boiling, laundering, 142
Boiling water starch, 169
Bolster case, weight, 180

Water temperatures:
  for enzyme detergents, 120
  for washing, 135
  for washing soda, 129
Water wax emulsion polish stains, 126
Wax, 112
  polish, 415
  to remove from furniture, 389
  to remove from woodwork, 434
Wax polish stains, 126
Wax proofing, 44
W.C., 346, 115, 124
Wear-resistant, 106
Wedding dress, to store, 389
Weedkiller stains, 256
Weight:
  approximate equivalents, 449
  avoirdupois, 448
  American equivalents, 451
  metric equivalents, 443
  special measures, 443
Weight of articles for washing machines, 180
Wellington boots, 210
Welvic, 279, 284
Wet look shoes, 207
Wetting agent, 126
Whipcord, 106
Whisky:
  glasses to a bottle, 447
  stains, 214
White buckskin shoes, 203
White fur felt hat, to clean, 191
White kid, to dry clean, 126
White satin shoes, 203
White sauce stains, 266
White sealer, 292, 370
White spirit, 133, 123
White straw hat, to clean, 192
White trousers, to launder, 177
Whitening, to make, 462
Whitewash, 437
  to clean, 389
  stains, 266
Whitewashing, 437
White wool:
  to dry clean, 126
  to launder, 183
  stole or shawl, 210
  toys, to wash, 382
Wickerwork, to clean, 389
Wildman Machine Company, 89
Wild silk, 86, 85

Honan, 48
Tussore, 100
Wilton carpet, to bind, 395, 39
Wincey, 106
Winceyette, 106
Windows, 390
  to clean, 126, 390
  cleaner, to make, 469
  paint stains on, 248, 438
  to prevent steaming, 390
Wine cask, to clean, 391
Wine, glasses to a bottle, 447
Wine stains, 266, 114, 212
  in decanter, 300
Winter cotton bedjacket, 140
Wollcrylon, 107
Women's Advisory Committee of the British Standards Institution, 10
Wood:
  block floors, 415
  bloom, 333
  bruise marks, 218
  floors, 415; paint stains, 247; to seal, 416
  to French polish, 438
  heat marks, 233
  limed oak, 348
  mahogany, 350
  oak, 354
  perfume stains, 249, 386
  panelling, 391, 354
  to protect, 438
  ink stains, 236
  stain, 433
  stains, 214
  teak, 378
  veneer, 385
  walnut, 385
Wooden kerb, to clean, 341
Wooden tableware, 391
Wool, 107
  to clean, 211
  to launder, 181
  taffeta, 91
  yellowing, 141
Woollen, 108
  baby clothes, 139
  bedjacket, 139
  gloves, 189
Worsted, 108
  trousers, 176
Woven vinyl filament, 284
Wringer, 180, 183
Writing, to revive when faded, 335